THE STRUCTURE OF INTERNATIONAL CONFLICT

Also by C.R. Mitchell

INTERNATIONAL RELATIONS THEORY:
  A Bibliography (*co-editor*)
NEW APPROACHES TO INTERNATIONAL MEDIATION
  (*co-editor*)
PEACEMAKING AND THE CONSULTANT'S ROLE

THE STRUCTURE OF INTERNATIONAL CONFLICT

C. R. Mitchell

Professor of International Relations
The City University, London

MACMILLAN

First edition 1981
Reprinted 1989

Published by
THE MACMILLAN PRESS LTD
Houndmills, Basingstoke, Hampshire RG21 2XS
and London
Companies and representatives
throughout the world

Printed in China

British Library Cataloguing in Publication Data
Mitchell, C.R. (Christopher R)
The structure of international conflict.
1. Foreign relations. Conflict
I. Title
327.1'6
ISBN 0-333-47413-9

To my parents, with much
love and affection

Contents

List of Tables

List of Figures

'. . . With the utmost reluctance we have been driven to begin active hostilities against your late ally, the Edinburgh and Glasgow Railway. All attempts on our part to bring about an agreement for an equitable decision of traffic common to the two lines are resolutely opposed . . . [The Edinburgh and Glasgow] . . . has commenced a series of aggressions. We shall discontinue hostilities when our opponents treat us with fairness . . .'

Letter to shareholders from the directors of the Caledonian Railway Company (1854)

Foreword

The Structure of International Conflict has been written mainly to
introduce undergraduate students in the social sciences to the ideas of
conflict research, and to its approach to the analysis of disputes
between humans, and between human groups or organisations. More
particularly, it seeks to apply some of the findings of conflict research
to analysing the nature of international conflicts, illuminating
structures and processes that appear in conflicts, irrespective of the
idiosyncratic factors that normally occupy the attention of more
traditional studies. Hence, it is not a book about a single dispute, such
as the Nigerian Civil War, nor a review of lethal conflicts since 1945.
Rather, it aims at gathering together ideas and theories from different
disciplines about various aspects of human conflict, and integrating
them into a coherent framework that will assist in the understanding of
future conflicts, as well as those that have already developed, been
fought out and terminated.

The idea of such a book occurred to me almost ten years ago, at a
time when the 'behavioural revolution' was beginning to make some
impact on the study of International Relations in the United Kingdom.
Anyone studying the discipline at this time could not help but be
influenced by the ideas of two scholars in the United States, namely
Karl Deutsch and James Rosenau, and I should acknowledge grate-
fully a long range intellectual debt to both of these writers (whether
they would wish to see their influence result in this present volume is
quite another matter!). More immediately, I owe far more in terms of
ideas, intellectual stimulation, constructive criticism and encouragement from my colleagues at the old Centre for Analysis of Conflict at
University College, London, namely; Reg Austin, Michael Banks,
John Burton, Tony De Reuck, Frank Edmead, John Groom and
Michael Nicholson. Without their influence and stimulation, and that
provided by my psychological mentor Bram Oppenhein from the LSE,
this present work would never have been started. More recently I have
benefited from conversations, discussions and arguments with my two
immediate colleagues at the City University, Peter Willetts and

Keith Webb, both of whom have opened my eyes to areas and ideas in political theory and comparative politics that I had been ignoring, or of which I had been totally ignorant. I am very grateful to both of them. I am more than grateful to my old friend Richard Little of Lancaster University who spent much time and effort with various draft chapters of the manuscript, and through his ideas and suggestions prevented the book from being more incoherent than it is.

Given the long gestation of this book, innumerable secretaries in various institutions from University College to City University have worked on different dafts, and I am duly grateful to all of them. I would particularly like to thank Norah Vas at City University, however, for her efficient and timely work on the tables and diagrams for the final draft of the work.

The final production of *The Structure of International Conflict* would not have occurred without the help of my wife and tolerance of my daughter, Emily, both of whom put up with long bouts of anti-social behaviour on my part to help me finish. In a more basic sense, however, the book is as much Lois's as mine, for her sensible comments and criticisms frequently underlined gaps or obscurities in the text, and caused me to look again, and usually to rewrite. The book would have been much less comprehensible without her help.

Introduction

Men have thought and written about the subject of conflict and war from Kautilya to the present day, while the phenomenon of organised violence has had a continuing interest for historian and philosopher, as well as for the statesman and man of action. However, it is only over the last three decades that scholars have engaged in an interdisciplinary approach to investigating the causes of conflict, violence and war and the problems of maintaining − indeed, defining − a condition of peace. Such work is known under a variety of labels, such as 'conflict studies', 'peace research', or 'conflict analysis'. In this present study the broad title of *conflict research* will be used, to convey the idea that the focus of a wide ranging research effort is on the phenomenon of 'conflict', wherever this might be found.

An initial difficulty in introducing conflict research as a new field of study is the changing and ambiguous use of labels, and the resulting problem of achieving an acceptable definition for a term such as 'conflict'. In everyday language, it tends to be associated with physical violence, but this 'common language' meaning of conflict is not the one generally adopted by conflict researchers (nor by this study), who are interested in a wider range of situations than those merely characterised by violent behaviour. Conflict research uses a broad approach to the question of what constitutes a conflict, one which attempts to encompass many of the features of terms used synonymously with 'conflict', such as 'competition', 'disharmony', 'tensions', 'antagonism', 'friction', 'hostility', 'struggle' or 'controversy'.

Moreover, any study of conditions precipitating human conflict leads on to consideration of the nature of co-operation, so conflict research also, perhaps paradoxically, demands of its practitioners an equal interest in the absence of conflict as in its presence. Hence, there is a dual interest in conflict and co-operation within the field.

Although this present study concentrates upon recent developments, we should warn against the assumption that little interest was taken in the subject of social or international conflict before the middle decades of the twentieth century. Robin Williams (1972) has condemned what

1

he calls the 'Columbus complex' in sociology, which holds conflict theory to be an invention of the 1950s, ignoring the vast legacy of sociological concepts, hypotheses and data in existence. Although conflict research 'came of age' in the United States in the mid-1950s, its intellectual roots go back to pioneering scholarship of the 1930s and 40s (Richardson, 1960; Wright, 1942; Sorokin, 1937), to the peace movements of the inter-war years and, some would argue, to European philosophers of the sixteenth and seventeenth centuries. What was unarguably innovative in conflict research during the 1950s was its eclectic and interdisciplinary approach to the study of all social conflicts, wherever these might occur.

A.   BASIC ASSUMPTIONS

One of the major spurs to renewed endeavour in the 1950s was the Cold War and the nuclear threat, which made a new intellectual effort to understand the causes and dynamics of war both pressing and immediate. A number of unique features in the work which resulted from this stimulus made the movement qualitatively as well as quantitatively different from previous intellectual enterprises, and while it would be misleading to assign common aims, methods or characteristics to the heterogeneous group of scholars who would claim to be part of 'the conflict research movement', nevertheless there are strands which are common to most, if not all, workers in the field.

1.   CONFLICT AS A LEGITIMATE FOCUS OF ENQUIRY

The first of these 'common strands' is a fundamental belief (and it can be no more than a belief at this stage) that 'conflict' can be extracted and studied separately from the rest of purposeful human behaviour, both individual and group.

The intellectual rationale for this belief is simply that there are no limits to how social phenomena (the 'referent' world) may be split up for study: any class of phenomena may be isolated from the remainder of perceived reality in order to facilitate closer examination. One may analyse a traffic system in a country town, while ignoring the workings of the town's industry served by a large part of that traffic system. One may study relationships within a family, to the exclusion of the father's relations at work or his childrens' life at school. One may focus upon the physiology of the brain and leave aside problems connected with the other (but highly related) parts of the body – respiratory system, nervous system, or circulatory system. It is important to recognise that there is no single 'right' way of analysing the real world, just ways that are more or less useful for different analytical and practical purposes.

Conflict research starts from the position that political and social processes can usefully be studied as various combinations of conflict and co-operation. Conflict researchers thus believe that conflict, while occurring at quite different social levels (from inter-individual to inter-national), nevertheless has sufficient common attributes to justify its study as a distinct field. It is assumed that it is useful to take 'reality' and isolate all those aspects which relate to the concept of ·conflict, even if this involves putting into one broad category such apparently diverse phenomena as the Russo-Japanese War of 1903–5, communal strife on the island of Cyprus, the Watts Riots, an industrial strike, and a fist fight between two individuals. It is argued that the common as well as the unique exists in all these diverse phenomena, and that the common is such as to make comparative investigation worthwhile. Naturally, the common elements shared by phenomena must be more than superficial to warrant the development of any new field of study. A grapefruit and a basketball are both round and have pebbly skins, but this obvious physical resemblance is worth little when problems of common structure and behaviour of both objects arise. 'Conflicts' as a social phenomenon must prove to have more than superficial qualities in common to justify their analysis as a class of things, and in part this study represents an effort to focus on these more-than-superficial commonalities, and show that conflict is more than just a '. . . promising theoretical focus . . .' (Mack, 1965, p. 336). A point that follows from our argument that conflicts are fundamentally similar phenomena occurring throughout society is that a war is a special case of this general phenomenon, and should be treated as a sub-class rather than a unique category in its own right.[1] Findings about conflict at other levels may thus be helpful in developing insights into the causes, processes and outcomes of international war. To take an extreme example, it may be that a study of the processes operative in a conflict among New York cab-drivers' organisations could con-ceivably contain elements similar to those present in a conflict between independent, sovereign states (Cassady, 1957).

Conflict researchers whose parent disciplines have been Politics or International Relations have pointed out that this represents a radically

new departure for both disciplines, but particularly for International
Relations scholars, who have conventionally (perhaps because of their
desire to have their own field of study accepted as a distinct discipline)
attempted to emphasise the uniqueness of events at the inter-state level.
Diplomatic practitioners have also tended, in the past, to begin their
activities with an assumption that international conflicts are the result
of forces which, either by their origin or their dynamics, are unique to
the international system. This led to the view that international
relationships of both conflict and co-operation must be studied as
distinct phenomena in their own right, without much reference to the
results of other fields of enquiry, such as sociology or social
psychology. Conflict research makes the opposite assumption: that
something which can, for convenience, be called 'conflict' exists
throughout human experience, extending from the individual to the
inter-state level, and amenable to comparative research wherever it
occurs.

2. A MULTI-DISCIPLINARY, MULTI-LEVEL APPROACH

Conflict researchers are also agreed that any attempt to understand
and analyse a complex phenomenon such as social or international
conflict must be multi-disciplinary in at least two senses:

(i) Scholars from diverse conventional disciplines can contribute
insights into conflicts normally regarded as outside their own
discipline or area of study. Psychologists, for example, may help to
throw light onto the processes of international negotiation over oil
concessions.

(ii) Patterns and processes that characterise conflict at one social
level also characterise it at other levels. This impels conflict
researchers to believe that concentration on conflicts in only one
area (conventional industrial conflict) will lead to a neglect of
findings relevant to an adequate understanding of conflicts in that
area. The only way in which a comprehensive analysis of industrial
conflict can be made is to inform such analysis by comparisons with
other classes of conflict.

A number of justifications have been advanced for adopting the
procedure of multi-disciplinary, multi-level analysis. Several are
particularly relevant for scholars interested in conflicts at the international level, where problems of conflict, co-operation and survival

appear most pressing. In connection with the transfer of findings and theories from one level of conflict to another, for example, it is argued that:

(a) The procedure increases the number of conflicts available for study.

(b) From the standpoint of the analysis of *international* conflict, many of the other levels of conflict are more amenable to direct study.

(c) Insights may transfer from one conflict level to another, and result in common findings at both levels.[2]

This procedure may seem unfamiliar and unjustifiable. However, the process of transferring findings and theories from one level of society to another (sometimes referred to as *analogue analysis*) is not new, and tends to be practised − at least implicitly − by many International Relations scholars, who use any number of crude analogies and metaphors to describe international processes and events: 'balance of power'; the existence of a 'power vacuum' which must be filled (with what?); or various organic or anthropomorphic analogies applied to entities like state, nation or class. Probably the most pervasive of these implicit analogies used by International Relations scholars is the 'domestic analogy', whereby assumptions that underlie many solutions to intra-state problems are unconsciously transferred to the inter-state level. (For example, the assumption that the creation of an international police force will keep the peace abroad is closely linked with the [probably false] assumption that domestic peace and tranquillity exist because of police enforcement at home.)

At a more systematic and sophisticated level, the recently developed field of cybernetics is based upon the conception that all organised entities communicate with one another by some means, so that one way to an understanding of behaviour of individuals, groups, organisations and nation-states is to study the communication patterns within and between them. Colonies of bees, human groups and business empires may thus all be analysed from the point of view of communications patterns, the exchange and interpretation of information and the use of stored information ('memory') in the interpretation of a changing environment. Thus, 'communications theorists' study their subject in any number of ostensibly disparate situations, and are interested primarily in those phenomena which fall within their particular selection from reality.

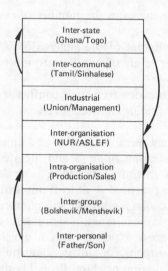

FIGURE I.1 Transferring findings

Conflict research rests heavily on analogue analysis, making comparisons between conflicts at quite different social levels, involving different types of participating parties, operating in different circumstances. This approach can be visualised as a ladder, with the transfer of insights or theories as a process of climbing up (or down) the ladder bearing different ideas, concepts and findings that might be useful at the other levels in understanding conflict structures and processes to be found there; in for example, transfers from a 'line vs staff' conflict within a complex organisation to a case of urban conflict between rival communities in an inner city area (see Fig. I.1). This practice is contrasted with the more familiar (and generally accepted) processes of generalising by transferring theories and hypotheses across to other conflicts at ostensibly the same social level, comparing for example the communal conflicts in Ulster and Belgium, or bilateral inter-state conflicts. Conflict research, on the other hand, makes the major *a priori* assumption that the same processes can be found at various levels of social conflict.

It is easy to argue that this assumption is fundamentally mistaken. If it is, then the possibility of transferring findings from cases at radically different levels, 'but also, be it noted, between those at similar social levels becomes difficult to justify. At present, the conflict researchers' case for doing this remains unproven.

3. CONFLICT AS AN ENDEMIC FEATURE OF SOCIETY

A final common assumption among conflict researchers is that the phenomenon of conflict, in one form or another, is an inevitable and ever-present feature of society and social inter-action. Conflict is inevitable because it can originate in individual and group reactions to situations of scarce resources; to division of function within society; and to differentiation of power and resultant competition for limited supplies of goods, status, valued roles and power-as-an-end-in-itself. One American sociologist argues, for example, that

. . . Since social organisations are characterised by both contact among members and competition for scarce positions and resources, the potential for conflict is a natural feature of human social life . . .

He also notes that the exercise of power in society generates opposition leading to conflict, particularly when losers decide their failure to achieve goals justifies overthrowing or ignoring rules designed to limit the nature of competition within that society (Mack, 1965, p. 334). Another states flatly that '. . . All interacting human populations exhibit many social conflicts . . .' (Williams, 1966, p. 718).

Conflict is also increasing. The twentieth century (called by Sorokin the bloodiest of all centuries) offers men increased opportunities for conflicts through processes such as industrialisation and urbanisation that encourage contact among people, competition, numerous forms of group differentiation (ethnic, occupational, status) and consequent visibility of inequities and stratifications within society. '. . . Since competition, contact and visibility are prerequisites for conflict', claims Mack, 'the mathematical possibilities of conflict increase both within and between societies under industrialisation . . .' (Mack, 1965, p. 335). Many conflict researchers agree with this thesis. Some would add that not merely industrialisation but a whole range of processes covered by the label 'modernisation' or indeed any rapid and widespread social change, such as the economic boom in Iran from 1973 to 1978, are likely to bring about an increased incidence of goal incompatibility between individuals and groups and hence an increased number of social or international conflicts (Burton, 1966, p. 370).

While it is possible to envisage a society free from conflict, such a society seems so remote from the world as we know it that the inevitability of continual and repetitive conflict seems a more sensible starting point. It is also open to doubt whether a conflict free society would genuinely be a Utopia. Robert Lee (1964, p. 3) remarks,

. . . Social conflict is a likely guest wherever human beings set up forms of social organisation. It would be difficult to conceive of an ongoing society where social conflict is absent. The society without conflict is a dead society . . . like it or not, conflict is a reality of human existence and therefore a means of understanding social behaviour . . .

A logical extension of the 'endemic conflict' argument is that there can be no abolition of conflict in any final sense, although specific conflicts may be temporarily resolved. Conflicts can always be avoided. One party may always obtain peace, and avoid conflict through the surrender of itself or its objectives. Conflict can be ended through the defeat of one party and the victory and success of another. (The German word for 'cemetery', *friedhof*, translated literally as 'court of peace'.) Conflicts may be settled by compromise, 'log-rolling', or an alteration of one party's perception and ambitions. Conflicts may be transformed to variable-sum situations, so that all parties gain. But always other conflicts will arise to replace those that have been avoided, suppressed, settled or resolved. Peacemakers will continue to be blessed, but also in demand; and if they are to have any success, their best policy might be to avoid efforts at abolishing social or international conflict, and devise methods whereby conflicts can be played out with a minimum of destructive side effects, or even (in some ingenious manner) rendered socially useful.

B.   INTRA-PERSONAL CONFLICT

The practice of multi-level analysis of social conflict raises the question of likely links with psychological conflict, and whether conflicts *within* a single individual should be included in any review of conflict research. We often speak of an individual being 'in conflict with himself' and psychologists and psychiatrists have made the concept of *intra-personal* conflict a relatively familiar one. On the one hand, such conflicts are exemplified by Freudian doctrines of the relationship between the *ego* and the *id* within the human psyche, or by personality conflicts that result from intense intra-personal stress or psychological imbalance (depression or schizophrenia). On the other, we need not go to the extremes of serious psychological disorder to acknowledge the existence of intra-personal conflict. The term *decisional conflict* describes very common situations in which an individual has to make difficult choices between competing and equally attractive (or unattractive) options. Any individual may simultaneously desire mutually incompatible objectives, and be subjected to considerable discomfort by the realisation that he cannot simultaneously fulfil all his desires. Cognitive balance and cognitive dissonance theory can be seen as an attempt to explain the nature and psychological effects of such decisional conflicts.

However, in spite of the extensive literature on various types of intra-personal conflict, and findings about its causes, course and effects, we will refer to it only peripherally in this study. Two factors justify drawing this lower limit to our ladder of levels of conflict. Firstly, grounds of practicality demand that some limits be set to the topics and issues considered. Secondly, there appears to be sufficient *a priori* justification for arguing that intra-personal conflict (of whatever variety) is significantly different on a number of key dimensions from inter-personal and inter-group conflicts (using 'inter-group' here to describe all conflicts above the level of two individuals), despite arguments that it is helpful to regard individuals as collections of social roles, or as the battle-ground of competing, unconscious forces. Hence, the decision to avoid intra-personal conflict, and to confine analysis to situations of mutually incompatible goals which involve (at least two) physically separate entities as parties to the conflict.

C. CONFLICT RESEARCH: THE FIELD OUTLINED

We have reviewed the major assumptions made by academic conflict researchers, and the remainder of this study discusses work in the field. It focuses on the problems of research, and suggests some possible means for overcoming these problems, both analytical and practical. The work adopts its own framework in an effort to integrate the relatively disparate aspects of conflict research into a coherent and comprehensible whole. Hence, it is idiosyncratic, and those who wish to obtain an overview of the entire field should consult one of the many review articles available.[4]

First we examine the conceptual problems faced by anyone attempting to analyse intranational and international conflicts. Difficulties include devising clear and useful definitions of terms; and identifying parties and issues (who conflicts with whom, when and over what).

Parts II and III discuss how parties conduct and conclude conflicts. Part IV considers methods of 'managing' conflicts and the problems of peacemaking. These final chapters concentrate mainly on making peace at the international level, but also introduce insights into ending conflicts from other social levels.

The scope of this study may appear very broad, and at times readers may feel that they are losing sight of the wood because of the number of trees. It may, therefore, help to keep seven basic questions in mind. These form the analytical themes running throughout the book and they are fundamental to any research on human conflict at any social level:

(1) What basic concepts are needed to analyse conflict?
(2) What types of conflict can be discriminated?
(3) What causes conflict?
(4) How do conflicts develop?
(5) What are the effects of conflict on both conflicting entities and their environment?
(6) What outside factors exacerbate, moderate or resolve conflict?
(7) Why and how do conflicts end?

The study may disappoint those who hope for clear findings and tested hypotheses about social and international conflict, or formal analyses of conflict structures and processes. The current state of the field makes it inevitable that a work such as *The Structure of International Conflict* must be conceptual, descriptive and taxonomic, rather than theoretical in any formal sense. The work is thus 'pretheoretical' in Eckstein's (1964) sense of that word, dealing with delimitation (the statement of the boundaries of the field), classification, analysis (in the sense of dissecting the subject into its components) and problemation (the formulation of specific problems, about which theories should be developed). At the same time, highly formal and mathematical approaches to analysing conflicts are avoided, not on the grounds that these offer no insights, but because we wish to study human conflicts largely as they appear to participants in the real world, with rough and ready guides to conduct being all that presently exist.[5] It is to be hoped that this attempt to examine conflict systematically, while retaining the human dimension, will help to throw new light on a familiar topic.

Part I: The Structure of Conflict

1 Structure

> . . . Conflict is a situation in which two or more human beings desire goals which they perceive as being obtainable by one or the other *but not both*. This compact definition can be opened out and clarified by saying that there must be at least two parties; each party is *mobilising energy* to obtain a *goal*, a desired object or situation; and each party perceives the other as a barrier or threat to that goal . . .
>
> Ross Stagner (1967a)

Considerable ambiguity surrounds the term 'conflict'. In everyday use, it is often taken to mean some dispute in which two or more parties are using violence as a means of winning, or more usually (as they perceive it) 'in self-defence'. Violence is normally used in the sense of physical damage, although it is becoming increasingly acknowledged that it is possible to speak of using *psychological* violence and causing *psychological* damage to an adversary. (It is not true that 'Sticks and stones may break my bones, but names will never hurt me!') However, a moment's reflection should be enough to recognise that a relationship of quite genuine conflict may exist, even though none of the parties behave in a manifestly violent manner. Two individuals in a legal case are undoubtedly 'in conflict', but both are using essentially non-violent methods in order to achieve their goals.

If the essential element of this common language meaning of conflict is the activity of the parties, this leads to an assumption that the term 'conflict' refers to actual behaviour (which often involves coercion and usually violence). The behaviour is aimed at least at preventing the opposing party preventing one from reaching one's own goals. Its absence is taken to be a sign that the parties are in a co-operative relationship, in a condition of peaceful co-existence, or 'at peace'. Concentration upon the behavioural manifestations of a conflictful relationship is extremely limiting, however, and leads to neglect of other aspects of that relationship. Is a conflict merely a particular (violent) kind of inter-action between parties, or also a psychological state of mind among their members? If a group of people hate and fear another group of people, are they not in conflict with them? And is a dispute over specific issues, which may involve no feelings of fear or hostility, or sense of personal threat, not conflict? There is little doubt that feelings of antagonism and other personal and emotional differences arising between humans, singly and in groups, are important aspects of human conflict, and form part of the meaning often attached to that concept.[1]

At the very beginning, then, we need to emphasise that such expressions as 'social conflict' or 'international conflict' are vague, even multi-meaning terms, presenting a challenge to devise clear definitions for what are normally ambiguous concepts. Partly because of the variety of phenomena commonly associated with such expressions, there seems little point in attempting a definition of conflict which is unitary as well as unambiguous. Instead, a multiple definition will be used throughout this study, in order to include a number of everyday connotations of the term, yet also to be able to discriminate between these aspects or *components*. When speaking of any conflict or dispute, fundamental distinctions will be drawn between the three inter-related components of:

(i) *a conflict situation;*
(ii) *conflict behaviour;*
(iii) *conflict attitudes and perceptions.*

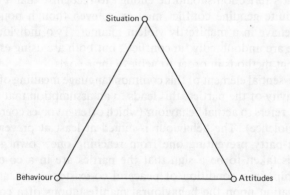

FIGURE 1.1 Triadic conflict structure

The three-dimensional format can be illustrated by a simple figure, adapted from Galtung (1969), emphasising that our three structural components may be analytically considered separately but that, in any real world conflict, all three are intimately connected with each other in complex ways (see Fig. 1.1).

A. CONFLICT SITUATIONS

Initially, a situation of conflict will be defined as:

> *Any situation in which two or more social entities or 'parties' (however defined or structured) perceive that they possess mutually incompatible goals.*

By 'goals' we mean consciously desired future outcomes, conditions or end states, which often have intrinsic (but different) value for members of particular parties, but which also bring with them other increased benefits or decreased costs for party members. Thus, the Palestinian goal of replacing Israel by a cantonal, secular Palestinian state is in conflict with the Israeli goal of the continuing existence of an independent Israel. The former in itself represents a valuable future achievement for many Palestinians, but also a wide variety of differentially distributed benefits for particular Palestinian groups. Compare the leadership of the PLO with existing Arab leaders in the West Bank area, or with the bulk of refugees in the Palestinian camps.

A simpler, more basic situation would be two small boys simultaneously wanting exclusive possession of a single rubber ball, a situation that might lead on to grabbing, name-calling, inter-party violence, an escalation in both inter-party hostility and intra-party anger plus appeals to superior third parties for assistance or arbitration. (The situation might also involve other factors, such as sibling rivalry and the need to demonstrate strength and intransigence to third parties.) Similar situations arise at other social levels. Divorced parents quarrel over custody of the child, and even go to such lengths as court cases and kidnapping in order to achieve their goal of possession (or denying possession to the other). The Japanese Government and the two Chinese Governments (Peking and Taiwan) all claim the Senkaku Islands in the East China Sea, which passed back into Japanese control in 1972 according to the terms of the US/Japanese Okinawa Agreement. All these cases involve circumstances in which parties possess goals which (apparently) cannot be simultaneously achieved, and hence a conflict situation characterised by incompatibility exists.

1. SOURCES OF GOAL INCOMPATIBILITY

Defining *conflict* situations as those in which parties come to possess mutually incompatible goals (whether the parties are individuals, social groups or organisations), immediately prompts a further question. What sorts of conditions regularly give rise to mutually incompatible goals? Attempting to answer this question would require a book in itself, but briefly, we operate on the assumption that the major source of incompatible goals lies in a mis-match between social values and social structure. Many conflict situations involve conditions of scarcity and values, which place a premium on the possession of the same resources or positions. Others result from value incompatibilities regarding use or distribution of resources, about social and political structures, or about beliefs and behaviour of others. Chalmers Johnson (1968) refers to such conditions as 'disequilibrated', emphasising that they arise most frequently in societies where rapid change is occurring (either in social structure or values). The conception of diverse sources may be included in Fig. 1.2 merely by adding a fourth element.

Inter-action between social structure and values producing conflict is well illustrated in a type of peasant social system known as a 'limited goods' society. In such a society, members hold acquisitive values, but also believe that every desirable social 'good' is in limited and fixed supply. Hence, there is a scarcity of such valued phenomena as security, health, safety, influence, manliness, honour or friendship, as well as such more familiar scarcities as wealth or land.[2] The values and perceptions in 'limited goods' societies are such that there is an inevitable process whereby individuals, families and factions develop goal incompatibilities, which arise when any other person or group increases its share of a valued commodity thus, by definition, decreasing the share available to others (Foster, 1967). In such cases, inter-personal and inter-familial conflicts arise (and also call forth social mechanisms for avoiding overt violence and coercion) through the inter-action of:

(i) existing value systems;
(ii) perceptions of scarcity;
(iii) physical limitations of the amount of material goods at any one point in time.

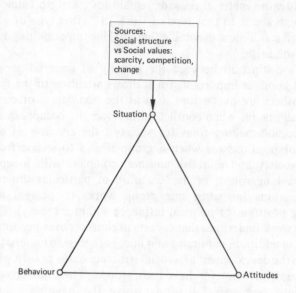

Sources:
Social structure
vs Social values:
scarcity, competition,
change

Situation

Behaviour

Attitudes

FIGURE 1.2 Sources and conflict structure

In more complex social settings, both intranational and inter-national, conflicts also arise from a (possible temporary) scarcity of goods, which existing value systems define as worthwhile or desirable, and over which competition occurs. Fred Hirsch has pointed out that circumstances of scarcity may arise both over *material* goods (oil wells, motor cars), and *positional* goods (roles as managers, permanent members of the UN Security Council), the latter being scarce in some absolute and final sense (Hirsch, 1977). However, beyond a certain minimum point necessary for physical survival, *both* types of goods are scarce at a given moment because value systems of various sorts persuade people that they *are* valuable and to be sought after; or because they bring about certain effects (admiration, social status, a sense of security) that people have learned to regard as desirable. (The fact that other value systems lead to contempt for, and rejection of, for example social status or material goods, underlines the argument that scarcity is brought about by an inter-action of social structure and social values. There is, as yet, no competition over the role of farm labourer because material rewards remain low, and no value system ascribes high status to that type of work.) If either type of goods is scarce, then it is almost inevitable that goal incompatibilities over distribution will arise.

Hirsch's distinction between the scarcity of material goods and positional goods is important, for it draws attention to the fact that many conflicts are over issues such as the *occupation* of particular scarce positions (as when conflict occurs over the occupancy of particular decision-making roles for society); the *creation* of alternative sets of positions (as when a group wishes to secede from one national society and establish another, complete with independent decision-making roles); or the *exclusion* of particular others from scarce positions (as when one group works to prevent another occupying positions of political influence within a society). Furthermore, his work underlines that success in conflicts over position often provides, in addition, continued and unequal access to material goods, leading to the development of a social structure based upon a whole set of have and have-not (or have-less) groups. These differences can stratify into permanent divisions where the have/have-not lines reinforce each other in some stratified social system based upon caste, race, language or class criteria. In such circumstances, goal incompatibilities tend to follow a similar pattern, and social entities possess whole inter-linked sets of goal incompatibilities leading to situations of almost wholly conflicting interests, with no shared goals to offset that conflict. Social structures are thus likely to be created which, given the values of those involved and the inability of that society to produce more of either the material or positional goods in dispute, lead to frequent, repetitive and often intense conflicts across apparently permanent cleavages within the social structure, as parties pursue goal incompatibilities that (in a very basic sense) arise from that structure and set of values. Cleavages in Ulster or in pre-secession Pakistan illustrate such structures. Alternatively, a social structure can emerge where the divisions into haves and have-nots cut across one another, the haves in one sense − social status − being the have-nots in another − material wealth or political influence. It is often argued that such a criss-crossing social structure while not necessarily diminishing the number of conflict situations that arise, has the effect of modifying the ferocity with which particular collectivities and groups pursue their interests – that is, of modifying conflict behaviour (Coser, 1956; McClelland, 1968).

This line of argument may offer insights into why much of the most violent human conflict occurs at the international level, where social structure is characterised by substantial 'vertical' cleavages between territorial state-based social entities; by inevitable development of mutually incompatible goals between these socially isolated and (often) highly cohesive units (only in a Utopia of limitless resources will conflicts not arise); by decentralisation of decision-making power; and by only the most rudimentary means for resolving disputes without resort to organised coercion or violence. Hence, the proportion of highly lethal conflicts at this social level, and the frequent replication of violent disputes when such conditions replicate themselves elsewhere, as within Nigeria, Vietnam, Cyprus or the Lebanon.

Given the approach to the sources of conflict outlined above, it will be obvious that this study is largely concerned with conflicts that are both realistic and – in some limited sense – rational (or at least 'instrumental'). Conflict situations arise from the pursuit of goals, and from goal incompatibilities, and in this minimal sense may be viewed as real. However, even at the level of basic goal incompatibilities subjective and psychological factors can be important. In certain cases parties may perceive that their goals are incompatible at a given point in time when, in fact, their perceptions are incorrect. Two possible examples of this are where parties act on the assumption that goals are logically mutually exclusive, when this is not the case; or where one or both parties misperceive the real nature of the other's goals, and perceive a conflict situation when, with perfect knowledge all round, none would exist. In the complex and emotional real world of human relations, neither situation is as rare as might appear, particularly given the propensity of goals to change over time, or the causes of a given situation to remain ambiguous or unknown. It can be argued that such 'unreal' conflicts should admit to an easy solution through correcting misperceptions, yet the practical difficulties of doing so may remain substantial.

2. TYPES OF GOAL

To a large degree, the nature of the parties' goals offers insight into the underlying sources of a conflict. The *kind of goals* held by individuals, groups and organisations are clues both to the underlying sources of particular types of conflict and the way the issues in conflict are presented. Goals can be classified as two major types:

(a) *Positive goals*, already referred to as consciously desired future states: increased wealth, favourable balance of payments, access to the sea, custody of the child, becoming head of state, seceding and establishing an independent country, achieving secure and defensible borders.

(b) *Negative goals*, which involve the avoidance of unwanted future states or happenings: avoiding bankruptcy, democrats coming to power, or the CPR being admitted to the UN.

To some degree, negative goals are automatically implied by a party's possession of positive goals. If Party A wants Goal X, then, logically, A does not want any Not-X. However, there is a practical difference between wanting a specific, positive goal as first choice and being unwilling to accept any alternative future state as second best; and wanting to avoid a specific future state yet perhaps being willing to accept almost any alternative if only that undesired can be avoided. The latter case can be illustrated by a conflict occurring annually on the US/Canadian border between North Dakota and Manitoba, when the spring floods fill the Pembina River (also the international boundary) and spill over onto the land of whichever side (Canadian or American) fails to build the higher dykes. The goals of both parties (local Canadian and American farming communities) are to avoid having the flood waters spill onto their side of the river and ruin the crops. To this end, dykes on both sides of the river are built higher each year (but apparently never high enough to contain the flood water completely). In recent years, farmers from both communities have taken to dynamiting the flood defences on the opposite side of the river in order to avoid the unwanted future state of flood and ruin on their side of the Pembina. It should be emphasised, of course, that the goal of both communities is not primarily to have the spring floods flow onto the land of the other community, but to prevent it flooding onto their own land. Hence, a whole range of other alternative outcomes become theoretically possible, most of them involving no loss or damage to the other party in this 'international' conflict.[3] The example suggests that conflicts involving negative goals for the parties may often be simpler to solve, mainly because they also involve the possibility of a number of alternative future states (some of which must be realistic as well as just theoretically possible), which would satisfy the parties by avoiding undesired outcomes.

The simple division of goals into positive or negative can be extended by the observation that parties in the real world seldom pursue single goals in isolation, thus becoming involved in situations where individual goals are mutually incompatible. A far more realistic view is one in which the parties possess a set, or schedule, of desired goals (both positive and negative), some of which are salient and highly valued, others desired but peripheral, and all held in (at least) some rough-and-ready order of importance. Circumstances will thus arise where parties possess a number of goals that clash, but the number and the salience of the clashing goals will vary from case to case. Similarly, other parties may find that while some goals they pursue are mutually incompatible, others are, in fact, compatible or congruent, their achievement even depending upon the co-operative behaviour of the other party. A mixed situation of conflict and co-operation often exists. One further line of thought arising from the conception of parties pursuing goal 'sets' is the nature of *non-conflictful* relationships between social entities, and how these differ basically from relationships involving conflict.

3. NON-CONFLICTFUL RELATIONSHIPS

That particular parties may possess and pursue congruent as well as contradictory goals underlines the simple fact that social entities, from individuals to countries, can be in co-operative as well as conflictful relationships, and frequently are in mixed situations of conflict and co-operation. Relationships of 'pure' conflict seldom exist, although it is logical to allow for circumstances in which all the goals of two parties are incompatible. Historically, situations of total conflict have occasionally existed between parties, from families (Montagues and Capulets before Romeo and Juliet reached puberty) to countries (Germany and the Soviet Union from May 1941 to 1945).[4]

While the world mainly proffers examples of mixed relationships between entities, it is interesting to consider the theoretical nature of pure conflict or co-operation, and to exhaust the range of social relationships that *can* exist, before concentrating upon those dominated by conflicting goals. Once again, in considering the nature of co-operation, common language approaches emphasise the behavioural aspects of the relationship (. . . '*cooperation*, the process by which social entities function in the service of one another . . .' Wright, 1951, p. 197), although psychological aspects are also commonly noted, such as mutual liking or role inter-dependence.[5] However, our discussion of goal compatibility and incompatibility leads to the conclusion that there are other components to the relationship of co-operation such as the nature of the parties goals, which need to be included in any analysis of pure co-operation.

Furthermore, it can hardly be argued that relationships of conflict or co-operation exhaust the possible range of circumstances. Countries, collectivities, groups and individuals '. . . may have non-interfering, private, disjoint goals . . .' (Lüschen, 1970, p. 24); may not inter-act at the behavioural level; and (in extreme cases) may possess no perceptions of, or attitudes towards, one another. In other words, parties may have no relationship at all, one with another, and hence be in circumstances of complete *isolation*. (Perhaps Japan under the Tokugawas comes nearest to the pure situation at the international level − that is, until Japanese isolation was broken through the action of Commodore Perry's fleet.) Hence, while bearing in mind the mixed nature of most real world relationships, we suggest the three relationships in Table 1.1 as 'ideal' types.

TABLE 1.1   Social relationships: Basic types

'Pure' situation	Goals	Characteristic behaviour	Characteristic inter-party attitudes	Characteristic relationship
Conflict	*Incompatible:* (i) in different order of importance (ii) Contradictory; mutually exclusive	Solely at own behest; blocking, resistant, interfering; cost imposing	Hostile	Enmity
Co-operation	*Congruent:* Identical, interdependent or complementary	Via consultation; concerted, or accommodative; benefit-conferring	Friendly	Alignment
Isolation	*Independent:* No inter-active effects; goals can be held simultaneously as none affects the other	None directed towards the other party	Ignorant or non-existent	None

Table 1.1 emphasises the central role of a party's goals in defining what sort of relationship exists between it and another party or, more

realistically, what degree of conflict and co-operation characterises the inter-party relationship. As we have argued already, 'pure' situations of conflict or co-operation seldom exist in real world relationships at any social level, even the international. The degree to which, in mixed relationships, conflicting relationships are off-set by co-operative ones (and vice versa) will have a considerable effect both on the attitudes of the parties towards one another, and to the behaviour they use to pursue their goals. These other components of conflict, *attitudes* and *behaviour*, must now be briefly introduced.

B. CONFLICT ATTITUDES

As we devote Part II of this study to considering the other two structural components of our overall concept of 'conflict', we can be brief in this present introductory section. The second of our major components of 'conflict' consists of those psychological states or conditions that accompany (and frequently exacerbate) both conflict situations and resultant conflict behaviour. We should emphasise initially that the main assumption of this study is that the 'psychology of conflict' is best regarded as an exacerbating factor, rather than a prime cause of social and international disputes. In other words, an *instrumental* approach is adopted to the main question of the sources of conflict, and the assumption made that conflicts are most usefully regarded as arising from a realistic pursuit of goals, no matter how oddly these goals appear to be selected. This approach is very much opposed to another main line of thought in research into human conflict, which may be characterised as the *expressive* view of the sources of human conflict. This is mainly espoused by those psychologists, psychiatrists and ethologists, who insist that human conflict is fundamentally an 'internally' generated phenomenon, its root causes lying in the emotional states of fear, hostility, anger or aggression shared by large and small groups of individuals. 'Wars begin in the minds of men . . .' is a crucial sentiment of the opening sentences of the UNESCO Charter. However, the exact interpretation of 'begin in . . .' is important. If it means that hostility, fear and aggression arising spontaneously within men are the prime underlying cause of conflict situations developing, or conflict behaviour taking place, then the whole drive of research into conflict must take one particular direction, as must practical efforts to solve conflicts and disputes.[6] If it means that fears, prejudices and assumptions inculcated into people in the past, or a current perception of threat and danger, can bring about or accompany violence or other coercive behaviour as a reaction, then quite different inferences for research and policy should be drawn.

It is worthwhile considering the *expressive* approach to the sources of social and international conflict, in connection with our simple 'model' of the major components of conflict. Basically, an expressive approach to conflict implies that the sources of a dispute lie in the psychological processes determining a party's emotions, attitudes and perceptions, and that these could, in turn, affect the selection of *an adversary*, and of *issues over which to differ*, as well as the kind of *behaviour* deemed appropriate. In short, the diagram would need to be altered from that appropriate for an *instrumental* approach to conflict, where the sources of conflict were those conditions in a party's environment leading initially to situations of goal incompatibility, and ensuing attitudes and behaviour, see Fig. 1.3.

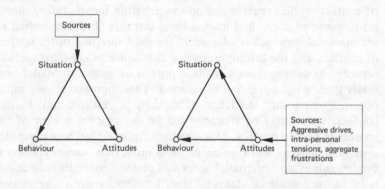

FIGURE 1.3   Instrumental and expressive theories of sources of conflict

This may seem rather an obscure distinction, although the second diagram in Fig. 1.3 represents the position taken by some psychiatrists, psychoanalysts and ethologists, who argue that the basic sources of war and other human ills brought about by unrestrained or lethal disputes, lie in human, genetically determined aggressiveness,[7] the death instinct (or some other manifestation of mental illness), or the normal (but regrettable) workings of the unconscious. It also throws light upon the arguments of conflict researchers who hold that some conflicts are, in a sense, *unreal* and thus require actions to end conflict quite different from those indicated by their ostensible causes. One example of *unreal conflict* is that caused by the process of scapegoating, the name given to the process by which the frustrations, fears and hostility generated within a particular group of people, either by continual stress and deprivation, or by specific events or actions by others, are redirected onto some easily available third party, which then becomes the target of accusations, competition, and (often) violence. Frequent cases of *pogroms* or disorganised violence carried out against ethnic or religious minorities during times of economic decline, high tension (war or an external threat) or severe frustration (by an untouchable ruling elite), are often quoted as examples of this process of redirecting hostility and energy away from the real source of fear and goal-frustration. If and when such a process occurs, it does, indeed, raise serious problems for anyone attempting to analyse the dispute. The basic causes of the overt behaviour may not be those consciously put forward by the belligerent party to explain that behaviour. (Individuals may be rationalising their own activity.) In this sense, then, the conflict may be 'unreal' and attempts to solve it by operating on the ostensible causes doomed to failure. It is argued by proponents of theories of unreal conflict that only when the original (and often hidden) sources of frustration, tension or fear are removed, will the redirected conflict behaviour come to an end. The problem for the analyst (and policy-maker) is to discover the actual source of these emotions, which usually involve salient goals not being achieved.

Even though a motive-oriented approach to conflict undoubtedly offers a number of promising insights into otherwise puzzling aspects of certain types of conflict (mainly individual and small group), nonetheless this study adopts a basically instrumental approach to disputes.

Conflict attitudes are regarded as those psychological states (both common attitudes, emotions and evaluations, as well as patterns of perception and misperception) that frequently accompany and arise from involvement in a situation of conflict. Conflict attitudes and perceptions are assumed to be factors arising through the stresses of being in a conflict, rather than factors fundamentally causing conflicts, although extreme conflict attitudes involving hostility, misperceptions and dehumanisation of the opposing party will obviously exacerbate any dispute. Furthermore, it is undoubtedly the case that previous experience of a conflict will leave residual elements of prejudice and hostility to affect future behaviour, and these may become contributory sources of future disputes. The long drawn out 'feuds' of Orangeman and Catholic in Northern Ireland, or Greek and Turk in Cyprus, are examples of this factor in operation.

Our choice should not be interpreted as downgrading the importance of psychological aspects of any conflict, however, nor an intention to neglect fear, hostility, suspicion, distrust and a sense of being under threat as important contributory factors in the continuance of a dispute. Conflict attitudes often become key factors in later states of disputes, and in the continuation (and even extension) of the conflict when the original situation has altered so that it no longer seems sufficient reason for continuing. High levels of hatred and anger may become of paramount importance, so that the conscious goals of the parties change to include those of defeating, punishing or humiliating the adversary. Recognition of the often crucial role of such psychological aspects of a conflict is of greatest importance in analysing any dispute, or in taking any action to bring about a solution (or merely an end to violence). If, for example, efforts are being made to remove the reasons for a conflict continuing, does one concentrate upon the situation of goal incompatibility, or upon the psychological condition and perceptions of the parties involved? The answer appears to be that, in most cases, both are important and inter-connected. Past experience of conflict (especially with the same adversary) will give people a set of expectations regarding the future; assumptions about their own nature and the nature of their opponents; and prejudices about other parties and peoples, all of which affect the likelihood of future conflict situations developing in the direction of coercion. Such behaviour will undoubtedly reinforce previously held beliefs and attitudes, and make participants ready to develop more extreme levels of intolerance, hatred and suspicion. A self-reinforcing process develops.

Implicit is the idea that, as conflict attitudes are regarded in this study, two distinguishable aspects are involved; an emotional, judgemental or *affective* element, and a cognitive or *perceptual* element. Both influence a party's view of its external environment, of itself and its adversaries, whether the party is an individual or made up of individuals. Both will affect the probability and intensity of subsequent violence. For the moment, therefore, we define *conflict attitudes* (employed as shorthand for 'conflict attitudes and perceptions') as: *Common patterns of expectation, emotional orientation, and perception which accompany involvement in a conflict situation*. At this point, it is sufficient merely to indicate that conflict attitudes include:

(i) Emotional orientations, such as feelings of anger, distrust, resentment, scorn, fear, envy or suspicion of the intentions of others.

(ii) Cognitive processes, such as stereotyping, or a refusal to accept non-conforming information in an endeavour to maintain a consistent structure of beliefs about the outside world (and especially about an adversary).

A number of specific 'images' are the result of these latter processes operating in a situation of conflict, but detailed consideration of these will be left until later.

D. CONFLICT BEHAVIOUR

Our third major component of 'conflict' consists of the actual behaviour of the opposing parties resulting from their possession of mutually incompatible goals and from their attempts to achieve those goals. *Conflict behaviour* may initially be defined as:

Actions undertaken by one party in any situation of conflict aimed at the opposing party with the intention of making that opponent abandon or modify its goals.

Several comments need to be made to clarify this working definition. The first is that it presents an immediate (and familiar) problem of interpreting the motivations of a behaving party; in this case, of 'getting behind' the action and determining whether an action was 'truly' intended to affect an adversary in such a manner as to bring about a change in goals and objectives. Use of the term 'truly' emphasises that *someone* has to make a judgement about the intention of the acting party and three possible answers exist to the question of who interprets the aims and intentions of the actor:

(i) The actor himself.
(ii) Some observing third party.
(iii) The target of the act.

It is quite possible that an action may be perceived by an adversely affected party as having the objective of forcing it to abandon a particular disputed objective, but that, in spite of such a perception this was not the underlying intention of the actor. A general warning issued by a minister of one country may be taken by another government to have been specifically directed against them, when the warning was, in reality, directed against a third government. Nonetheless, it seems from a common-sense point of view that *conflict behaviour* should consist of actions aimed at affecting the other party, either directly or indirectly, but certainly by intention. The particular individual, group, organisation or country should be trying to raise the costs to its adversary of the latter's continuing to pursue its own goals, and should be conscious that this is its fundamental strategy. The parties' intentions and objectives underlying particular actions are, however, crucial elements in the definition. Conflict researchers have indeed, made a distinction between *conflict*, implying behaviour aimed at affecting an opponent, and *competition*, where behaviour is aimed directly at achieving particular goals. (For instance, a fist-fight contrasted with a foot-race.)

The second point about our definition is that actions do not necessarily have to be violent to be counted as conflict behaviour,[8] although they may be so. Violent behaviour does not automatically arise from any conflict situation, nor, indeed, does conflict behaviour necessarily have to involve any coercive element, or strategies that raise the opponent's costs of continuing to pursue his own goals to such a level that the pursuit will be abandoned. This may seem perverse, as conflict behaviour is normally taken to mean some form of action containing a coercive element, threatening or imposing costs on an opposing party. Furthermore, any definition of conflict behaviour which does not limit the category to that involving coercion places us in the paradoxical position of arguing that *all* behaviour in a conflict situation, provided it is aimed at the opposing party, is conflict behaviour, even if this involves retreat, compromise or behaviour which confers benefits on an adversary. According to our present definition conflict behaviour can involve threats of negative sanctions, offers of alternative benefits, discussion, persuasion, appeals to common values, or common sense, and a whole range of non-violent behaviour, even though the ultimate threat of future violence may be constantly in the background to act as implicit coercion should any of the non-coercive acts fail to achieve their desired objective.

Apart from the crucial element of deliberate intention, and the unimportance of violence as a criterion of conflict behaviour, a third major implication of our working definition is that conflict behaviour can take on a wide variety of forms in addition to the classical ones of physical damage to other people and property on a large or small scale. Often, these forms can be extremely bizarre. For example, one small section of the pacifist sect known as Doukhobors, now resident in western Canada, practices a wide variety of conflict behaviour in order to force the remainder of the sect (and ultimately, the other inhabitants of British Columbia) to abandon material possessions which threaten 'the spiritual life'. The 'Freedomites', as the radical section of the Doukhobors is called, have blown up schools, public buildings and other churches, as well as burning down their own villages and starting major forest fires. However, one of their most frequent forms of social protest is to appear in the nude, in order to emphasise their contempt for material possessions and their desire to convert others to sharing their values.[9] Undoubtedly, such action falls within our present working definition of conflict behaviour; a situation of goal incompatibility exists between orthodox and radical Doukhobors, and the radical Freedomites are using this particular form of behaviour, among others, to influence their adversaries to abandon their goals.

Paradoxically, other forms of conflict behaviour can be intended to have a primary effect upon the opposing party, but result in an even more drastic secondary effect upon the party taking the action. One example is self-destruction (or the threat thereof) through: (i) suicide, as in the case of a number of Buddhist monks in South Vietnam in their struggle against the Catholic-dominated regime of Ngo Den Diem; or (ii) hunger striking, as in the case of many suffragettes in England during the struggle to obtain the franchise before World War I, or various Catholic prisoners during the current troubles in Northern Ireland. Both types of action may be seen as behaviour aimed at changing the goals, decisions and behaviour of an adversary (usually a much stronger one). The 'coercion' in such cases is not easy to identify — at least in any everyday sense of that word — although some may be exerted through loss of reputation, or through the anticipated negative reactions of influential third parties. Physical damage occurs mainly to the behaving party. However, self-destruction by some members of a party in conflict can prove a very potent strategy in achieving 'victory' for those of the party who remain.

When confronted with such strange examples of conflict behaviour, a sense of intellectual simplicity arises when considering more 'orthodox' forms by parties in a conflict situation. However, even the more straightforward types of conflict behaviour, involving coercion, cost-imposition and (ultimately) violence, are all, to some degree, culture bound. Hugh Foot, for example, describes how, during his early years as a colonial administrator, a traditional form of conflict behaviour between *hamoulets* (family farms or holdings) in Samarian villages was tree cutting, whereby injury was inflicted upon an enemy by cutting down or burning fig or olive trees belonging to the rival hamoulet (Foot, 1964, p. 45). Sanctions against villagers who gave evidence about such behaviour to colonial authorities consisted of further bouts of tree cutting as a warning. Tens of thousands of pounds worth of damage was inflicted annually by this activity.

E. SUMMARY

This opening chapter has introduced some of the conceptual complexities that attend any study of the basic structure of social and international conflicts, and in doing so has advanced the conception of three inter-related components in what everyday language means by 'conflict':

(i) A situation of incompatible goals.
(ii) A range of psychological conditions experienced by the parties involved.
(iii) A set of related behaviours used to achieve the disputed goals.

Working definitions were suggested for these basic components, a short discussion undertaken of possible sources of social conflicts, and some consideration given to questions of non-conflict relationships.

All of this may seem academic in the worst sense of that word, and to have little connection with the realities of either conducting a conflict in a cause deemed just, or of managing conflicts which threaten to be damaging for the society in which they occur. However, discussions of fundamental terms and concepts, and attempts to achieve initial clear thinking should be sympathetically considered. Clear analysis should always precede action, and this is the case whether one is trying to understand a conflict, win it, or find a solution before it becomes too destructive. Consider the prime problem of how a society, intra or international, can cope with intense conflicts. To a large degree, the manner in which any social system attempts to deal with conflict depends upon the dominant theories in that society about the nature of the phenomenon, about its structures, and about the way in which it develops (perhaps in 'undesirable' directions). To take a crude example of this principle, if certain conflicts within society are regarded as stemming from ineradicable human qualities such as greed and envy then they are defined as sins, crimes or social deviance, and are 'managed' by coercion or punishment and the imposition of law-and-order policies through deterrent police forces. If, by contrast, conflicts are deemed to be caused by inadequate socialisation then a solution is sought by efforts to improve the inculcation of approved norms, beliefs, and patterns of behaviour within new members of society. If another society holds the theory that conflict becomes unavoidable because of inherent aggressive drives in men, then the best way of managing conflict in that society becomes the provision of 'safe' opportunities whereby such aggressive drives can be released in ways that cause minimum destruction to the social fabric, and to others in society. If, finally, the view is prevalent that conflicts are basically instrumental, and occur because of a rational pursuit of goals in conditions of scarce resources, then conflict management becomes a matter of resource redistribution, or the inculcation of different sets of values, such as frugality and asceticism.

Adopting an initial approach that suggests that what are normally called 'conflicts' are complex and multi-dimensional phenomena, consisting of at least three basic components, we imply that efforts to analyse disputes must take account of the existence of these three components, and their inter-relationships. Similarly, attempts to prosecute disputes, or to manage them so that they become productive (or at least less harmful) must also take account of the three components discussed in this chapter.

Unfortunately, a number of other complexities regarding the basic nature of conflicts between human individuals and groups remain to be discussed before proceeding to more detailed analysis of the realities of international and intra-national disputes. For one thing, it is manifestly the case that conflicts are not static phenomena, and hence the dynamic aspects of conflict which alter both structure and inter-party relationships over time, are essential aspects of any satisfactory analysis. The necessity for considering the nature of basic *conflict processes*, both inter-party and intra-party, is unarguable. Again, we have tended to discuss the basic structure of conflicts in isolation from any consideration of who takes part in such inter-actions, and of what sorts of social entities engage in conflict, with what differences in behaviour and results. The remainder of Part I therefore considers such fundamental topics as the nature of conflict situations and conflict processes, the nature of parties in conflict, and the dynamics of conflict. We begin with a more detailed discussion of the issues in conflict.

2 Conflict Situations

> . . . the only war I ever approved of was the Trojan war; it was
> fought over a woman, and the men knew what they were fighting
> for . . .
>
> William Lyon Phelps

The decision to define *conflict situations* as circumstances in which
parties possess mutually incompatible goals, frequently arising from a
mis-match of social values and structures, is an arbitrary one, as are all
definitional decisions. Furthermore, it may be controversial, as there
are other possible approaches to defining the basic structure of conflict
and distinguishing the different types that exist. It could be objected,
for example, that a definition relying upon overt goal incompatibility
between social entities as an indicator of the presence of 'conflict'
might well be misleading, for it obscures an important difference
between disputes over things, and disputes over ideas or values. This
familiar distinction in the literature on conflict contrasts *conflicts of
interest* and *value dissensus* (Aubert, 1963), or *competition* and
ideological conflict. Is such a distinction a valid one, and does it affect
our decision to identify a conflict situation by the existence of goal
incompatibilities?

A. CONFLICTS OF INTEREST OR VALUE

The distinction between conflicts of interest and ideological (or value)
conflicts is often made on the grounds that some disputes are
characterised by a disagreement about the distribution of some scarce
resource which the parties all value highly, while others are more
'fundamental', and arise from parties possessing wholly different sets
of beliefs and values about desirable future social structures, ways of
achieving these, and the basic nature of the circumstances within which
relationships exist. In the case of ideological conflict, the parties
fail to '. . . share the same conceptualization of the situation . . .'

(Druckman and Zechmeister, 1973, p. 450) and are working towards objectives that, while certainly incompatible, also involve no shared values permitting some compromise solution based upon sharing prized (but disputed) resources. Glenn *et al.* (1970) use as an example of conflicts over basic values, two individuals quarrelling about the details of work arrangements within a marriage, while the 'real' conflict arises from wholly differing conceptions of the husband and wife roles in such a relationship.[1] At another social level, we might find 'liberal' and 'Marxist' academics in dispute over a university policy on student admissions, where the basic conflict stems from wholly different views about the short-term role of universities in society. Again, domestic political controversy over a particular piece of government legislation might arise from fundamentally different conceptions about the nature and reasons for social problems; one ideology might hold that problems arise from a social structure that should be changed, another that they arise from people not adjusting to the system (Druckman and Zechmeister, 1973, p. 451). An excellent international example (apart from the frequent ideologically en-gendered disputes that characterised the sixteenth and twentieth centuries) arose from the wholly different approaches of the Bolsheviks and the German and Austrian delegates to the Brest Litovsk peace talks in 1917–18. The representatives of the Quadruple Alliance operated on the basis of a traditional value system, which involved advancing the interests of their national state (and hence perceived the negotiations as being mainly concerned with wringing the maximum concessions in terms of territory, economic resources and 'in-dependent' client states to serve as buffers against adversaries). The Bolsheviks (at least in the initial stages of the talks) operated on an ideology of transnational class conflict and the overthrow of French and British, as well as German and Austrian capitalism, irrespective of 'national' interests. Hence, their goals were peace without annexa-tions, but also maximum delay and opportunity to undermine German capitalism and militarism via massive propaganda, so that their class revolution would spread to the remainder of industrialised Europe and obviate the need for any traditionally conceived 'peace settlement'. The account of the early discussions makes a fascinating example of the way in which clashing goals can arise from wholly differing ideological positions, and be the overt source of continuing conflict (Wheeler-Bennett, 1938).

While a case can be made for differentiating between conflicts where: (i) the parties basically agree about the value of some position, role or resource, and conflict over who obtained most of it (a *conflict of interest*); and (ii) the parties differ fundamentally about the nature of desirable end states or social and political structures (a *conflict of value*), it does not seem to be a distinction that necessarily invalidates our contention that all conflicts can usefully be viewed as relationships involving incompatible goals. Whether we consider circumstances where two social entities differ about desirable social structures, behaviour and values, or where two factions within a single entity cannot agree about legitimate goals for that entity because of opposed ideological positions, such circumstances eventually produce situations of overt goal incompatibility. Parties that possess wholly different value structures (and possibly, as a result, a different definition of their existing relationship and the problem facing them) will inevitably also hold particular goals arising from these values. Hence, conflict may still usefully be considered a matter of goal incompatibility *if* these resultant goals (a means of achieving some ideologically determined end state) are indeed, mutually incompatible at that point in time. (The actual goals of two parties with quite differing ideologies may not conflict; there is no logical reason to rule out the possibility that differing ideologies could give rise to compatible goals although this is probably rare.) In many cases particular value structures call for conforming behaviour or even conversion of others (or, failing this, their physical destruction). Then, goals of conversion clash with other goals of retaining one's own pattern of beliefs or behaviour.

Although basic similarities exist between inter-party relations that develop when social entities possess widely different value systems, and those that develop when they share fundamental values, but clash over distribution, priority or even means of attaining goals, this is not to argue that the circumstances giving rise to goal incompatibilities are irrelevant for resultant disputes. For one thing, ideological differences frequently give rise to very many intense goal incompatibilities. Wright (1951, p. 186) comments that, historically, '. . . radical differences of religion, ideology or institutions have tended to induce conflict . . .' while others have argued both that ideologically derived goal incompatibilities are likely to result in more intense disputes, and that such conflicts are ultimately more difficult to resolve than those where the involved parties share, at least, basic value orientations. According to Druckman and Zechmeister (1973, p. 454), '. . . Conflicts of interest between parties from opposing ideological "enclaves" are more threatening to the stability of the social system than is competition between parties within an "enclave" . . .'. Such a view is hardly surprising, given some of the customary attitudinal and behavioural patterns associated with extreme ideologies and their tendency to produce patterns of instrumental goals likely to clash with those produced by other ideologies.

However, while the historical linkage between ideological differences and major goal incompatibilities can be accepted, there is no logically necessary connection. Wright (1951, p. 196) has noted that differences in ideology tend to induce conflict, but he adds that they '. . . do not . . . necessarily do so, nor does conflict, if it occurs, necessarily eliminate the differences. Consequently, it is unwise to *identify* inconsistencies of opinion with conflict. . . .' For this reason, it seems appropriate to retain the definition of a conflict situation as being one involving some form of goal incompatibility, which may arise from holding similar values or widely different ones, leaving an analysis of the actual issues in dispute to determine whether a conflict is over resource distribution, role occupancy, the existence of a perceived threat to already obtained and enjoyed resources, or conversion to, or retention of, a fundamental pattern of belief, behaviour or social organisation.

B. CONFLICTS OF ATTRIBUTION AND MEANS

A similar line of argument can be used with regard to two other forms of conflict, both of which can, ultimately, be regarded as resulting in situations of goal incompatibility. The first of these is what Joann Horai (1977, pp. 88–91) refers to as *attributional* conflict, or a dispute over what has given rise to the set of circumstances from which a dispute or problem arises. At an inter-personal level, Horai gives the example of parents disagreeing about the source of undesired physical symptoms displayed by their child, and coming into conflict about whether the cause of a rash might be insect bites or some form of psychosomatic disturbance. At the intra-societal level, similar disagreements arise over the causes of large scale unemployment, while in international relations, disagreements about the fundamental causes of Third World poverty have produced causal analyses ranging from those which point to the detrimental effects of the capitalist system in exploiting Third World resources and their peoples, to those which underline the Third World's initial poverty, over-population, traditional values, and general misgovernment and instability.

Disagreements about *why* particular undesired conditions exist produce a number of phenomena which influence the future course of attributional conflict. First, relations between the parties disagreeing over attribution are likely to deteriorate as each party begins to hold the other responsible, via its faulty analysis and actions on that basis, for the continuation of the undesired situation:

> . . . the party who rejects the remedial initiative proposed by the other may be perceived as a continuance cause, held responsible and blameworthy for causing the problem to continue by failing to do what the other perceives the situation requires. . . . (Horai, 1977, pp. 89–90)

Secondly, as with fundamentally differing views about the nature of the issues in conflict, one strategy often adopted by parties in an attributional conflict is to attempt to foist their analysis: (i) on to their adversary (if successful, such a strategy can be useful in shifting or avoiding any blame for the situation attaching to one's own party, in shifting responsibility for the major remedial effort onto others, or in placing one's own party in an advantageous bargaining position with others in attempting to find some solution to the problem); or (ii) on to observing and interested third parties (if successful this strategy can avoid a negative image of faulty motivation, neglect or incompetence).[2] Finally, the parties in an attributional conflict often disagree about the nature of the most effective remedies to be put into operation. Attributional conflict is therefore accompanied by disagreements over *means*, so that while parties may agree about ultimate goals, they fundamentally disagree about both: (i) the root causes of their problem, and (ii) appropriate means for dealing with it.

Disputes about means need not, however, be accompanied by attributional conflict. It is perfectly possible (and frequent) for parties to agree about the goals they wish to achieve (the goals may be identical, complementary or inter-dependent), yet disagree violently about the most effective, least costly manner of achieving them. Even if parents agree that the source of their child's rash is, in fact, mosquito bites, it is still possible to disagree about the most effective treatment (Horai, 1977, p. 89). Similarly, in apparently united groups and organisations there may exist a complete consensus over the goals that should be pursued on behalf of the organisation, yet such disagreement about the most appropriate means to be used that major cleavages develop within the party, and a major intra-party dispute develops. As Hammond (1965, p. 46) observes, in connection with international differences over what solution is 'best', conflict over means '. . . can be as dangerous as any other kind; it can and does rapidly proliferate into self-contained systems of thought, which harden into ideologies . . .'.

While 'conflicts of means' exist both between and within parties apparently agreed about the nature of desirable ends, they can exist for a variety of reasons. One is that the parties or factions within parties may genuinely disagree about the probable outcome from the range of courses of action confronting them. In other words, people may agree completely about what they want, but disagree about what to do to obtain it by disagreeing about the likely effects of proposed actions. There exist '. . . differences in predictions only . . .' (Marwell, 1966, p. 430). On the other hand, it may be that intra-party cleavages and conflicts over means develop because those proposed impose costs of action in the pursuit of the agreed goals, and these are differentially distributed among those involved. Pursuit by one means may impose low costs on the bulk of the people involved, but heavy costs on a small subgroup; pursuit by another might cause the elite to suffer considerable losses in status and possessions yet the bulk of the rank and file to sustain minimal loss; a third method may push the bulk of the costs on rank and file, while the leaders suffer not at all.[3] The effects of such differentially distributed costs in arousing a conflict over means will obviously be most frequently observed in circumstances where the relevant social entities already suffer from major cleavages (a country divided upon religious lines, a group made up of several families, or a community clearly split along class lines); or where separate parties are agreed upon complementary goals but not means, as in an inter-party or inter-governmental alliance.

Whatever the basic reasons for disagreements over means, or the dimensions that underlie such disputes, there can be little doubt that they are frequent and can be intense. Many conflict researchers feel that conflicts of means pose as large a threat to international peace at the present time as more traditionally conceived conflicts over goals, ends or 'the spoils'; and that an international consensus may be emerging about the nature of common problems and of desirable, shared goals, but that countries and communities will remain dangerously divided '. . . over political solutions to those physical, biological and social problems . . .' which threaten all of them. Hence, there will be a change '. . . to a future in which there will be agreement over ends (world security), but . . . conflict over means (how to get it) . . .' (Hammond, 1965, pp. 45–6).

There is undoubtedly some validity in this view, and it need not necessarily be confined to conflict over methods and means at the international level. Conflict over means can be intense, and lead to the further development of antagonistic feelings and patterns of behaviour in much the same way as can situations of basic goal incompatibility (although there is [initially] less likelihood of violent conflict behaviour developing over shared goals accompanied by differing means, than over fundamentally opposed goals). The attitudinal and behavioural results of a conflict of means do not, however, appear fundamentally different in kind from those of a straightforward incompatibility of goals. Furthermore, conflict over means can simply be regarded as another case of goal incompatibility between factions where the *issue* is the strategy to be pursued by the party to which those factions belong. The goal of one faction is to make their party adopt strategy A1, and success in this will prevent another faction achieving the goal of making the party adopt strategy B1. While both factions may be agreed about the overall goal for their party, they possess additional and incompatible goals that give rise to a situation of conflict at a different analytical level. For all these reasons, it seems reasonable to ignore the conflict of ends/conflict of means distinction, and regard both as straightforward cases of goal incompatibility.

In summary, all of the different types of conflict discussed above can be encompassed by the 'incompatible goals' formulation of a conflict situation, even though it may be true, as Table 2.1 illustrates, that there are interesting differences between the manner in which goal incompatibilities come about, and these will obviously have an effect upon the subsequent development of the dispute.

C. ISSUES IN CONFLICT

The conception that a conflict situation consists essentially of parties holding (and probably pursuing) mutually incompatible goals simplifies the analytical task of delineating the *issues* in any conflict – in plain language, what the conflict is 'about'. This is always one of the most familiar questions asked about any dispute, and the query 'What are the issues in conflict?' can be answered by reference to salient goals that are incompatible. In other words, 'issues' refer to the inter-related goal incompatibilities of adversaries. In many cases these can be

TABLE 2.1 Types of conflict situation

Conflict type	Values	Causal agreement	Goals	Means	Related concepts
Value	No necessary agreement on basic values and ends	No	If incompatible arise from different values and definitions of nature of problem	Not applicable	Value dissensus (Aubert, 1963); ideological conflict
Interest	Agreement on basic values and ends	Yes	Incompatible, arising from scarcity of similarly valued resources	Not applicable	Competition
Attribution	Agreement on basic values and ends	No	Compatible or shared (i.e. removal of the problem)	Disagreement on basis of different predicted outcomes	Causal conflict (Horai, 1977)
Means	Agreement on basic values and ends	Either	Compatible or shared (i.e. removal of the problem)	Disagreement on basis of (i) predicted outcome or (ii) differential cost distribution	Cognitive conflict (Hammond, 1965)

regarded as subject *dimensions* upon which parties take up opposed positions because of their conscious goals. (The Indian goal of forcing a substantial devaluation of the Pakistani rupee in 1948, compared with the Pakistani goal of maintaining it at more or less its existing exchange value.) In others they may be simple either/or *dichotomies*. (The US goal of maintaining Taiwan's occupancy of the Chinese seat in the UN compared with the CPR's goal of occupying that seat itself.) It is commonplace that issues vary markedly from conflict to conflict, and can change radically over time in what is ostensibly the same conflict, once the parties' original goals are modified, abandoned or supplemented. As a case in point, the basic issues in the dispute in

Northern Ireland have changed radically, several times, between 1967 and 1978, moving from questions of civil rights for the Catholic minority back to the old question of the political regime suitable for the area, and its relations with Britain and Eire.

1. TYPES OF ISSUE

Issues in conflict may be classified in a wide variety of ways. One simple division is into disputes over limited resources, where one party will win, absolutely or relatively, and the other will lose, but both will exist at the end of the conflict (*resource conflict*); and disputes where the continued existence of one of the parties is at issue (*survival conflict*). This distinction can be exemplified by contrasting conflicts over who controls the political system in an existing state (via an election or a revolutionary war); and those over the continued existence of that state (a secessionist war, for example, such as the Nigerian–Biafran struggle, or the breakaway of East Pakistan to become Bangladesh). Often, survival conflicts are more intractable, even when the survival in question does not involve the physical survival of a category of individuals, but the continuance of a particular social organisation or political structure (the 'survival' of the state of Israel, or of unified Nigeria). It is often felt that civil wars offer no intermediate outcome between victory and defeat, if partition is not possible for geographical reasons.

However, not all conflicts centre around issues of survival or resource scarcity, or even over material resources or positional goods as Hirsch (1977) argues. Something more than a simple two-fold classification of issues is required:

(1) Issues concerned with the (exclusive) use, or ownership of resources (goals of obtaining land, raw materials, water supplies, access routes, houses, jobs).
(2) Issues concerned with the exclusive right to resources, or the control of both existing resources and potential future resources (goals of obtaining legal right or 'sovereignty', political power or control). One factor exacerbating the dispute over the Senkaku Islands is the possibility that rich deposits of oil might exist under the sea-bed of the nearby continental shelf.
(3) Issues concerned with the continued existence of one of the parties in its present form, or in some form acceptable to members of that party ('goals of survival'). Leaders often attempt to portray

issues in many conflicts as 'really' being those of survival, in order to increase solidarity, effort and support within the ranks of their own party.

(4) Issues concerned with status, prestige and precedence (goals of coming first, doing better than, depriving the other of, or not losing face because of).

(5) Issues concerned with the beliefs, attitudes, behaviour and (often) socio-economic organisation of another entity, with efforts to make that entity conform to desired and 'desirable' standards. This appears to be the basic implication of an 'ideological' conflict, exemplified by goals of converting Protestants to Catholicism and vice-versa.[4]

2. THE ISSUES: DIFFERING INTERPRETATIONS

One notable feature of many disputes is that the parties involved often disagree on what the conflict is 'really' about, one side defining the issues as being a set of (to them) salient problems, the other claiming the 'actual' core issues as something completely different. In psychological terms, the parties have *opposing 'definitions of the situation'*. One national government may see a conflict as a dispute about an attempt by a neighbouring government to deprive one of the latter's minority communities of its right to self-determination, while the rival government may view the dispute as a claim to state territory or an attempt to undermine national unity by attacking the integrity of the state.[5] One example of such a clash of perceptions may again be seen in the re-opening of the communal conflict in Ulster during the mid-1960s. To the early Catholic activists, the issues in dispute were discrimination, social reform and their community's lack of genuine participation in Ulster politics. At this early stage there was no mention of the boundary problem or unity with Eire. However, the Protestant majority defined the issues as the traditional ones of unification vs the continuation of Ulster's British connection, so that Catholic activity was perceived as yet another attack on the integrity of the state.

The existence of opposing definitions of 'what the conflict is about' implies that one way of gaining one's own goal in such a conflict is to influence the other party so that the latter accepts one's own way of regarding what issues are in conflict. Hence, a common tactic for gaining an advantage in a dispute is to have one's definition of the issues in conflict accepted by an adversary. Fisher (1964) has pointed to the general principle that 'issue control' is of vital tactical advantage in prosecuting a conflict successfully, a view which echoes Herbert Simon's dictum (1957, p. 233) that '. . . influence is exercised through control over the premises of decision . . .'. Once a party accepts its adversary's definition of the issues in conflict, it will often be at a marked disadvantage, seeking to justify both to itself and others, its own goals and behaviour in terms of its rival's underlying values. The process of justification often proves impossible, and leads to the phenomena of a 'loss of will' or 'crisis of confidence', preparatory to conceding the conflict to the opposing party. The use of this tactic of *conversion* is normally more successful in intra-national conflict, where the means for persuading an adversary to accept one's own definition of the situation are more readily available, usually including: (i) a generally shared value consensus within which limited conflicts occur; and (ii) rules and opportunity for debate, or exchange of information and views between the parties. In international disputes, such facilities for converting one's opponent are few, and attempts to force one's definition of the issues on another party are usually rejected with ease. 'National' minds are not often changed by an enemy. However, a supplementary strategy is to convince interested, and potentially influential third parties (other governments, the UN Secretariat, other international organisations) of the correctness of one's own definition of the issues in conflict. This strategy is often used by parties trying to obtain international support for their position in any dispute, so that indirect influence may be brought to bear on their adversary. If, for example, one government can convince others that the dispute in its border region involves a territorial claim by its neighbour, rather than a secessionist movement by an oppressed minority, the reaction of other governments is more likely to be favourable. If a salary claim can be presented as a matter of justice rather than greed, war as a matter of self-defence rather than aggression, a dispute over fishing grounds as a matter of survival rather than profit, a quarrel as forced rather than sought, then the reactions of third parties towards the convincing party are likely to be favourably affected.

D.   SUMMARY

This chapter has explored the idea of a situation of conflict and, while discussing various other formulations of *conflict situations* such as conflicts of values, means or attribution, has concluded that each of these can be regarded as a case of goal incompatibility, the *issues in conflict* falling into different types. We have also made the point that issues in a conflict can vary widely, and that it is possible for parties to have different views about what are the issues actually in conflict. This last point underlines that even an approach to conflict that emphasises goal incompatibility as a basic condition does not imply that conflict is always wholly realistic. Subjective elements creep into even such a basic process as the parties defining what the conflict is about. Misperceptions and confusions, particularly about the goals of the adversary, can often lead to widely differing views about the issues at stake, quite apart from the purely tactical question of attempting to present the conflict situation in the most favourable light to outsiders and followers in one's own party. The former process is particularly likely to occur when conflicts arise involving a number of inter-connected issues which the adversaries regard in different orders of importance; or when the conflict extends over a long period of time and the issues alter as time goes on. (Note how the issues in dispute between Israel and Egypt have changed radically since the June War of 1967.)

A final comment on the question of parties' definitions of the issues in conflict is that the goals of conflicting parties frequently become highly inter-dependent, particularly as the conflict proceeds over time, and fresh issues become involved in the dispute.[6] In such situations one party will develop subsequent goals: (i) because conditions have altered and new issues arise, *or* (ii) because of perception of the tactical and strategic goals (and motivations) of the opposing party and of the necessity for preventing attainment of these goals if one's own ultimate ambitions are to be fulfilled. It may happen that a manufacturer confronted with a strike has the primary goal of defeating the strikers, but the secondary goal of maintaining plant-running. He may attempt to bring in non-union labour to fulfil this latter goal, in which case the response of the union will be to prevent the non-union labour from entering the factory. This behaviour, in turn, may induce in the manufacturer the further goal of involving national law and order forces in order to maintain only peaceful picketing, and so on. The example merely shows that conflict has a dynamic aspect, and changes of issue may occur over time so that any static analysis which ignores change must be incomplete and misleading. The various processes by which conflicts change over time, as well as the *conflict situation* at any single point in time must be analysed if any useful understanding of a dispute is to be gained. The following chapter deals with some of these dynamic aspects of conflict.

3 Processes

Insisting upon the importance of the dynamic aspects of conflict is splendid in principle, but advancing knowledge of such dynamic processes has proved difficult. It is a commonplace that conflicts change over time. The most obvious aspect is change in the behaviour of the parties as they alter strategies and react to each other's actions, making minor escalatory or de-escalatory moves, or initiating major changes such as adopting coercion instead of conciliation. These behaviour patterns of the parties in conflict constitute a *process* that changes over time as the conflict develops giving rise to questions such as 'Is the conflict repetitive and cyclical, or characterised by a linear pattern of escalation?' or 'To what extent is the pattern of inter-action between the parties symmetric and to what extent one-sided?'

As our hypothetical example in chapter 2 indicates, however, the dynamic aspects of a conflict are not merely confined to the changing patterns of behaviour displayed by the parties, nor the relatively stable or unstable characteristics of inter-action patterns between them. Conflicts consist of the three basic components which can alter steadily over time or alternatively become wildly unstable. Conflicts can be dynamic in that issues and attitudes, as well as behaviour change markedly. Other aspects of a conflict also alter over time and radically change its nature and salient characteristics. Morton Deutsch has pointed out that destructive conflicts particularly have a tendency to 'expand' and 'intensify' along a large number of different dimensions, including the intensity of negative attitudes towards the adversary, the salience and number of issues making up the situation, the costs that parties are willing to bear, the number of parties (and principles) involved, and the tendency to rely more and more on behaviour involving threats, coercion and deception (Deutsch, 1969, p. 11).

Dynamic processes in conflicts may be sought in three major areas:

(a) *Within the parties themselves*, as goals, attitudes and behaviours change, or party structures alter in response to changes in adversary or environment. For example, hostility towards an adversary can grow slowly or rapidly within a party, or the sense of in-group solidarity show rapid increase at the start of the conflict to be followed by a gradual decline and final disintegration.

(b) *Between the parties*, as differing patterns of communication and inter-action emerge over time, and the conflict escalates, de-escalates, intensifies or dies down, expands or contracts in the attribute spaces it occupies.

(c) *Between the parties and their environment*, as the latter reacts to the conflict in ways ranging from efforts at quarantine to the involvement of third parties in roles such as supplies of resources, interveners, intermediaries or imposers of limits on behaviour or settlements.

With all three areas, the crucial problem is to find out what changes over time, and why, and what are the relationships between changes in various aspects of a conflict and between the rates of change. *What* increases or decreases in a conflict, and how are these changes inter-related? Unfortunately, in no other aspect of conflict research is the field more deficient in research findings than in the analysis of conflict processes. It is commonplace and commonsense knowledge that conflict situations often bring about a marked increase of coercive or violent behaviour by one or both parties, and that this phenomenon is frequently accompanied by an increase of hostility, hatred and suspicion as well as increasingly distorted perceptions of an enemy among members of parties in conflict. Similarly, studies have shown that the patterns of communication between parties in conflict alter considerably and diversely, ranging from a decrease in the subtlety and range of information communicated to a complicated alteration in the balance of information exchanged by adversaries, usually involving an increase of communication accompanied by a greater proportion characterised by expressions of negative affect or coercive statements.[1] However, the general level of knowledge about conflict processes is extremely patchy and uncertain, seldom going beyond the anecdotal or the hypothesis drawn from a single case.[2]

Given this lack of systematic analysis of conflict processes, the remainder of this chapter focuses on a limited number of dynamic processes that often occur when situations of goal incompatibility initially arise and lead to inter-action between parties, whether in-dividuals or made up of individuals. Two major processes are the familiar ones of *conflict widening* and *conflict escalation*, but we begin with the development of a conflict in a sequence of stages, and conclude with a short discussion of the nature of conflict cycles or spirals.

A. DEVELOPMENT PROCESSES

One fundamental dynamic aspect of social and international conflict involves the development of all three conflict components discussed in chapter 1. Classification into three basic components in a conflict implies that it is possible to have one or two components existing at a particular point in time without the others, and also that there might be some 'ideal' sequence in their development. The triadic structure of conflict and the idea of a sequence of development are also helpful in tackling the problem of how an observer can be sure that a conflict exists if there are no obvious signs of such a conflict through the behaviour of those involved.

This is not necessarily a trivial problem, for Marxist sociologists and others have pointed out that an extreme goal incompatibility (a situation of conflict) can exist between groups in a given society, and yet no sign of this deep-seated conflict be evident to outside observers searching for manifest signs of such a goal incompatibility. Similarly, all may be 'peaceful' between two countries, and yet the apparent peace mask intense differences of objectives, and a feeling of considerable mutual antagonism between citizens of the countries ostensibly 'at peace'.[3]

This problem is often debated as the difference between *manifest* and *latent* conflict, and definitions of the two exist.[4] A simple solution is to define *latent* conflict as the existence of a situation of conflict (parties possessing mutually incompatible goals); and *manifest* conflict as conditions in which parties possess incompatible goals and are pursuing some overt strategy *vis-à-vis* their opponent in order to achieve those goals. Thus *latent* conflict may be regarded as a conflict situation, while *manifest* conflict is a conflict situation accompanied by overt behaviour.

The major drawback of such a simple distinction is that it offers no clue as to why conflict behaviour is absent in spite of parties possessing mutually incompatible goals; or what circumstances prevent recognisable conflict behaviour in some intense conflict situation. Three sets of circumstances in which possible conflict may remain 'latent' can be suggested, namely conditions in which:

(a) A conflict situation is not recognised by one or both parties, but where their actual values and goals are mutually incompatible, so that if this were recognised, conflict behaviour would follow. (This is defined as *incipient conflict*.) This is a difficult situation to envisage, as it implies a complete misperception of a situation by somebody, but it is connected with the Marxist concept of 'false consciousness', and it is possible to imagine a situation in which one group of people aspired to a higher standard of living, but had yet to realise that this goal was being frustrated by another group either delaying technical innovation, or taking a disproportionate percentage of the wealth of the society.

(b) The conflict situation is recognised as such by both parties, but because too many other goals would be sacrificed if the mutually incompatible goals were to be pursued, no conflict behaviour occurs. (Each party's *own* goals are mutually incompatible.)

(c) The conflict situation is recognised, but actual conflict behaviour in pursuit of the party's goals is impossible, owing to the coercive power of potential opponents. Hence, all appears 'peaceful' (there is no apparent coercion or violence), but only because the potential costs of pursuing the desired goals are perceived as being too high to justify the attempt (for example, loss of freedom, approval of friends, status in society, possessions, life). This could be termed *suppressed conflict*. Perhaps the most obvious instance is the situation in the South African Republic where 'peace' and a relative absence of violence were a function of police efficiency, coercive sanctions, and a resultant lack of organisation and apathy.

Such distinctions may help in envisaging conflicts passing through a number of stages, although there is every possibility that particular conflicts may not develop beyond the preliminary stages, or be resolved (or resolve themselves) before reaching the stage of overt conflict. First there may exist some co-operative stage, in which parties possess complementary goals. From this relationship may arise circumstances in which certain interests, goals or objectives become mutually incompatible, even though this is not recognised immediately by one or other party to the relationship; conditions of *incipient conflict* will then exist. When both parties recognise the existence of mutually incompatible goals between them, conditions change to those of *latent conflict*, while both parties consider what action (if any) to take in such circumstances. Finally, parties may initiate action in order to achieve their own goals, and make the opponents abandon theirs, or give up some of their own objectives and search for a compromise settlement. The four stages and the analytic thresholds can be illustrated as a progression. However, there is nothing deterministic about the progression; not all conflicts pass through this complete process, although many do so. (See Fig. 3.1.) Others, as we argue above, either remain incipient through ignorance or through one party's manipulation of information and beliefs, so that one party recognises goal incompatibility while concealing this situation from others. Finally, conflicts may remain latent or suppressed, or return to being latent or suppressed, depending upon how they are dealt with by the society as a whole, or conducted by the parties. The development of real world conflicts is, once again, far more complex than suggested by our simple sequence, although the latter does form a useful framework for discussing the developmental dynamics of any dispute.

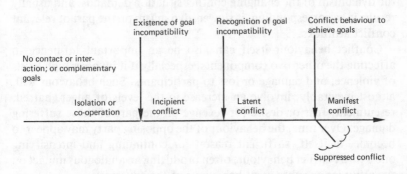

FIGURE 3.1   The developmental stages of conflict

B.   INTER-ACTION BETWEEN COMPONENTS

Any conflict that develops through the suggested sequence will eventually reach a condition where parties possess mutually incompatible goals, accompanying negative attitudes and display some form of behaviour, often of a coercive nature, in pursuit of these goals. In such circumstances, another important aspect of conflict dynamics is the process by which the basic components of a conflict affect each other, sometimes bringing about major transformations in the structure of the dispute.

It is important to emphasise the inter-relations of the three components of conflict, and the way in which these are closely linked in the real world. Analytically, it may be useful and justifiable to separate various aspects of the overall conception of a 'conflict' and by isolating them to achieve a more precise definition of each, emphasising distinctions between them. However, the three components isolated for separate study are inter-related parts of the same phenomenon, and in any analysis of an on-going dispute, they cannot be taken in isolation. For example, fear and hostility developed at some previous time can affect parties' perceptions of the situation confronting them, as well as their behaviour, both active and reactive, towards each other. Similarly, as the situation of conflict alters over time, and new issues and additional parties become involved, previously held attitudes and perceptions may alter to conform to changed conditions. In this way, the dynamism of the changing conflict situation demands, and usually results in, a corresponding, if slower, dynamism on the part of relevant conflict attitudes.

Conflict behaviour itself can also be an important influence in affecting the other two components, especially if it involves high levels of violence, and damage or loss to participants. Such behaviour will, almost inevitably, involve an increase in the levels of anger, hatred, resentment, fear or desire for revenge on the part of those suffering damage. Over time, the behaviour of the opposing party may appear to become, in itself, sufficient reason for continuing and intensifying one's own conflict behaviour, often producing an analogous impact on the attitudes or subsequent behaviour of the adversary.

In a similar fashion, changing patterns of inter-action between parties may raise new issues in the dispute, and alter the underlying situation of goal incompatibility itself. For one thing, the original issue may become 'elevated' from a specific goal incompatibility to one involving a clash of principle which affects not merely the original parties, but others who will have an interest in the outcome and thus be available as allies or patrons (Deutsch, 1969, p. 28). (If an instrumental conflict between members of two races becomes 'a racial conflict' then the scope has altered so much as to justify treating it as a different conflict.) For another, the tactics of conducting a conflict may develop new goals, as the parties seek to undermine each other's position of tactical advantage. Means- or sub-goals often take the form of preventing an adversary from retaining a position of tactical advantage in some area. To take a trivial example, a national government may attempt to hold elections in a dissident province seeking the ultimate goal of secession so that a major sub-goal of the movement directing the secession struggle will become the disruption of that election. The dissident leadership may be arrested by the political incumbents, so that a major sub-goal of the remainder of the party becomes one of securing the release of its imprisoned leaders. Usually, the process of adopting a tactical sub-goal is regarded as being merely a temporary expedient. New goals are seen as a means to an end, as ways of achieving original goals and aspirations. On occasions, however, they take on such a salience for the members of a particular party, both leaders and followers, that they replace that party's original goals. The conflict behaviour, although performed by the same party, is directed towards a wholly new set of goals; the issues change fundamentally. For example, between 1967 and 1977, the stated goal of the Egyptian Government of ending the existence of the state of Israel changed to a grudging acceptance of Israel's existence, and the goal of bringing about Israeli withdrawl from Egyptian territory in Sinai, plus some recognition of Palestinian rights. Equally, goals may, because of costly conflict behaviour, alter to those of peace, simple survival and some end to the conflict inter-action.

Alternatively, rather than gradually substituting wholly new goals for the originals, the evaluation of the original goals underlying the conflict situation may alter, or a re-ordering of overall preferences give greater prominence to some goals under direct threat from the other party's behaviour. It is a commonly observed phenomenon that conflict and a real threat may heighten attachment to goals and values previously taken for granted. Hence the behaviour of another party may increase the perceived value of threatened goals to one party, and their evaluation may increase yet again because of efforts made to defend them, or the alternative goals sacrificed in that defence.

In a slightly different fashion, the behaviour of the opposing party in many conflicts becomes, after a time, sufficient reason in itself for intensifying one's own conflict behaviour and altering one's own goals, particularly if the opponent's behaviour involves widespread violence. Many people have suffered and wish to retaliate, so that the goal of hurting the opponent, and 'making them pay' becomes salient. Many people have made sacrifices and wish to see some recompense for them, so that the goal of extracting physical and psychological 'reparations' from the opponent becomes important. Many people have directed their own fears, suspicions and hostility onto the opponent, who may thus become some monstrous, dehumanised figure, driven solely by greed, ambition and implacable hostility to oneself, so that the goal of humiliating the opponent and reassuring oneself of fundamental safety and superiority becomes an end worth striving for. Numerous examples of this process in operation demonstrate that, while conflict behaviour normally arises instrumentally from holding incompatible goals, it can also be affected by the adversary's previous conflict behaviour.[5]

Conflict behaviour may also become the source of future conflict attitudes and behaviour, irrespective of any future development of mutually incompatible goals. The best example of such a process in operation is found in the feud in tribal and agrarian societies. In a feud, A's behaviour (perhaps the murder of B) becomes the reason and justification for B's family's subsequent hostility and violence towards A, and towards A's relatives. A's relatives become involved through B's family's efforts to harm A in retaliation, and a complicated action-reaction process of injury and counter-injury develops, often lasting well after A and B's original quarrel has disappeared, or A and B themselves long vanished from the scene. For Montagues, the mere presence of Capulets has become the reason for conflict behaviour, from thumb-biting to sword-play, unless restrained by some ducal third party.

In less extreme situations, the behaviour of others as a determinant of attitudes is a phenomenon supported by both casual and systematic observation as well as experimental information. Deutsch uses all three types of data to support the contention that conflictful behaviour and inter-action between parties tends to produce an increase in perceptions that another party is constantly motivated by malice or is in opposition across a wide range of issues, and a willingness to exploit the other's needs or respond negatively to the other's requests (Deutsch, 1973, pp. 29–30). In contrast, co-operative behaviour produces trusting and friendly attitudes, as opposed to suspicious and hostile ones, and a high degree of sensitivity to common values and beliefs based upon open communication.

The above discussion can be summarised as a number of simple propositions:

(a) *Situations affect behaviour* (goals, especially salient goals, being frustrated call forth intense efforts to achieve those goals).

(b) *Situations affect attitudes* (goal incompatibility is likely to increase suspicion and mistrust).

(c) *Behaviour affects situations* (success may bring more issues into the dispute as demands escalate).

(d) *Behaviour affects attitudes* (destruction increases anger, success can affect the sense of in-group solidarity).

(e) *Attitudes affect behaviour* (expectations that . . . 'Our traditional enemies the X's are up to no good again' will affect defensive preparations and contingency plans).[6]

(f) *Attitudes affect situations* (More issues will be perceived to be in dispute with an adversary, so that a long drawn-out confrontation may develop).

The essential argument can be clarified by modifying our simple model of conflict structure to illustrate inter-dependencies among the components, and the ways in which change in one component feeds back to affect others. (See Fig 3.2.) The model helps to emphasise the existence of such linkages, although it does not suggest the complexity of many of the feedback processes involved, the difficulties of tracing out the linkages, and the differential time lags almost certainly involved in one component bring about changes in others.

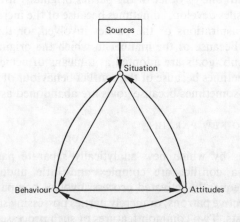

FIGURE 3.2 Basic conflict structure

C. WIDENING CONFLICT

Many inter-actions between the components of conflict discussed in the previous section contribute to the enlargement of the original conflict in different ways. *Conflict widening* can take a variety of forms, and it might be more appropriate to consider it as a shorthand term for a number of analytically separate processes (probably causally linked). However, the idea of a conflict 'widening' seems an intuitively familiar one, so the term is retained in this discussion.

One of the commonest interpretations of a conflict widening or becoming more 'complex' is through other parties becoming involved in the original situation of goal incompatibility, either because they possess complementary goals, or because their interests dictate the support of one side rather than another. Other interpretations of the concept are possible, however, some of them obviously inter-related:

(a) Existing parties take up new issues, and thus become parties to new conflicts.

(b) New parties are formed to take up existing issues and purposefully pursue goals.

(c) Other parties are drawn into the conflict as protagonists, either through a process of searching for allies, or because objectives coincide with one or other of the parties originally involved.

(d) New issues develop, sometimes because of the increasing hopes, plans and aspirations of the parties involved, or their numbers, sometimes because of the manner in which the original conflict is pursued ('sub'-goals are adopted as a means of achieving original goals), sometimes because of the conflict behaviour of the opposing party, and sometimes because goals are abandoned as too costly.

1. INVOLVING NEW PARTIES

The processes by which new analytically separate parties become involved in a conflict are complex and little understood. One apparently frequently activated process involves one party calling in allies or protective patrons, or merely parties possessing strong links or similar interests. Two common features of such processes·are that the patron so involved frequently has major linkages of various types to the client party (Russett, 1963), and that it is often the weaker party, perceiving itself as the object of a major threat or as about to suffer complete defeat, that first calls in 'outside' help and begins the process of widening the conflict. Once this first stage is reached, the adversary responds by mobilising its own patrons, colleagues or allies, and the process can continue until the two parties consist of rival coalitions involving a large number of separate groups, organisations or governments. The classical instance of such a process of international conflict is the conflict between Austria and Serbia over Bosnia and Herzegovina in 1914, when the process of conflict widening rapidly involved the major powers of Europe – and eventually the Ottoman Empire, Japan and the USA – in World War I. However, the process can take place in almost any conflict at any social level. Strikes in a single firm can widen to involve other firms, other unions and ultimately result in situations resembling the General Strike of 1926 in Britain. Even apparently simple industrial conflicts can widen to involve parties far beyond those initially involved in the situation of goal incompatibility between workers and management. A dispute between workers and management in a small engineering firm at St Brieuc in Britanny in the spring of 1972 widened dramatically before it ended, partly because the local management was represented by a Paris-based industrial group, the Compagnie Général d'Electricité. The strike was prolonged and bitter, with the plant being occupied by the workers until they were ejected by local riot police, and the courts used to condemn workers for 'restraint of work'. The French Ministry of Labour put pressure on the management, the local authorities acted as mediators, and numerous outsiders intervened on the side of the strikers, becoming parties to the conflict: local farmers' organisations brought in food and supplies for the strikers, shopkeepers extended credit, the town council voted subsidies for the strike fund (which, by the end of the strike stood at 900,000 Fr) and opened school canteens to strikers' children, and the mayors of five other local towns shipped five tons of free food to the strikers. Eventually the conflict ended through the mediatory efforts of the local authorities and the pressure of the Ministry of Labour, but not before what had appeared to be a simple two-party 'industrial conflict' had involved half the countryside and numerous parties in the distant capital.[7]

The introduction of new parties further complicates the original conflict in another way. New parties in any coalition are likely to have goals of their own to pursue, so that the number of issues in dispute increases usually in the sense that other goal incompatibilities become involved, and often in the sense that a coalition's priorities alter from those held by the original party. The addition of new parties makes the issues in conflict more complex, and this can call forth new strategies and patterns of conflict behaviour appropriate for achieving the range of goals now being pursued. In many cases of intra-national conflicts, the process of widening a conflict involves more militant groups, aiming to bring about radical changes in the social structure and having a propensity to advocate, and use, more violent methods. The involvement, sometimes even the existence, of more extreme allies often alters the course of the conflict by making the original parties less willing to compromise, both because of their ability to use their own extremists as a bargaining counter, and because of fears that their adversary's extremists make compromise with moderates irrelevant.

2. CONFLICT WIDENING IN PRACTICE

That involving new parties and widening the issues making up a conflict are inextricably connected, helps to account for the dynamism of conflicts that begin over certain issues pursued by rival parties, yet end with wholly different parties clashing about wholly different issues. An example can be found in the May Events in France during the summer of 1968 which severely shook the foundations of the French Fifth Republic. Originally, the conflict began over university issues such as student participation in the running of university affairs, greater freedom for political expression within universities, and more contacts between staff and students. As more radical student groups became involved, the issues changed to the radical reform of French society along participatory lines. Violence erupted as the unlucky university authorities, acting for the French Government, called in the police, who acted throughout the Events as an almost autonomous party in their own right, determined to put down student radicalism by violence. Other parties subsequently drawn into the conflict, included both Catholic trade unions, demanding participation in industrial management for their members, as a pre-emptive tactic to gain the support of their members, and the Communist unions making more conventional demands for shorter hours, higher wages and better working conditions. Finally, left wing political parties and organisations saw the situation as an opportunity to undermine the Gaullist regime, and became involved in the conflict to pose a political threat to the Government.

One interesting feature of the process of conflict widening in the May Events was that, while it is certainly true that the issues changed, they did not necessarily change in a more radical direction. Once the unions and the leftist political parties and groups became involved in the dispute, many of the more radical student goals were abandoned. The issues became switched from a total transformation of French society and grass roots participation in all institutions from universities to government, to more conventional ones, such as greater economic benefits and political reform. On this occasion, new parties came into a conflict and, while taking it over and re-defining the issues, moved it into more familiar and far less radical directions, a move symbolised by the ending of violence that had characterised the radical second stage of the conflict between students, police and government.

3. POLARISATION

A final way in which conflicts can be said to 'widen' involves neither new parties nor the development of new issues as a result of direct inter-action between parties. Frequently, conflicts are spoken of as becoming 'polarised', as the parties move further apart in some fashion and some 'gap' between them widens.

There are at least two aspects to this process. The first is that conflicts change over time because parties become more absolute in the positions they take up regarding particular goals. A party can change from demanding *some* of a value to demanding *all* of it, or from being willing to compromise over a given issue to being unwilling to make any concessions. On issues where an initial demand has been made for higher wages or shorter hours, for example, later demands could involve even higher wage claims, demands for shorter hours and for longer holidays.

The alternative interpretation of polarisation consists of parties becoming adversaries across a wide *range* of issues, so that the original dispute 'widens' in the sense of involving opposition on a larger number of ostensibly unrelated issues. Sometimes the contest, or confrontation, remains closely related to the original conflicting goals, as when political parties take up widespread adversary positions in pursuit of the original goal of achieving political power. At others, the business of taking up an opposition position, or 'lining up' on opposite sides of issues, takes on a dynamic of its own, and becomes connected with the goal of defeating the opposing party, or 'opposition for the sake of opposition'. Feuds represent this form of behaviour, while at the level of international conflict such confrontation can develop into massive regional or global rivalries, such as the 'Cold War', the conflict between the Arabs and Israelis or, at a lower level, the confrontation between Indonesia and Malaysia in South East Asia.

Such processes are usually accompanied by increases in negative attitudes and coercive actions. Hence, this definition of polarisation usually involves changes not merely in the number of issues involving the same two parties, but also in the latter's attitudes towards each other, and the nature of intra-party behaviour.[8]

D. ESCALATION

Apart from the involvement of others in a conflict, the best known if least understood dynamic aspect of human conflicts is their tendency to 'escalate' or, on rarer occasions, de-escalate (Bonoma, 1976, p. 6). These two concepts have become part of the general vocabulary of international politics since World War II. Normally, the term 'escalation' is used in a confined sense to refer to a process by which the parties to a conflict embark upon a mutually destructive process of increasing the level of coercion or violence in the threats or actions they direct against each other.[9] Escalation refers to escalation of behaviour along a violence dimension, either in the sense of increased destruction or the involvement of more individuals in destructive activity.

A much wider range of phenomena can, however, be implied by the term. Some writers use it to refer to an increase of stereotyped perceptions or of feelings such as frustration, anger, fear or hatred among members of a party, either in the sense of more individuals experiencing such emotions, or experiencing them with a greater intensity. Escalation can also be viewed as a negative process, as an increasing inability to empathise with an adversary, or to inform one's activity by understanding their problems and internal conflicts. Alternatively, as Edelman points out, escalation can be seen as the mobilisation of wider support within a party for the goals of 'the party', or the 'national interest', or some other form of objective usually selected by an elite within that party (Edelman, 1969, pp. 234–6). Escalation, in such a view, represents the increasing crystallisation of support within a party, and the mobilisation of effort for the pursuit of party defined goals. As Sisson and Ackoff (1966, p. 195) express the idea, escalation is the increasing degree of support for shared or super-ordinate goals within the party.

Even within a narrow, behavioural definition of the term, escalation can possess a number of different aspects, particularly if it is regarded as an increase of coercion rather than simple violence. It is perfectly possible, for example, to escalate a pattern of conflict inter-action by expanding all the spheres of inter-action in which coercion occurs; conflict behaviour can begin with verbal attacks, and later involve economic sanctions or military action. Equally it can be asymmetric by escalating activity in one such sphere – increasing economic sanctions – while de-escalating it in another – stopping military attacks.

From the parties' viewpoint, escalation normally involves committing additional resources to the conflict. Parties may choose a number of basic forms of escalation:

(a) Intensifying an existing strategy.
(b) Employing the same strategy in different geographical localities, where the adversary may prove more vulnerable.
(c) Employing wholly different strategies, either in the original locality or in some new locality.

These forms of behavioural escalation are either complementary or competing alternatives. For example, in an industrial conflict the union side may decide to begin coercing the management with a 'go-slow' or work-to-rule, then wish to escalate the conflict and put further pressure on the management side by instructing its members to go-even slower, extend the go-slow to other plants or branches of industry, call for a complete stoppage, use flying pickets against other plants, or attempt to involve other unions, or the national government, in the dispute. In war, the level of violence may be increased by attacking new targets, introducing new and more devastating weapons, opening a new front, or simply by employing more men and material.[11]

Apart from being a pattern of behaviour and occasion for choice by the parties involved, escalation and de-escalation involve changes in the *pattern* of inter-action between the adversaries, and have frequently been analysed as a process rather than a form of behaviour. Not all inter-action processes between parties appear the same, however. Some exhibit a symmetric pattern of behaviour while others show an asymmetric one, depending upon how a party responds to the actions of its adversary. For example, an escalatory pattern implies a pattern of inter-action that changes through both parties *increasing* something that they exchange in the inter-action. This may not be the only way in which a conflict process can be characterised, however, and three basic inter-action patterns may be suggested:

(a) A *repetitive* pattern of inter-action, which involves an exchange of similar actions over a long period of time. This type of 'tit-for-tat' exchange can be exemplified by the exchange of fundamentally similar propositions during disarmament negotiation, in which none of those involved has any real intention of disarming.

(b) An *intensifying* pattern of inter-action, in which parties exchange qualitatively similar actions with greater frequency or intensity over time. An arms race following an escalatory pattern described by Richardson is such an intensifying pattern of behavioural change. Similarly, the tariff wars that took place in the 1880s and 1890s were characterised by countries acting and reacting by often rapid increases in the amount of tariffs imposed upon each other's exports. The tariff wars admittedly covered a wide range of goods, but they were confined to one type of economic sanctioning behaviour, and none 'escalated' in the sense of involving qualitatively different forms of behaviour, such as military threats or diplomatic sanctions (Nicholson, 1967a, pp. 26–30).

(c) A *developing* pattern of inter-action, in which the actions exchanged alter over time both qualitatively and quantitatively. For example, a rejected wage claim could develop into an industrial strike, which might then develop into a lock-out, violent picketing or .strike-breaking, and the final introduction of the police or army on the side of managers.

A similar classification could be made of changes in attitudes during a dispute, with hostility or distrust increasing or decreasing; or with wholly new attitudes and beliefs about the situation and the adversary emerging within both parties. (Experience suggests that any changes in the psychological aspects of a dispute are likely to take longer and thus lag behind behavioural changes.) Undoubtedly one of the features of human conflict is that the participants learn over time, and change their attitudes and perceptions as well as often modifying their goals and behaviour as a result of altered perceptions. The learning process may involve the adoption of alternative patterns of behaviour if those previously adopted prove unsuccessful. Alternatively, as Bengt Abrahamsson suggests, a process of *reinforcement* can take place. Whenever a pattern of behaviour is perceived as being successful, a party is likely to repeat the pattern in the same or future conflicts; if the behaviour is coercive then coercion will become an accepted pattern of response. 'Conflict habituation . . . might be caused by the success of a number of aggressive acts . . .' (Abrahamsson, 1972, p. 77).

It may, of course, be argued that the 'pattern' mentioned in (c) can hardly be described as a pattern, save in the sense that the (perhaps widely) different forms of behaviour are exchanged between the same parties; or that (a) hardly deserves being labelled 'dynamic' (behaviour having reached some stable equilibrium), even though inter-action is undoubtedly taking place. However, the scheme is a useful one especially when considering various possible interpretations of the blanket term 'escalation'. It is also useful in drawing attention to the final question about conflict processes, which is whether there are any common features of such inter-actions that enable us to talk about cycles or spirals, and recognise familiar patterns of conflict inter-action when they occur.

E. CONFLICT SPIRALS AND CYCLES

One of the implications of much of the discussion in this chapter has been that particular patterns of behaviour by one party in a conflict bring a limited range of reactions from an adversary, so that an equally limited range of inter-action patterns occurs in conflict situations. Coercion tends to bring forth a response of counter-coercion plus increased hostility, to be met in turn by increased coercion and further hostility. In contrast, positive sanctions and co-operative behaviour spark off a co-operative process with increasing exchange of rewards and the increase of positive attitudes. Although many people argue that a wide variety of factors make co-operative inter-action patterns less likely than conflictful ones (for example, Boulding's argument that harm can be done faster than good), nonetheless both patterns, once embarked upon, tend to become self-reinforcing. '. . . While the exchange of rewards tends towards stability and continued inter-action, the exchange of punishments tends towards instability and eventual failure of inter-action in escape or avoidance . . .' (Homans, 1961, p. 57). The self-reinforcing nature of much human inter-action has led many writers to talk of conflict situations leading to the development of *malign* or *benign spirals*, and to emphasise that the existence of a situation of major goal incompatibility between parties predisposes them to enter into a *malign spiral*, from which it is difficult to escape. Escalation becomes easy, de-escalation difficult.

Both types of spiral depend very much on factors that make for positive, reinforcing feedback, which can, in the case of malign spirals, prove disastrously costly to the parties involved, in terms of abandoned alternatives and, in some cases, the survival of the parties themselves. In such cases, the pattern is often held to develop through a number of stages, beginning with efforts to find a solution to a newly recognised conflict situation via negotiation and compromise which usually breaks down on the 'intransigence' of the adversary; the growth of hostility and use of coercive sanctions; the escalation of negative sanctions sometimes culminating in violence, followed by either the withdrawal of one party or stalemate and exhaustion; renewed negotiations and either a compromise (often similar to that discussed at the earliest stage) or breakdown and a return to the stage of mutual coercion. The simple process is usually represented in a figure such as Fig. 3.3.

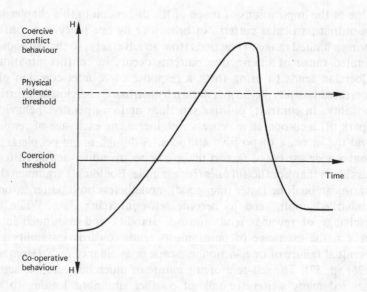

FIGURE 3.3   Standard conflict profile

Numerous suggestions have been made about factors that contribute to such a malign spiral. Many observers, such as Phillips, argue that the major factor in such a spiral is the inter-active effect of the parties' behaviour and that the major determinant of a party's decision to continue the spiral rather than reverse it lies in the previous behaviour directed at it by the opposing party (Phillips, 1970). In analysing dyadic conflict exchanges between national governments over a limited period of time, Phillips finds evidence that the bulk of conflict behaviour can be explained by the previous conflict behaviour received from an adversary, a finding which echoes Richardson's argument that the dynamics of arms racing stems from each side's reaction to the other's previous increases in the arms level (Richardson, 1960).

By contrast, others argue that there are many *intra-party* factors that contribute in a complex and subtle way to the development of a malign inter-party spiral. Both Edmead and Deutsch point to the importance of *previous* investment of intra-party resources as being the crucial factor pushing inter-party exchanges to new heights of malevolence. Writing of the escalating US commitment to South Vietnam in the mid-1960s, Deutsch argues that the stated reasons for further US involvement often took the form of decisionmakers' *previous* commitments of men and resources which 'could not' be sacrificed, because they had been made already (Deutsch, 1969, pp. 16–18). This case illustrates Edmead's more general point that resources previously expended in pursuit of goals increase the evaluation of that goal, and justify yet further sacrifices (Edmead, 1971). Both ideas are expressed in Festinger's dictum that '. . . rats and people come to love the things for which they have suffered . . .', and both illustrate those intra-party factors that many feel to be important in establishing malign spirals of inter-action.

A third point of view is exemplified by David Singer who emphasises inter-action between intra-party and inter-party processes, and the way in which these reinforce one another to produce malign spirals in conflict situations. Singer suggests that spirals of escalating coercion and violence in international conflicts can be the result of positive feedback processes:

(a) Intra-party opposition, which makes options of responding to an external adversary's demands by conciliatory moves too costly, and intransigence probable by making it more attractive in terms of domestic support, at least in the short run.
(b) Moves to prepare party members both psychologically and militarily in order to bargain with an external adversary, which then give intra-party hawks greater backing for intransigence as well as

the adversary a reason for beginning similar mobilisation processes.
(c) Media activities and values that lead to the dissemination of
information arousing negative evaluations of 'outsiders' and
reinforcing hostility towards leaders not defending the party's
interests.
(d) Tendencies for the existence of an external threat to party goals
to bring to power those concerned with defending parties' interests
through coercion, who then develop an interest in the maintenance
of the threat and expansion of the machinery for coercive activity
(Singer, 1970, pp. 165–7).

Edelman has also pointed to the manner in which any increase in the
influence of more militant, hawkish factions within one party can
strengthen the position, credibility and influence of similar elements in
the adversary, so that militants amplify the successes of their counterparts in an adversary in order to widen their own political support.[12] In
a curious way, the position of militant factions becomes inter-
dependent; change in the fortunes of one group has a positive feedback
effect on the positions of their counterparts (Edelman, 1969, p. 233).

The idea of *conflict spirals and cycles* can be interpreted in a slightly
different way if the relevant time period is expanded. Often, the same
parties become involved in repetitive cycles of conflicts at different
times and over new sets of issues. To some degree, this kind of
extended *conflict cycle* resembles long drawn out family feuds, where
residues of hostility and mistrust remain from previous disputes over
particular issues, and help to exacerbate relations between the parties
should their interests diverge at some future time over new issues. One
necessary condition for this type of repetitive cycle of conflicts between
the same parties is that the latter remain in some kind of continuous
relationship involving inter-action on some common task or within a
common institutional setting (although our previous comments on
international cold wars or confrontations indicate that the institutional
setting need not be highly structured). Walton, for example, has noted
such cycles of inter-personal conflict within organisations which
consist of a series of linked 'episodes' over different issues, each being
set off by a triggering event followed by conflict behaviour and
consequences for participants and issues (Walton, 1969, pp. 71–5).
The relationship then ceases to become conflictful until the next
triggering event, but the next episode is affected by residual memories
of previous episodes and the attitudes and perceptions engendered.
Walton does not explicitly state that there is a strong likelihood that

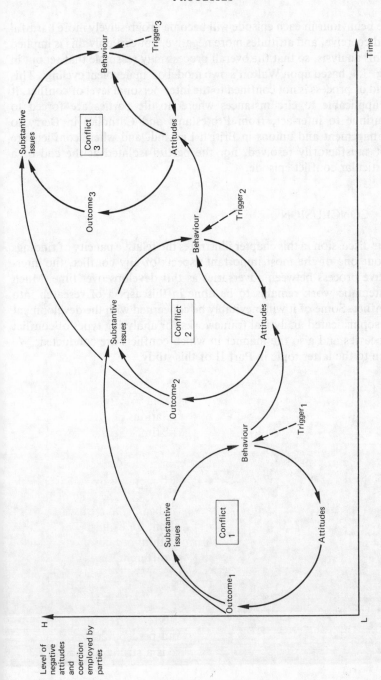

FIGURE 3.4 Conflict cycle between linked parties

the behaviour in each episode will become progressively more harmful and coercive, and attitudes more negative, but certainly this is implied in his analysis, so that the overall process may resemble that set out in Fig. 3.4, based upon Walton's own model of 'malevolent cycling'. This kind of process is not confined to the inter-personal level of conflict. It is applicable to circumstances where hostile parties are forced to continue to inter-act, from Protestants and Catholics in Derry to management and unions in British Leyland, and where conflicts are not satisfactorily resolved, nor the parties isolated at the end of a particular conflict episode.

F. CONCLUSION

Our discussion in this chapter illustrates the relative paucity of findings about one of the most important aspects of any conflict, the inter-active process between adversaries as this develops over time. Much systematic work remains to be done in this aspect of research into conflict. Some of it will inevitably be concerned with the development of sophisticated analytical frameworks for analysing types of conflict processes and also the manner in which conflicts are conducted. We turn to the latter topic in Part II of this study.

Part II: Conducting Conflict

4 Psychological Dimensions of Conflict

What do you mean, 'My country right or wrong?' Since when has our country ever been wrong?

Cartoon in *The New Yorker*

In Part I we argued that conflict attitudes could best be regarded as a set of psychological processes and conditions that accompany involvement in a conflict, particularly an intense one, where levels of personal involvement are high, and participants experience a marked degree of personal tension brought about by the existence and actions of a threatening adversary. Many writers on conflicts at various social levels have referred to 'negative feelings' or to 'emotional antagonisms' between members of the conflicting parties. Mutual fear and hostility are marked characteristics of parties in conflict, while such relationships also intensify the tendency for the same external 'reality' to be perceived quite differently by involved groups. An inter-related cluster of emotions, attitudes, prejudices and perceptual distortions accompany most forms of conflict, and lead to its continuation and exacerbation.

While such emotions and cognitive processes are essentially characteristic of individuals, nonetheless they can be shared by a large or small group of people. There is considerable evidence that images, attitudes, prejudices, emotions and beliefs can be relatively homogeneous across a great number of individuals just as, by contrast, people in the same group can possess diametrically opposed beliefs. Hence our working definition of conflict attitudes stressed that they were '. . . *common* patterns of expectation, emotional orientation, attitude, and perceptual conditions and processes which accompany involvement in a conflict situation . . .'; the twofold implication of 'common' being both that they arose *frequently*, and could be found *simultaneously* among numbers of people.

However, the psychological processes and conditions that accompany involvement in a conflict are more complex than suggested

71

by this definition. Members of parties involved in a conflict situation are likely to possess complex cognitions and evaluations about themselves and their own party; the opposing party, its leaders and membership; and the environment within which the conflict situation arises. Furthermore, each party will sub-divide its views of itself and its adversary into numerous aspects, such as the goals and motivations of its adversary; its own level of internal unity; the manner in which third parties perceive the conflict; the divisions (or lack of them) within the adversary; and a range of other images, both of attributes and behaviour. The basic division is into images of self, adversary and environment of the conflict, but the details are complex.

These complex cognitions and evaluations necessitate a more detailed consideration of the nature of conflict attitudes, their causes and common features, the manner in which they develop and change over time, the way in which they affect various forms of *conflict behaviour*, or act as a hindrance or help in efforts at finding a solution to the conflict. Material used in this chapter is drawn from the growing literature on the psychology of being 'in conflict'.

A.   CONFLICT ATTITUDES: UNDERLYING PROCESSES

Providing a simple framework to summarise psychological processes relevant to conflicts is not easy. A starting point might be the common observation that most human individuals try to minimise psychological discomfort. A general human tendency is to reduce psychological strain as far as possible (both consciously and unconsciously), coping with one's environment by avoiding tension and anxiety, reducing levels of uncertainty and ambiguity, lessening any sense of insecurity, and avoiding, as far as possible, irreconcilable pieces of information and uncomfortable complexities. The crucial element in this process is that individuals try constantly to make their own behaviour and that of others more predictable. Success in minimising psychological 'stresses and strains' or 'keeping a mental balance' may be equated with avoiding physical discomfort, although the analogy is misleading if carried to extremes.

This principle in operation can be observed in a wide variety of circumstances. For example, common psychological reactions emerge frequently during intense crises in relations between rival groups, organisations or countries. In such circumstances, the individuals involved confront a sudden and immediate threat to some highly valued goal or object, with no previous warning of this particular threat, and little time to decide (August 1914, the period immediately before Pearl Harbour in 1941 or Cuba 1962). Levels of uncertainty are likely to be high for decisionmaking elites, while anxiety and general psychological stress induce them to activate psychological processes for relieving strain and tension. During any intense crisis the sense of being the target of a serious and continuing threat will increase anxiety, and lead to such a high level of stress that response may be ill-considered and violent. Milburn has argued that the use of deterrent threats leads to a high level of anxiety on the part of individual decisionmakers, so that the result is 'expessive' (tension relieving) rather than 'goal oriented' behaviour (Milburn, 1961). The use of threats by one party may thus set in operation a series of psychological processes designed to avoid or minimise high levels of stress by individual leaders (and sometimes by the mass of their followers).

On the other hand, it is equally obvious that the process of avoiding stress and psychological discomfort is not the only one underlying individuals' efforts to cope with their environment. On other occasions it is clear that they seek out difficulties, place themselves in situations of uncertainty, and receive stimulation from mild amounts of stress and strain in their environment. (Much experimental evidence exists that mild degrees of stress increase efficiency in performing physical, computational and intellectual tasks.) Many people argue that this tendency to seek out problems and challenges which impose varying degrees of tension as a stimulus underlies much of human creativity, and man's ability to understand and change his environment (Storr, 1968). Applying this argument to conflicts implies that conflict may be *functional*, both in the sense that it stimulates people to engage in creative thinking, and that they obtain psychological rewards from participating in conflicts. In certain circumstances, conflict can be a stimulating, exciting, stress-reducing, even happy phenomenon, sometimes for all those participating, at others for certain members of a party in which others may be suffering considerable discomfort, both physical and psychological.

With this argument in mind, we need to amend our previous contention about the basic process underlying the development of recognisable, repetitive conflict attitudes being those with the function of reducing unacceptable levels of stress. If, under different circumstances, people actually seek out stress to achieve stimulation and psychological benefits and if, on still other occasions, the tendency is not to avoid stress altogether, but merely to reduce it to an acceptable level, then the basic principle underlying those psychological processes whose operation leads to the development of appropriate attitudes to deal with any environment must be an attempt to achieve an optimum level of stress or stimulation. Instead of dealing with stress-avoidance as a key conception, a process which could 'go either way' exists, either attempting to reduce stress and discomfort, or seeking out stimulation and benefit. Hence, it might be better to employ the label of *stress-optimising* to describe the principle, whether applied to individuals or groups of individuals in conflict.[1]

1. CONFLICTS AS STRESSFUL ENVIRONMENTS

While it is undoubtedly the case that human individuals optimise the degree of stress and stimulation from their environment, and that individuals differ in what is regarded as an optimum 'mix', it is equally the case that certain kinds of environment are very likely to call forth processes to reduce levels of stress as they present, for most people, an unacceptable level of psychological discomfort. Consider the problems facing a Negro policeman charged with policing a Negro community on behalf of a white-dominated society. Many such roles and situations exist. Obviously certain individuals will be able to resist the discomforts of stressful roles better than others, and to tolerate uncertainty, contradictory information and fear, without immediately resorting to particular protective mechanisms in order to reduce strain. However, the tendency to use such processes if discomfort becomes too great is present in all of us, so that, in many situations imposing a high level of stress and discomfort, common psychological patterns are likely to reveal themselves, sooner or later. Everyday observations of people conforming to group norms, expectations or attitudes at periods of high anxiety, or of others searching for evidence to show that they have made a correct decision (thus relieving uncertainty and anxiety) bear this out. In many situations, the social pressures on an individual to conform to the beliefs as well as the behaviour of the group becomes overwhelming, and considerations of both psychological and physical comfort create an environment in which only the most determined individuals can resist pressures towards consensus. This can occur over a very short time span, and even in relatively unrealistic settings. A *simulated* prison study by Zimbardo placed students in roles as 'prisoners' and 'guards' in an artificial prison situation. Before the experiment was completed, the constraints of even such artificial circumstances were beginning to force both groups towards patterns of behaviour and sets of attitudes akin to those existing in a real-life prison. 'Guards' were intimidating and acting with cruelty towards 'prisoners', while the latter were being subservient towards but developing intense hatred of the 'guards'. A simulated situation had produced a remarkably realistic set of stereotyped views of prison behaviour by activating psychological processes customarily activated by real situations (Zimbardo, 1972).

While a wide range of circumstances can provide stressful environments for human individuals, singly or in aggregate, conflicts are among the most likely circumstances to impose high levels of psychological stress and discomfort and thus to call forth 'discomfort reducing' processes with great regularity for those individuals involved as members of opposing parties. High levels of frustration, of threat to highly valued goals, coercive (and perhaps physically damaging) behaviour, uncertainty about future outcomes, and the knowledge that another person, or group of people feel hostility and suspicion about oneself and one's group are likely to produce considerable uneasiness, which will increase as the levels of perceived threat, uncertainty and coercion increase. As Stein (1976, pp. 156–7) argues in his survey of the cohesion inducing functions of conflict, conflicts frequently produce stress, tension, fear and a sense of frustration which act as intervening variables between degrees of conflict and psychological reactions at both individual and party level. Experimental findings also support the contention that conflicts bring about recognisable patterned psychological reactions, both cognitive and evaluative. Mazur (1973) for example used a sample of Jewish–American academics at the time of the 1973 Arab–Israeli war, and found that the tendency towards cognitive balance increased during stressful conflict. Others have noted the constant tendency of all groups and their members to misperceive and misunderstand an adversary's position or proposals, even though the former believe that they have a very precise understanding. This inability to understand an out-group's position occurs even in simple experimental situations (Blake and Mouton, 1961). Add to this evidence the frequent, if *ad hoc*, observation of repeated psychological reactions by participants in a variety of conflicts, and the argument that common patterns of cognition and evaluation arise during conflicts is hardly novel or surprising.

Other factors besides being in conflict obviously affect the degree of stress reducing reactions displayed by individual participants. For example, while there is undoubtedly a generally shared tendency for all individuals to reduce unpleasant levels of psychological discomfort and develop ways of coping with environmental stress, it is also the case that individuals differ in their levels of toleration for situations where they are subjected to high levels of anxiety, uncertainty and ambiguity. Some individuals show a great need for a structured and well-ordered environment, as well as a low tolerance of stress and a need to reduce uncertainty. Often, the last is achieved by a process of excluding certain features of the environment from attention, so that some people are more 'closed' in what they permit to enter their conscious awareness. The extent to which this process of defensive selection occurs depends upon a number of factors, and not merely upon whether the individual involved has an open rather than a closed mind (Rokeach, 1960) or a low or high tolerance of ambiguity (Frenkel-Brunswick, 1949). The need to implement protective psychological processes in order to achieve 'balance' depends on an interaction between the personality of the individual and the demands made on him by his total environment.

Our basic argument regarding the formation of typical *conflict attitudes* is thus somewhat more sophisticated than merely stating that conflicts produce stressful environments and protective psychological reactions as a response:

(1) Many common psychological processes come into operation in order to reduce psychological stress in individuals and groups faced with a particular range of circumstances.

(2) Many factors which result in the activation of such processes (tension, stress, a high degree of uncertainty) are frequently found during conflicts.

(3) A conflict is likely to bring such psychological processes and their resultant attitudes into play more frequently and with greater intensity than other situations or forms of inter-action.

However, the degree to which stress reducing processes need to be employed will additionally vary according to:

(i) The degree of psychological flexibility of individuals.

(ii) The intensity of the conflict situation (the value of the goals seen threatened and the intensity of the threat).

(iii) The conflict behaviour of the adversary.

(iv) A variety of social factors, including the position of individuals within the involved parties (the degree of each person's exposure to stress) and the efficiency with which the party is structured to cope with its environment and avoid further stress-inducing factors such as information overload and in-fighting.[2]

Put another way, conflicts (especially intense conflicts) create for those involved a greater *need* to activate certain psychological processes, and develop particular ranges of beliefs and attitudes; and provide greater *opportunities* for the easy (and justifiable) utilisation of a range of defensive processes and development of a range of attitudes to cope with the situation. Hence, people placed in circumstances of conflict are likely to react psychologically in similar ways.

2. STRESS AND COGNITIVE CONSISTENCY

The general principle of *stress optimising*, or even *stress avoidance* does little more than provide a starting point for describing the processes by which individuals attempt to achieve a balance between the stresses imposed by their environment and the level of psychological discomfort (or stimulation) that they tolerate. Providing even a simple framework for the large number of complex processes adopted by individuals in different circumstances as they try to achieve an optimum level of stress is not easy. The most basic, protective process for helping an individual involved in a conflict reduce the level of environment-imposed stress to an acceptable level involves reducing the complexity and contrariness of incoming information about the conflict, thus ensuring that the conflictful environment presents a consistent and orderly pattern to the perceiver. This process underlies a whole range of current psychological theories about achieving consistency in one's image of the environment, from Osgood's concepts of congruence and incongruence, to Heider's theory of cognitive balance and Festinger's (1957) theory of cognitive dissonance. The process is referred to hereafter as the individual's preference and search for *cognitive consistency*.

Under this general heading, three inter-related sub-processes are discussed; those associated with *selective perception*; those with *selective recall*; and those with *group identification*. The last concerns the development of an individual's self image and the image of his party (and, by implication, other parties) and his own place within it. The two former processes are more concerned with environmental perception. All, it should be recalled, share the characteristic that they are efforts to reduce the complexity, contrariness and stress of an environment containing a significant conflict with another party, and hence to minimise (rather than optimise) levels of anxiety, uncertainty and insecurity, see Fig. 4.1.

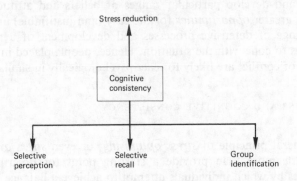

FIGURE 4.1 Protective psychological processes

B. PERCEPTION AND COGNITIVE CONSISTENCY

A number of processes fall under this heading, all sharing the characteristic that they fulfil the function of avoiding stress by:

(a) Reducing the amount of information from, and about the environment which contradicts what individuals feel they already know about that environment or

(b) Enabling an individual simultaneously to hold contradictory information about aspects of that environment without becoming uncomfortably aware of contradiction.

At their most basic, such cognitive processes (which all have to do with the recognition and interpretation of incoming information), enable an individual to ignore that which does not conform to what is already 'known' as 'the truth' about any situation. At a slightly more complex level, an individual tends to seek out confirmatory information for reassurance, avoiding cognitive dissonance or achieving cognitive consistency and thus minimising stress by efforts to achieve 'balance' in his perceptions and evaluations of the environment. Major psychological processes in this regard include those, such as selective perception, denial or stereotyping, that assist in *developing* a consistent image of the environment, including the adversary; and those that assist in *maintaining* one.

1. DEVELOPING COGNITIVE CONSISTENCY

The key process by which individuals in conflicts achieve acceptable levels of psychological stress is through the ignoring of or the rejecting of information about the environment which does not fit in with existing beliefs and images, and hence is disturbing. Different individuals possess a greater or lesser propensity to exclude non-conforming features of their environment or to re-interpret incoming information, so that it is easy to maintain intact their 'image' of the world. White calls this process selective inattention (White, 1970). By it members of a colonial nation ignore or minimise the cruelties of colonialism to the colonised (especially as these are caused by 'our' soldiers and administrators) as this does not 'fit in' with the colonialists' image of the relative 'benefits' of order and civilisation that follow from their rule. Similarly, a man in love will be able to extol the virtues of his beloved, while·being unable to admit (or even notice) that she has certain unlovable characteristics, obvious to the non-infatuated.

Selective perception is a commonplace of psychology, and is used in other fields, such as political science, international relations, and conflict research, where writers (Boulding, 1956; Holsti, 1967)[3] emphasise:

(a) The relative rigidity of an individual's image (or 'cognitive structure'), so that certain individuals are more easily able to indulge in 'selective inattention' than others, thus maintaining intact their beliefs about their environment; and
(b) The importance of expectations, derived from past experiences, in determining current perceptions.

This latter factor is particularly important with all types of perception, whether concerned with straightforward physical properties or more complex personal or social phenomena. Experiments have used playing cards with wrong coloured suits (black diamonds or red spades flashed quickly at observers) to demonstrate that, even at simple cognitive levels dealing with physical properties, expectations about what things should look like influence what people actually perceive (and remember). At a more sophisticated level, Allport conducted a series of experiments involving childrens' perceptions of a picture of a Negro and a white man fighting in a subway[4] to show that individuals become conditioned at an early age to anticipate seeing certain phenomena, and hence actually 'see' them (Allport, 1954). A similar process of filtering out non-conforming information is found when data is transmitted orally rather than visually, and particularly when the information contradicts strongly held beliefs and attitudes about the social and political (as opposed to the physical) environment (Festinger *et al.*, 1956).

Individual abilities to ignore non-conforming information on receipt, especially while in circumstances of stressful conflict, do not exhaust participants' capacity for self-delusion. It is equally common for individuals in conflict to indulge in *selective recall* and distort recollections of past events to fit in with current images of the conflict or adversary. *Repression* is the unconscious process by which non-conforming information which usually redounds to one's own or one's party's discredit, or contradicts the simple, black and white cognitive structure developed to deal with a complex situation, is not remembered. At a more general level, it is a process helping an individual to exclude disturbing thoughts, feelings or events from the level of consciousness.

A similar process, but one which occurs at the conscious level, and with the knowledge and intention of the individual concerned, is *suppression*. For example, a person can make a conscious decision not to think about something, such as the approaching death of a close friend, or an unpleasant piece of double dealing by his own government – or the consequences of doing badly in forthcoming examinations. In a conflict situation, both suppression and repression can remove from immediate awareness events showing one's party in a bad light, or acting cruelly or unjustly, or behaving against its stated principles, or acting dishonestly or in bad faith. Success in repressing such information will, of course, make it all the more difficult for the members of one party to understand the way they are regarded by their opponents, and thus further confirm the latter's essential malevolence.

Underlying all these processes that select only aspects of reality that conform to already firmly held beliefs, is the tendency to over-simplify a complex and contradictory reality. Unacceptable levels of psychological stress – brought about by ambiguity or uncertainty – are avoided by this general tendency to employ overly simple categories when evaluating one's environment, or to force events, people and motivations into relatively few and grossly over-simplified cognitive categories. One way of labelling this process is to use the term 'black-and-white thinking', or adopt Charles Osgood's concept of *psychologic* (Osgood, 1962). In essence, all of these terms stand for the process of taking the line of least resistance when confronted with contadictory, 'cognitively inconsistent' information, and avoiding stress by retaining a simple cognitive structure, based upon few categories. According to Osgood, *psychologic* starts from an individual's tendency to perceive a simple, black-and-white world, and to indulge in 'evaluative polarity' by constantly employing only two contrasting categories along simple dimensions. For example, as 'our' party are known to be good, fair and just, it follows that our enemy must be bad, unfair and greedy. This process of simple categorisation and evaluation operates on all incoming information in any intense conflict, affecting interpretation of the information. Complex situations are over-simplified, judgements made upon caricatures of the opposing party, its acts and estimated intentions. Information that might complicate this simple, comfortable picture of the conflict is ignored, rejected or re-interpreted so that it does not damage existing beliefs. The process helps to set up a double standard of morality in evaluating one's own (or one's party's) activities and those of the enemy, as well as excusing otherwise inexcusable actions: 'We know that our own actions are motivated by good intentions and just objectives, hence theirs must be motivated by the exact opposite!' Osgood refers to such simplifying processes as being founded upon 'psychologic' because they reveal a curious consistency, but an emotional rather than rational one. All positively evaluated acts and qualities are connected, as are all those which are negatively evaluated. However, the connecting link is *who* acts or *who* possesses the quality.

Apart from general processes of selective inattention and recall, and the operations of psychologic, psychologists have drawn attention to a number of other more limited processes that commonly operate in conflicts. All can produce widespread misperceptions serving to exacerbate any conflict. They add complexity to the basic proposition that favourable information emanating from, or about, the enemy will be rejected as inaccurate because it clashes with the hostile evaluation of the opposing party's nature, objectives and behaviour. Ralph White, for example, emphasises the operations of *bolstering* or seeking out evidence to support a position already adopted in order to justify that position to self and others; and *separation* or defending an existing negative image of the adversary by failing to give credit for an undeniably good action — attributing the act to others, or to force of circumstances, for example. Thus the bad enemy and the good act are kept separate (White, 1970, pp. 256–64).

One of the commonest of these simplifying processes helping to achieve cognitive consistency is *stereotyping*, or simplifying cognitive categories referring to groups of people. Stereotypes normally concern social groups or categories, particularly ethnic groups such as Negroes, Jews or Orientals or national groups, such as Chinese, French or Italians. However, they can also be held about religious, age, sex or class groups. Stereotypes may be widely held among members of a given group, as they are based upon the common cognitive process of selecting particular attributes, traits or characteristics apparently shared by another group and then: (i) expecting all members of that group to exhibit the stereotyped characteristics and (ii) tending to play down the differences between individual members of the stereotyped group. Hence, Turks are cruel, Russians humourless and Japanese industrious. The simplicity of such cognitive categories is obvious, but the process of categorising groups of people in such a manner assists in developing an individual's ability to cope with a complex environment. The tendency to stereotype increases when high levels of tension are experienced, so that simplifying the key attributes of another, rival group and ignoring differences and divisions within that group are processes likely to increase during any intense inter-group conflict. All Germans become militaristic, all Japanese become treacherous, all strikers become deluded or selfish, all Ulster Catholics become potential rebels.

Other slightly less familiar processes which are important aspects of the psychology of conflict include a lessening of participants' *ability to empathise*, an increased tendency to *universalise one's own frame of reference*, a likelihood of the development of *tunnel vision*, and an increased probability of perceived *polarisation* of the environment within which conflict occurs. In the first process, firm adherence to a consistent image of the conflict renders it difficult to empathise with the opponent's genuine fears, suspicions, grievances or beliefs about one's own goals and intentions. For example, many Soviet citizens undoubtedly saw the placing of missiles in Cuba in the context of their own party's peaceful objectives and continuing US threats which had to be met in kind. The missiles were to *deter* acts by the USA (White, 1965). Hence, the action was justified, with no need to excuse a move so eminently justifiable. In the Middle East, Arabs are wholly unable to appreciate the depths of Israeli fears about actual, physical destruction, the Holocaust being merely an incident in recent history, while Israelis remain largely insensitive to the Arabs' sense of humiliation and outrage arising from the manner in which the state of Israel was established.

The fact that members of one party hold a consistent image of the environment means that in conflicts, these members will tend to universalise their own image and believe firmly that the adversaries must 'really' perceive the environment and the conflict as 'we' ourselves perceive it. Opponents must really see events and statements within the framework of 'our' peaceful intentions, non-aggressiveness and justifiable goals! If they pretend that they do not (publicly, at least), 'we' know that 'they' do secretly, and are only pretending that there can be other ways of viewing the problem.

A final process for simplifying a complex environment and reducing the stresses caused by an excess of information is through the process known as *tunnel vision*. This phenomenon has been observed in both intense, real world conflicts (usually during periods of intense crisis) and also in controlled experimental conditions, such as complex simulations, or decisionmaking 'games'. Tunnel vision denotes a tendency by decisionmakers to concentrate upon a few specific aspects of their environment (usually what they define as salient to their winning, or settling the conflict successfully) to the exclusion of all else. Hence, the concept is rather wider in its implications for ignoring non-conforming information than *selective perception*, where certain types of information are ignored or rejected because they do not conform to what decisionmakers already 'know' about a situation. Instead, tunnel vision implies the ignoring of all information not perceived as having a bearing on the immediate problem facing decisionmakers, so that their concentration becomes narrowed to a few salient issues, objectives, inter-action patterns, or relevant parties, to the exclusion of all else. In one sense, the tendency towards tunnel vision is present in all situations of intense crisis, often accompanied by a *time-foreshortening* factor, when decisionmakers in parties become concerned solely with the immediate, rather than the long-term future, and to see the time available for decision as shrinking rather than expanding.

2. MAINTAINING COGNITIVE CONSISTENCY

Many of the processes discussed above are also important in maintaining a consistent and non-stressful image of the environment, but a number of others are more frequently directed towards enabling individuals to keep a sense of cognitive balance, once this has been achieved. White (1970, p. 264) while noting that the process of *separation* can often be used to 'defend the enemy-image against contamination', also emphasises that another common technique for avoiding cognitive stress during conflicts is to take deliberate steps physically to avoid the source of dissonant information, whether this is a person or any other provider of discomforting data. *Avoiding the communicator* can be a matter of deliberate avoidance of an individual whose ideas differ from those generally held within a party (thus, incidentally, providing a social sanction against non-conformity) or of confining one's reading, listening or viewing to sources which confirm what one already 'knows' about a conflict, or an enemy. Both methods enable participants to maintain cognitive consistency much more easily than by exposing themselves to contradictory information.

A similar function is performed by a process of using language to obscure a real situation that exists, or the actual consequences of actions upon others. What some psychologists refer to as the *use of meaningless assigns* often appears to be a form of propaganda aimed at changing outsiders' perceptions and evaluations of the conflict. In reality it is much more a process by which those directly involved in a conflict, particularly a violent and destructive one, maintain a desirably low level of psychological stress in highly distressing circumstances. It is typified by the constant use of euphemism, or abstract labels to obscure or soften the real meaning of an event or situation which might otherwise be unpleasantly disturbing. For example, the constant use of 'ICBMs', 'enhanced radiation weapons', 'nukes' or even 'mini-nukes' instead of 'bombs' can help to lessen the impact of any discussion of the weapons' use. The label 'overkill' has sufficient distance from the reality of incinerated bodies, and sufficient vagueness to enable 'rational' decisionmakers and strategists to discuss the concept without becoming paralysed with horror. The process involves the use of softer, vaguer, and hence more acceptable euphemisms to describe unpleasant and stress-provoking events (or possibilities), as when the total destruction of station, equipment, track, vehicles and the death of railway workers is described as 'taking out the rail system'. The idea that language can be used in such a fashion is by no means new. In the 1940s George Orwell pointed out that, when a political leader says: 'We must deal with such dissident elements and restore internal stability at all costs', he really means, 'We will take some people, shoot them and so terrify the rest that they will do what we want them to do' (Orwell, 1953). However, the first version sounds less cruel and horrible, as it is full of vague, non-specific concepts like 'deal with' and 'dissident elements', rather than words like 'kill' or 'blood' that have an immediate and stress-inducing impact on people. A similar process operates in the assigning of labels to the enemy, or even apparently innocent bystanders, who are being killed (or 'wasted') by the activities of one's own 'defenders'. If one can unconsciously emphasise the essential alien-ness or 'other-ness' of members of the other party, then this moves psychological barriers and moral restraints that might otherwise cause stress at the thought of appalling treatment to people 'like us' (Kelman, 1973). A tendency develops to use names that call attention to both the opponents' lack of shared qualities with 'us', and their basic lack of humanity. One is psychologically justified in killing or injuring 'fascists', 'subversives', 'imperialists' or 'Zionists', when the same treatment of 'fathers', 'fiancés' or 'neighbours' might appear inexcusable or at best dubious. The two most frequent forms that such a process of dehumanisation takes are either to emphasise the monstrous and inhuman nature of the enemy ('the beastly Hun' of 1914 becomes the robot-like 'Nazi fanatics' of 1940); or to make the adversaries much less than human in situations where one is in an undeniable position of advantage over them and has to justify appalling behaviour (the treatment of Jewish minorities in Nazi Germany and many other places). The process of reducing psychological stress by turning the enemy into lower beings sharing none of our qualities and thus justifying different treatment can be seen in many colonial situations, and recently in Vietnam, where feelings about taking human life were dealt with by depriving local Vietnamese of their human status, so that there need be no qualms about killing 'gooks', 'slants', 'dinks' or 'Cong' as opposed to 'men'.[5] Excusing the killing or injury of the enemy thus becomes partly a matter of verbally downgrading an enemy group, a concomitant of any strong process of identification with an in-group (Tajfel, 1970).

C. THE DEVELOPMENT OF GROUP IDENTITY

Other major processes relevant to conflicts are those which have the effect of developing a gratifying sense of belonging to a group. 'The search for group identity' is exemplified by such familiar processes as the growth of nationalism, ethnocentrism or race prejudice, a sense of superiority and hostility towards an out-group, and the elevation of group interests (or the 'national interest') to the supreme good of a particular set of individuals.

Again, the process of identifying with and belonging to groups is not one which is merely associated with people in conflict situations,[6] nor are the sole results of this general tendency among humans the exacerbation of conflicts. Individuals obtain their identify from others with whom they inter-act and they are defined as persons by the roles they play within a wide variety of groupings, both formal and informal. However, the process of being involved in a group with similar interests and attitudes frequently has implications for involvement in conflicts.

Like the processes connected with an attempt to optimise stress by constructing a consistent and unambiguous image of the environment, processes which establish a satisfactory group identity are numerous and interconnected. They are particularly influential in situations of conflict, both in the sense that they:

(a) Determine the psychological response and subsequent behaviour of individual members of any party to a conflict; and

(b) Affect the manner in which the party behaves as a result of the conflict situation having arisen. The more individuals making up a party are affected by processes of group identification, the more energy that party can mobilise in order to 'win' the conflict, and the more sacrifices leaders can demand – and receive – from followers.

1. 'OWN-PARTY' IMAGES

It is a commonplace that one means of achieving a greater sense of security (and sometimes of achievement) is for the individual to identify himself with a prestigious grouping. Feelings of being accepted as a member of a larger grouping, of being a part of a powerful collectivity which in some sense represents an individual and protects him, are intensely comforting, particularly in an uncertain and threatening environment.

If an individual finds it helpful to identify with a larger group, a number of factors follow from the initial identification process:

(a) Membership of some larger collectivity or grouping satisfies an intense desire to belong, to be accepted by other people, common in every individual; hence identification and acceptance lessen a sense of isolation for individuals, whether faced with a conflictful environment or not.

(b) If identification with a particular collectivity or group is also a means of increasing self-esteem and security, then it is preferable that the group is seen to possess desirable qualities and is a success, in its own terms and in the terms of the individual group member. Individuals would like to be identified with a grouping which appears worthy − in terms of their own values. Many individuals cannot, of course, choose their own groupings but belong to ascribed categories. (Few individuals, for example, actually choose their own national groupings.) However, a common tendency for individuals in ascribed membership groupings is then to emphasise the desirable qualities of their group to themselves and others. (Kelman, 1969).

(c) The desire to avoid thinking badly about one's own group is related to an individual's desire to think well of himself. If the group is regarded as an extension of the individual (the 'self-writ-large') it follows that each member would like it to be perceived by other members (and outsiders) as possessing desirable qualities and behaving in a worthy manner.

(d) Because of the need to continue to think well of himself the individual will tend to exalt the qualities of his group, and ignore information about events or actions or attributes that do not reflect credit on the group and (by implication) on him as a member of that group.

(e) Dividing people into 'us' and 'them' almost inevitably involves some down-grading of 'them', so that 'we' can be satisfactorily upgraded. Experimental work by Tajfel indicates that the mere act of dividing individuals into categories on some quite arbitrary basis is enough to begin processes of evaluating aspects of 'our' group more positively than 'theirs', and that there exists 'a generic norm of outgroup behaviour', irrespective of the nature of the groups in question (Tajfel, 1970, p. 102).

(f) Group identification is often so strong that the values and objectives of the group are internalised by individual members and become their values and objectives. Furthermore, individuals begin to identify with group symbols (especially in larger and more complex groups such as nations and subnational 'communities'), so that these symbols (flags, leaders, land) come to have a high significance for all group members, from the leaders to the followers (Kelman, 1969).

(g) Hence any threat to the group (or any of its values and objectives) will be treated by individual members as a threat to them, and to their own values.

Group identification as a commonplace psychological process leads, in turn, to the activation of other, related processes which allow a 'good' group member to enhance his own group's value, in his own eyes by justifying its behaviour and goals, constantly emphasising its qualities and achievements, and demonstrating that other groups are different and usually inferior in both qualities and attainments, as well as unprincipled in behaviour.

At the international level, the most obvious examples of group identification are the extreme forms of nationalism and xenophobia periodically affecting all national groups, and often resulting from external threats. Numerous examples of group identification also occur at the subnational level, from the development of strong group loyalties called 'primordial ties' by Geertz (1963) within ethno-linguistic groups in Southern Asia (Tamils in Ceylon) to the remnants of tribal groupings in some of the newly independent African countries (Ibos in Nigeria).

2. MAINTAINING A POSITIVE 'OWN-PARTY' IMAGE

Once an individual has identified strongly with his group, sharing that group's attitudes, definition of the environment, and basic expecta-tions (as well as beliefs about the nature and intentions of other groups in that environment), a number of other processes operate, especially in times of threat, to maintain a high level of group conformity, in perception and attitude as well as behaviour. These processes may be either sociological or psychological. Pressures towards group con-formity in attitudes and beliefs can be group-imposed or self-imposed as a reaction to, or anticipation of group sanctions.

(a) *Self-imposed*. In this case the processes operate (often sub-consciously) so that an individual continues to conform to the per-ceptions and evaluations of his own group. Some psychologists have called it a process of 'unconscious self-monitoring', as if the individual had acknowledged the need to conform to the beliefs of his own group, and was carefully ensuring that his perceptions and attitudes fall into line with those generally held. (Naturally, the range of permissible attitudes and perceptions will vary from group to group, and within the same group according to circumstances; groups in conflict and under major external threats tend to be less tolerant of different beliefs and deviant behaviour than do groups where levels of general security, success and prosperity are high.)

Another way of looking at the manner in which individuals within a group ensure that their views conform with that is approved (or permitted) is to suggest that the group members had internalised (to a greater or lesser degree) the value of being a loyal group member, so that the individual's own cognitive and evaluative structure (his belief system) tended to take over the function of both censor and propagandist in order to exclude non-conforming information about the group, its environment and its enemies.

(b) *Group imposed.* Intra-personal psychological processes tending to make for conformity in views and attitudes among the individual members of that group are customarily reinforced by processes which become most relevant when a group is facing a major external struggle with a threatening adversary. For one thing, all groups from the smallest religious sect to the largest nation, possess norms and approved patterns of behaviour which are inculcated into group members, young and old, from the time they first become members of that group. Secondly, each group tends to have a shared pool of 'private' information and beliefs that help to interpret new data, and fit it into the group's existing 'dogma'. Often, the group's belief system will be flexible, permitting a good deal of non-conformity in behaviour, and opportunity for individual members to hold widely differing views, attitudes and expectations. However, even the most open-minded groups, communities and societies tend to limit freedom of thought in times of severe crisis, and to insist upon a high level of conformity. Anyone arguing that Hitler was a tolerable chap in England during 1940 would have received a highly unsympathetic hearing, while toleration of non-conforming views was not a notable characteristic of either Calvin's Geneva, nor France under the Jacobins.

What sanctions can groups impose upon deviant attitudes and behaviour at times of acute perceived threat or crisis? Exclusion or isolation of the deviant – a cutting off of communication and then membership – is one obvious reaction. Other sanctions are the physical ones imposed by the threat (or fact) of bodily harm, or loss of property or freedom.[7] However, most group sanctions – and probably the most effective – operate more subtly. The mere knowledge that his views are at variance with the majority of the group is highly disturbing, and often enough to bring intense pressure for conformity upon an individual.[8] The psychological stress of even being minimally isolated from one's chosen group is enough to make most people readjust their views to those of the group. Well-known experiments by both Sherif and Asch indicate that many individuals, placed in a situation where they first hear others give views which blatantly contradict their own, will often change their expressed views so that they conform with the majority. This was the case even when many of the individuals in question were convinced that their view was 'right' according to their perception (Sherif, 1936; Asch, 1955).

The kinds of social pressure placed upon an individual to obtain conformity in both beliefs and behaviour vary from group to group, and within the same group according to the nature of its environment. Asch's experiments seem to show that a significant amount of conformity can result from minimal social pressure, involving mere disagreement with one's fellows over a relatively minor matter of fact. It can be imagined that, in real-life conflict situations involving considerable ambiguity, pressures towards conformity of beliefs and opinions will be even stronger. An individual member of a group in conflict will not merely wish to avoid the embarrassment and psychological discomfort of contradicting the views of the majority. Threats may be made, and actual physical coercion be applied, ranging from isolation through imprisonment to actual physical violence. To the psychological stresses of non-conformity may be added the actual physical discomforts of being the object of sanctions from one's fellow group members, or from the leaders of the group, perhaps ending up as the victim of a witch-hunt, or a search for 'heretics' or 'traitors'.

One further psychological process may be added to this list of those *aiding* in the maintenance of group conformity. This is the strong tendency towards obedience in many individuals, amply observed in real-world situations, and also experimentally in Milgram's studies of students taking part in a psychological 'learning-teaching' laboratory at Yale University. Milgram's basic finding was that a large number of people are willing to obey 'legitimate' instructions, in spite of their own discomfort in so doing and the fact that they seemed to be causing pain to other people by such obedience. The crucial factor bringing about a high level of obedience were that the instructions were issued by a person of some (apparent) status in the academic world, and that, for many individuals, the orders were 'legitimised' to such an extent that doubts were suppressed and instructions obeyed (Milgram, 1974).

If high levels of obedience can be obtained by a mere academic experimenter in a white coat, the chances of even greater obedience if orders come from a high government source (or from some other person with status and prestige within the group, community or nation), are extremely high.

All the processes mentioned above have either helped (i) to achieve, or (ii) to maintain a high level of conformity between an individual and his group, such conformity being perhaps in terms of behaviour, but especially of perceptions, beliefs and attitudes. The process of identification with some larger group or collectivity is particularly relevant to situations of conflict, and affecting and being affected by the conflict interactions between opposing parties. The remainder of the processes discussed below assist the individual group member to continue to think well of his group (whether chosen or not) and to make it continuously worthwhile for him to identify with it, sharing its strength, status and successes.

3. MAINTAINING A POSITIVE 'OWN-PARTY' IMAGE: THE ROLE OF THE ENEMY

The importance to an individual of identifying with some larger collectivity possessing valued qualities which both represent and make up for the lack of any qualities in the identifying individual has already been emphasised. *Rationalisation* is a process by which the individual is helped to retain his image of his group as being essentially worthy and prestigious, and to avoid (or cope with) any information that might contradict this positive image.

On the individual level, *rationalisation* is an unconscious process of explaining behaviour that is unacceptable to oneself by either assigning 'logical' reasons for the behaviour, or by excusing it. Often the process is so internalised that an individual will excuse his own actions only to himself, rather than seeking to justify them publicly to an offended person. If the second party then reacts in a hostile fashion, the first is apt to see this reaction as totally unjustified 'in the circumstances', and to react himself with further (justified) hostility. Thus, an interpersonal conflict situation might be made more intense by a psychological process that functions to maintain self-esteem through finding 'reasonable' explanations for actions based upon unacceptable motives.

At the group or organisational level, the process is needed because (perhaps unfortunately) no group, organisation, community or nation can possibly appear to be benevolent, or strong, or successful, or superior on every occasion. Nor is it inevitable that a group, or its representatives, will always behave or speak according to the expectations of all individual group members, or in accordance with the values and beliefs officially espoused by the group in question. Hence, group identification is always accompanied by the possibility of both general psychological stress and particular painful feelings of guilt caused by the actions of individuals representing the group and acting in the group's name. Confronted with such a situation, there is a personal need to discover good reasons to justify otherwise unacceptable action, and individuals customarily indulge in a search for acceptable reasons to explain away unpleasant facts that do not fit in with their positive image of the group. On many occasions, especially in a conflict, a group, community or nation (or its officials or symbolic representatives) perform some unacceptable action. Both the rank-and-file membership and the leaders of a group rationalise this, and justify any group actions which conflict with the values and standards of that group. '. . . National leaders are very likely guilty at times of rationalising past injustices committed by their governments . . .' (Nye, 1973), and this process is likely to reinforce the tendency of group and national leaders to play down their own mistakes and crimes and, by falling victim of their own rationalisation processes and propaganda, be unable to understand why their opponents should distrust them, or call their present motives into question. In the Vietnamese struggle after 1954, both sides were apt to ignore their own failure to implement particular provisions of the Geneva Agreements. (In the south, the Saigon's regime's failure to hold elections; in the north, Hanoi's refusal to withdraw all guerilla units.) When these omissions were brought to anyone's attention, the tendency was to rationalise the failure away on the grounds that this failure occurred as a result of the (prior) failure by the opposing side.

This example illustrates another psychological process which often accompanies and reinforces *rationalisation*, that of *projection*. At a purely individual level, this involves a tendency to achieve psychological comfort by 'projecting' onto others the characteristics and traits in oneself of which one feels most ashamed, and which one wishes to deny. For example, in order to deal with his own hostile feelings towards another individual or group, a person may convince himself that the group in question is, in fact, hostile towards him. In this way, his own feelings towards the other is *projected*, with the possible result that:

(a) The first individual can now justify his (counter) feelings of hostility or aggression against the other group/individual.

(b) The other group/individual may come to hold hostile feelings towards the projector, and thus, through a process of *self-fulfilling prophecy*, confirm those traits, attitudes or behaviours that were first assigned to him by the original projector.

Two further psychological processes relevant for the manner in which a high level of group loyalty and identification are maintained are those of *transfer* and *displacement*. The meaning of the two terms at the individual level may be illustrated by a person who is frustrated in obtaining goals by some other person or group. If the latter cannot be dealt with directly, it is often the case that rather than admit that (for reasons of relative lack of power, or unwillingness to admit hostility to a person of superior status or position) it is impossible to deal with the source of the frustration directly, the frustrated individual will redirect his feelings of hostility (and his antagonistic behaviour) on to some available third party, whose relative lack of status and strength permits such a response. A distinction is normally made between:

(a) *Transfer*, where the substitute person or group resembles the original source of the frustration in one or more significant characteristics (in one sense, therefore, forming a 'rational' substitute) and

(b) *Displacement*, where the feelings of hostility and frustration may be directed on to any convenient person or group, without them necessarily resembling the source of the frustration in any significant respect.

A similar process acts at the level of the group, the community or the nation, except that at these different levels the frustrating agent may be a set of non-human conditions (for example, conditions in the economy) as well as another identifiable group. In such circumstances, aggregate frustration may build up because: (i) the actual cause of the frustration conditions may not be known; or (ii) it may be impossible to take action against the identified cause of the frustration. In either case, frustration and hostility may be displaced or transferred to another group, another community or another nation, the process being accompanied by:

(1) A belief that there is genuine and justified reason for the transferred hostility or the (displaced) aggressive behaviour.

(2) A release of tension, because something is being 'done' by oneself or one's group to deal with 'the problem'.

(3) A heightened level of self- or group esteem, because action taken against a scapegoat group will prove that the acting individual or group is powerful, aware, and not to be trifled with.

There is impressionistic evidence that a similar process might take place at the national level, where a defeat or setback in one area of foreign policy may lead to a high level of frustration in top decision-making circles, so that the frustration (and attendant energy or 'will to succeed') is transferred on to another, more amenable government or country. Ross Stagner quotes a passage from the Washington columnist, James Reston, detailing the frustration in top American decisionmaking circles following the Bay of Pigs fiasco in Cuba, and the determination to 'do something' against a more 'reachable' enemy to make up for the failure in Cuba (Stagner, 1967b, p. 76). Much of this desire for successful action must have involved support and international credibility, but there appear to have been some elements of transfer in the desire to 'take action in Laos to make up for Cuba'.

One final, crucial problem is likely to confront any individual member of a group (or a nation) striving to maintain his image of the group with which he identifies as being essentially fair, just, strong-but-peace-loving, and highly principled. This dilemma arises constantly when the individual and his group or nation are in intense conflict with another party, for almost inevitably both sides will employ violent forms of conflict behaviour that run counter to accepted norms of permissible behaviour held within the group. Especially in wars or communal conflicts, representatives of the involved parties are almost bound to act in a careless, cruel, destructive and generally appalling manner, and to put into effect policies that involve physical damage and death. The problem for the individual member of that group is how he can maintain his 'good' self- or group-image in the face of such information. An essential contradiction arises between the belief in the fundamental goodness of the group, and the inexcusable badness of the group's acts in many conflicts. For the individual who identifies with a particular group (and its desirable qualities) there is a pressing need to explain the group's failure to live up to its own standards, and to relieve psychological discomfort by explaining and justifying the dubious behaviour and removing any feelings of guilt (Sanford, 1971).

This contradiction is another aspect of the *cognitive consistency* problem, and the psychological task is to reduce the inconsistency between beliefs about the group and facts about current behaviour by its representatives. In many cases, the solution is found in the process of *dehumanisation*. Fundamentally, this is a matter of convincing oneself that the enemy group is inhuman, or sub-human; or so cruel, barbarous and uncivilised that the customary standards of ethics and morals that apply within our (more civilised) group (and between that group and all 'really' civilised peoples) do not apply to the enemy. This is because that enemy has put himself beyond the pale of 'normal' considerations and treatment, either by his characteristics or behaviour.[9]

Successful use of the dehumanisation process fulfils several functions. For one thing, it removes the inconsistency between knowing that killing human beings is wrong (this generally violates moral codes) and the knowledge that one belongs to a group that is killing human beings, perhaps in large numbers. Dehumanisation does this by removing the killed from the category of 'human being', so that normal moral standards need not apply. Secondly, it is much easier to plan, order and carry out what would be regarded otherwise as a cruel and vicious policy, if the policy is operating against a group or a nation whose alleged behaviour or inherent characteristics have put them so far outside the pale of human civilisation that they are no longer covered by 'our' code of ethics relevant to the right treatment of human beings. The achievement of dehumanisation is one of the side effects of war-time propaganda. Efforts during World War I to portray the Germans as monstrous barbarians (because of 'behaviour' within Belgium), were echoed in the American view of the Japanese during World War II. A similar process operated at the height of the Cold War. As White comments:

> . . . modes of perceiving which limit the category 'human' to citizens of our nation and which view citizens of Russia as less than human will foster the displacement of aggression on to the Russians. Conversely, if they are encouraged to view us as 'bad, imperialistic, war-mongering capitalists' who lack human attributes, it will be easy for them to express their hostilities in the form of violence against us . . . (White, 1970, p. 292)

One implication of arguments outlined above is that there may be many positive psychological advantages to possessing (and if not possessing, actively creating), 'an enemy'. A party in conflict that fills the role of enemy can serve as a scapegoat upon which unrelievable frustrations or feelings of aggression may be directed. Any need to project undesirable and inadmissible feelings may be simply filled, if some unpopular out-group is conveniently available to serve as an object for the projection. Again, possession of an enemy group helps to increase the value of identifying with a strong, and essentially good grouping, while action taken against the threatening and aggressive enemy group can begin to take on the chacteristics of a 'crusade'. Psychological satisfaction can be derived from a feeling of superiority towards the enemy, and from a self-righteous feeling of sacrifice for 'the cause' and identification with group effort, while the process of dehumanisation of the enemy enables one to destroy without any of the normal qualms of conscience. In short, the presence of an enemy (or even an alien out-group) may be highly functional for the individual and collective members of a group, because it may enable a number of psychological processes to work effectively in relieving psychological discomfort in frustrating circumstances (Gladstone, 1959).

D. SUMMARY AND CONCLUSION

It may be helpful to conclude this chapter by referring back to the original simple figure dividing relevant protective processes into efforts to maintain cognitive consistency by selective perception, selective recall and achieving a satisfactory form of group identity, and adding the processes discussed above under appropriate headings (Fig. 4.2).

However, the clear-cut division made above is not as clear-cut in reality. Many common psychological processes can simultaneously contribute to simplifying perceptions of the environment and to increasing the degree of group identification, either by an individual or by many members of a party in conflict. Rigid distinctions, in this regard, would be misleading. Rationalisation of one's leaders' behaviour as they order a particularly unpleasant form of conflict behaviour may help to remove cognitive inconsistencies, but it also assists individuals to maintain a high level of loyalty to their party, and a sense that the party itself continues to pursue a course of action essentially justifiable. Similarly, stereotyping may occur in order to simplify a complex environment yet have the parallel effect of

between groups likely to develop a clearer perception of out-
groups. Even discussions of pressing international conflicts,
complex, however, the adaptation observed in some is not
helped at all to be obtained help.

Discussion of implicit knowledge of problems, a barrier to
conflict-wary analysts, application of the scientific results, these
understandings to the interpretations and contributions that result in
conflict.

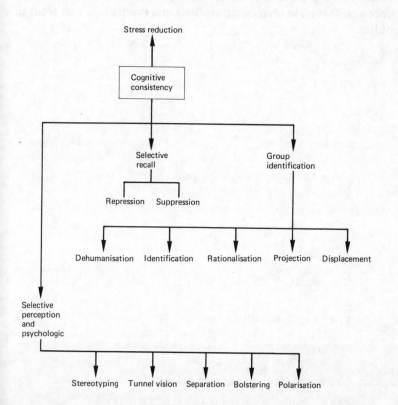

FIGURE 4.2   Conflict attitudes: Underlying processes

increasing group identity by drawing a clearer boundary round a group. Protective psychological processes are inter-connected in complex ways. However, the suggested classification scheme is sufficiently clear to be of some help.

Our discussion of the major psychological processes activated in conflicts now leads to a consideration of the specific results of these processes; that is, to images, perceptions and evaluations that recur in conflicts.

5 Perceptions During Conflict

In chapter 4 we argued that a number of inter-related psychological processes concerned with the alleviation of excessive stress occur frequently within human individuals, whether leaders or followers, successes or failures, activists or passive supporters. Furthermore, involvement in conflict situations and processes brings many of these processes into operation: (i) more frequently, (ii) with greater intensity and (iii) across a wider range of individuals than do co-operative situations, where there are seldom the same levels of fear, suspicion, threat or hostility. We now outline in more detail some of the perceptual and evaluative results of psychological processes previously discussed as efforts to establish and maintain cognitive consistency. Most illustrations of results from relevant stress-reducing processes will be taken from international conflict. However, the same general type of perception and evaluation frequently occurs in intra-national conflict, even though exact content might vary. Chapter 5 therefore discusses common phenomena of group perception during a conflict, and distortions or misperceptions caused by high levels of tension, fear, suspicion or anxiety.

A. SELF-IMAGES

Perceptions which result from the activation of psychological processes may be classified into those which concern the perceiver's own self or group, the adversary and third parties in the overall environment within which the conflict occurs. This first section reviews some common perceptions (and misperceptions) concerning one's own party; the next various types of 'enemy' images; and the final section how these two categories of image are closely related to one another.

1. IMAGES OF AN EXTENDED SELF

In conflict, one important aspect of group identity is the apparently universal phenomenon that individuals identify not merely with a set of other similar individuals but with symbolic objects which come to represent the set, as much as the individuals in it. The 'self-image' or 'group-image' comes to include elements apart from the people in the group. At the purely individual level, this is a familiar process. Kurt Lewin, for example, described how a person's clothes come, psychologically, to be part of 'the person' (Lewin, 1935), while Robert Ardrey has suggested that a person identifies his car, his house, his office desk and other salient possessions as part of 'himself', to be kept inviolate from trespass or use by others (Ardrey, 1966). In international as well as other disputes, one crucial aspect of the process of identification is that which occurs between an individual, a group, and what the group defines as 'its' territory. The identification between an Englishman and the boundaries of the British Isles (even if apprehended only through maps) and an Irishman with the boundaries of Ireland (including both Eire and Ulster) is important. It is a frequent phenomenon that territory becomes thought of as part of the 'national self' (Kelman, 1969), so that group identity involves (among other features) a sense of being at one with a defined piece of territory and hence a 'territorial' self-image.[1]

At the international level, it is obvious that conflicts will arise (or, at least, be exacerbated) in situations where two national groups possess territorial self-images which 'overlap' as, perhaps, in the case of an Englishman and an Irishman over Northern Ireland. Ralph White has suggested a list of areas in the world which have been the source of constant dispute, where parties involved have undoubtedly perceived the disputed area as part of 'themselves', and the activity of their adversary as affecting that core value, the integrity and security of 'the national self'. These are zones of overlap, as one nation's territorial self-image overlaps with that of another.[2] A parallel phenomenon is one in which a national group has a self-image which includes a particular area as essentially 'ours' and involving concomitant exclusive rights to do as 'we' choose; but where others possess an image of the same area as being excluded from the territorial boundaries of the first nation, and hence subject to other rules about use, exploitation or potential ownership. (The Egyptian perception of the Straits of Tiran as being part of Egypt is not one shared by either Israelis or Jordanians.)

It would be interesting to consider why a group of individuals come to identify with a particular piece of territory as being part of 'themselves', but the effects in worsening – or, some people have argued, causing – a conflict situation cannot be denied. White links the concept of *territorial images* and *zones of overlap* to a process mentioned earlier, arguing that the rigidity that often accompanies rival claims to the same territory is the result both of identification with a group symbol (territory) and tendency towards 'black and white' thinking. The clarity with which a territorial dispute can be defined ('It can only be ours *or* theirs, and their claim has no shred of validity') removes all strain from understanding the complex situation that might exist within the disputed area, and helps to make the conflict easily understood in terms of 'us' and 'them', of allies and enemies, and of straightforward cognition and evaluation.

2. VIRILE AND MORAL SELF-IMAGES

One vital element of the positive image held about one's own group (or nation) particularly exacerbates tendencies to respond forcefully and aggressively to perceived threats by another group, or any situation in which one's own goals are thwarted by the activities of another. White calls it the *virile self-image*, and notes that it is connected with pride in the qualities of one's own chosen group, and associated with the process of rationalisation. The latter transforms pride into a set of supportable and justifiable reasons for taking actions, which can then be further rationalised as 'defensive'. In many situations people are convinced by leaders (or manage to convince themselves), that their group or nation's reputation as a strong-but-wise, tough-but-peace-loving entity is at stake and that this, rather than the actual details of any current problem, is what matters. White connects the idea of group virility (that the group's 'manhood' is at stake, so that it must demonstrate its courage and toughness to the adversary and others), with the concept of overlapping territorial self-images, arguing that a result of the conjunction of both is the feeling – and the policy – that 'we' must demonstrate firmness and resolution by expelling the intruder from 'our' territory. Once this act has been carried out successfully, the group's toughness, determination and virility will have been amply demonstrated to the intruder, to the outside world, and to 'ourselves', reinforcing the knowledge that 'we' are members of a worthy group and also (vicariously) our own self-esteem. However, the tendency to try to demonstrate group virility is not confined to territorial disputes as any study of the international news will show.

In addition to a virile self-image, it is important for members of any party in conflict to maintain their perception that their party is also essentially moral in its dealings with others (even the adversary). Thus, actions against an adversary are always interpreted as being principled and lacking in evil intent or ultimate effects. Americans' perceptions of their role in Vietnam were initially based upon the assumptions that this arose from the pursuit of wholly honourable and disinterested motives, and obligations to principles that could not be avoided. A similar *moral self-image* was obviously genuinely held by the leaders (and, naturally, the followers) in North Vietnam. Ho Chi Minh in an interview with Felix Greene in 1965 clearly perceived the presence of North Vietnamese regular army units in the south solely as an aid to southerners in resisting US aggression and a counter to illegal and unwanted US military intervention in the south of the country (White, 1970, p. 98).

3. INTRUDER SELF-IMAGES

Given that many groups of individuals find it comforting to identify their group symbolically with a particular piece of territory, the presence of people obviously not of 'our' group on that territory, no matter how long these 'aliens' have been there, leads to the development of a related image concerning outsiders on 'our' territory. In situations of territorial overlap it becomes obvious to both sides that, as the territory in question is part of 'us', any encroachment on it must be an alien invasion to be expelled, back to the 'outside' from which the invaders come. It becomes a duty to expel the alien intruders and easy to become angry at their effrontery at existing as intruders on our land. The territorial self-image can lead to an *alien intruder* image.[3] The implications of this kind of thinking for situations of intra-national conflict defined as involving help from a neighbouring country (Vietnam or Ulster), or of a secessionist movement in a remote region (Biafra or Eritrea) need not be emphasised.

However, the spatial boundaries of a party are not the only ones that can be 'penetrated' by outsiders, and in many conflicts it becomes obvious that disturbing self-images arise from perceptions that important group boundaries have been breached. One extension of the alien intruder image has been noted during intra-national conflicts, when it becomes apparent that a faction within one's own party is discontented or, worse, 'on the side of the enemy'. Rather than face the stressful realisation that some genuine discontent might underlie agitation or dissent (which is thus a sign that something is seriously wrong) and the equally uncomfortable task of doing something about the sources of the discontent, an easy reaction is to delude oneself that there is no serious discontent, nor a need for basic change or reform. The only reason for otherwise loyal and sensible group members behaving in this strange manner is because they have been 'stirred up' and pushed into action by outside agitators, sent for the express purpose of fomenting discontent where none exists. White mentions:

(i) White southeners in the US convincing themselves that the local Negro community had been stirred up over civil rights only because of northern agitators, who knew nothing about the 'real' problems of the south.

(ii) Militant communists in developing countries who see every manifestation of local opposition to their aims as stirred up by American imperialists.

(iii) Militant anti-communists in Vietnam and the USA who saw the Vietcong as North Vietnamese outsiders, backed by Chinese interventionists and a world-wide, militant Marxist movement (White, 1970, p. 315).

In a similar fashion, during a strike in the British building industry, employers were attributing workers' discontent and disruption to the influence of sinister 'outside elements' coming 'into' the building industry and onto local building sites to create trouble where none had existed before.

One effect of possessing such an image is that it helps to relieve a feeling of psychological discomfort by 'exonerating' most of those who (actually) constitute an opposing party. It is also possible to reinforce one's own self- or group-image as being basically fair and well-disposed, tolerant of a misguided faction and hostile only towards the *alien* agitator. In essence, hostility is transferred onto outsiders, and the alien agitator image acts as a substitute for empathy and remedial action. As long as a person believes it, '. . . he does not have to understand what made that group receptive to outside influence, or to anything drastic to relieve their sources of discontent . . .' (White, 1970).

Closely connected with the *alien agitator* image is another form of group-image, also functioning to maintain belief in an essentially good and uncorrupted group identity. White calls this the *traitors-in-our-midst* image, and notes that it manifests itself at times of extreme stress. He instances the great Stalinist purges in the 1930s; the Nazi success in scapegoating Jews, liberals and communists during the same period as the elements that had 'stabbed Germany in the back' in 1918; and the McCarthy period of communist witch-hunting in the USA at the time of the Korean War in the early 1950s. Minor examples are the frequent accusations of American politicians as being 'soft on communism', during the 1960s and the attitudes among the militant Protestant community in Northern Ireland towards liberal Protestants who joined with Catholics in the Northern Ireland Civil Rights Movement in the period 1966–8.

The extremism of some of these 'witch-hunting' outbursts reflects two elements. The first is a desire to purge the group identity of unworthy and contaminating elements presented by people and factions who disagree, and who might represent the enemy within 'our' (otherwise basically worthy) group.[4] In this sense, the image is a product of all the emotional investment connected with a successful search for group identity (and the maintenance of purity once this is found). Secondly, the discovery of 'traitors-in-our-midst' represents yet another attempt to reduce discomfort induced by ambiguity in a complex situation. It is simpler and more comfortable to reduce the manifold divisions of opinion and action into two simple categories, pro and con. This simplifies the way people should be regarded and treated. People in 'our' group should be on 'our' side in all disputes, and hold 'our' views in any disagreement. The discovery that some do not can be disturbing and frustrating. These feelings can be converted into hostility towards those who break up the simplicity of the situation. The attitude may be summed up in the old adage: 'Those who are not for us are against us'! This may be bad tactics, but seems to be a good strategy for relieving ambiguity and any resultant psychological discomfort.

B. ADVERSARY IMAGES

Most of the 'images' discussed above concerned a group's perception and evaluation of itself, and its qualities, as well as resultant actions. The next set are those which appear frequently in one group's evaluation of a rival and the latter's characteristics, motives and behaviour.

1. BLACK-TOP IMAGES

Two major enemy images are apparently contradictory ways of minimising potential discomfort caused by consciously acknowledging that oneself and one's group or nation are hated and feared by a large number of people. The first of these methods is called the *black-top* image, a belief that the enemy can be divided into two categories:

(1) The evil leadership, who hate and fear 'our own' group and who are responsible for deluding their followers about 'us' and our aims and ambitions – as well as our basic goodwill towards their group or nation.

(2) The mass of the followers, who are basically good, and only hostile towards us because of the activities of their leaders.

Examples of the black-top images are the British belief in World War I that the Kaiser and the German militarists were the 'real' villains of the war; and the apparent ability of both Soviet and US citizens to differentiate between the leaders of the other side (the evil capitalists of Wall Street, and the tyrannical and ambitious men at the head of the Communist Party in the Kremlin), and the basically benevolent mass of the people, who would be friendly if only permitted to be so by their leaders.

The advantages of holding such an image are many and obvious. In the first place, it enables people to ignore the fact that some of the goals valued by the mass of both parties may actually be in conflict, and genuinely irreconcilable, at least at one particular point in time. Secondly it is always unpleasant to contemplate the knowledge that large numbers of people are hostile towards one's own group. This throws some doubt upon its worthiness and that of its members. Hence, it is possible to escape the dilemma by assuming that the mass of people (the mass of the Vietnamese peasants), are 'really' friendly, while only the leaders are 'truly' hostile (the villains of the National Liberation Front); and this latter fact can easily be explained away by their essential evil, which one can only expect from some small group of deluded men. Finally, developing a black-top image of a rival group enables those holding that image to deal with a high degree of ambivalence in their feelings about another (often large) group of people, as well as maintaining a consistent self-image as remaining basically friendly and tolerant in spite of provocation. For example, with help from American propaganda, US citizens could cope with ambivalent feelings about the Soviet Union (part friendly, part hostile, part fearful, part virile) by concentrating hostility on the leadership and friendly feelings (mixed with some pity) for the bulk of the Soviet people. This gave a legitimate means of expression for both positive and negative feelings about the USSR. It also enabled people in the USA to continue to picture themselves (and their national group) as being consistently friendly towards the vast majority of the human race (including the mass of the Russian people), especially those who are oppressed; and as being consistently hostile towards the minority oppressor groups throughout the world. (No doubt, a similar argument could be put forward for people in the Soviet Union.)

The black-top image (which functions as a way of avoiding the horrid possibility that 'we' are hated and disliked by a vast number of people) is related to another image. This is the *pro-us illusion*, an unquestioning conviction that the bulk of the people involved in some conflict situation must 'really' be 'for' our group, or at least agree with the things we stand for, and are trying to achieve. This particular image has manifested itself in a number of ways in many international and intra-national conflicts. For example, the illusion persisted for over 20 years in 'the West' (and particularly in the USA) that not only the 'satellites' in Eastern Europe but the Soviet Union itself were seething with suppressed discontent (based upon the peoples' inability to achieve what observers with Western values thought they ought to want to achieve). Hence, the bulk of the Soviet and East European people were basically 'on our side' and against their own leaders in the Cold War, and only waiting for help from outside to rise and throw off the tyranny of their leaders. Again, the Bay of Pigs operation was launched upon the mistaken premise that the Cuban exile groups were right,[5] in that the bulk of the Cuban people did not 'really' support Castro; while in Vietnam the initial belief that the vast majority of the peasants in South Vietnam were anti-Vietcong and pro- the Saigon regime (and its American patrons) vitiated any attempt to arrive at a more accurate assessment of the actual range of opinion and attitudes in the South Vietnamese countryside.

We should not be mistaken about this argument, however. No doubt there are situations in which the leaders of a group, community or nation have lost the support of their followers, as well as some in which that support remains strong, if not obvious. The point is that there is often a strong tendency to assume (for reasons of psychological comfort) that the vast majority of people are 'really' pro-us, and cannot genuinely disagree with us or hate us in the manner which they publicly appear to do. There may frequently be a 'silent majority', but it is false to assume that it is automatically 'pro-us'. There are at least two other major possibilities: (i) it is really anti-us and pro-them; or (ii) it is really indifferent to both sides, and wishes everyone would just go away. White argues that this last was the situation in the South Vietnamese countryside by 1969, although earlier the American estimate of support for Saigon had been quite wrong, and peasant support for the Vietcong had been roughly between three and four times as strong as that for the Saigon Government (White, 1970). This, of course, is the most realistic possibility; that levels of support and conflicting attitudes differ over time, so that the population are seldom totally 'for us' or 'for them'. If one can tolerate some complexity and ambiguity, the most realistic assessment seems likely to be one which refuses to categorise people into dichotomous types.

Finally, in this group of images that attempt to reduce ambiguity by tampering with the perceived possibility that 'we' are genuinely hated and feared by a large number of people, is the *puppet-enemy image*. This is complex, but in outline implies that a complicated relationship of co-operation and conflict (or domination and insubordination), between allied groups or nations is simplified into a straightforward master-slave, or 'puppet' relationship. In this fashion, it appears that the dominated puppet cannot 'really' be regarded as an independent actor (with confusing and ambivalent motives and characteristics different from its 'master') but merely as an extension of the main enemy. Examples of this image are numerous. The Chinese Government in Peking was seen by many Western leaders as a mere puppet of the Soviet Union throughout the 1950s. Soviet leaders still appear to perceive the UK and the remainder of western Europe as an extension of American dominated capitalism. Arabs tend to see Israel as an extension of either western colonialism or American imperialism, while both US and South Vietnamese leaders apparently saw the Vietcong as a simple extension of the North Vietnamese Government in Hanoi.

While not denying that there are numerous situations in which the actions and statements of one group, community or government are strongly influenced, even dominated, by the wishes of another (although influence is a two-way process and the tendency seems always to be to over-estimate the degree of control from the puppet— master to the puppet),[6] the present question is why the image is so prevalent in situations of conflict. The puppet-image may be yet another way in which the complexity and ambiguity of most real-world conflict situations is reduced, so that, once again, there appear to be only two undifferentiated parties. However, an additional reason may be that this type of image is yet another means of avoiding the unpleasant realisation that a large number of people might hate and fear 'our' party and its activities. In this case, one does not need to feel hostility towards the 'puppets'. They are only puppets, doing what they are told. (At the same time there is, as in the *alien* agitator image, no need to try to empathise with them and to try to understand why they behave as they do!) Similarly, it may be a relief to recognise that the puppets only 'pretend' to dislike and fear us, because they are so instructed by the leaders of the 'real' enemy who control their behaviour and attitudes. Thus, once again, the number of people with genuine feelings of hatred towards us (and the possibility of a genuinely felt conflict of interests) is neatly reduced, and with it, the level of potential psychological discomfort which accompanies an awareness of being widely opposed and disliked.

2. THE 'UNIFIED ENEMY' IMAGE

In direct contrast to the cluster of images differentiating an opposing party into distinct categories (the few that are really our enemies, and the mass who are not), is an image which sees the enemy as a single, unified entity, the members of which are all equally bent upon our downfall, equally evil, and equally implacable in their pursuits of a set of unjust and immoral goals. This 'homogenous enemy' image runs directly counter to the black-top image just discussed, and there is as yet only the observed fact that either image can exist during a conflict, with no indication of factors that make one reaction more likely than the other. Both are obvious attempts to reduce ambiguity in the conflict situation, and examples of black-and-white thinking. In the case of the 'unified enemy', it is simpler (if less comforting) to think of the enemy as a single group, to retain a belief in the total unity of the adversary, and to fail to see divergences and subgroups within an opposing party. It also enables all enemies to be treated exactly the same ('They are all equally guilty') without having to go into troublesome problems of differentiating between individuals, or taking into account individual qualities which might reveal that some of the enemy were human. Belief in a unified enemy leads to such stereotyped judgements as: 'The only good X is a dead X' — which simplifies the conflict considerably.

At a slightly more sophisticated level, the unified enemy image leads to a belief that the opposing party is not only more regimented than ourselves, but that it does not suffer from the same splits and internal divisions that beset 'us'. Often allied to this perception of an enemy's possession of a high level of internal unity are a number of other elements:

(a) A tendency to under-estimate the possibility that the opposing party can genuinely perceive 'us' as a menace.

(b) A tendency to over-estimate the degree to which the opposing party acts in response to what 'we' do ourselves, and to perceive the opponent's attention as constantly directed towards 'us' and 'our' actions.

(c) A tendency to have difficulty in realising that issues and events important to us may be of much less relevance to the opposing party (Jervis, 1968).

Again, the unifying element in such tendencies is yet another effort to exalt one's chosen group and increase its perceived self-importance by assuming that everything and anything it does or says (or its leaders do or say), must be of central importance to both the adversary and to relevant third parties (Jervis, 1968). Such a set of beliefs places 'our' party right in the centre of the stage, with a suitable amount of prestige and influence. Similar tendencies among participants have been reported from simulation studies of international crisis situations. The 'Conex' experiments, for example, showed that participants had quite unrealistic expectations about the general success of their diplomatic initiatives during the course of the simulation, while, specifically, there was a distinct tendency for the senders of messages to give the exact composition of their messages far more attention than they ever accorded incoming messages from other parties (Banks *et al.*, 1968).

C. INTERDEPENDENCE OF SELF/OTHER IMAGES

The perceptions and attitudes resulting from individual (but widely shared) processes activated in conflict situations emphasise the manner in which perceptions of self and adversary tend to be inter-dependent, or at least complementary. Each depends, in many instances, upon the nature of the other, but particularly in the way in which perceptions of the opposing group result, in some curiously 'logical' way, from the images an individual holds of his own group.

1. SELECTIVE PERCEPTION AND INTERPRETATION

One of the most common and significant ways in which individuals (and groups) manage to misperceive a situation, or others involved in a dispute, is by the process of *selective perception*. The operation of this process is obviously not confined to the members of one party in conflict. (The members of one side do not see everything accurately, while their adversaries constantly misperceive, no matter how much this may seem to be the case to those directly engaged in the dispute.) Hence, it is likely that, in any ambiguous situation the parties may well attach quite differing interpretations to actions or statements by themselves, their adversaries, or relevant third parties. This process of slanted or inter-dependent interpretation can be illustrated by considering rival Soviet and US interpretations of various actions in the Cold War.

Slanted interpretation can occur over a place, a policy, but most particularly over an event which has to be set in a context of perceptions and expectations, and then evaluated as part of a meaningful pattern. However, as at least two parties are carrying out the interpretation, the chances of the two contexts being widely different are high, so that the same event can take on widely differing meanings. The U2 incident, for example, was interpreted by the Soviets as a gross violation of Soviet territory by a threatening and dangerous spy-plane, quite unlike the defensive espionage carried out by the USSR, but equally something only to be expected from aggressive and hostile capitalists. To Americans the incident was a regrettable measure undertaken defensively by the USA because of the paranoid secrecy of the Soviet leaders (who must obviously have something to hide because of their concern over secrecy) and the need to gather information about Soviet aggressive preparations. Furthermore, it was the equivalent of Soviet espionage activities in the late 1940s and early 50s, and hence essentially reactive. Similarly, quite different interpretations of German re-armament and membership of NATO were prevalent following 1955, one Soviet, and one American. To US decisionmakers and their public, re-arming West Germany was seen as a matter of forcing reluctant Germans to do their share in building up Western defensive strength against the looming Soviet threat, thus shifting some of the military and financial burdens of European defence. For the Soviet public, on the other hand, German adherence to NATO could only represent an alliance between basically good (if misguided) Americans and the unspeakable German aggressors who had nearly destroyed the Soviet Union in World War II. Other contrasting interpretations of the same event or situation are numerous and not merely confined to international conflicts (see Table 5.1). Inability to

TABLE 5.1 Interpreting Cold War events

Stimulus	Soviet interpretation	US interpretation
Soviet role in Eastern Europe	Leadership	Subjugation
Placing MRBMs in Cuba	Deterrence, and the equivalent of many US actions	Aggression and a whole new type of action in the Cold War
Berlin	Outpost of an enemy: centre for dangerous espionage and source of propaganda: remnant of World War II	Surrounded outpost of freedom

empathise with an adversary, to see one's own actions in the context of their set of assumptions, is a recurring feature of all conflicts. Role reversal becomes more difficult the more intense the conflict. Kennedy Trevaskis has recounted how a face-to-face meeting with tribesmen rebelling against British rule in the hinterland of Aden brought him to a recognition of the way in which what had seemed to colonial rulers eminently sensible and enlightened acts had been perceived and evaluated totally differently by local inhabitants using a wholly different frame of reference:

> . . . It was the road which McIntosh had made through their country in 1951, to link the Upper Aulaqi Sheikhdom with Aden. This was their country and within it they alone had the right to propose or dispose. By making a road through it, McIntosh had been as much an aggressor as if he had invaded their encampment and stolen their goats . . . As I listened to them plunging noisily about in protest, I began to realise that this was no mere fanfaronade. To examine their complaints with cold, official eyes was to see nothing more than a threadbare pretext for doing Asshami's bidding in return for rifles and ammunition. But looking at it as a tribesman would, it seemed different; and I began to understand what our brusque intrusion would mean to the . . . tribes whose country had customarily been as inviolate as an Englishman's home . . . (Trevaskis, 1968, p. 85).

2. MIRROR-IMAGES AND INTER-DEPENDENCE

Interpreting incoming information in context (or in accordance with some pre-existing structure of knowledge), has formed the basis of much of our discussion of psychological processes underlying conflict attitudes. However, it does little to explain why the original assumptions about the bad-faith, aggression and inherent untrustworthiness of the opposing party are created and subsequently reinforced. One suggestion is that this process is almost inevitable, given the inter-dependence between one's self-image, the probable behaviour of others, and the images formed of those others from deductions about their behaviour in the light of one's self-image. As a simple example, an essential element in any Soviet citizen's perception of the USA as posing a threat would be his own perception of his country as obviously peaceful. Furthermore, if the Soviet citizen (identifying with his national group) assumes that Americans perceive the USSR as he himself does, this would keep him from imagining that any Americans might genuinely fear a Soviet attack. Further assuming that the Americans cannot really be afraid of an attack, a Soviet citizen would be wholly unable to suppose that American bases, ICBMs and 'containing' alliances were actually intended to be defensive, so that he could hardly reach any conclusion other than that all US military preparations were essentially unprovoked aggression. Hence the argument that '. . . the chief factor determining the Soviet people's enemy image (or their receptivity to official propaganda about that enemy), is their own self-image . . .' (Bronfenbrenner, 1961, p. 45).

The Soviet–American example neatly illustrates that complementary self- and enemy-images produce a circular, cause and effect relationship. Given that, through the processes of group identification, individuals possess an image of themselves and their own group as peaceful and reactive, the power-orientated actions of an opponent cannot be perceived and evaluated as anything other than aggressive; and given the image of the opposing party as threatening and aggressive, then the power-orientated actions of oneself and one's group are perceived as reactive, defensive and wholly consistent with peaceful intentions. The two images are '. . . mutually complementary and thoroughly interdependent . . .' (Bronfenbrenner, 1961).

The ultimate sophistication of this process of inter-dependent image-building may occur when two sides to a conflict develop mutually uncomplimentary images of one another, in which the details of one tend to be the reverse of the details in the image held by the enemy. This phenomenon is known as a *mirror-image*, and Nye describes it as '. . . the fact that each opposing side has certain views of itself and of the opponent which are reversed from those held by the other side . . .' (Nye, 1973, p. 15). The development of perfect mirror-images in every type of conflict is obviously unlikely, but more likely in highly symmetrical conflicts. The perceptions of the Americans held in Hanoi and those of the North Vietnamese held in Washington are likely to diverge widely, as are those held by Israelis of Arabs, and Arabs of Israelis. However, even in this type of symmetrical conflict, some elements in the contrasting images are likely to be the same, and to result from this basic complementarity of self- and enemy-images. In the case of the images held within the main protagonists in the Cold War, the details of the mirror-image are uncannily similar (see Table 5.2).

TABLE 5.2   Mirror-images in the Cold War (Stagner, 1967)

American image of USSR	Soviet image of USA
(1) They (the rulers) are bad. The men in the Kremlin are aggressive, power-seeking, brutal in suppressing Hungary, ruthless in dealing with their people. They are infiltrating the western hemisphere to attack us. They engage in espionage and sabotage to wreck our country.	(1) They (the rulers) are bad. The Wall Street bankers, politicians and militarists want a war because they fear loss of wealth and power in a communist revolution. They are surrounding us with military bases. They send spies (in U2 planes and otherwise) to destroy the workers' fatherland.
(2) They are like the Nazis – an aggressive expansionist dictatorship. They are trying to divide us – split NATO, stir class hatred.	(2) They are like the Nazis – re-arming the Germans against us. They are trying to divide us – split off Yugoslavia and Poland, incite rebellion against our government.
(3) They are imperialistic. The communists want to dominate the world. They rigidly control the satellite puppet governments.	(3) They are imperialistic. The capitalist nations dominate colonial areas, keep them in submission. The Latin-American regimes (except Cuba) are puppets of the USA.

TABLE 5.2—cont.

American image of USSR	Soviet image of USA
(4) They exploit their own people. They hold down consumer goods, keep standard of living low except for communist bureaucrats.	(4) They exploit their own people. All capitalists live in luxury by exploiting workers who suffer insecurity, unemployment etc.
(5) They are against democracy. Democratic forms are mere pretence; people can vote only for communist candidates. Rulers control organs of propaganda, education and communication. They persecute anyone favouring western democracy.	(5) They are against democracy. Democratic forms are mere pretence; people can vote only for capitalist candidates. Rulers control organs of propaganda, education and communication. They persecute anyone favouring communist ideas.
(6) They distort the truth. They pose as a friend of colonial peoples in order to enslave them.	(6) They distort the truth. They falsely accuse the USSR of desiring to impose ideology by force.
(7) They are immoral, materialistic, atheistic.	(7) They are immoral, materialistic, selfishly individualistic.

While evidence from other conflicts such as that between Vietnamese and Americans in Vietnam (White, 1970), and Indians and Pakistanis on southern Asia (Haque, 1973) offer support for Bronfenbrenner's original hypothesis about the formation of mirror images during conflicts, other studies have tended to modify the idea slightly. Salazar and Marin (1977) attempted to see whether mirror images developed among participants in the conflict between Venezuela and Colombia over their joint boundary in the late 1960s. They found that, while there were elements of a mirror-image in the way in which Venezuelans and Colombians perceived themselves and one another there were other results that did not fit the original hypothesis. They suggested that this might be because the close geographical and cultural proximity of the two groups enabled a much more accurate image of the characteristics of the adversary to be formed, so that the mirror-image could in some cases merely apply to the evaluative elements of their mutual stereotypes. The result of this work suggests that mirror-images are common effects of groups being in conflict but that previous lack of direct contact and low levels of communication (plus low intensity of conflict) are more likely to lead to a mirror-image on both descriptive and evaluative dimensions. Closer contacts lead to a mirror-image merely in evaluative aspects.

3. MAINTAINING INTER-DEPENDENT IMAGES

Two final processes which also hinge upon the inter-dependence of parties' interpretations of the situation and the manner in which their image of the adversary depends (to some measure) upon their self-image are: (i) the process of *issue polarisation*; and (ii) the perception of *different degrees of freedom of action* held by one's own party and by the enemy.

Issue polarisation theory in its basic form, argues that there is often a strong tendency for parties in conflict to perceive that even more interests and issues are mutually incompatible than is actually the case. Given this psychological tendency, a dispute is likely to widen to include many new issues, and to create rivalries where none existed before, or where (in other circumstances) none might have developed. In practical terms, finding oneself opposed over a particular issue is likely to arouse hostile feelings and produce a tendency to range oneself on the opposite side to the original adversary on any new issue (provided this does not involve going against a major value, or abandoning a salient objective). Hence, a process of expanding confrontation begins and accelerates, covering numerous issues. In many cases the level of negative inter-action begins to outweigh positive inter-action in mutually collaborative endeavours. Cold Wars or 'confrontations' begin to develop, where the mere fact that the 'old enemy' has taken up one position, or is espousing one cause, is enough to justify taking the opposite position, or supporting the rival party. Justification becomes a matter of *who* holds particular goals, or *who* pursues a particular line of action, irrespective of the nature of the goals or the action.

In a slightly different fashion, the possession of some complementary goals has a reverse effect on two parties, and the development of strong mutual interests tends to be self-reinforcing in much the same fashion as strong mutual incompatibilities. Similar goals will reinforce a perception that more goals are complementary than is originally the case, and this perception will set up a form of *self-fulfilling prophecy* ensuring that goals and actions will fall into line with the original perceptions of shared interests and expectations of co-operation. Both this process, and the negative one involving polarisation present no surprises. Both follow from principles of *cognitive consistency*, and resultant pressure to remove the ambiguity of another party being in conflict over one set of issues, yet in collaboration over another. It is far less stressful to believe that an enemy on one issue is an enemy on others, and that a friend in one area is going to be a friend in another. As Jervis (1968) has noted, there seems to be a distinct tendency at the international level to perceive that allies have more interests in common with one's own country than is actually the case. This is a comforting belief for one who does not want the stress of dealing with an ally who opposes some of one's actions or to come into conflict with that ally's actual interests.

Finally, one curious complementary process often appears simultaneously within both parties in intense conflict. As the level of tension increases, so does the perception that one's own range of options is closing and that of the opposing party expanding. The phenomenon, which we have called the *freedom-of-action differential*, has been noted in crisis simulations, in historical analyses of conflict interactions, and in casual observation of decisionmakers under high levels of stress. In some versions of the process, the range of alternatives open to the adversary is only relatively greater than 'ours'; in other versions, 'our' range of options contracts while that of the opposing party expands absolutely. Whatever the details, the principle seems to remain constant; adversaries always possess greater freedom of action than 'we' do.

That parties in conflict frequently attribute greater freedom of action, and even free will, to their adversary seems, on closer examination, to be merely part of a much more universal tendency to ignore very real constraints operating on the other party, while remaining conscious of, even exaggerating, those factors that limit one's own freedom. In part, this is caused by the general tendency to overlook the situational factors that constrain the behaviour of others when judging that behaviour. What Ralph White calls the 'Jones/Nisbett Principle' states that, when judging its own behaviour, a party will tend to regard such behaviour as inevitable, even natural, given its own situation. The usual reaction will be: 'Well, what else could you expect us to have done?' However, in judging the behaviour of an adversary, given the normal lack of empathy experienced during conflicts, the latter is likely to be seen as not (or at least less) constrained by his own environment, and responding to it in a manner he also deems inevitable and natural. It is particularly difficult to see the other's behaviour as reaction to something that one's own party has done in the recent past; or that by altering one's own behaviour a marked change of behaviour in the adversary becomes possible. White comments that just as Arabs are unable to perceive that many of Israel's actions are responses to Arab actions ('. . . fear of people like him is the mainspring of everything he hates most in Israel's behaviour . . .'), so are Israelis unable to perceive that the worst Arab excesses of violence are regarded by the Arabs as responses to Israeli 'provocations' (White, 1977, pp. 201–5).

Furthermore, many observers have noted a tendency on the part of parties in conflict to assume too readily that adversaries' actions are always the result of careful consideration and clear-cut decision processes. In other words, there is an increasing tendency in conflicts to *over-rationalise the adversary's position and policy*, and to assume that actions and statements are always intended and planned, rather than *ad hoc* or reactive. In Raymond Bauer's words, 'each party attributes to the other a degree of omniscience and omnipotence that he knows is impossible in his own situation . . .' so that the perceiving party cannot bring himself to believe that his adversary's policymaking is, in fact, '. . . the complex shambles that it often is . . .' (Bauer, 1961, p. 225). The result of this tendency is another facet of the freedom of action differential. 'We' know that our own stances and acts are frequently affected by the accidental and contingent, as well as the stresses and compromises brought about by internal disagreement. However, our need for cognitive clarity is such that it enables us to banish such factors from our image of the adversary, attributing to his decisionmaking processes and behaviour a far greater degree of control, calculation and rationality than might be the case. The point is not that such differentials never exist, but that the psychological tendency is to try to make sense out of a complex set of circumstances by assuming less randomness, accidental happenings and unintended consequences when viewing any adversary. The safest course is to assume rationality in thinking and behaviour.

The interesting general principle that appears to underlie these perceptions is that parties in conflict (and elsewhere) abandon the idea of *inter-action* when considering the activities of others, and switch to the alternative approach of *behaviour*. That is, when reviewing their own activity, parties are perfectly capable of recognising that an entity's behaviour is the result of an inter-action between itself and others, particularly salient others in its environment; *behaviour is reaction*. However, this principle is forgotten when viewing the activity of others, particularly adversaries. In such cases behaviour is perceived to arise from a set of relatively unchangeable characteristics of the others (Israelis are aggressive and land hungry, and will continue to use force and violence to obtain more Arab land) rather than from the others inter-action with a complex environment, including our own party. In this version, *behaviour is purposeful action*, determined by basic characteristics and by unconstrained, rational choice.[7]

Once again, conflicts bring about or reinforce a psychological double standard, whereby one's own party's behaviour can be explained as necessity, and one's adversary's by choice. Given such a process, both cause and blame can be shifted firmly onto an adversary, and discomfort avoided by the perception that certain (possibly reprehensible) actions were forced on our side through lack of choice, so that our response was thoroughly reasonable, given the kind of circumstances which we ignore in the case of our adversary's actions. This cluster of inter-dependent and complementary attitudes is once again related to the general principle of minimising unpleasant levels of psychological stress, this time by avoiding blame and responsibility for action in a dangerous and ambiguous situation. The underlying *rationale* is one that relieves responsibility and feelings of guilt, both for unpleasant policies and for damaging outcomes. The implications of the perception is that 'we' react in this (admittedly rather unpleasant) fashion because we have to; there is no alternative for us. On the other hand, the enemy act as they do through choice. They had alternative possible courses of action (unlike our own party), and chose not to take them. Hence, everything is their fault, and they will have to take the ultimate blame. Adoption of this particular perception becomes a neat way of: (i) justifying policy – even inaction – as inevitable; and (ii) shifting the blame for any disasters into the opposing party, who becomes responsible for the outcome of the conflict, and always for forcing 'us' to take particular actions by leaving no choice.

D. SUMMARY

The discussion has highlighted some of the results of the psychological processes activated by being in conflict that were reviewed in chapter 4. The major points arising from this review of images and perceptions accompanying conflict are firstly, their structural similarity; while the actual *content* of many of the images obviously varies from conflict to conflict as details of issues, parties and circumstances alter, nevertheless the *structure* of many of the images remains sufficiently similar to justify our original decision to refer to such phenomena as *conflict attitudes*. This point is reinforced by the frequency with which such images and perceptions occur in conflicts. Common patterns of self- and enemy-images recur time and again, no matter whether we analyse the psychological aspects of international, inter-communal, inter-group or inter-personal conflict. Finally, the review emphasises the degree to which many of the images are closely inter-dependent and form a psychological structure of considerable complexity, highly functional for individuals in conflicts, whether they be leaders or followers, combatants or spectators, decisionmakers or decision-takers. Images of the enemy to a large degree depend on images of self, and vice versa.

From discussing conflict attitudes it is a small step to considering *conflict behaviour*. The two obviously inter-connect in complex ways. Images of the enemy depend to some degree on enemy behaviour, while images of an enemy affect expectations and one's own anticipatory behaviour. The latter, in turn, affects both the enemy's perception and his reaction. The next chapters discuss the nature of behaviour during conflicts, the forms it may take, and various ways in which it may be analysed.

6   Conflict Behaviour

> . . . We all have the feeling that we are living in an unprecedentedly
> violent world. But what is really unprecedented is not the violence,
> but our awareness of it . . .
>
> Brian Magee MP

We have already noted that the basic, everyday implication of the word
'conflict' is that it refers to behaviour involving physical violence. This is
held to distinguish conflict from other forms of human activity whether
it merely involves a fist fight between two individuals, or a full-scale
military campaign with deaths running into hundreds of thousands, and
damage worth billions of pounds. However, it is an inadequate conception. At the very least, it leaves out of consideration all essentially non-
violent activities such as persuasive arguments, sit-ins, industrial strikes
or economic boycotts that are part and parcel of many intense conflicts.
There is admittedly an important behavioural component in any
conflict, although in the stages of *incipient* or *latent conflict* no
observable behaviour occurs to enable an outside observer to identify
parties and issues with ease. The *manifest* stages of any conflict is
identified by the existence of some structural organisation actively
pursuing goals, and hence by behaviour undertaken as part of that
pursuit. Overt behaviour in any situation of conflict does not necessarily, however, need to involve violence, or damage to one's adversary.
It can take a wide variety of forms, some even involving damage or the
threat of damage to the acting party itself, rather than the 'target' party.
By no means all involve coercion. The crucial factor is that the behaviour
should be *aimed* at the adversaries, in the sense of attempting to make
them alter or abandon their goals, or modify their own behaviour in
pursuit of those goals. We have suggested a working definition of the
behavioural component of conflict covering these diverse elements:

> *Conflict behaviour consists of overt actions undertaken by one party
> in any conflict situation, aimed at an opposing party with the
> intention of making that party abandon or modify its goals.*

120

In improving this – admittedly broad – definition of conflict behaviour, a number of troublesome problems arise. Some definition is needed broad and flexible enough to encompass all the varied phenomena already noted as possible forms of conflict behaviour. The major problem is to decide upon criteria to discriminate between conflict behaviour and other kinds of activity.

One simple way of avoiding this problem is to regard all behaviour by parties in a dispute as conflict behaviour, no matter what overt form this takes. Thus, behaviour ranging from the most peaceful attempts to achieve a compromise solution by negotiation and concession, to violent coercion or use of organised physical force is classified as *conflict behaviour*, provided the two parties indulging in such behaviour possessed mutually incompatible goals, and are trying to achieve these goals by influencing the opposing party. Such a definition would mean that all speeches (hostile or conciliatory), threats, warnings, promises, acts conferring benefits, acts imposing costs or causing direct physical damage, would be regarded as conflictful, if the parties utilising such behaviour were in a situation of conflict. In short, the *setting* within which the action occurred would be an outer limit for defining the nature of the behaviour, rather than any intrinsic quality in the behaviour itself.

Paradoxically, in adopting such a basis for definition, acts of conciliation or gestures of friendship would count as conflict behaviour because they occurred within the context of a conflict situation. Similarly, acts of self-destruction, such as an attempted or successful suicide, or a hunger strike would equally count as conflict behaviour and be equated, in some sense, with acts harming members of the opposing party, such as assassination, imprisonment or campaigns of indiscriminate terror. This latter point may not seem quite so paradoxical by recalling the two Price sisters undertaking a hunger strike in 1974 in order to try to force the British Government to transfer them from a prison in England to one in Northern Ireland.

The alternative approach to distinguishing conflict behaviour from other types would be to take the presence or absence of some essential characteristic of behaviour (such as physical violence) as the criterion of whether that behaviour is 'conflict' behaviour or not. However, given the obvious fact that conflicts are themselves characterised by behaviour ranging from violent physical destruction; through verbal persuasion or the withholding of symbols of support, to the promise of material or psychological rewards for desired changes, the search for such unvarying criteria seems a fruitless one. Hence our adherence to the basic principle that *conflict behaviour is behaviour that occurs in conflict situations*, although it is possible to broaden our original definition to include a large number of familiar aspects of human behaviour in conflicts:

> *Any non-legitimised[1] action by a party in a situation of conflict, aimed at an opposing party, with the intention of:*
> (i) *making the opponents modify or abandon their goals;*
> (ii) *countering the actions of the opposing party; or*
> (iii) *punishing the opposing party for its behaviour.*
> *These intentions may be achieved by:*
> (a) *threatening or imposing an unacceptable level of costs;*
> (b) *offering or providing alternative benefits; or*
> (c) *offering or providing concessions by abandoning some of the goals in conflict.*

Although this definition can be faulted in numerous ways, it possesses a number of advantages, not least that it is broad enough to encompass a wide variety of forms of behaviour, from turning the other cheek to hitting back hard (both methods of imposing different kinds of cost); and that it sets some limits on types of activity excluded from the category of *conflict behaviour*.

A. CONFLICT BEHAVIOUR AS TACIT BARGAINING

The definition is also helpful in that it begins to sort out the various forms that conflict behaviour can take, suggesting that alternative strategies can be employed either consecutively or simultaneously by parties in conflict. The first of these (threatening or imposing costs) is usually known as a strategy of *coercion*; the second (offering or providing benefits) as a strategy of *reward*; and the third (seeking compromise by abandoning some goals) as a strategy of concession or *settlement*. The fundamental feature of a coercive strategy is that each party to the conflict attempts to force its opponent to abandon its goals by imposing unacceptable costs on goal-seeking behaviour. Rewarding behaviour, by contrast, involves achieving similar ends by making alternative decisions, behaviours and outcomes more attractive. Finally, settlement strategies involve behaviour aimed at some compromise solution to the dispute; one which may not completely fulfil the goals of either party, but such that both parties achieve some, if not all, their original goals.

Analysis of international conflict has a tendency to concentrate upon the coercive aspects of conflict behaviour, especially on strategies that involve the use of violence to impose unacceptable costs on an opponent. In Clausewitz's terms, '. . . if an opponent is to be made to comply with our will, we must place him in a situation which is more oppressive to him than the sacrifice we demand . . .', and the underlying assumption of such doctrines is that a coercive strategy is usually both cheaper and more effective than any involving positive sanctions. A Brookings Institute study published at the beginning of 1977 reported that the USA had deployed its military forces for a political impact abroad on at least 215 occasions since World War II, while the Soviet Union's record involved at least 115 cases in the same 30 year period. However, it is not automatically the case, even at the international level, that coercive strategies are employed once a situation of latent conflict develops and social 'safety mechanisms' fail to prevent it moving into the stage of overt action. At this manifest stage, once the parties begin to take action to influence each other's objectives and behaviour, they (or their leaders) are continually confronted with a choice among four basic forms of action:

(a) Using, or continuing coercive behaviour, in the hope that the costs inflicted upon the opposing party will cause its leaders to decide to abandon goals and behaviour.
(b) Using positive sanctions in the hope of arriving at some similar outcome.
(c) Attempting to reach some form of bilateral compromise solution through proffered concessions, via negotiation; or
(d) Using third parties to assist in arriving at a similar compromise solution.[2]

The first two of these options are colloquially known as 'altering price tags on options', but the whole process of acting to influence another's decisions and behaviour is usually referred to as *tacit bargaining*, mainly to differentiate it from *negotiation*, a similar process taking place upon a face-to-face basis.

The conception of tacit bargaining emphasises that conflict behaviour is, in one sense, a process of affecting another's behaviour by one's own activity. It operates through its effects on the target's evaluation of the situation, the condition of the opponent and the costs and benefits of the range of choice available. This agrees with our conception of conflict behaviour being essentially *aimed* at the opposing party with the objective of modifying that party's behaviour, and underlines that a process of tacit bargaining can be regarded basically as a two party process in which actions affect attitudes, and attitudes, reactions (see Fig. 6.1).

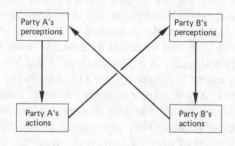

FIGURE 6.1   Basic conflict behaviour

As Roger Fisher has emphasised,[3] the use of any strategy (coercive or rewarding), is intended to influence Government B to take a decision which is favourable to Government A, and skilful conflict behaviour is that which achieves a decision to modify goals or behaviour in a favourable direction with the minimum of cost and of uncertainty. A similar point could be made about conflict inter-actions at any social level. Just as strikes are intended to affect the perceptions of alternative options confronting management and bring about a decision to take action favourable to the strikers, so are the threats of a child to scream if he (or she) is not allowed to stay up and see family visitors, and the counter threats of the mother to send the child supperless to bed. Similarly, offers of aid and assistance are made to persuade the recipient to take some action, or make some statement, desired by the donor. Conflict behaviours designed to coerce or persuade the opposing party to make a desired decision, or to undertake a desired act, can often take curious forms. Thus, the behaviour of the Emperor Henry IV, standing penitently in the snow outside Innocent III's camp at Canossa may be regarded as one form of conflictful behaviour, as can the threat of a desperate lover to shoot himself at the feet of his hitherto indifferent beloved unless she returns some of his affection. Both are behaviours aimed at another party with the objective of making them abandon or modify current goals or behaviour – though in neither example is overt violence being used on or threatened *against* the opponent, the costs being of a more subtle nature.

B. TYPES OF CONFLICT BEHAVIOUR

Confronted with such a bewildering range of behaviours open to parties in conflict situations, can anything be said about classifying conflict behaviour into types, *all* of which having as their objective the modification or abandonment of opponent goals? One rough division of behaviour is into strategies involving coercion, positive sanctions and concessions-through-negotiation. Ignoring this final category, observers of tacit bargaining processes have suggested further interesting distinctions between types of conflict behaviour. One frequently used distinction is between *threats* or promises and *acts*, differentiating behaviour according to whether it takes the form of:

(a) Overt physical activity that results in costs being intentionally and visibly imposed upon the opposing party, or
(b) Verbal or written references to some future state of affairs[4] which will adversely (or beneficially) affect the circumstances of the opponent through the action of the threatener or promiser.

This distinction is a fruitful one. There are fundamental differences between the announcement of an intention to impose costly sanctions under certain circumstances at some future time, and the actual imposition of such sanctions. For one thing, the likely reaction of the party threatened with or actually suffering the costs is likely to be markedly different, both as regards psychological response (degrees of fear, hatred, determination) and behavioural reaction. For another, the employment of threats or promises regarding future behaviour raises problems of convincing the adversary that the threat or promise is a serious one, especially if carrying out either will impose obvious costs on the actor as well as on the target.

Using these distinctions, a promising approach to classifying conflict behaviour begins by considering the kind of inter-action between parties that the behaviour initiates, modifies or disrupts. In such a framework, the question of how parties impose costs on or extend benefits to their rivals is answered by reference to the inter-actions, or lack of them, that result from efforts to make an adversary change goals or behaviour. A basic distinction can initially be made between behaviour which initiates a new form of inter-action, and that which alters an existing one. However, it is possible to alter an existing inter-action in either a positive (beneficial) or negative (costly) manner, and one party can extend or disrupt a given inter-action.[5] Furthermore, the disrupted inter-action can be an existing one that confers either benefits[6] or costs. A final element can be added to this scheme by recalling that behaviour may be performed or threatened. This further dimension completes our overall scheme which may be clearer if set out in a table, with some examples of conflict behaviour from inter-personal, industrial and international conflicts, see Table 6.1.

This framework has the advantage that it is straightforward in principle, yet comprehensive in its ability to include the wide variety of behaviours, familiar or bizarre, encountered in conflict situations. For example, the terrorist campaign waged by the Basque ETA against the Spanish Government (or the campaign of counter terror waged against Basques by the so-called 'Guerrillas of Christ'), could be classified in our third category. The with-holding of student grants by university authorities facing a student rent strike, would fall within category 2. At a different level entirely, threats by British trawlermen at the beginning of 1977 to use their boats to block European fishing ports provide an example of behaviour falling again within category 3, the threat being innovative and cost-imposing. Similarly, the action of fishermen from Filey in Yorkshire in dumping a variety of obsolete consumer durables such as old gas ovens into fishing grounds 'trespassed' on by their Scarborough rivals would be similarly classified, the essential dif-ference being that the former activity remained a threat, while the latter was actually put into effect.[7]

The scheme is also appropriate for conflict behaviour at the inter-national level. The gradual imposition of sanctions against the other Occupying Powers by the USSR over Berlin in 1948 provides an excellent example of conflict behaviour moving from the interruption of beneficial inter-action to its complete severance. Stage one of the Berlin blockade consisted of the Soviet announcement on 1 April that Allied military traffic into Berlin would be subjected to Soviet inspection. At the same time impediments were set up to overland and waterway traffic into the city, and subsequently rail lines between Hamburg and Bavaria and Berlin were closed, all rail freight being routed through Helmstedt. When the Allied Powers responded by

TABLE 6.1 Bilateral conflict behaviour

| Type of behaviour | Individual | Industrial | International |
Verbal: Threaten or promise Physical: Perform			
(1) Slow down or lower an inter-action conferring benefits on an adversary	Stop talking to other person after a quarrel, save for minimum exchange	Work to rule	Delay aid deliveries
(2) Stop completely an inter-action conferring benefits on an adversary	'Send to Coventry'	Strike	Stop aid or trade. Break diplomatic relations
(3) Begin an inter-action imposing costs on an adversary	Make verbal attacks damaging adversary's reputation and self-esteem	Take union leaders to industrial court	Nationalise other's investments. Confiscate financial reserves
(4) Intensify inter-action imposing costs on an adversary	Physically assault adversary	Physical assault by hired strike breakers on pickets	Use armed forces to damage adversary's members or possessions
(5) Slow down or lower an inter-action imposing costs on an adversary	Stop verbal attacks on adversary except as direct response to latters' verbal attacks	End physical occupation of plant by strikers	Abandon or slow down particular military tactic (e.g. a bombing pause)
(6) Stop completely an inter-action imposing costs on an adversary	End verbal harrasment or 'haunting' of adversary	Stop legal proceedings against union leaders	General cease-fire or armistice
(7) Begin an inter-action conferring benefits on adversary	Find explanations or excuses for previously condemned actions of adversary	Limited return to work	Resume trade or aid
(8) Intensify existing inter-action conferring benefits on adversary	Praise activity or character of adversary	Produce and implement new pay and productivity agreement	Increase trade or aid to new levels

going ahead with the planned currency reform which had triggered this Soviet behaviour, the USSR went beyond a mere slowing down of a beneficial inter-action. At the end of June the blockade became a full one. All rail links with West Germany were cut, all supplies of food-stuffs into Berlin forbidden, and road traffic from the west into Berlin completely halted. Two days later all supplies of coal and medicine were stopped as was waterway traffic into Berlin. By 30 June the blockade was complete; all beneficial inter-actions from the west to Berlin had ceased, and it was only with the success of the Berlin airlift that the USSR gradually ended the blockade and reversed the process by permitting the resumption of a beneficial inter-action.

More generally, our framework enables us to categorise and ask questions about the various forms of economic pressure used by parties to international, transnational and domestic conflicts. Apart from straightforward economic warfare accompanying military coercion, writers divide such pressure into three basic forms: specific economic embargoes, general economic sanctions and tariff wars (Wallensteen, 1968). All of these prove, on closer examination, to involve the cessation of previously beneficial inter-actions between the party imposing the embargoes, sanctions or tariff barriers, and some target party or parties previously involved in the benefit-conferring relationship. The severance of trade with Rhodesia following UDI in 1965 is only the best-known recent attempt to coerce a country in this manner. League of Nations sanctions against Italy over the seizure of Ethiopia is probably the most famous historical example of such conflict behaviour. A more comprehensive list of recent sanctions is outlined in Table 6.2. All share the feature that one party to a conflict was trying to bring about conforming behaviour from another by reducing or stopping an inter-action that had been beneficial to both at some previous time.

The conception that the use of such behaviour by parties in conflict involves the end of an *inter*-action suggests lines of thought about the almost total lack of success of such methods, at least at the level of inter-national conflict. For one thing, the lessening of any beneficial inter-action has, by definition, a two-way effect, so that the party imposing the embargo, as well as the target party, loses something. The question always arises as to the relative *balance of loss* sustained by the two parties, whether counter sanctions are imposed or not. Wallensteen suggests that, at least in international conflicts, cost-imposing parties usually make sure that their losses will be minimal compared with that of the target party, and that only parties where a suitable economic or trading imbalance exists will use this particular form of conflict

TABLE 6.2 International sanctions: 1945–70

Dates	Target	Sanctioning parties (main sanctioner)*	Nature of sanctions	Objectives	Later military sanctions	Outcome
1948–55	Yugoslavia	Socialist bloc (USSR)	Complete trade embargo; debts ignored; borders sealed	End Yugoslavia's independent line; bring down Tito's regime	No	Failure and trade normalised in 1955
1951–	Israel	Arab League (Jordan)	Complete boycott of trade and severance of communications	Weaken Israel's economy and Israeli stand on Palestinians	Yes	Failure, except in damaging trade potential
1960–	Cuba	USA	Trade and diplomatic relations severed: Cuban assets in US frozen	End Cuba's expropriation of US assets and alter socialist direction of Cuban regime	Yes (Bay of Pigs)	Failure to change Cuban regime; alternative outlets provided by USSR
1960–2	Dominican Republic	OAS (USA)	Embargo on arms and war material; later petrol and oil products	Change Dominican external policy to one no longer 'threat to peace and security of hemisphere'	No	Success(?): sanctions ended with fall of Trujillo family's regime
1961–	Albania	Socialist bloc (less Poland and Czechoslovakia) (USSR)	Reduction of trade; suspension of aid/credits; end of training facilities, visiting experts	End Albanian adherence to CPR in Sino-Soviet split	No	Failure: Albanian remained in close contact with CPR until 1977
1961–77	South Africa	UN Security Council (UK)	Security Council recommended embargo on all arms and military vehicles (made *mandatory* in 1977)	End S African policy of apartheid	No	Failure; only partially observed by key UN members
1962	Cuba	OAS	Embargo on arms; diplomatic relations severed; suspension from OAS; later, all trade save food, medicine and medical equipment	End Cuban policy of 'subversion'; change Marxist nature of Cuban regime as this incompatible with inter-American system	No	Failure, except in sense of raising costs of Cuban support to USSR

TABLE 6.2—cont.

Dates	Target	Sanctioning parties (main sanctioner)*	Nature of sanctions	Objective	Later military sanctions	Outcome
1963–5	Portugal	UN (General Assembly)	Embargo on arms/Military material for use in Portuguese Overseas Territories	Induce Portuguese regime to accept principle of self-determination for POT	No (support for guerrilla units)	Failure, ignored by Portugal and key UN members
1965–	Rhodesia	UK (UN)	Gradually imposed (by May 1968) complete trade embargo save medical supplies and educational material; sever communications	End UDI and white rule in Rhodesia	No	Failure, support from South Africa and 'sanctions busters'
1963–6	Malaysia	Indonesia	Complete trade embargo and ban on shipping/carrying trade; end of credit arrangements; nationalisation of Malaysian (mainly Chinese) owned enterprises in Indonesia	End incorporation of North Boneo state in a federal Malaysia; end Malaysian links with UK	Yes infiltration of raiders/guerrillas into N Borneo and Malaya itself	Failure to bring down Malaysian Federation: considerable damage to Indonesian economy (inflation, loss of exports) and to Singapore
June–August 1967	UK, France, W Germany	Arab states (Arab oil producers, especially Saudi Arabia)	Ban on oil supplies (rec. for nationalisation of oil installations and ban on imports/exports not approved by Arab states)	Retaliation for west European support for Israel during 'June War'	No	Abandoned after 2 months because of damage to economies of Arab oil exporters
1967–70	'Biafra'	Federal Nigeria	Economic blockade of 'Biafra' (air and sea ports) save initially for oil; ban on foreign currency transactions; cutting of incoming communications	End secession of Eastern Region from Federal Nigeria	Yes full-scale military campaign to end secession	Although circumvented once full-scale war started, successful in weakening Biafran economy/finances and supplementing military pressure

* Country suffering major disuption of inter-action and heaviest costs of imposition.

behaviour. However, his research also suggests a number of reasons why, even in such imbalanced situations, the use of sanctions usually fails. These include the availability of alternative, often clandestine sources of supply for the target party, the offsetting of imposed costs by other benefits, such as an increase in intra-party solidarity and support for leaders (Galtung, 1967) and the fact that the imbalance in vulnerability of the parties involved is frequently counteracted by an opposite imbalance in the salience of the issues to the parties (Wallensteen, 1968). For example, the issue of continuing white rule in Rhodesia was really of peripheral concern to the UK Government and the vast majority of the British people, whereas it was perceived as of burning, almost life and death importance by white Rhodesians.[8] It seems that, when considering the likely success of sanctioning behaviour, account should always be taken of:

(a) The relative size of the costs sustained by both parties.
(b) The salience of both the threatened inter-action and the issues in conflict to the target.
(c) The distribution of the imposed costs or benefits within the target party. (Simply, who suffers or gains most, and how relatively powerful they are within the target.)
(d) The degree of unity within the imposing party regarding the issues in conflict; a party which is polarised over whether to pursue a goal in dispute or allow the other party to achieve its aims (as in the case of the United Kingdom over ending white rule in Rhodesia) is often liable to choose some form of benefit-withdrawing behaviour as a compromise between complete inter-action and cost imposition via physical force.

These factors may indicate possible reasons for the failure of sanctioning behaviour in international conflicts. Some writers suggested that the use of sanctions or embargoes is, in fact, a sign that the parties using them are not particularly committed to success in pursuit of their goals, but use sanctions more as a symbol of a disapproval not sufficiently intense to go further. The issues in conflict are not salient enough to warrant more costly strategies. Where they are, parties rapidly move beyond behaviour that ends beneficial inter-action (sanctions) on to that which is overtly and violently cost-imposing (war) (Wallensteen, 1968). In the former circumstances, it is often open to the target party to determine what level of sanctions can be used against it, for war or other forms of open violence can always be threatened if particularly damaging sanctions are being considered. Such a threat can be potent if, as is frequently the case, the imposing party is not prepared to risk moving to a strategy of direct and violent cost imposition. Mussolini was able to avoid having an oil embargo added to League of Nations sanctions against Italy by credibly conveying to the British and French Governments that he would consider going to war were such an embargo implemented (see Eden, 1963 on this). In short, when issues in conflict are salient, conflict behaviour imposing high costs will be rapidly employed rather than that withdrawing benefits; while a decision to employ some form of benefit-withdrawing sanction usually indicates that the motivation to pursue goals is low, but that some unconventional and public symbol of disapproval for the adversary is required which may prevent the possibility of having to employ physical coercion in the conflict (Hoffman, 1967).

Similar arguments can be made about another form of international conflict behaviour, breaking diplomatic relations. Often, this is an indication that governments are prepared to go no further than a symbolic gesture of disapproval, or are too weak to do anything more. Alternatively, the action may be a move in some intra-national struggle, with a government seeking to divert support from a critical, and often more radical, opposition faction by a show of low cost radicalism abroad; or further signalling the defeat of intra-party rivals by breaking relations with outside governments previously supporting those rivals (Gitelson, 1974, pp. 453–5).

The framework can also encompass forms of civil disobedience and non-violent behaviour often employed by weaker parties in intra-national conflict. Much of this consists of efforts to influence an adversary by benefit-withdrawing or cost-imposing behaviour, involving disruption of existing or potential inter-actions. A rent strike or boycott, for example, involves the disruption of an inter-action that confers benefits on an adversary, as do such other familiar forms of civil disobedience as mass resignations or refusals to participate in common activities (the sports ban on South Africa, for example). Stay-at-home strikes, protest emigrations, refusals to pay taxes or debts, general withdrawals of labour, boycotts of elections or legislative bodies, withdrawals or expulsions from international organisations, or actual physical interventions, such as sit-ins and non-violent occupations,[9] are all examples of disruptive behaviour. A familiar version of the last tactic has been traditional in agrarian societies, where peasants employ the strategy of non-violent land invasion against landlords or local political authorities in order to put pressure on their adversaries and draw attention to their goals. Huizer (1972) has pointed out that such occupancy normally starts peacefully, and only becomes violent through the employment of violence by those 'occupied' or their allies. Given that occupied lands are usually uncultivated, the initial non-violence of the land invasion seems likely, but the action is undoubtedly cost-imposing on the adversary in the sense that it changes the condition of the disputed land from satisfactory (unoccupied and clearly in the landlord's ownership) to unsatisfactory (occupied by peasants who customarily begin immediate subsistence cultivation and call title into question through squatting). Land invasion as cost imposition could therefore be contrasted with the original boycott in Ireland and similar behaviours as a form of benefit-withdrawing.

Many strategies of civil disobedience do, however, introduce a further complication into efforts to categorise forms of conflict behaviour, for it is clear that they involve coercion of, or reward to another party by some *indirect* effect. In other words, a third party (or many such parties) may become involved in conflict behaviour, changing the relationships from a direct, two party inter-action to a matter of indirect influence, involving the third party as recipient or transmitter of costs or benefits. Many non-violent activities connected with civil disobedience involve behaviour that affects non-involved parties who will, it is often hoped, put pressure on the adversary because of these effects. Almost all civil disobedience campaigns involve forms of disruption of existing inter-actions between adversaries and outsiders, as when demonstrations or 'interjections' result in large masses of people occupying a space or facility, denying its use to others.[10] It is therefore necessary to devote some consideration to the situation of third parties in different types of conflict behaviour.

C. CONFLICT BEHAVIOUR AND THIRD PARTIES

Third parties become involved in conflict inter-actions in various ways. Their roles often take the form of some intermediary behaviour to bring the parties together to work out some compromise solution. On the other hand, third (or *n*th) parties may become *victims* of the conflict, in the sense that costs are imposed upon them, either unintentionally or by design. A third alternative may involve third parties

indirectly in one party's attempts to alter the behaviour or goals o:
another, so that they become secondary actors in the conflict itself.

1. INDIRECT CONFLICT BEHAVIOUR

Many types of conflict behaviour can be used to influence the goals and
behaviour of an adversary *indirectly* − that is, by influencing the per
ceptions, attitudes or behaviour of relevant third parties (often those in
a good position to bring direct pressure to bear on the adversary)
Hence, conflict behaviour can be aimed *directly* or *indirectly* at an
opponent. This dichotomy provides another useful distinction for ou:
classification of conflict behaviour, which thus can either be:

(a) Aimed directly at the opposing party, its members, interests o:
resources or
(b) Intended to affect some third party in such a way that it acts, in
turn, upon the opposing party, the ultimate target.

At the inter-personal level, the latter behaviour might involve some
body trying to persuade a father to use his influence over a small son to
make the latter return a disputed object. At the international leve:
examples of this indirect type of conflict behaviour are not infrequent
Israeli raids on Lebanese territory (especially the raid on Beirut airpor
in January 1970) were made with the objective of coercing th(
Lebanese Government into curtailing the activities of the Palestinia:
guerrillas operating from Lebanese bases. In such circumstances, th(
objective of the Israeli strategy was to prevent further guerrilla attack
on Israel, but the method was the indirect one of imposing costs upo:
the Lebanese Government as third party, in the hope that the guerrill:
behaviour would be changed by the Lebanese Government itself t(
avoid these costs. For a short time, Israeli strategy appears to hav(
succeeded, and offered a good example of indirect conflict behaviour
involving successful coercion. This impression did not last.

Not all indirect conflict behaviour involves physical violence an(
damage to third parties, even at the international level. Much wil
involve costs and coercion, however, as the interests of third parties ar(
sometimes damaged in an effort to make them use their own influenc(
on the target party.[11] Boycotts can be accompanied by blockades tha
successfully reduce a beneficial level of action between an adversar:
and any number of third parties. Picket lines can seriously disrup
inter-action between the firm directly subject to strike action and othe

unions or firms not directly involved in the conflict. At the international level, an example of this type of conflict behaviour can be found in the Arab League's attempted economic blockade of Israel in which all firms in third countries trading or having economic connections with Israel have been ordered to sever their links, or be blacklisted by Arab League members who then boycott the blacklisted firms. (Firms affected by the blockade have included Ford, ICI, Air France, Renault, RCA and Coca-Cola.) In 1967 it was reported that 67 Canadian firms were on the Arab League blacklist (Doxey, 1971, p. 29). A better known example of applying indirect pressure to Israel by the Arab states was the oil boycott of the USA, Britain and West Germany following the 1967 Middle East War in retaliation for their 'support' of Israel and as a warning regarding future policy. Leaving aside the punitive and expressive elements in this action, and the fact that it was a lamentable failure that imposed greater losses on Arab states than on the three industrialised targets, the boycott illustrates the nature − and the pitfalls − of coercive indirect conflict behaviour as a means of bringing influence to bear on an adversary. A similar move in the more favourable economic circumstances of 1973 was more successful, at least as regards undermining support for Israel.

2. THIRD PARTIES AND NON-COERCIVE ACTION

Indirect conflict behaviour need not always involve some form of coercion, or cost-imposition on third parties. In many conflicts, parties adopt a strategy of 'making a case' to an audience of third parties, justifying their own position, goals and actions and calling into question those of their opponents. Initially, the strategy may be intended to win support and approval from neutrals, or even from those whose sympathies lie with the adversary in the dispute, by convincing the audience of the justice of one's own case and behaviour.[12] Success may indirectly influence the opposing party by weakening its own sources of support (and its sense of certainty), and winning over third parties who might then be expected to try to persuade the opposing party to accede to the demands of the first. Removal of approval and visible support may have a marked effect upon a target, but the technique may be even more effective if third parties can be moved towards employing negative or positive sanctions themselves to coerce or persuade the opponent into abandoning key goals. In this case, third parties are again influenced into themselves decreasing the benefits or increasing the costs to the adversary of continuing to pursue the disputed goals.

In some conflicts, parties using such a *persuasive* approach may have their task simplified for them by the fact that relevant third parties, while not directly involved in the conflict, may share or approve of the acting party's goals and thus be more willing to forgo otherwise beneficial inter-actions in order to ensure the achievement of the approved goals. In the case of the white Rhodesian declaration of UDI, for example, the original strategy of the British Government was to interrupt a beneficial inter-action between the UK and Rhodesia. Only at a later stage in the conflict over UDI did the British request other UN members to help implement mandatory sanctions on a world-wide basis against the white regime in Rhodesia. The gradual escalation of British action against Ian Smith's regime involved an initial slowing down of beneficial inter-action, a second stage total stoppage, and a third stage extension to influence third parties (other UN members) to bear costs themselves by severing beneficial connections with Rhodesia (Strack, 1978). In other conflicts, governments may be persuaded to approve exclusions from international organisations, forgo investment opportunities, suspend or slow down aid shipments (which are frequently highly beneficial to the donor's economy), or break diplomatic relations as a symbol of disapproval.

Naturally, in the case of indirect conflict behaviour either involving *persuasion* or *coercion*, the calculation of the actual loss of benefits to third parties becomes crucial in determining whether an indirect strategy can be mounted successfully, let alone succeed in its objective. The Israelis were able, for a time, to impose high costs on the Lebanon, just as they were in their efforts to make Egypt and Jordan control their Palestinian refugees on the West Bank and in the Gaza Strip prior to the 1956 war. Indirect strategies using less damaging means are more problematical. South Africa's refusal to end a beneficial inter-action with Rhodesia – and willingness to increase inter-action by replacing others as market and source of supply – together with other third parties' less blatant refusal to end beneficial exchanges, rendered sanctions against Rhodesia ineffective for over a decade, and ensured that white Rhodesian rule would be ended largely because of the direct violence of black Zimbabweans. Similar remarks could be made about the attempt to end Italy's conquest of Ethiopia in the 1930s.

However, while the actual success of indirect conflict behaviour may remain problematical, the concept nonetheless is a useful one in understanding why parties in conflict behave as they do. Acknowledging its importance necessitates adding a number of categories to our previous classification of bilateral direct conflict behaviour, see Table 6.3.

TABLE 6.3 Trilateral or n-person conflict behaviour

Type of behaviour Verbal: Threaten or promise Physical: Perform	Individual	Industrial	International
(1) Persuade or coerce a third party into slowing or stopping a beneficial inter-action with the target party	Persuade daughter to stop seeing an 'unsuitable' boyfriend	Picket power stations and other coal users during miners strike	Persuade other governments to implement economic boycott on key goods
(2) Persuade or coerce a third party into beginning or intensifying a cost-imposing inter-action with the target party	Ask parent to punish child for non-attendance at school	Induce other unions to strike 'in sympathy'	Persuade others to make embargo total and freeze assets
(3) Persuade or coerce a third party into slowing or stopping a cost-imposing inter-action with the target party	Persuade third person to stop slandering target	Persuade other unions to end 'sympathy' strike	Persuade others to end or relax embargo
(4) Persuade or coerce a third party into beginning or intensifying a beneficial inter-action with the target party	Ask friend to make a loan to target	Persuade other unions to join in productivity deal	Persuade other governments to provide aid or arms for defence to target

3. THIRD PARTIES AND MULTI-LEVEL CONFLICTS

Furthermore, it is obviously the case that introducing indirect conflict behaviour complicates our overly simple model of dyadic conflict inter-action. Situations where indirect forms of conflict behaviour are employed are at least triadic in structure, and involve a three-way inter-action, as when the Icelandic Government, during the conflict with the UK over the extension of Icelandic territorial waters to 12 miles, put indirect pressure on the UK Government by threatening to close down the main US base in Iceland, unless the US Government used its influence on the British to persuade them to accept Icelandic claims. The inter-action may be represented in the more complex pattern of Fig. 6.2. A similar pattern may obviously be involved whenever one country

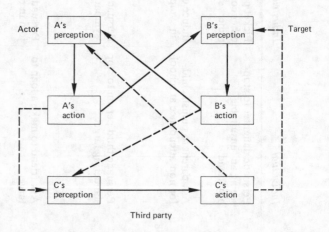

FIGURE 6.2   Indirect conflict behaviour

prevents the exchange of trade between two others by imposing a blockade or economic sanctions. In this case, the costs of the first's actions are shared by both the latter two. However, it is less obvious that similar triadic or *n*-party situations may exist in circumstances that initially appear to be strictly bilateral, until it is recognised that parties may themselves be split into (often rival) factions and agencies, and that conflicts can be *multi-level*. Take, for example, conflict behaviour that ends some beneficial inter-action through the boycott of another country's goods. Considered at the inter-governmental level, this appears to be a simple two party inter-action. However, if one alters the level of analysis, and avoids viewing the situation as being one involving entities labelled 'Iceland' and the 'UK', or 'Rhodesia' and 'Zambia', then it may well become a pattern of multi-party inter-action. If Country A (Rhodesia) stops all trade with Country B (Zambia) in order to influence the behaviour of Government B (to make the Zambian Government withdraw support from the African guerrilla organisations based in Zambia), then it may be interfering with exchanges between a trading group within its own country, and Zambia. In other words, it may be imposing costs on a potentially powerful sub-faction within its own party (Rhodesian Railways, or particular industrial organisations). Hence, the costs of A's action will be borne not merely by the Government of B (which may or may not take the desired decision to alter its behaviour in the direction favoured by A), but also by a faction within Country A itself. Furthermore, this faction may: (i) disagree with its government's policy of stopping the beneficial inter-action (especially if losses are substantial), and (ii) try to influence its own government to restore the status quo (a policy also, presumably, desired by Government B). In this respect, Government A and its inter-party faction possess mutually incompatible goals, and are in a situation of conflict. A similar analysis could be made with respect to the target, Government B. One might find that A's action had created a dispute involving at least four parties, with an economic faction in B suffering heavy costs, and trying to influence its own government to restore the previously satisfactory inter-action with the faction in Country A. The situation would then have to be considered as a four-party inter-action, rather than one involving merely the two governments.

Even this brief discussion emphasises once again the differences between simplifying analytical frameworks and the complexities of the world they are intended to illuminate. While an observer may be able to distinguish various individual strategies or isolate patterns of conflict behaviour, a similar luxury is seldom available to groups and individuals actually engaged in the complexity of a dispute, where a variety of issues and parties are involved, and numerous patterns of conflict behaviour occur simultaneously and confusingly, setting up complicated patterns of acts, events and processes. However, to understand such a pattern necessitates some effort to separate and classify, and in such an effort the taxonomy of types of conflict behaviour outlined above may serve as a useful point of departure when relationships between party strategies and conflict termination, or party structures and patterns of conflict behaviour tentatively begin to be expressed as formal hypotheses and theories.

D. SUMMARY

This chapter has concentrated mainly upon the conception of conflict behaviour being directed, instrumental behaviour undertaken by parties in conflict, although it was acknowledged that symbolic and expressive elements could also form part of behaviour in conflicts. An attempt was made to provide a classification of the wide range of behaviour that could occur during conflicts at various social levels. The result was mainly intended to help in analysing the nature of that behaviour but also in considering likely effects, successes and drawbacks. In addition, the indirect nature of some kinds of conflict behaviour was underlined, as were the different ways that third parties could become directly involved in a conflict.

However, even though the scheme is comprehensive, it remains inadequate for many purposes. For one thing, it fails to make any distinction between conflict behaviour which is intended to compel an adversary to do something (*compellent* behaviour) and that which is intended to prevent him doing something (*deterrent* behaviour). As Schelling argues, this distinction is often a crucial one. The problems of compelling an adversary to act in a desired manner are far more complicated than those involved in deterring an adversary, so that he refrains from an undesired action. This distinction is particularly important with the use of conflict behaviour to alter the goals and behaviour of large and complex parties (Schelling, 1966).

Similarly, the scheme does not encompass a whole series of behaviours employed in conflict situations involving no obvious attempt to offer benefits or impose costs on an adversary. Conflict behaviour by human groups and individuals is a far more complex matter than the mere production and use of 'carrots and sticks'. Our scheme fails to take any account of:

(a) Those types of conflict behaviour that involve efforts to influence not the behaviour of an adversary, but the values underlying that behaviour. In other words, the whole dimension of *conversion* implied in philosophies of non-violence from Gandhian *satyagraha* to Quaker 'friendly persuasion' is neglected, and with it a complete arsenal of behaviours which are often employed in any situation of conflict to obtain one's goals. These include such behaviours as public debate or persuasive speeches, actions within the framework of a system of law, written statements of intent, advertisements, vigils, peaceful and legal demonstrations and a further range of demonstrative and symbolic acts called 'mass-based, secular prayer . . .' by Oglesby and Shaull (1967, p. 145). While it is undoubtedly the case, in spite of much that has been written to the contrary, that some aspects of such techniques, particularly *satyagraha*, are coercive (Klitgaard, 1971), the basic objective of this form of non-violent conflict behaviour is either to alter the views and underlying values of an adversary, or to bring the existence of a possibly suppressed conflict to the attention of some public in such a way as to mobilise sympathy, as well as recruit adherents to one's party and maximise *ésprit de corps*.

(b) Those related behaviours that seek to persuade the adversaries that the fault for particular circumstances arising lie largely with them, so that the cause of the conflict is attributed to them and the solution becomes mainly (or solely) a matter of adjusting their behaviour or objectives. Persuasive behaviours that result in a limited *conversion* of an adversary (or at least to the point where that party is willing to admit blame for the conflict situation arising) are less rare than might be supposed, even at the level of international conflict, but they occur mainly in social systems where opportunities for contact, open communication and a sympathetic consideration of other's point of view are possible. 'Managing' attributional conflict as it is called (Horai, 1977, pp. 91–5) depends on there being opportunities for relatively friendly persuasion and conversion. It also depends on the recognition that, in complex phenomena such as human conflict, mono-causality (and hence easy attribution of blame to one party) is unusual, in spite of all the psychological predispositions towards such analysis by participants.

(c) Those symbolic behaviours during a conflict that can only be included in the scheme if the conception of 'imposition of costs' is taken to include psychological costs of shame or regret, sense of loss, or activation of conscience and guilt, such as might occur when a respected individual or group resigns, renounces honours, or commits some form of self-injury. Such symbolic behaviours are only genuinely effective when some relationship of respect and mutual regard exists between at least some adversaries, so that the psychological cost in terms of increased self-doubt, sense of disquiet, loss of reputation or a tarnished self-image become active; or where the effects are made manifest through the reactions of some third parties affected by the symbolic act. Nonetheless, such strategies have been part and parcel of many conflicts, and so form part of the total arsenal of conflict behaviour open to adversaries.

In addition, one neglected major aspect of this subject is the comment made early in our discussion, that the basic purpose of conflict behaviour was to change the perceptions, behaviour and goals of another party, or, at least, of the key leadership groups and factions in the party ultimately the target of the conflict behaviour. Regarding conflict behaviour in this light raises questions about the manner in which behaviour or goals can be modified, the best ways of achieving this objective with particular types of target, and how coercive or persuasive messages can best be passed to an adversary in order to have maximum impact. If conflict behaviour is a form of tacit bargaining and designed to '. . . influence Party B to take some decision that is favourable to Party A . . .', then it has to be considered as a process of communication, with all the latter's attendant problems and opportunities for error. It is to this approach to conflict behaviour that we now turn.

7 Conflict Behaviour as Communication

> . . . You can't make people do things with military force. You can only threaten to hurt them, to destroy what they value, and hope that, to avoid the pain and damage, they will do what you ask. But you can't make them. If they are obstinate, or heroic, or dumb, or if they are politically or administratively inflexible, or if, rightly or wrongly, they believe you don't mean it, your threat won't work . . .
>
> Thomas C. Schelling (1968)

The major theme of this chapter will be how conflict behaviour can be used to influence the decisions of leaders of rival parties. Even the most violently destructive strategy will succeed in its objective only if it: (i) totally destroys the opposing party, or (ii) so affects the other party through its leaders that they comply with the wishes of the influencing party by taking a decision to abandon or modify goals. For this reason, our discussion treats even violent coercive strategies as a form of communication, the success of which depends partly upon the clarity with which alternative options are transmitted by one party, and received or interpreted by the other.

A. COERCION AND REWARD

If two parties, for example national governments, find themselves in conflict, what forms of behaviour are open to them to achieve their disputed goals? Two potential strategies are:

(1) Behaviour to achieve some compromise solution through negotiation. This has the advantage that neither party will incur the costs of using coercive or collaborative strategies, but the disadvantage that a compromise solution by definition involves sacrifice of some of the disputed goals. In many cases, national

governments are initially unwilling to settle for less than 'a whole loaf' and as many conflicts are (at least initially) defined as constant sum situations, one or both parties may refuse to negotiate. Given this refusal to negotiate, a second possibility is:

(2) The long-term alteration of the values or *conversion* of the other party, so that the opponents (or at least key leaders) come to recognise the underlying 'justice' of the objectives sought. This strategy is common in domestic politics (note, for example, the gradual acceptance of the idea of the 'welfare state' in western European countries). At the intra-national level an underlying structure of common values often holds together a political community, no matter what divisions and disputes affect different sub-factions, so that a gradual socialisation process may lead to a change in values over a (relatively) short time period.

However, divisions within international society, the absence of any substantial underlying feeling of in-group solidarity and loyalty, and the lack of common socialisation processes, make such a possibility remote at that level. One has only to recall the failure of propaganda campaigns in time of war to recognise that processes of group identification make this particular strategy of little practical use, although it has been argued by some writers that use of western values of 'democracy' and 'self-determination' did, at least, accelerate the process of decolonisation when skilfully used by nationalist leaders in colonial countries.

Given that long-term alteration of values is an ineffective strategy at the international level, and that negotiations often seem more effective after a period of intensive conflict inter-action than before, alternatives open to the parties in conflict are reduced to coercive or rewarding strategies, or some mixture of both. In practical terms, this involves attempting to alter the decisions, and behaviour of the opposing party by:

(a) Issuing *warnings* about probably costly outcomes of non-compliance, either because of third party reaction or 'natural processes'.

(b) Making *threats* of negative sanctions which will impose costs on the opposing party through one's own actions, undertaken deliberately to cause harm.

(c) Offering the *inducement* of positive sanctions, by promising some form of behaviour conferring benefits upon the opponent in exchange for their abandoning the goals in dispute.

(d) Putting into *effect* threats of behaviour that impose high costs upon the opponent as a penalty for non-compliance, or actually supplying the benefits predicated on the opponent's compliance.

1. REWARD AS CONFLICT BEHAVIOUR

In spite of the weight of scholarly interest in coercive strategies, their subtleties, implications and potential success at the international level, it may be that this level is no different from others and that collaborative strategies are used more frequently (statistically speaking) than coercive strategies.[1] David Baldwin has suggested that the very failure and frequent implementation of threats at the international level makes them more noticeable. In domestic society, the high rate of compliance with implicit threats makes them less obvious, and further reinforces the perceived prominence of positive sanctions.[2] However, it must also be admitted that it is far less easy to legitimise positive sanctions in international conflicts than in domestic ones, and that international moral imperatives make it more acceptable to threaten an adversary than to buy him off. One should (very properly) deter a nuclear attack rather than bribe a potential attacker, so that there may be good reasons for an actual imbalance. It may also be that the general tendency to confuse the concept of 'influence' with the threat or use of violence is misleading, both in a definitional and statistical sense. All influence need not be based primarily upon negative sanctions, nor on deprivation and damage. If positive, rewarding strategies are being pursued by one's opponents in any conflict, then being the recipient of an influence attempt may be quite pleasant. Positive sanctions influence behaviour by providing a pleasant experience which encourages conformity with the rewarder's goals. They avoid many of the drawbacks of negative sanctions, such as the engendering of stress or a reduction of problem solving capacity in the target (Milburn, 1961) and convey a sense of sympathy and concern rather than indifference and hostility. Furthermore, they tend to affect future behaviour in a positive fashion by colouring the target's perception of the actor (Deutsch, 1958).

Not unnaturally, the use of rewarding strategies is often difficult, practically and politically. At the receiving end, national leaders and their followers tend to distrust Greeks, or anyone else, bearing gifts. Furthermore, acceptance of positive benefits in return for abandoning a party's previously clear, articulated goals often appears to be only marginally better and usually worse than abandoning a goal under the threat of coercion. Most national governments have, at one time or another, refused to abandon a national goal in return for some 'sordid bribe' – often of an economic nature. (Although this has often meant that the 'bribe' was not large enough, or in the wrong medium of exchange, or made in too crude or public a manner.) Part of the problem seems to be that the costs of being seen to be 'bought off' usually outweigh the benefits offered, unless some formula for making the offer acceptable to the vast majority of the opposing party – and not merely its leadership – is found. The only acceptable collaborative strategy might prove to be one in which the positive benefits offered by Party A to Party B represent a genuine sacrifice (with high costs) to A; and that this major 'sacrifice element' is recognised generally within B, by leaders and followers.

From the viewpoint of the party using positive inducements, there is often a strong and widespread feeling that the opposing party ought not to be offered benefits for its 'outrageous' ambitions or 'wicked' behaviour. The tendency, in such situations, is to feel that one's own conflict behaviour should contain a variety of elements:

(a) *Instrumental*, designed to make adversaries abandon their own goals, and lose the conflict.

(b) *Punitive*, designed to impose high costs on opponents as a punishment for holding unrighteous goals or daring to behave in an aggressive manner, and to provide psychological satisfaction that the wicked have received their just deserts. In other words, there is a common psychological tendency in conflicts to perceive any opposing party's goals and behaviour as necessarily immoral and perversely wicked, and to argue that it is both morally and tactically wrong to reward such people for behaving wickedly.

(c) *Demonstrative*, designed to avoid the impression that 'our' only answer to conflict situations is to reward opponents. The assumption is that if parties pursue a strategy of rewarding its current opponent, future opponents will assume that they will receive similar treatment. One does not wish to gain a reputation for 'softness', or giving in to blackmail. There is an almost universal norm, particularly in international society, that toughness and negative sanctions are honourable, while buying one's way out of a fight demonstrates weakness. 'Appeasement' is hardly a term of diplomatic abuse by chance. Such considerations can be seen at work in the arguments within the USA against the provision of 'aid' to North Vietnam after the cease-fire agreement in 1973.

The use of collaborative, rewarding strategies will also depend upon: (a) the nature of the issues involved, and their salience to the parties and (b) the type of relationship existing between the involved parties prior to the development of the conflict situation. Strategies open to traditional allies, or parties in normally collaborative relationships, do not exist in confrontations between traditional adversaries, or even recent enemies. A party's reaction towards positive strategies is strongly affected by *who* is utilising such techniques. Even the most tempting inducement from an opponent is likely to be rejected in conflicts which have continued for considerable periods of time, and in which hostility has reached a high level, attitudes hardened, perceptions become rigid, communication broken down and the enemy become merely a group deserving coercion, punishment and defeat. On occasions, a third party can take it upon itself to offer rewards on behalf of one of the parties in conflict to try to bring about a solution to the dispute. In 1976, for example, the US Government considered a scheme to offer large-scale financial recompense to Rhodesia's white minority in order to persuade them to leave Rhodesia or to remain under black majority rule. Parts of the proposal eventually became incorporated in the US/British peace plan unveiled a year later by the British Foreign Secretary. Again, US promises of large quantities of military and economic aid to both Israel and Egypt cannot have been entirely unconnected with the eventual conclusion of the bilateral peace treaty between the two countries in March 1979.

In normal conflict situations it should not, however, be surprising if the use of bilateral collaborative strategies is difficult and subtle. Promising some future benefit is, if anything, an even more delicate strategy than threatening some future cost, especially between parties whose relationships are traditionally conflictful and hostile, or where levels of trust are low. Using positive sanctions raises the question of credibility in an acute form; how do leaders convince themselves – and their followers – that an offer of future benefits from an adversary is genuine and will probably be fulfilled when that adversary has recently employed all manner of damaging coercive strategies against them? Material rewards offered by one party as a means of settling an intense conflict will often be rejected as a bribe (as was President Johnson's offer to the North Vietnamese in 1965). Hence, offering such rewards often becomes merely a tactic to demonstrate the intransigence of the adversary, the offer being made in the certain knowledge that it will be refused.

Rewarding strategies involving positive sanctions thus seem much more likely to work successfully either: (a) in the early stages of a dispute or (b) where there is a recent history of friendship, or at least co-operation, between parties. As a general principle, however, it is much less effective to influence via threats or other coercive strategies, or from a position of a perceived enemy or rival. We listen more kindly to our friends, and in such relationships influence over the goals, decisions and actions of others can be more easily obtained by positive sanctions than by threats or abuse. However, using strategies of reward in international conflicts, although a common feature of such disputes, tends to have been analytically neglected in favour of the study of coercive strategies, particularly manipulation of the threat or use of force as a form of conflict behaviour.

2. COERCIVE CONFLICT BEHAVIOUR

Underlying much analysis of coercive conflict behaviour is the assumption that both the threat and use of physical force may best be viewed as an attempt to manipulate another party so that that party's behaviour complies with that desired by the threatener. The key process involves Party A trying to get its adversary, Party B, to do something that B otherwise would not have done. This can occur because of A's manipulation of:

(a) Threats of a changed or costly inter-action in the future.
(b) Promises of some beneficial inter-action in the future.
(c) Actions, which either involve the employment of violence to impose damage, or of positive acts to confer benefits.

Cost-imposing sanctions may be employed with the objective of bringing about:

(1) Cessation of present behaviour or refraining from future un-desired actions – (*deterrence*).
(2) Commencement of some desired action, probably costly to the compelled but beneficial to the compeller – (*compellence*).

The successful use of violence, threat of violence or threat of sanctions to deter or compel are examples of manipulating threats to influence some person to make a decision desired by another party. Coercive strategies often involve either the destruction of life or property, or the infliction of some form of pain or order: (i) to stop some persons acting in a way which poses a threat to one's own goals or (ii) to force them to act in some new way (a more positive and difficult process). Schelling has pointed out that the power to cause grief is a form of bargaining power, and that its use is often a strategy to emphasise (sometimes to third parties) a willingness to cause damage and pain, an ability to do so, or the consequences of provoking the user.[3] The process of using coercive strategies as *compellence* is to manipulate successfully the threat of pain or damage. The strategy is difficult but often used in international conflicts. '. . . Military potential is used to influence other countries, their governments or their people by the harm it *could* do them . . .' (Schelling, 1966). Those on the receiving end of a coercive strategy have options of: (i) defence, to minimise the costs and pain; (ii) counter-violence to force the adversary to cease his own coercion (causing more pain to him than he does to you); or (iii) compliance, to bring an end to the opponent's coercive behaviour.

However, force and its threat suffer from serious limitations. Even leaving aside problems arising from the process of *deterrent behaviour* (the fact that one can never be sure of a successful effort at deterrence, only of an unsuccessful one) and concentrating upon *compellent behaviour*, limitations remain serious. For one thing, the manipulation of force, violence and damage as a coercive strategy is fundamentally negative. It can only be used as a successful compellent strategy if people are sufficiently afraid of what it will do.

3. COERCION AND BARGAINING: ESSENTIAL ELEMENTS

In its simplest form, coercive behaviour is an attempt to manipulate the behaviour of a target party by operating upon that party's evaluation of the future consequences of its own actions. The compellent party attempts to influence the adversary to abandon its own goals (or, at least stop its undesired behaviour) by acting upon: (i) the latter's definition of the situation and (ii) its decisionmaking process — (mainly by altering the relative attractiveness of the various options it sees as open to it). The following discussion will refer to the use of coercive strategies involving deterrent or compellent behaviour which is designed to *reduce* the attractiveness of various options, but a similar analysis could be made of strategies to influence Party B's behaviour through increasing the attractiveness of options.

In either coercive or collaborative case, conflict behaviour can be regarded as a form of physical or verbal action intended to manipulate an adversary by altering three basic factors in the latter's view of the situation:

(a) The perceived benefits to be gained from undertaking or continuing a particular course of action.

(b) The perceived costs incurred by so doing, and risking retaliatory behaviour from Party B. (A will always incur costs whatever course of action is decided upon, even if these are only opportunity costs, but the eventual level of costs will only be decided by the interdependent decisions and actions of A and B.)

(c) The perceived risk of attaining low benefits and high costs through pursuing alternative courses of action.

The basic problem of successful conflict behaviour (that which manipulates the prices on B's options so successfully that he ceases contemplating behaviour in pursuit of that goal as no longer worthwhile) is that it involves a process influencing the opposing party's intentions by signalling costs to be imposed or benefits offered. This implies that the attitudes of the party to be influenced become of paramount importance, in that Party A is essentially trying to affect Party B's decision through B's perceptions of the benefits likely to be achieved, or the costs sustained, and the risk that A will do as threatened. Conflict behaviour by A will be selected on the basis of A's perception of B's perception of the options confronting B, and of the benefit-cost-risk calculation attending those options. This central fact makes the *successful* use of either coercive and collaborative strategies a highly uncertain matter. Both A and B may have different perceptions and evaluations of benefits likely to accrue to B through one course of action, often because B's value structure is not the same as A's. Many colonial governments could not believe that local nationalist leaders valued independence more than the economic benefits of remaining part of an existing (and, in some cases, liberalising) empire. Similarly, A may evaluate the costs to B of pursuing a particular course of action as being too high to contemplate 'rationally' (that is, according to A's perception of the situation and A's value system). To B, the cost may not seem high, or at least lower than those imposed by any available alternative. (The Jewish garrison at Masada preferred mass suicide to surrender to the Romans!) Finally, parties' perception of the risk involved − the likelihood that A will, indeed, carry out the threat and impose pain and damage − may be totally different. A may be fully determined to put his threat into effect, so that A's perception of the subjective probability is very high. B, on the other hand, may believe A neither capable nor willing to carry out the threat, in which case B's subjective probability will be low. In such a situation B may act, or refuse to act, and A's behaviour will have failed in its original objective. The problem is A's failure to convince B that A will indeed carry out the threat of imposing costs should B not comply with A's demands. Convincing B, changing B's evaluation of the risk into a certainty, is a crucial element in successful coercive behaviour.

The problem of using either coercive or collaborative strategies is, therefore, a complex one, open to innumerable uncertainties, especially as behaviour to alter both parties' cost-benefit-risk formula depends upon two sets of perceptions and not upon any 'objective' reality. (A's action depends upon A's perceptions of B's evaluation of the cost-benefit-risk formula facing B and vice versa.) Deterrence and compellence or collaboration are complex, psychological relationships involving problems of accurate communication, perception and values, with a particularly important problem arising over the credibility of threats or promises (Milburn, 1961, p. 3). In considering such a psychological relationship, any party contemplating the use of coercive strategies must always take into account the other's subjective evaluations of: (a) what is threatened, and in what circumstances (b) how it is valued, compared with the benefits to be gained from ignoring the threat and proceeding and (c) how credible is the threat (Milburn, 1959, p. 138). The actor's problem is to increase the subjective costs to the target of failure to comply, to decrease the value of the pay-off through non-compliance and to increase the credibility of the threat or offer being made. In all of these tactical moves, A is always handicapped by having to operate on his own, usually imperfect image of B's evaluation of costs, benefits and risks. This estimate is inevitably highly uncertain. For one thing, a party's evaluation of both costs and benefits alters over time, and there is little evidence to link particular predetermining factors with regular changes in evaluation. One familiar process once a party has experienced some form of coercive strategy and hence some cost, is the desire to cause damage to the adversary in revenge for those injuries already suffered. The very act of damaging the opposing party may become valuable in itself, adding to the original instrumental value of trying to attain one's goal. Alternatively, part of the reason why the evaluation of any particular goal changes over time is that the value of any course of action, or outcome, may be altered by:

(a) The amount of resources already expended, or the level of costs sustained, in pursuit of the disputed goal.
(b) The additional value conferred upon the continued pursuit of the disputed goal by the disutility of a publicly admitted failure and
(c) The additional value accruing to the continued pursuit of a disputed goal through the 'demonstration effect', both to the current adversary and to potential future opponents.

One important point to emerge is the paradoxical one that, by using coercive strategies to impose a high level of sacrifices on the opposing party, the coercing party may be increasing the value to the adversary of the goal pursued, thus making that party's abandonment of the goal less, rather than more, likely (Edmead, 1971).

Complexities similar to those discussed above attend efforts to analyse the use of collaborative strategies and positive sanctions that make desired courses of action appear more attractive. A's perception of the value to B of a particular outcome may be incorrect. A may have misjudged B's evaluation of the benefits to be gained by complying with A's wishes. To B, the proffered 'rewards' may not be benefits at all, or may have so little value as to be wholly offset by the costs incurred in complying. However, the most uncertain element in the use of both coercive and positive strategies lies in the perception of the other party's *evaluation of probability*, and in the fundamental problem of how one party makes an offer or threat credible to the target. Paradoxically, successfully convincing another party of the credibility of both capability and intention of implementing threat or promise may often be a matter of the acting party's reducing its freedom of decision, so that no alternative to carrying out the threat or promise exists, should the target not act in the desired manner. (For a discussion of the problem of *commitment*, and conveying successful threats or promises, see Schelling, 1963; Boulding, 1962.) Convincing an adversary is, however, part of a much broader problem of communicating intentions to the target party in such a way as the desired effect on the latter's perceptions of choices confronting him is achieved. Coercion or reward depend upon communication as much as do persuasion and conversion.

B. CONFLICT BEHAVIOUR AS COMMUNICATION

If an essential aspect of conflict behaviour is its use as a form of communication, a fruitful way of regarding behaviour in conflict is as a process of signalling between the parties. For the parties, the problem takes the form of discovering how to signal effectively, so that the opposing party, in fact, abandons the goals or behaviour it was supposed to abandon. Verbal and physical acts become signals between Party A and Party B, or vice versa, intended to influence (i) perceptions of the current situation; (ii) expectations about future outcomes; and, ultimately, (iii) goals and objectives.[5] In other words, A tries to influence B's decisionmaking process through the symbolic effects of statements and actions, and the communication of views and intentions by messages and symbolic gestures, hoping to affect the future behaviour of his target in a desirable manner; and B tries to do the same to A.

1. PROBLEMS OF COMMUNICATION IN CONFLICTS

Conflict behaviour may thus be regarded as a process consisting of a number of separate elements:

(a) Communication of intentions (threats, promises, and warnings of *future* actions by *present* messages or acts).
(b) Communication about capability of implementing these intentions and
(c) Physical actions which are also forms of communication about *future* physical actions, their extent and likelihood of occurrence.

The success of such signalling often depends upon the perceived credibility of both capability and intentions, and much behaviour is undertaken to increase the level of credibility for a party's stated strategies. Often this leads to situations in which one party acts in the present to reinforce credibility for the future. The French Government intervened militarily in the civil war in Chad in 1968, partly at least to demonstrate that France would keep its commitments to the rest of

Francophone Africa, as well as to support the threatened political incumbents in Chad.

Through a 'communications' view of conflict behaviour, a number of new problems arise for a party engaged in a conflict, most concerning the successful manipulation of signs and symbols so that signalling to an adversary is clear, accurate and understandable, and the verbal or physical behaviour employed has the effect intended. Three serious difficulties arise in accurate signalling between parties in conditions of conflict.

(1) Convincing the opposing party that messages and symbolic actions about intentions are not bluffs.

(2) Faulty reading of actual intentions as well as commitment by the target. This is a particularly difficult problem as often the physical difficulties of communicating, and the psychological distortion to which messages and actions are prone, militate against an adversary building up any kind of accurate picture about either intentions or determination.

(3) Using appropriate messages and actions to affect a complex decisionmaking process within the opposing party in a desired, not counter-productive manner. This is often discussed as the problem of assuming 'rationality' on the part of the opponent's decision-making elite, but in reality it involves the influencing party making a serious effort to 'role reverse', and to evaluate its own behaviour (and the possible options open as a result of that behaviour) within the decisionmaking framework of the adversary. This is not an easy operation. It involves understanding the opponents' own definition of the situation, their goals and objectives, values and preference ordering, decisionmaking processes, internal political pressures on the leadership group, and (often) the psychology of key leaders.

Accurate signalling between opposing parties to a conflict poses most problems at the international level, where the magnitude of 'normal' cross-boundary communication is relatively low, compared with that of intra-national communication, and subject to distortion. International diplomacy is still the major form of communication between adversaries, designed to convince an opposing party of something about the actor's wishes, intentions, capability or determination. This view of diplomacy as communication applies both to formal, official, government-to-government diplomacy, and to non-official (although sometimes officially sanctioned) behaviour by organisations or individuals within the country concerned.

That diplomatic and non-diplomatic acts carry a symbolic signal apart from their overt effects is explicit in much of Schelling's work on 'tacit bargaining'. The key point is that any form of action has at least two effects; the effect upon 'concrete reality', as when a decision to supply food as aid to another country increases the supply of food available in that country; and the symbolic message attached to the action, perhaps that the donor has decided to change its policy towards the recipient, and is now attempting to establish friendly relations, extend its area of protection/interference, or warn off its international rivals. It is the symbolic meaning that is often the most difficult to discern, and remains open to the most contradictory interpretations, which may be quite different from the meaning that the initiator of the action was trying to signal. However, no matter what the difficulties in interpreting such signals, symbolic actions are designed to influence others by signalling something, even though the signal is open to misinterpretation because of the different frame of reference of observers,[6] and even though an act not intended to signal anything specific may be seized upon by another party and misinterpreted as some definite signal. Any increase in a military budget may have been decided upon in response to internal pressure by the armed forces, but the signals sent out by such an act may (a) reach and affect other parties that were never intended to be affected and (b) be interpreted in a manner adverse to the interests of the government implementing the original budgetary increase.

2. MULTIPLE AUDIENCES

One major difficulty is that any leadership group is always engaged in a complex process of signalling to multiple audiences, and in today's open communications system it is difficult to ensure that the signals are picked up by, and affect, only the audience(s) they were intended to affect. Most leaders, whether governments, trade union officials or community leaders, find themselves trying to signal in at least two directions at once: (i) *inwards* to their own domestic supporters and (ii) *outwards*, to the party with whom the dispute exists. Often, national leaders make statements aimed at domestic constituents, pressure groups or opposing factions which, when perceived by an external government, are highly detrimental to the successful influence of that government's behaviour — unless, of course, relations between the two are good enough for the receiving government to recognise that the statements are made purely for domestic consumption. Some of the statements about Cuba made early in his Presidency by John F. Kennedy were primarily designed to ward off Republican attacks that he was 'soft on communism'. However, when these (mainly internally directed) communications were picked up by the Cuban Government, they can only have confirmed the Cuban's original, hawkish impression of the Kennedy administration reinforced by the Bay of Pigs invasion.

In conflict situations, considerable effort is often expended in trying to separate, and keep separate, different communications networks, especially those directed inwards at domestic supporters, and those aimed outwards towards an adversary. Hence the continuation of such processes as secret negotiations or communication between adversaries, denied by leaders to their followers if these are ever brought to light before completion; efforts to maintain sagging support among the party's rank-and-file, without indicating to the adversary that such efforts are becoming necessary; or efforts to reassure a potentially dangerous faction that the conflict is being prosecuted with vigour without completely closing the door to a negotiated settlement with an adversary. On occasions, it is possible to 'insulate' some of the signals from targets that would be 'adversely' affected by their receipt, so that the signals have an effect on (for example) the adversary's leaders, but no undesired side-effects on opposition factions or rank-and-file support within either party. In general, and given the growing 'openness' of global communications, successful insulation is difficult, even at the level of national governments, where the inspired leak, particularly to intra-party factions, is a commonplace method for defeating disapproved inter-party initiatives. In many other cases, and at many levels other than the international, this mixing up of communications intended for different audiences is a major factor in ensuring that signals between parties are misinterpreted, misunderstood, disbelieved or otherwise fail to have the intended effects upon the original target — or the intended effects *solely* on the original target. Unintended side-effects from acts and statements in conflict situations appear to be the rule, rather than the exception.

3. INEFFECTIVE SIGNALS

Using conflict behaviour to signal is thus beset with problems inherent in the nature of any communications process. However, this is only one kind of problem. Another involves circumstances where the signal has been – roughly – successful in 'getting through' intact to the opposing party. The threat has been clearly made, the warning understood or the promise received more or less in its intended form. What factors then prevent the signal having the desired effect on the decisionmakers within the opposing party? Often the impact can be adversely affected by some combination of factors, especially when the party acting as the target is a complex organisation, containing factions within the decisionmaking elite, a mass following, and a communication problem between leaders and followers:

(a) *Inertial factors.* These apply particularly in situations of compellence, or whenever one party is trying to make the target party *reverse* some decisions already taken. The problem is that the adversary's decisionmakers will already have discussed the costs and benefits of their proposed course of action, will have come to a decision, and will have psychologically 'closed the book' on that decision. To re-consider will mean to re-open an old discussion, possibly take a decision contrary to the one already taken and, perhaps, admit a previous mistake. Forces acting against this will be strong, and must be overcome by a strong compellent threat or promise. Should a threat fail, a similar, inertial factor operates in the party making it. The decision to make the threat is often taken as a decision to implement it. Again, this is often because of inertial factors in group decisionmaking, and a refusal to re-open old arguments, or to recognise that, with the failure of the threat, a wholly new decision situation has arisen.

(b) *Demonstration effect factors.* This is sometimes called the 'not giving in to blackmail, or threat of force' effect. It stems from the target party's concern with its overall bargaining reputation. Leadership groups usually place a high value on showing clearly that they do not surrender, or even negotiate, under duress, nor do they appease bullies. Partly this is to resist the current opponent, but it is also intended as a demonstration to future adversaries.

(c) *Credibility factors.* Targets often question the rationality of effecting a threat: 'Why should our opponents carry out their threat when they see it has failed? They may do so because of the demonstration factor but there are other factors influencing and reducing the likelihood.'

(d) *Overall cost factors.* Carrying out the threat, or continuing the policy of inflicting pain or destruction is costly to the imposing party, in terms of direct and opportunity costs. A target's decisionmakers may believe that these costs will soon outweigh those imposed on them. Hence, the imposing party may give up first.

(e) *Counter-cost factors.* The argument here is that while the carrying out of the threat will hurt one party, the carrying out of counter-threats will hurt the other party even more, and force them to give up. (Increases in North Vietnamese aid to the South was obviously intended to put up the costs of involvement to the USA.)

(f) *The moral cost factors.* There seems to be a general 'norm' against the use of force or the infliction of pain or destruction merely to demonstrate that one can and will use force. Hence part of the costs of implementing a threat to use force will be in declining prestige and even in internal support within one's own party. As Schelling (1966) says, 'Deliberate pain, whose only justification is to extort a decision, too closely resembles torture.' The moral cost element probably helps to explain the US Government's need for the 'interdiction-of-supplies-and-men' *rationale* to justify the initial bombing of North Vietnam.

(g) *Sunk-costs factors.* Such factors tend to apply after a conflict has continued for some time. The argument is usually that the conflict has cost the target party much but that they have 'invested' their losses in final success. It becomes impossible to surrender now when they have sacrificed so much previously. Furthermore, they would not give up earlier when they had more to lose, so why give up now? Allied to this argument is what may be termed the 'marginal losses' factor. Compared with what the party has lost *overall* during the dispute, the extra, or marginal loss that the opponent inflicts may seem small. Hence the threat of further harm and destruction may seem minor and able to be ignored when compared with any aggregate sacrifice over a long period of time − or it may not.

The final five factors all concern the outcome of some anticipated cost-benefit calculation made within the target party, and of the relative attractiveness of the options perceived as open. Another set of factors, often relatively neglected, may negate even the most successful use of conflict behaviour to communicate clearly the existing or potential configuration of costs and benefits facing leaders of an opposing party. These are all concerned with what may be termed 'stickiness-in-group-decisionmaking'. They came about through the operation of processes which affect group decisionmaking in committees, cabinets, advisory councils, high commands or politburos and which militate against any rapid or 'rational' response to coercive or rewarding conflict behaviour. They include such factors as:

(1) Personal fears of showing weakness, or of being labelled the first wishing to compromise, or fall in with the demands of the adversary.
(2) Group fears of intra-party retribution if compromise, 'surrender' or abandonment of party goals is contemplated.
(3) Group fears of loss of intra-party control, or of being easily replaced by other opposition factions.

Factors contributing to 'stickiness-in-group-decisionmaking' tend to be those which have often been ignored in much of conflict research by the implicit assumption that influencing a group of leaders to take some desired decision is much the same as influencing an individual to take a similar decision. This is the problem of 'changing a party's mind', when 'the' party might consist of a group of leaders, a set of rival subfactions and a large number of rank-and-file followers, as opposed to a single individual.

C. 'CHANGING A PARTY'S MIND'

If the instrumental element in any form of conflict behaviour has, as its primary objective, to alter 'the mind' of its opponent, questions arise about: (i) the manner in which different kinds of party 'change their minds' regarding the issues in conflict and their opponents, and (ii) the constraints (individual, group and organisational) on mind-changing. In much of the tacit bargaining approach to conflict behaviour, decisionmaking is assumed to take place in some centralised and calculated manner, so that the behaviour of parties to any conflict tends to be explained according to what can be called the 'Rational Actor' mode. According to this, the process of decisionmaking can best be understood as an anthropomorphic one, in which some unified entity considers the available options, cogitates, and decides upon an optimum course of action according to consciously specified values. Hence, the underlying assumption that affecting any party, no matter how large or complex, is a matter of changing that party's 'mind' by coercion or collaboration.

Nowhere is the use of this anthropomorphic metaphor more in evidence than at the level of international conflict, where it is probably least appropriate. It is common to speak of 'changing a government's mind' when, in reality, no government has a 'mind' to change, and some other model of the process is more appropriate. Even success in changing the minds of some of the men who make up a government may be a necessary rather than a sufficient condition for that government to take a positive decision to change its behaviour, cut its losses or abandon some of its objectives.

If this is the case − and it seems a more reasonable starting point than any Rational Actor approach − then a major problem for a party using any form of conflict behaviour to influence a leadership group in a target party is that, to 'signal' successfully, there must be some prior understanding of the structure and processes of decisionmaking within the target and of the nature of the intra-party influences to which leaders will be susceptible. It may be, for example, that the effect of a coercive strategy is mainly suffered by groups of people within the rank-and-file of the target who, while highly conscious of the costs imposed on them, are wholly incapable of influencing their own leaders to change their party's goals or ameliorate the effects of the coercion. In the mid-1960s, the imposition of sanctions by the UK Government upon Rhodesia placed a high level of costs upon both Rhodesian tobacco farmers and business interests. However, neither of these groups was able to muster enough influence within Rhodesia to change the Rhodesian Front regime's policy in the direction desired by the UK Government.

This line of thought underlines the need for a more realistic model of decisionmaking by parties in conflict, a model which takes account of some of the organisational and intra-party factors that affect a party's ability to respond to the strategies of another party and − perhaps − to 'change its mind'. No government or leadership group arrives at a decision in the same manner as an individual, in or out of government. 'Collective' decisions depend upon the intra-party politicking and bureaucratic processes within the overall party, upon hierarchies, and lines of communication, upon structure and the existence of rival factions within that structure, and upon group and individual values and ambitions. Hence, something akin to a 'Bureaucratic Politics' model of decisionmaking for parties in conflict − unless those parties *are* individuals − is a realistic starting point. In complex parties, such as nation states, processes within the leadership group:

. . . are characterised by politics and bureaucracy, personal careers and rivalries, leaders and interest groups and formal mechanisms like chains of command, voting procedures, committees within committees, and overlapping committees; and numerous individuals who have their own sources of information, their own lines of ideology, their own measures of boldness and timidity, their individual capacities for boredom, sickness and even death . . . (Schelling, 1968, p. 10)

Using some form of Bureaucratic Politics model as starting point (Allison, 1971) makes the process of a leadership group or government 'changing its mind' in some major fashion far more complex than suggested by any Rational Actor model. The process of bringing about change is inevitably more difficult. In many cases, the only processes through which a leadership group or government can 'change its mind' in some significant manner are either:

(a) For that particular government to be replaced by a new set of individuals, or representatives of factions, with quite different preference orderings, or given that the old set of leaders have 'changed their minds' and are looking for a way of cutting losses.
(b) For the government's environment (including 'public opinion among its followers, and the power and cohesion of rival elite factions) to be significantly altered, so that concessions can be made, or a compromise settlement arrived at without making too heavy a sacrifice in terms of the leaders' domestic position.

The first of these processes is common when major alterations in strategy are demanded from a leadership group. Frequently, 'changes of mind' are preceded by a significant change in the composition of a party's leadership. Individuals with a particular configuration of goals and preferences are replaced by others possessing different goals or different preference orderings. Alternatively, some major shift occurs in bargaining power, authority or influence among rival factions within the party. Or the entire leadership group is replaced by another.[7]
There are indications that this 'change of mind/change of personnel' process is frequently found where one or both parties wish to terminate the conflict, or arrive at some kind of compromise settlement, agreeable to both. On occasions, the desire for a compromise will be mutual. On others, one party may have successfully coerced the target into a position where the latter perceives it must cut its losses, abandon its goals, or surrender. In either case, there is some truth in the rule of thumb that governments who fight wars rarely make peace. When the time comes to stop fighting and begin negotiating, new governments

are formed, especially when negotiations are to be carried out from a position of relative weakness. This process is also common at other social levels.

Essentially, the entire process of restructuring or replacing a leadership group is part of the much larger problem of *terminating conflict behaviour*, to which we turn next. This involves the dual question of:

(1) What combination of factors helps to persuade at least some leaders in one party that the time has come to abandon apparently unsuccessful coercive (or rewarding) strategies designed to make the opposing party give up its own goals and instead make efforts to achieve a compromise settlement by negotiation, and the sacrifice of some goals?

(2) What problems arise within the party when some of the leadership group reach such a decision, and are faced with the problem of persuading others that the time has come to abandon coercion and adopt some form of concession?

The simplistic view of a group, an organisation, a community, or a national government 'changing its mind' in the face of coercive or collaborative strategies in an analogous fashion to an individual, is so simplistic as to be dangerously misleading. At present, little comparative information is available to discredit this all too common analogy, which should be treated as a metaphor, and little more. Schelling knows of no area in which conflict theorists

. . . are more deficient in their theory than in understanding the ways that different governments can respond to the threat or use of force; more important, I know of no place where the policies and actions of governments may be more seriously deficient than in not thinking through the mechanism by which the influence of force is supposed to be translated into action within the target government . . . (Schelling, 1968, p. 12).

Part III: Ending Conflict

. . . To enter into war needeth no counsel, but how to end war with
honour and profit men must needs study . . .

Henry VIII

8   Conflict Termination

... To make defeat palatable may require as much effort as to make war desirable ...

Lewis Coser (1961)

One paramount problem for parties employing coercive or persuasive strategies in a conflict is when to give up — at the international level, the familiar problem of how to 'make peace' or of 'arriving at a decision to compromise through negotiation'. The more general process relevant to conflict at all social levels can be called *conflict termination*, a matter of at least one party in conflict determining to abandon coercive behaviour and adopt some form of settlement strategy, through concessions and conciliation. Rather than continue costly, and possibly ineffective, military operations either because a perceived stalemate exists or because defeat seems more likely than victory, a national government may take the difficult decision to send out peace feelers to the adversary through a neutral government, or prepare to make a direct compromise offer to the opposing party. In both examples, the objective will be the *termination* of both parties' conflict behaviour and the development of a compromise solution involving an abandonment of some goals underlying the original conflict situation.

An important characteristic of conflict termination, as defined here, is that it is basically a bilateral process, the main roles being played out directly by adversaries. This is hardly surprising. There have been many unilateral declarations of war, but none — if one excepts the initial Bolshevik efforts at Brest Litovsk in February 1918 — of peace. It does take one party to make a war, but at least two to make a peace. (Trilateral efforts at peacemaking involving intermediary parties are discussed later.)

A.   TERMINATION: COMMON ELEMENTS

The generality of the problems and processes of termination may be illustrated by the final abandonment, in August 1973, of one of Britain's longest running strikes involving workers at Fine Tubes Ltd in Plymouth. This industrial conflict was ended by the strikers after three fruitless years. It began over a pay and productivity agreement, and developed into a question of union recognition when strikers were dismissed and replaced by a new labour force. The striking workers were unable to obtain support from other plants for the 'blacking' of Fine Tubes' output, and hence their strike turned out to be an ineffective form of conflict behaviour. As a coercive strategy, it was unable to impose a high level of costs upon the management of the firm, while the costs (for example, in lost wages) suffered by the strikers themselves[1] were large.

Once it had become obvious to the strikers that their tactics were no affecting their adversary in any degree, the question became one o conflict termination, or deciding when 'enough is enough'. The decisior to terminate (especially when this involves a tacit acknowledgement o defeat), is a most difficult one to reach, and usually takes a considerabl time. In the case of the Fine Tubes strikers, it took three years ol unsuccessful picketing, being 'let down' by other unions, and dwindlin numbers[2] before the remnant made a decision to cut their losses an terminate the conflict − in this case by abandoning the dispute com pletely, rather than attempting to negotiate further with the opposing party. In international parlance, the conflict had ended with the 'unconditional surrender' of one party.

The example of the Fine Tubes strike underlines both the difficulties of making a decision to terminate a conflict through compromise and that similar problems arise in conflicts at different social levels. To a degree, problems of termination all share common features making the modification of coercive strategies, acceptance of some measure of failure or a need to compromise, and abandonment of at least some of the goals for which conflict behaviour was begun and costs and hard-ships borne, a long drawn out and divisive process.

Conflicts that can be ended at some unambiguous and readily available termination point are rare.[3] Usually, parties to a conflict are faced with the problem of ending their conflict by working towards some settlement by an indeterminate, almost trial-and-error process. The exact nature of this termination process is dependent upon numerous inter-related factors, the most important of which are the parties' evaluation of their position of relative advantage in the on-going conflict and the structure of the parties themselves. However, while the precise nature of the difficulties will vary according to circumstances, fundamental aspects of the termination process remain the same, no matter what kind of conflict is involved, or what stage the conflict has reached. Thus, whether facing a situation of perceived advantage, disadvantage and defeat, the basic question facing parties and their leaders is always when to accept the terms the adversary offers, given that circumstances may change disadvantageously, so that later terms may be worse. The problem concerns the stage in a conflict when it becomes best to abandon some goals as unattainable and conclude a second or third best arrangement. Such an action involves accepting settlement terms offered explicitly or implicitly by an adversary, and concluding a compromise.

No matter what the circumstances, decisions about 'when?' normally involve some cutting of losses in order to salvage other objectives. Sometimes the sacrifice can be small, as when the Allies at the end of the World War II allowed the Japanese Emperor to remain as head of state. At others it can be large, as when the Bolsheviks at Brest Litovsk gave up vast areas of European Russia to safeguard their revolution. But always the problem facing parties to a conflict is when to give up and start compromising, unless rare circumstances exist in which one party is in such an overwhelming position of superiority that it can achieve the disputed goals without any acquiescence from its adversary.[4]

Short of achieving this unambiguously overwhelming position, however, the difficulties of deciding when to offer or accept a compromise are likely to be profound. The major one will be that of estimating accurately the relative position of advantage of the adversaries, and forecasting how these relative positions may change. This problem of estimation is one in which there is the greatest possibility for uncertainty, especially when a party's leaders consider the range of the bargains that might be struck with an adversary. To a large extent, this potential range depends upon the past damage already inflicted by and upon the adversary, and the perception of the future damage which continued conflict will inflict. Leaders who wish to continue the conflict behaviour will argue that 'fighting on' will improve the eventual outcome. Those wishing to terminate the conflict will argue that the costs and risks of prolonging the conflict far outweigh those of compromising now, and that the, admittedly uncertain benefits of a settlement soon also outweigh more uncertain benefits to be obtained at some unspecified future time, when an even greater position of dominance may have been gained over the opposing party. The differences in estimates of a party's position of relative advantage can be illustrated by the assumptions and contrasting views of likely costs and benefits held by factions within the French Government during June 1940, when the question of making a separate peace with Germany after the military disasters of the previous month was being considered. The pro and con arguments of those wishing to terminate France's part in the war (the pro-peace faction, led by Marshal Pétain) and of those wishing to fight on (members of the French Cabinet wishing to widen the war) show clearly the dilemma facing a leadership contemplating a compromise, especially from a position of marked disadvantage *vis-à-vis* the opponent, see Table 8.1.

TABLE 8.1   The French dilemma, June 1940

Pro-continuation (Make the war 'total')	Pro-termination (Acknowledge defeat on best possible terms)
Premier Reynaud, Mandel, Monnet, Marin, Dautry	Marshall Pétain, Gen. Weygand, Chautemps, Baudoin, (Laval, Marquet)
Strategy: Long term: uncertain, but very large benefits	Strategy: Short term: relatively uncertain, minor benefits
Assumptions: Britain will continue the war, even without France; the Allies can eventually win the war; the USA will enter war; Hitler's terms will be unacceptably harsh	Assumptions: Britain will very rapidly be defeated, or sue for peace; the USA will not inter-vene; Hitler wants a swift, cheap and com-plete 'victory' in the West
For: Continuing the struggle would:	For: Making a quick peace with Germany would:
(a) Lose Allied support if separate peace were made; French interests would not be con-sidered at final peace settlement if Allies won	(a) Lead to an end to French dependence on untrustworthy coalition partner (Britain) and an uncommitted neutral
(b) Maintain France's alliance commitments and gain her leaders an eventual share in the Allied victory over Germany when peace could be made on favourable terms (i.e. reverse the outcome)	(b) Avoid total disaster in France (including complete destruction of armed forces) and the extension of the war to vulnerable French overseas territories in N Africa (especially if Spain joined the Axis)

TABLE 8.1—cont.

Pro-continuation (Make the war 'total')	Pro-termination (Acknowledge defeat on best possible terms)
Premier Reynaud, Mandel, Monnet, Marin, Dautry	Marshall Pétain, Gen. Weygand, Chautemps, Baudoin, (Laval, Marquet)
(c) Maintain French morale and national pride	(c) Take advantage of French war-weariness and unpopularity of the war to transfer domestic support to pro-termination faction
(d) Not reveal current French helplessness at the negotiating table	(d) Gain easier terms for France by offering a speedy end to the war and (at least) reasonable returns for offering to quit a losing alliance *first*. (Hence the need for a speedy termination and no hanging on)
(e) Avoid the total discrediting of the Third Republic, and the emergence of an indigenous right-wing regime (supported by Germany): a *German-imposed* regime would lack real support in France	(e) Avoid a social and political breakdown inside France and a move to the extreme left; provide the opportunity for a regime of 'national regeneration' (right wing and Christian) after the 'chaos' of the Third Republic

Against: Continuing the struggle would:	Against: Making a quick peace would:
(i) Lead to the possible loss of all metropolitan France and at least the devastation of large areas of the country	(i) Lead to a heavy blow to national pride and morale
(ii) Risk the loss of parts of France's N. African empire	(ii) Lead to loss of British and (potential) US support and help
(iii) Inevitably result in a harsh German occupation of (part of) France	(iii) Confront France with inevitably disadvantageous peace terms dictated by Germany — possibly including occupation
(iv) Involve inevitable costs in further death and destruction	
(v) Lead to virtually complete dependence upon alliance partners	

TABLE 8.1—cont.

Pro-continuation (Make the war 'total')	Pro-termination (Acknowledge defeat on best possible terms)
Premier Reynaud, Mandel, Monnet, Marin, Dautry	Marshall Pétain, Gen. Weygand, Chautemps, Baudoin, (Laval, Marquet)
Assets: for continuing the war:	Assets: For concluding a good peace agreement:
(a) Basically, latent mobilisable strength – large overseas empire and an undamaged navy	(a) Residual resistance of Allied forces in France
(b) British potential strength and possible US intervention.	(b) Threat of a possible continuation of the war from N Africa (supported by Britain, the French fleet and Colonial Empire) against the offer of a quick and cheap peace for Germany (if desired by Hitler)
	(c) Providing Germany with the opportunity to concentrate upon ending war with Britain, either by force or negotiation. (Hence, again, the need to make peace before Britain opened negotiations or began to gather strength from the British Empire)

It may be that some kind of realistic calculation can often be made about the relevant advantages enjoyed concurrently by the rival parties, and hence of the relative advantages of terminating in the present rather than in the future.[5] Aristotle recounts how Eubulus of Atarneus offered to surrender his town to the besieging Persian leader, Autophradates, immediately, for slightly less than the latter's own calculation of the costs of a long drawn out siege. After reflecting for some time on the implications of this early form of cost-benefit analysis, Autophradates abandoned the siege of the town.[6] More recently, efforts have been made to elucidate the level of costs in terms of casualties suffered that commonly lead to nations at war abandoning their goals and terminating the conflict. Lewis Richardson, for example, argued that '. . . the amount of suffering at the time of the defeat can be crudely expressed by reckoning the war dead as a percentage of the total pre-war population . . .' and arrived at the conclusion that a population loss between 0.05 and 5.0 per cent was a critical level (Richardson, 1960b, pp. 298–9). Steven Rosen, by contrast, has argued that the ability to tolerate costs in terms of casualties may often be higher, and that it is a form of advantage in any conflict, closely related to the relative salience of goals to the parties in conflict in terms of what or who they will sacrifice to achieve them (Rosen, 1971; 1972). The idea may best be exemplified by Ho Chi Minh's comment, '. . . In the end, the Americans will have killed ten of us for every American soldier who died, but it is they who will tire first . . .'

Unfortunately, no clear pattern emerges from any of this work. Rosen finds that winners frequently suffer a higher percentage of casualties in war than losers. There appears to be no unambiguous level at which national decisionmakers give up, either in respect to battle casualties, or casualties as a proportion of overall population. Of recent major wars, it is true that Germany lost the equivalent of 3.9 per cent of its population between 1914 and 1918, the Confederacy a similar proportion in the American Civil War while the figures for Germany and Japan in World War II were approximately 6.1 and 4.3 per cent (Klingberg, 1966, p. 171). Against this, however, should be set Soviet losses of over 9 million people in World War II, and the fact that in the 'Lopez' war between Paraguay and the alliance of Argentina, Brazil and Uruguay (1865–70), Paraguay's population went down from over 1.25 million to just under 0.25 million before peace was finally concluded.

The major drawback with such approaches is that actual casualties among the members of a party in conflict are only one form of cost, so that they become only one element in any cost calculations about carrying on with a conflict or not. Normally, such calculations are dominated by essentially ambiguous elements and are inevitably highly subjective. At any one time, it is quite possible for individual leaders within the same party to come to wholly different conclusions about the desirability of continuing or terminating their struggle. On occasions, uncertainty about relevant information for such a decision is so high as to make almost any assessment feasible. Most uncertain will be one party's estimate of how its own coercive strategies are affecting the resources, unity and, above all, determination to continue the contest of members of the opposing party.

Nothing gives rise to greater intra-party disagreement than the search for the answer regarding under what circumstances should conflict behaviour best be terminated in order to give a maximum pay-off of one's party. The ambiguity of any estimates of the relative advantages of the two parties makes any clear-cut conclusions unlikely, while personal and political factors make it probable that there will seldom be unanimous support for either the view that now is the time to terminate, or that continuing the conflict is more beneficial. At one stage in the French debate about a negotiated settlement in June 1940, General Weygand accused Premier Paul Reynaud: 'You want to go on to the bitter end . . . but you are *at* the bitter end!' – a comment which illustrates the wide difference of evaluation that can underlie debates about whether a party has any alternative to compromise and negotiation.

In whatever circumstances, decisions about ending conflicts involve calculations concerning (i) benefits to be gained from continuing the conflict compared with those gained by making a settlement and (ii) cost incurred through continuing, relative to those suffered should the conflict end in a compromise.[7] Often the calculations also involve consideration of additional (or marginal) rather than overall costs or benefits, as these have the greater impact on leaders' calculations.[8] The decision is difficult even when one party is in a relatively unambiguous situation of advantage, while its adversary faces the failure of its efforts. Leaders of the successful party must still decide whether they have gained sufficient to make a settlement the sensible, if not optimum, solution. As with all problems of termination, termination after success often presents a situation in which it can be argued that enough of the sought-after goals can be achieved, so that termination of conflict behaviour should occur; while equally it can be argued that a continuation of the coercive strategies will bring yet further benefits, probably with a minimum of exertion and low costs. This decision is not made any easier by the common phenomenon of a party's goals 'expanding' with success in the conflict. As one party's tactical position improves, so do its aspirations and demands.

The situation at the point of success is simply that one party has succeeded in coercing its adversary into making peace on favourable terms. For the successful party, the problem presents itself as one of 'enoughness', or of choosing the point at which maximum achievable gains can be obtained. The leaders have to decide that their party has reached a position of maximum benefit, and that failure to terminate, a policy of 'hanging on', will result in fewer benefits and higher costs. Emphasising the uncertainties which attend such calculations, and the fact that a leadership group always deals in uncertain probabilities when making such calculations, the dilemma can be illustrated as in Fig. 8.1.

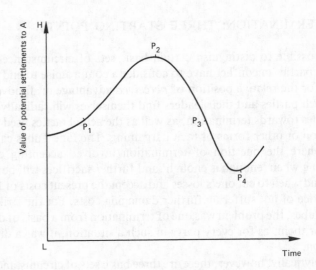

FIGURE 8.1 The dilemma of deciding when to settle

The dilemma for Party A is to decide whether they are at P_1, P_2, P_3, or P_4 and to act accordingly. Unfortunately, unless a leadership group is united in its interpretation of the situation confronting it, the chances are that some will see their party as being at P_2, and at the brink of losing considerable net benefits, while others that their party is at P_1, and will act and argue accordingly.

The dilemma of where to end a conflict is particularly acute for a party facing the probability of failure (P_3). Failure is seldom self-evident. All the problems about uncertainty of evaluation and lack of definite information arise, and underlie widely differing views among leaders regarding the relative fortunes of the parties. Add such psychological factors as the tendency to hope for success and assume that genuine defeats are merely temporary setbacks, and organisational ones whereby mainly positive views and evaluations are passed up any organisational hierarchy as 'sycophantic feedback', and the difficulties of confronting a need to compromise because of failure become apparent.

B. TERMINATION: THREE STARTING POINTS

It is possible to distinguish certain basic sets of circumstances from which parties in conflict have to consider a compromise to end a conflict, for the relative position of *perceived* advantage or disadvantage in which parties and their leaders find themselves will radically affect attitudes towards termination, as well as the actual tactics used to end coercion or other forms of tacit bargaining. The Fine Tubes case was one where the question of termination involved accepting defeat, knowing when 'enough is enough' and further sacrifices will be pointless, and when to cut one's losses and accept the present costs of failure as a price of not suffering further damaging costs. For the strikers at Fine Tubes, the problem was one of termination from a basis of defeat, and for them, as for every party in such a situation, it was a difficult decision.

Analytically, however, there are three basic sets of circumstances for parties bent on ending conflicts; of perceived success, of perceived stalemate and of perceived failure.[9] The problems of bringing a conflict to an end in these circumstances of victory, stalemate or defeat produce different orientations to the basic problem, particularly in the kinds of cost-benefit calculations carried out by leaders considering a compromise.

1. CONFIRMING VICTORY

It may seem surprising that any successful party ever offers a compromise to a defeated opponent. Certainly, the management side in the Fine Tubes conflict did nothing of the sort. Why should any compromise be offered by a party to a dispute which believes that its successful use of coercive strategies will put it in an even stronger bargaining position at a later date, from which it can dictate any terms it chooses? One possible explanation for a relatively successful party offering a negotiated compromise to its opponent is that victory is often merely 'the price of admission', meaning that negotiations at the end of a conflict are carried out under the shadow of one side having, by its previous coercive success, put itself in the position to inflict enormous harm on its opponent without running much risk of suffering counter-costs in exchange. If, indeed, the purpose of utilising coercive strategies is to make an adversary abandon certain goals, then it is only in the final stages of a conflict that the absolutely certain threat of one party causing immense damage to the other, unimpeded by that opponent's counter-strategies, can force decisions to alter behaviour and goals on the vulnerable party. Schelling insists that the key factor in successfully concluding a conflict inter-action is that the '. . . power to hurt could be brought to bear only after military strength had achieved victory . . .' (Schelling, 1966).

A 'compromise' settlement can, therefore, be dictated by the dominant position of one party, and although negotiations for a settlement may be unaccompanied by the use or public threat of further coercive behaviour, nonetheless it is the threat of this in the background which causes some solution to be formulated. These ideas can be illustrated in a more formal fashion, and thus provide clues to conditions that will encourage a successful party to contemplate offering a negotiated settlement to a vulnerable adversary. Implicit in Schelling's theory is the idea that both parties to a conflict must perceive that the conflict interaction has reached the stage at which Party A can, from that point on, inflict massive costs on Party B, without B being able to inflict anything equivalent on A. This is the situation which normally exists as a background to surrender negotiations, but a recognition of this highly asymmetric ability to impose costs by continued coercive strategies is a pre-condition for either party contemplating the offer of some negotiated compromise. Assuming, for the sake of argument, that we could calculate the level of on-going costs of conflict, the situation might be illustrated in an admittedly highly artificial manner as in Fig. 8.2. In this situation, after a certain point in the conflict, the perceived marginal costs to B are increasing rapidly, while those to Party A_1 are decreasing. (The costs to A_1 will never quite vanish, no matter how helpless B becomes, as the costs of continuing to inflict damage on B will always have to be met.) The actual slope of the perceived cost curves will vary from stage to stage and there is always the possibility that in future the trends will be reversed, but given the circumstances illustrated there is a very high incentive for B to achieve some form of compromise before the costs inflicted by A_1's strategies become astronomical. The French Government confronted such a situation in the summer of 1940, when their military ability to damage Germany had apparently vanished, while France was almost wholly vulnerable to the military costs the German army might be ordered to inflict. A similar situation faced the new Bolshevik regime in their negotiations with the Germans and Austrians at Brest Litovsk in 1917, where the head of the German delegation, Count von Kuhlmann, was heard to remark of the Bolshevik's negotiating position that 'The only choice they have is what sort of sauce they will be eaten with . . .'[10] (Wheeler-Bennett, 1938).

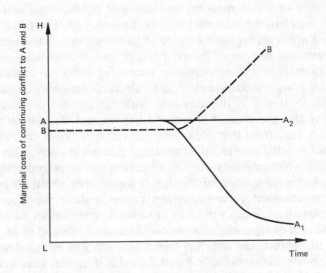

FIGURE 8.2   Altering marginal cost ratios

If the mounting costs suffered by B make that party willing to accept a compromise solution, what gives the successful party an incentive to accept some negotiated settlement which may still leave a number of its goals unfulfilled? One possibility is that, in spite of A_2's relative success in the use of coercive strategies, these are perceived as progressively more costly, so that both A_2's and B's perceived total costs continue to rise as the conflict drags on. In such a situation there will be a strong incentive to both sides to accept some form of compromise settlement.

An alternative explanation depends upon the benefits likely to accrue to the successful party, should its members decide to continue to coerce their adversary. If Party A is to have a real incentive to discontinue the conflict inter-action, and offer some compromise settlement to the defeated B, then it seems important that members of Party A must perceive that the benefits to A will not markedly increase from that point on, no matter how successful the continuation of coercive strategies. In many ways, the German position following their victory in France in May–June 1940 placed them in such a position. The completeness of their *blitzkrieg* victory meant that any continuation of operations to coerce the French Government could only have brought minor additional benefits in desired concessions.

However, in many cases the marginal benefits gained by continuing the conflict may not be so minimal. Consider two extreme cases illustrated in Fig. 8.3.

In the first it is likely that A_1 will offer to terminate the conflict interaction and begin negotiations, as the gains from continuing will be slight. However, in the second, A_2 is likely to continue to coerce B, at least until A_2's members perceive that the marginal benefits of continuing the inter-action begin to decline.

For any unsuccessful party facing a situation such as that illustrated in the second case, the prospects appear grim indeed, for its opponent has every incentive for continuing to coerce until the members of the defeated party are forced into a position of unconditional surrender. However, even in such a situation, the unsuccessful party may still be in a position to extract concessions from the victor through the cost element. As Schelling emphasises, the important point about costs is that, even in defeat, a loser may still be able to make victory cost more or less. It is the loser's ability to inflict further undesirable – because, from the victor's point of view, unnecessary – costs which often persuades even the most completely victorious party to offer compromise terms to its adversary, rather than just demand total surrender of decisionmaking power, so that it can achieve any goals it pleases. Sometimes, this ability to inflict further costs may be minimal, and appear to amount to nothing more than 'nuisance value', but even this ability may be significant in dealing with a successful, but possibly weary opponent, wishing to stop suffering further costs of continued

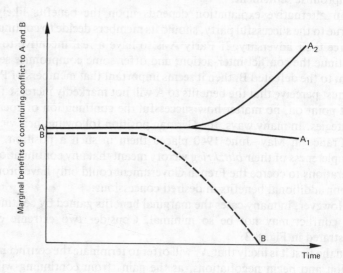

FIGURE 8.3   Altering marginal benefit ratios

conflict. The basic strength of the unsuccessful can consist of the capacity to withhold co-operation in reaching a final settlement. This capacity is a useful bargaining counter, in spite of the fact that, in normal circumstances, the victor has far less to lose by any failure to co-operate than the defeated. Even in a situation such as that confronting the Japanese Empire after Hiroshima, the defeated party may not be wholly without bargaining resources. In 1945, the US wanted to finish the war quickly, without having to invade Japan and without too much reliance upon Soviet intervention, which would have allowed Stalin a larger say in any final Japanese peace settlement. However, the alternative policy of slowly bombing Japan to pieces (in the event of some fanatical Japanese leadership failing to offer peace) would have been costly to the USA. Furthermore, American decisionmakers did not want the problems of dealing with a large Japanese army in Manchuria, or of clearing out small but well-armed Japanese garrisons from innumerable Pacific islands. Hence they needed a viable Japanese Government to conduct an orderly surrender. This last factor implied the preservation of some form of recognisable Japanese Government with which to negotiate, which need gave the Japanese authorities some further bargaining power. Kecskemeti generalises such circumstances into the principle that:

> . . . All the loser can do during the terminal stage is to obtain a political payment for the service he renders the winner by renouncing the use of his residual strength . . . (Kecskemeti, 1958, p. 123)

Many of the points made about balancing marginal costs and benefits apply equally to the defeated, although the problem there presents itself as minimising losses, making defeat less bad than it might otherwise have been, rather than maximising gains. Similarly, the approach can also be applied in situations where there is no clear winner or loser, and a situation of stalemate exists. Difficulties of making clear cost calculations are increased in the latter circumstances, and the chances of both parties arriving at a similar evaluation of their relative positions in the dispute correspondingly diminished.

2. ENDING STALEMATE

If the difficulties of terminating a conflict inter-action from a position of perceived, but fairly unambiguous, success are as complex as those suggested above, the difficulties of arriving at a compromise settlement in a situation where neither side has any clear advantage are even greater. For one thing, unless the stalemate is one of exhaustion, factions within each party arguing for a continuation of the coercive strategies, for 'more of the same', for 'a little greater effort to bring final success' will be stronger and more persuasive. Given the ambiguous position of the two parties in the conflict, such factions will also be even less easy to refute by pointing to the benefits of termination and the costs of continuing.

Many factors tend to make parties 'fight on', even when they appear to be in total stalemate, and it is likely that continuing coercive strategies will bring only marginally increased benefits. A major factor is, of course, the ambiguity which attends calculations of relative advantage in the struggle. In highly indefinite situations, such as those in which it is obscure who has 'lost' or 'won', a number of other 'inertial' factors appear frequently, and affect a leadership group's willingness to take a positive decision to quit:

(a) *The search for a 'better' post-conflict situation*
In conditions of stalemate, a phenomenon common to both sides appears to be a mutual desire that, at the very least, the outcome of the dispute should somehow represent a markedly 'better' situation than existed before the conflict developed. The twentieth century has seen wars fought with the avowed object of establishing 'a lasting peace' or of removing the threat from the adversary 'once and for all'. The idea that, after all the sacrifice and struggle, things might only go back to what they were before, and may even be worse, seems to affect both leaders and rank-and-file to such an extent that they are willing to continue the conflict until there appears to be a definite chance of some improvement − at least on the pre-conflict situation.

(b) *The desire to prevent future conflict*
One specific feature of this general desire for a settlement bringing a 'better world' is the frequent demand from members of a party in conflict that one of the results shall ·be the prevention of future conflicts, or, at least, future conflicts with the current adversary. Hence, prolonging the conflict may be partly with the objective of improving the party's position in any future conflict, for example by achieving a reputation for being a strong and ruthless opponent; or of achieving a compromise settlement that will leave one's party at a permanent advantage over the current adversary. In many wars, the aim of preventing future wars often comes to complement, and sometimes overshadow, the issues initially underlying the start of the struggle. Parties seem willing to risk losing the on-going struggle in order to improve their relative positions in some hypothetical future conflict.

(c) *The need for a 'victory' to justify sacrifice*
Up to the point at which it becomes generally recognised that they are facing a serious defeat, many parties to a conflict relate the level of costs incurred and the sacifices they have made to the kind of settlement that will ultimately be 'acceptable'. The general rule seems to be that the higher the sacrifices involved, the more the people will feel that some significant gains must be achieved in the final settlement to make up for all they have endured. The more prolonged the conflict, the more difficult it becomes for the leaders to accept anything short of a

significant improvement on the pre-conflict situation as a final settlement. The problem for the leaders then becomes one of presenting the final compromise outcome as a significant victory, and the achievement of the party's major goals.

One effect of the combined influence of these factors may be to prolong the use of coercive strategies beyond the point at which the conflict brings benefits to either party. In extreme cases, if one of the stalemated parties allows such influences as the desire for a 'victory' to dominate its evaluations of alternatives before it, that party may find itself going down in ruin while searching for a settlement guaranteeing 'lasting peace'. Alternatively, it may merely render the achievement of future reconciliation with the adversary more difficult and, ultimately, more costly. However, the factors discussed are more often crucial when one party is facing the possibility of compromising from a position of comparative weakness. When there is no clear-cut situation of dominance and inferiority, the question of when to give up is not often considered. The problem presents itself in the form of *how* best to force the adversary to improve his offer of terms for a 'satisfactory' compromise settlement.

Thus, in conditions of stalemate when the initial surge of confidence that the party's chosen strategies will bring quick success has worn away, the most common response seems to be escalation, even though it is always difficult to estimate to what degree further, or fresh, coercive strategies will improve the terms for a settlement.

3. ACCEPTING DEFEAT

Many of the points made previously concerning the inherent difficulties of terminating a conflict apply with particular force to situations of failure. In such circumstances, the problem of when to cut one's losses by accepting an often highly unfavourable compromise offer are especially acute. A list of relevant problems would include:

(a) As in the case of stalemate, the fact of failure is seldom immediately evident.

(b) The leaders of the party in conflict are being called upon to make a public admission of the failure of their policies and their choice of primary objectives. Furthermore, it is unlikely that there will be any visible rewards for all the previous efforts and sacrifices made to achieve those desired goals.

(c) The post-conflict situation, even if a compromise is successfully worked out, may be considerably worse, at least for many members of the losing party, than that existing before the dispute.

(d) Sheer inertial factors in any complex process of decisionmaking make it easier to continue a policy than to reverse it, especially when the change of policy, a negotiated, compromise settlement, is so dramatically contrary to previous policy.

(e) Opposition factions within the party find it easy to cry 'Betrayal' in situations of imminent defeat, and to find support for their own aims and ambitions among the party's rank-and-file who have suffered and sacrificed, and who now have to face an outcome denying them the rewards to which, they have constantly been told, they are entitled.

(f) Allied to any intra-party conflict for power and status is the probability that the costs of abandoning goals are likely to be asymmetrically distributed among various groups and factions making up a complex party; while the benefits of continuing to conduct the conflict, rather than terminate it, are equally likely to be felt more by certain groups than others. Hence a number of markedly different evaluations about continuing or terminating are likely to exist within the same party, and different individuals, groups or factions will have clashing views about the desirability of ending the conflict and compromising, or continuing and (perhaps) 'winning'. We return to this point in Section C.

For any kind of termination process to begin, therefore, a number of conditions have to be fulfilled:

(1) The leaders of the party confronting failure must be agreed that they have, in fact, failed.

(2) The loser's leaders must take a decision to make the best of some compromise settlement rather than 'fighting on', in the hope that some near-miracle will save them.

(3) The definition of the current situation of success and failure held by *both* parties' leaders must be similar, in that one side has recognised the symbols of defeat (the loss of the capital, the defeat of the army in the field, the defection of a key ally), while the other recognises that these are, in fact, symbols of defeat for its adversary.

In such circumstances, some kind of process for bringing the conflict to a conclusion is initiated, and the search for a compromise settlement begins.

However, even though these might be *necessary* conditions for termination, the fact that leadership groups within the contending parties possess similar evaluations of their relative positions of advantage in the dispute does not constitute a *sufficient* condition for beginning a search for compromise. Serious obstacles remain from the point of view of the leaders of the defeated party, and some of these also constitute problems for the leaders of the successful party. One involves making the fact of failure sufficiently palatable to the rank-and-file of the defeated party that the conclusion of a disadvantageous compromise settlement becomes acceptable. The eventual achievement of some final, compromise settlement may depend upon a victor's ability to ease the loser's position, and enable the latter's leaders to 'sell' the final outcome to their supporters and intra-party rivals. The successful party must always distinguish between the will to make peace in its opponents and the will to accept defeat, and recognise that while one exists, the other often does not (Coser, 1961, p. 252).

Even if the leaders of the successful party agree to make every effort to minimise the extent of their victory, and their opponent's failure, the task of the leaders of a losing party in persuading their followers to accept the necessity for a compromise is never an easy one. It is particularly difficult following a long and costly conflict, in which major sacrifices have been demanded of the followers by the leaders. One common tactic in 'selling' a compromise settlement to a potentially discontented following is to have the settlement concluded or endorsed by some individual whose role, or previous personal history, makes it impossible to contemplate that he would be party to some 'betrayal'. The tactic might cynically be entitled 'the role of the hero as peace-accepter'. Examples include the appointment of Marshal Pétain, the hero of Verdun, to head a French regime capable of making peace with the Germans in 1940; the re-assertion of Imperial power and the decision to make peace by the Emperor Hirohito of Japan in 1945, when the time had come to make the Japanese people, and some of the more fanatical factions within the armed forces, accept the consequences of the Allies use of nuclear weapons; and, more recently, the role of President Bhutto in persuading West Pakistan to accept the secession of Bangladesh. The provision of a new leader to sell a peace to the remainder of the party is another example of the rule that existing leaders rarely change policy and seek to make peace, but that a new leadership comes to power when the time has come to end a conflict. One positive factor in the process of seeking some compromise is the new regime's ability to disown or even condemn its predecessor's policies, and to argue with the adversary for a 'new start' or some major reconsideration as a result of the changed circumstances brought about through its accession to power. The argument also applies to cases when a new regime comes to power in a relatively successful party. The Sudanese military regime that seized power in the 1969 coup could, to some degree, disown the previous harsh and repressive policies in the south of the country by the preceding regimes. President Nimiery was able to present himself and his regime to an admittedly suspicious South Sudanese Liberation Movement as a relatively fresh set of leaders with new goals and policies, with no responsibility for the previous behaviour of the Khartoum Government, and this undoubtedly helped in concluding the 1972 Addis Ababa Accords. Similar arguments hold good for new leadership groups in defeated parties. Their relative lack of responsibility for the fact of failure often helps in selling a disadvantageous compromise to their followers.

Such tactics may not work, of course. A wide variety of factors exacerbate the problems of unsuccessful leaders, who wish to remain in power, yet to search for a compromise settlement from a highly disadvantageous position, while their followers still wish to continue the struggle:

(1) The leaders must, in many cases, accomplish a complete 'U-turn' in policy, and yet carry the bulk of the rank-and-file supporters with them. At the beginning of the struggle the task of the leaders was to convince their followers that the sacrifice demanded would be to their benefit, and that the dispute concerned the wide interests of all, rather than the narrow interests of the leaders. When defeat becomes a possibility, the leaders have to convince their followers of just the opposite, namely, that the acceptance of defeat is desirable for the whole party and not merely from the point of view of special leadership interests.

(2) Leaders will differ from the led not merely in the interests they pursue and wish to preserve, but in the information available to them. An elite's evaluation of the course of the conflict may differ markedly from that of the rank-and-file, and they may be able to foresee a defeat not yet visible to their supporters. The problem then becomes one of convincing the followers of the need to make a compromise settlement, while defining the defeat in such a way as it still appears a partial victory. Often, this proves an impossible task, which is why leadership groups tend to change when the time comes

to make peace. Leaders have to explain to followers why what the latter experience as a loss is 'in reality' a partial victory. They often fail to soften the blow of impending defeat by manipulating its symbols into those of success, and so are rejected by an enraged set of followers, some of whom may wish to fight on until the promised victory has been achieved.

C. TERMINATION AND INTRA-PARTY FACTIONALISM

Analysis of the problem of ending conflicts which concentrates upon perceptions of the positions of relative advantage enjoyed by parties in conflict has a number of disadvantages. Chief among these is the unrealistic assumption that there exists some unified entity as the party in conflict, possessing a single preference ordering and an ability to take 'rational' decisions about termination, based upon cool evaluation of alternative outcomes. The whole idea of a 'decision to terminate' implies some central, powerful leader or elite, weighing relative costs and benefits of continuing the conflict against those of ending it, then choosing upon the basis of this complex, but essentially rational evaluation.

Conflicts do occur in which parties are like this, but in most they are more complex than such an approach suggests. When discussing problems of 'changing a party's mind' in chapter 7 several difficulties were noted in this Rational Actor approach to parties in conflict. Particularly it ignores the existence of intra-party factions having a large impact on a terminate-or-continue debate, the neglect of which makes many decisions about ending conflicts wholly inexplicable.

A more realistic approach is one which acknowledges that many parties in conflict have a more complex structure than that of a single individual, and takes into account such factors as intra-party conflicts and rivalries, the distribution of factional influence, bureaucratic factors making for slow decisionmaking, and differing perceptions of the adversary held by separate intra-party factions. At the very least, such an approach emphasises the necessity for the disaggregation of cost-benefit calculations, given that in complex parties, costs and benefits are likely to be unevenly distributed and result in divergent views about the value of continuing or compromising. In addition, observers using this framework are able to consider the effects of differing intra-party evaluations on the inter-party situation, and on the ability of parties to end their conflict. In short, it is more appropriate to apply some form of Bureaucratic Politics approach to terminating conflict, to abandon restrictive and often misleading assumptions about common goals and single, shared preference orderings within a party in conflict, and to concentrate on intra-party cleavages and their effects on bringing conflicts to an end.

1. CLEAVAGES AND TERMINATION

The difficulties of a leadership group selling a disadvantageous settlement have already been mentioned, but these can be seen as part of a much larger problem caused by internal dissension within a party. Although entry into a dispute often tends to integrate a group, community or nation, this is not always the case. An external threat does not automatically create unity, nor does it banish forever the contests and conflicts that arise from divisions within an embattled party. A major problem in terminating a conflict is that there may already exist serious internal cleavages and disputes within a party in conflict and competing factions may utilise efforts to reach a compromise settlement in the inter-party conflict in intra-party struggles.

Even if there were no significant cleavages in the party structure before it becomes involved in a conflict, the very act of prosecuting a conflict may bring cleavages into existence. In complex parties any decision to indulge in coercive strategies, involving organised sanctions and violence, often causes a radical alteration in the balance of influence within the party. The conduct of a conflict, especially a war, usually involves a transfer of decisionmaking power to those agencies whose function is the professional conduct of coercion, and the relative abdication of responsibility of others responsible for the conduct of normal external relations. This structural change means the emergence of a set of influential leaders, whose values and orientations are coloured by the nature of their function – that is, to coerce an adversary. Hence, there will be a tendency for decisionmaking to become primarily focused upon considerations as how best to coerce the adversaries, or deal with their counter-strategies. This is not to argue that 'military' men are less prone to consider the termination of a conflict, but merely that the nature of their task, as they and others define it, prevents them devoting much time to considering how the purposes of coercion change, how a compromise settlement can best be achieved short of an ill-defined 'victory', or at what point political, as opposed to tactical factors indicate that the use of coercive strategies be abandoned.

Even if the divergence between tactical–military and strategic–political thinking about a conflict is minimal, and being in conflict results in intra-party disputes being ignored, cleavages are likely to reappear when problems of ending a conflict have to be confronted. Even where no significant intra-party differences existed before the start of the conflict, they are likely to develop when the problems of compromise or surrender approach. The most integrated party will exhibit signs of internal disunity when the need to make a possibly disadvantageous compromise becomes pressing. Things will fall apart, cleavages and splits appear, and factions arise as the party goes through the process of deciding upon what terms it should settle, given that it is hardly bargaining from a position of strength. Factions will form around the questions of whether the situation is bad enough to consider making a compromise peace, and what terms will be minimally satisfactory for the final settlement. One of the easiest and most effective tactics for one faction of an embattled party is to accuse its rivals of preparing a premature 'sell-out' to the enemy, after all the previous struggles and sacrifices, for purely factional advantages. Hence, before any compromise settlement can be made, an intra-party struggle between 'hawks' and 'doves' (or between self-defined 'patriots' and 'traitors') may have to be decided.

The existence and intensity of such an intra-party struggle will vary from conflict to conflict. In each case, a crucial determining variable will be the existing internal cohesion of the party engaged in the conflict, and whether this can be maintained. This is particularly so in the case of the party deciding that its position in the conflict demands its seeking an offer from its adversary. Even in the case of a dispute involving two individuals, the problem of when to ask for an offer of terms involves a decisional conflict, and this is analogous to the idea of different factions within other parties possessing differing interests and evaluations of the need to continue or to terminate a costly conflict.

2. PROBLEMS OF ADVOCATING COMPROMISE

Whatever the circumstances of the inter-party conflict, or the nature of the intra-party structure, any group of leaders determined to seek a settlement suffers from a number of disadvantages in its search for an end to the conflict. For a start, no individual or faction within any party will relish being the first to advocate that goals be abandoned and defeat accepted, particularly if the sacrifices made during the course of the conflict have been heavy, and the commitment to the party's goals in the conflict emphasised frequently. There are both practical and ideological aspects to this problem. First, if the elite faction deciding that the time has come to accept failure is the same that entered the conflict in pursuit of goals, then defined as non-negotiable it will lay itself open to charges of folly, mismanagement and duplicity, both with respect to the goals that it chose to pursue, even in the face of the adversary's strong opposition, and its assessment of the likelihood of successfully achieving these goals at a reasonable sacrifice. Throughout the conflict, the leadership group will have emphasised that the party's goals are those worth sacrificing, suffering and perhaps dying for. When the time comes to terminate the conflict from a position of disadvantage which can seldom be fully revealed to followers, these goals must be de-emphasised to the advantage of other, alternative goals. For any leaders this will be difficult. For the original leadership it may prove disastrous, and they are likely to be replaced.

Again, any faction seeking to end a conflict before some victory has been achieved will lay itself open to the dangerous charge of betrayal — or even treason in the case of a nation at war. The form of betrayal may vary. It may be betrayal of those ideals for which sacrifices have been made; of a trusted ally or group of clients; or of those factions who still adhere to the original goals for which the conflict is being conducted, who have remained 'true to their principles', and are intent upon 'maintaining the national honour' in spite of treason within the party. This is, perhaps, the most damaging charge of all. Being accused of treachery or betrayal serves as a strong deterrent to any compromise moves towards an enemy, even long after it has become apparent that continuing the conflict can only lead ultimately to a worse settlement.

Any leadership faction, whether newly in power or responsible from the start for the conflict, will thus always find it difficult to abandon popularly accepted and supported goals. Hence, it is especially easy for a faction wishing to fight on to level the charge of faint-heartedness against one wishing to compromise, and to have such a charge generally accepted. Two further advantages lie with hard-liners in any conflict. The first is that they will often have control of the party's coercive apparatus (the institutions responsible for putting coercive strategies into effect), or at least, they will enjoy major support from this quarter. Hence, 'hawks' can use this control (or support) either to:

(a) Coerce the 'doves' into silence, or assent for continuing the struggle or

(b) Prevent or ruin any compromise moves by a more vigorous prosecution of the struggle.

A common tactic associated with this second strategy is to argue for, or launch without full consultation, a 'final effort' to improve the party's position at the negotiating table, which even the most hawkish may see as inevitable. The fact that much experience shows that last offensives serve only to infuriate the adversary and increase the severity of the compromise terms offered, seldom acts as a deterrent to their proposal.

The second advantage enjoyed by many hard-line factions is that there usually exists great difficulty in publicly debating the possibility of a compromise settlement. A number of arguments are customarily advanced against any open consideration of the changing nature and worth of the goals of the party. One is that discussion and disagreement about the making of some compromise can only display intraparty dissension to the adversary, and that this will indicate weakness and a willingness to compromise, thus leading to the adversary contemplating harsher terms. There is considerable justification for this argument, as the beginning of internal dissension is often one of the symbols of success commonly sought in conflicts. Indeed, in many conflicts, one of the chief tactics available to both sides is to encourage internal cleavages within the opposing party to cause weakness of purpose. The other major argument concerns the effects of any open debate on the party rank-and-file rather than on the opponent. Here, the problem is whether open, or even semi-secret, discussion of the possibility of compromise will have a detrimental effect on morale, and cause individual members to slacken efforts in anticipation of a settlement, or merely because they are unable to see why they should continue their efforts when their leaders appear to be discussing some form of 'sell-out'.

3. FACTIONAL COMMITMENT TO CONTINUING

Even if most members of a party in conflict perceive the situation confronting them as calling for a re-evaluation of aims, and the possibility of compromise can be freely discussed, there is no guarantee that all factions will evaluate the situation similarly, or that 'the party' can arrive at a consensual decision for continuing or terminating. A major factor underlying any factional commitment to continuing is often that the costs of surrender will be asymmetrically distributed among the factions within the party. By definition, defeat and even compromise will impose losses, but these will not necessarily be borne equally. Those who stand to lose most by giving up will, almost inevitably, oppose the suggested compromise, and among such are usually those whose leadership positions will be threatened or lost by the defeat. One condition of arriving at a compromise solution is the prior removal of the leaders responsible for beginning the conflict. Victors dislike dealing with governments against whom they have been fighting a war, so that one set of leaders may have to be replaced before another can begin to negotiate with the adversary. Inherent difficulties attend this process of replacing current leaders as a preliminay to debating or concluding a compromise peace. To make peace may require:

(a) That the party removes its current leaders, but the latter can hardly demand from their advisers or colleagues a *frank* debate on their own removal.

(b) The abandonment of goals for which many are being asked to sacrifice and even die, but if the 'dove' faction denigrates these goals, they are asserting baldly that the sacrifices are in vain, and this is not a psychologically easy, nor a politically safe position to adopt.

(c) The disbanding, or substantial reduction of the fighting forces, but it is difficult for civilian and military leaders to debate freely how to abolish one another, or curtail each other's power and position.

Moreover, individuals, groups and factions may receive both material and psychological rewards from their part in the conduct of the struggle, and these may be lost once peace comes. Political power, status and economic wealth may accrue to certain individuals, factions or agencies while the conflict continues, but all these may be re-distributed in time of peace and such rewards vanish. Generals may be retired into obscurity, leaders of guerrilla groups return to being unknown citizens instead of powerful leaders or celebrities, factions find that their interests have been ignored in the interests of gaining a peace which they will inevitably regard as unworthy and purchased with their sacrifices. Hence, opposition factions form to prevent an 'unworthy' settlement and ensure the achievement of 'peace with honour'.

The importance of different individuals, factions and agencies possessing their own range of benefits and costs for the existence and continuance of any conflict lies in these factors' tendency to undermine the ability of any complex party to achieve a general consensus about the relative position of advantage of 'the party' in the conflict, and hence about the optimum point for terminating conflict behaviour. In addition to inherent ambiguities attending attempts to evaluate such an optimum point, the fragmentation of the party into factions or separate agencies, each with its own evaluation of the advantages and disadvantages *to it* of terminating the conflict at any particular stage, will militate against the formulation of any coherent view of termination strategy.

4. FACTIONALISM IN AN ADVERSARY: SOME PROBLEMS

From the viewpoint of a successful party in a conflict, serious internal cleavages in an opponent (either built into that party's structure or brought about by failure and possible defeat), present a difficult problem when making peace. This is not merely a problem that arises when a position of acknowledged dominance has been achieved, and an advantageous compromise settlement become a signal possibility. Much of one party's conflict behaviour consists of a continuous process of communication to affect perceptions, decisions and behaviour of the rival 'party'. With many complex parties, however, the process must consist of simultaneously trying to affect a number of different individuals and factions. This involves taking into account the differing circumstances, objectives and evaluations of separate, often rival factions, or at least tailoring one's own activity so that its major impact is upon those factions and individuals perceived as having the greatest effect on the other party's behaviour. To take an extreme example, those in the US Government trying to influence the Japanese Cabinet prior to the outbreak of World War II had to contend with the fact that the moderates, whose behaviour they were trying to influence, had always to consider the possibility that any move viewed as wrong or dishonourable by extremists might result in the moderates' assassination. (One assumes that this might have been rather a large factor in the moderates' calculations of the costs of giving in to foreign persuasion.)

The problems are no less complex when a conflict has continued for some time, and members of both parties wish to arrange a compromise. For the successful party's leaders there is, initially, the purely practical problem of getting into contact and then communicating clearly with the opponent's 'dove' faction. This is not to argue that substantial physical difficulties always exist. There are usually channels by which one leadership group can communicate with the leadership of its adversary. Third parties are always ready to act as intermediaries, if only to pass messages through their own channels. Direct communication is often possible. However, difficulties arise when the cental leadership is split into factions, for the problem is one of communicating with 'doves' regarding possible terms for a settlement without: (a) letting hard-liners know that such contact exists (or else 'doves' will be open to the damaging charge of trafficking with the enemy, and be discredited within their own party); and sometimes (b) without letting one's own hard-liners, or the rank-and-file supporters, know that contact exists, for fear that similar charges of a 'sell-out' may ruin the chances of any contemplated compromise.

A second and probably trickier problem for a party whose leadership has made contact with 'doves' within an adversary, is to decide upon 'reasonable' terms which the opposition's doves might be able to persuade their own rank-and-file followers to accept. Doves in a disadvantaged party first have the task of finding out whether their opponents will put forward 'reasonable terms', which will enable them to win support for their otherwise dangerous efforts at compromise. If the initiating party's leaders wish to make such a compromise, rather than dictating at a later stage, then their best strategy may be to help the opposing doves and they can do this by not insisting upon terms which are too obviously brutal.[11] However, the problem will then be of 'heading off' their hard-liners who will argue either that the terms should be as harsh as feasible, or that the struggle should be continued until the opponents were ready to 'listen to sense' and accept harsher terms. If the hard-liners are successful, it may be that their terms are so harsh that even the opposing 'doves' will reject them, or feel that there is no alternative but to continue.

One of the most difficult types of party with which to conclude any compromise settlement is a coalition representing widely divergent interests, whose major chance of staying united and, perhaps, in power, is to maintain an existing status quo by refusing to 'betray' the interests of constituent factions by gaining one set of goals at the expense of others. Certainly the intransigence of the Israeli coalition government between 1967 and 1973 offers some support for this contention, even though there were obviously other factors at work in this case. Even in less extreme examples, major intra-party opposition to a leadership group always possess a real threat to possible external compromise, for it can usually mobilise rank-and-file antagonism to concessions and abandoning goals. The history of efforts to revise the Panama Canal Treaty between the USA and Panama from 1964 to

1978 reveals a pattern of both parties' inability to make constructive compromises and concessions when in a position of domestic weakness. At one stage, intense domestic disapproval forced President Robles of Panama to begin 're-negotiations' of an agreed draft; at another, the Watergate scandal wrecked Secretary of State Kissinger's efforts to find a satisfactory compromise.

The Middle East offers an example of yet another problem affecting the achievement of a compromise settlement. This may be seen by looking at the situation through Israeli eyes, at the disunity among the Palestinian organisations. For the Israeli Government, one central problem, in the event of the Israelis eventually deciding to make some compromise settlement that would be recognised as a compromise by their adversaries, is to find a party sufficiently unified and organised to conduct peace negotiations. The next problem is to sell the terms of any final compromise agreement to all the other factions involved in the dispute. Even were the Israeli Government merely interested in coming to some compromise with the Palestinians, the problem would be with whom to communicate, and then negotiate, in the hope that the chosen faction among the Palestinians would be able to persuade all the Palestinian factions and organisations to accept a final compromise. Expressed in such a way, the often repeated questions of Israelis about whom they are to negotiate with, takes on a realistic note. In the event, Israeli Governments appear to have taken the option of negotiating with their enemies one by one, on an ad hoc, opportunistic basis, partly with the objectives of splitting the Arab coalition and isolating the Palestinians.

The line of thought leads to the somewhat paradoxical conclusion that it may be in the interests of a unified − and successful − party wishing to make a compromise settlement, to help to create (or, at least, not to hinder the development of) a more unified opposition. The development of a united opposition may be a pre-requisite to finding an answer to the question: 'With whom do we negotiate?' One necessary condition for the negotiation of a lasting compromise agreement may be the creation of an opposition party with a leadership that can conclude an agreement, and then enforce the terms of that compromise onto its followers and rival factions wanting yet more favourable terms. Thus, a successful party wishing to compromise with a split, disunited, opposition may find some advantages in assisting the enemy to find unity, perhaps by deliberately playing up the role and importance of one of the rival factions within the opposing party in order to strengthen the intra-party influence of that faction.[12] At other times, the successful party may assist third parties in bringing one faction to the top by encouraging third party contact with one or other 'suitable' faction or organisation, and holding out the hopes of recognition of this faction as the representatives of the diffuse interests of the opposing party. This may sound far-fetched, but there is little doubt that the civil war in the Southern Sudan was only successfully brought to a negotiated close when the Southern Sudanese factions were united into one, fairly cohesive, organisation, the SSLM, that could realistically negotiate with the Sudanese Government in Khartoum. In addition, Major General Lagu's group could claim to represent nearly all the people and groups in conflict with that government and was able to make any agreement it recognised as satisfactory actually work. While not arguing that the Khartoum Government had any direct hand in the achievement of unity among the South Sudanese, there can be little doubt that it recognised the advantages of having a single opponent with which to negotiate, *when* it decided to negotiate.

D. CONCLUSION

The main argument of this chapter is that the process of terminating any conflict is complicated by a number of common and intractable factors arising, in various forms, wherever the conflict occurs:

(a) Difficulties of arriving at an agreed and unambiguous view of the relative positions of advantage of both adversaries, and of the probable future course of events.

(b) Difficulties in calculating the relevant costs and benefits of various compromise solutions that might be arranged.

(c) The fact that increased recognition of sacrifices necessary to achieve goals in dispute is often offset by the involvement of other costs which would be incurred as a result of terminating the conflict obviously short of success.

(d) Uncertainties about the circumstances in which considerations of *overall levels* or *marginal increments* of costs and benefits play the greater part in influencing calculations about the desirability of termination.

(e) Doubts about the stability of parties' preference orderings of goals over time, and about the factors which contribute to alterations in such orderings.

In addition, ending a conflict presents special problems, depending upon whether a party begins the process from a position of perceived advantage, disadvantage or stalemate. A cursory review of these problems indicates that the problems for a defeated party are most intractable. In all circumstances, the process can be complicated by intra-party cleavages and by the fact that continuing a conflict may suit some factions while others would benefit greatly from the conclusion of some reasonable compromise. Such complications do not merely affect the party suffering from major cleavages and factional disagreement; they are also relevant for an adversary seeking to arrange a settlement with a divided party, and having to search out a satisfactory strategy for dealing with a party particularly prone to repudiate or be unable to carry out compromise settlements arrived at through delicate peacemaking processes.

Much of our discussion has concentrated upon the difficulties of arriving at an initial decision to seek some bilateral compromise. This represents only a preliminary stage in the process of bringing a conflict to an end. The central process is that of actually negotiating the terms of the settlement, and bargaining to obtain the best compromise possible for one's party, irrespective of the relative balance of advantages in the conflict process. Our next chapters discuss this process of bilateral, face-to-face bargaining.

9 Settlement Strategies

Given that parties to a conflict have decided to end their conflict, both, at some stage in the proceedings, will usually have to abandon the process of long-range tacit bargaining as their main strategy, and send representatives to engage in face-to-face bargaining over a negotiating table. This kind of direct meeting is usually difficult to arrange and conduct. The very fact that the parties are in often intense conflict with one another, and hence not communicating with ease, makes it difficult even to set up a suitable meeting. Again, any conflict process consists of a series of actions and reactions, as both parties try to achieve their respective goals, and at any point of the process one or both parties may still perceive that they are more likely to achieve their ultimate objectives through their chosen coercive strategies, rather than through negotiated compromise. However, given that parties even to international conflicts *do* engage in negotiations at numerous stages during a conflict, and that some negotiations eventually achieve what appear to be relatively satisfactory compromises, it is important to analyse the negotiating process and understand its structure and dynamics as well as its relationship to the broader process of ending conflicts.

A. THE NATURE OF NEGOTIATION

Even in its common-language sense, 'negotiation' consists of a number of separate, but inter-related elements. The first is that it necessarily involves some form of direct, face-to-face contact between representatives of the rival parties, who meet to exchange compromise offers and counter-offers, both trying to get the best final outcome for their party. Secondly, this process is usually accompanied by attempts to argue the opposing representative out of any rigid, uncompromising position on salient issues, often backed up by appeals to shared standards of morality, concessions already proffered, general conditions outside the negotiating chamber, and (sometimes) an external audience, if the opponent proves recalcitrant and unyielding.

196

However, concentrating upon 'within-chamber' inter-action between formal negotiators may lead to the neglect of other aspects of the overall negotiation process. One view of negotiation is of a process achieving '. . . an agreement between parties, settling what each shall give and receive in a transaction between them . . .' (Deutsch and Krause, 1962). Certainly some concentration upon the *outcome* of a negotiation is necessary to remind us that negotiations frequently deal with relative distribution of something in dispute, although (a) such an agreement could be achieved without any kind of face-to-face contact and (b) the overall process of tacit bargaining itself could be viewed as a strategy to lead to some such final agreement.

Broadly conceived, the term 'negotiation' could be taken to mean all the strategies and inter-actions previously considered as long-range, tacit bargaining that precede and often accompany any actual face-to-face efforts to argue with, and modify the position of, leaders of an adversary. Intermingling of the concepts of tacit bargaining and negotiation also occurs in two other ways:

(a) All tacit bargaining may be viewed as a process leading up to (and directed towards) a final negotiation, and hence as a series of manoeuvres designed to allow one's representatives to enter the negotiating chamber in a position of marked advantage.

(b) Tacit bargaining 'outside the negotiating chamber' may well continue while the negotiation takes place, and its outcomes will affect the relative positions of the parties' representatives, and hence the negotiating process.[1]

The first point may prove to be less of a definitional problem than appears initially. The very fact of engaging in formal negotiations would indicate that, on most occasions, the parties involved have decided to attempt to find a solution through means other than coercion. Hence, the nature of their behaviour in the conflict situation is often marked by noticeable changes, such as formal ceasefires or unilateral restraints on further coercion – although any failure to achieve some satisfactory compromise may lead them to revert later to a process of coercive tacit bargaining once more. For this reason, it is justifiable to set up a temporal limit on the negotiating process; and to regard all activity up to some preliminary agreement to meet and talk as being best classified as *tacit bargaining*; and behaviour thereafter as being part of a general settlement strategy focused on substantive *negotiations*.

The problem still remains of integrating into a negotiation *process* those activities outside the negotiating chamber which affect either by accident or design the on-going process of negotiation about a solution. Such activities include acts or statements designed to alter the relative position of advantage of the negotiating parties; behaviour intended to influence third parties who might have some impact upon the course and outcome of the negotiations; and actions or statements intended to affect leaders and followers within the party whose representatives are engaged in face to face discussion. One of the first incidents to threaten the Anglo-Irish peace talks in October 1921 occurred not in 10 Downing Street, but completely outside the formal negotiations when De Valera in Dublin sent, unasked, a telegram to the Pope commenting on the latter's message of goodwill and encouragement to George V (Pakenham, 1972, pp. 136–9). De Valera was undoubtedly trying to affect both the status of Sinn Fein, as well as the negotiations, but the problems raised for the actual Irish delegation were, for a time, severe.

In circumstances such as this, it seems unarguable that, to be realistic, such external activities and strategies should be reckoned part of the total negotiating process, so that it is best to adopt a broad definition of the overall process including '. . . all actions or communications by any party made within the negotiating situation and intended to influence its outcome . . .' (Sawyer and Guetzkow, 1965). Given this broad approach, the process of negotiation will contain these elements:

(a) Face-to-face bargaining between representatives of the parties (which raises questions about whether the former are *representatives* or *delegates*, and what difference to outcomes might result from any combination of the differing roles).

(b) A concentration upon substantive issues, without much attempt to probe the goals, motivations or perceptions of the opposing party (except in the sense of exposing weaknesses that might be exploited).

(c) A frequent assumption that the conflict is of a constant-sum type, and that the function of the negotiator (team or individual) is to 'win' as much as possible.

(d) A process based upon exchange of concessions[2] or compromise offers with the adversary;

(e) An accompanying process of action and counter-action outside the negotiating chamber designed to place one's own delegation in a position of greater advantage or lesser disadvantage, and to affect the adversary's delegation in the opposite manner.

B. CONDITIONS FOR NEGOTIATION

Aspects of any decision to negotiate a solution to a conflict have already been discussed in considering conflict termination, including factors in the relationship between conflicting parties that might bring about some decision to compromise. As negotiation is the final stage in a process of conflict termination, many remarks about ending conflicts from positions of advantage, stalemate and disadvantage apply to final negotiations arising from such situations. The basic question of why parties decide to negotiate may then be expressed in terms of at what point in the conflict process do parties, either singly or mutually, decide to try to open negotiations. Undoubtedly one of the crucial factors in any decision to negotiate remains the perceived positions of relative advantage on the part of those actively involved in the conflict. Hence, decisions to begin moving towards a negotiated settlement rather than victory may be affected by such factors as the perceived costs and benefits involved in 'cutting losses', or the effects of recent success-through-coercion on increasing one's demands and on expectations of success because of previous success. This argument raises again the familiar attitude towards compromise by negotiating ˝from strength', emphasising that much tacit bargaining may be seen as a direct effort (i) to place one party in such a position of advantage outside any formal negotiating chamber that it can determine the terms of a settlement agreement virtually unilaterally or (ii) to 'level up' from a position of marked disadvantage, so that it is possible to begin some compromise process on more equal terms, rather than dealing with an opponent enjoying marked tactical superiority. In many ways, President Nasser's behaviour in the weeks preceding the June 1967 War can be interpreted partly as an effort to get back onto something like an equal footing with the Israeli Government preparatory to beginning a negotiation from a less disadvantageous position,[3] although attention is usually directed to other aspects of the removal of UNEF, closing the Straits of Tiran and moving two divisions of troops into Sinai, such as the need to reassert Egypt's position in the Arab world or to take Israeli pressure off Syria.

It is obvious that there are numerous obstacles even to beginning a process of negotiation. Such factors as the issues in conflict, the current positions of relative advantage of the parties, internal constraints within each party operating against compromise and difficulties of communicating a desire to compromise to the adversary without giving the impression of weakness or lack of resolution, can combine to prevent any negotiation taking place until one or other party reaches the point of exhaustion. However, the fact that negotiated settlements *do* occur indicates that there must be circumstances in which parties are prepared to cut losses, abandon goals, and compromise, even if the precise combination of circumstances are rare. This is not to argue that negotiated settlements are simple matters to arrange. One writer makes the point that:

> . . . compromise requires two agreements between the parties; both . . . must initially agree that a partial withdrawal of demands or positions is preferable to continued conflict, and only after this decision has been reached can they began discussing the substantive terms of a compromise agreement . . . (Holsti, 1967)

In many circumstances, both parties can arrive at the first 'agreement' regarding their preference for abandoning some goals separately, but the problem then becomes one of communicating this conclusion to the other party clearly and without appearing to be weakening. This often has to be done, at least in the initial stages, without any very certain knowledge that the opposing party has come to a similar conclusion.

In plain language, then, for negotiations to occur both parties have to have reached a stage where a compromise settlement offers a potentially better alternative than a continuation of tacit bargaining, although whether this potential is maximised will depend upon the nature of any final compromise agreement. The features of a *potential* negotiating situation are likely to include the following:

(a) Parties perceive that there is a chance of reaching an agreement in which each would be better off − and no worse off − than if no agreement were reached.
(b) Parties perceive that there is more than one agreement that can be reached.
(c) Parties perceive each other to have conflicting preferences with regard to the different agreements that might be reached.

A simple diagram can illustrate and contrast two alternative pre-negotiation situations, in one of which a potential for a negotiated compromise exists, see Fig. 9.1.

In Fig. 9.1(a) both parties have mixed motives towards one another because of the maximum level of concession they are prepared to con-template before returning to the status quo:

(i) Each has to co-operate with the other in reaching *some* form of agreement but,

(ii) Each has conflicting interests with the other regarding the precise nature of the agreement eventually concluded.

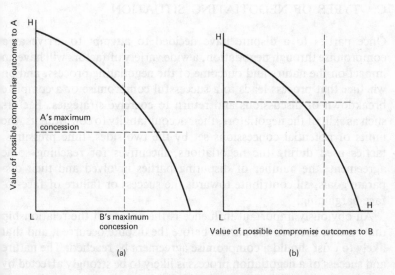

FIGURE 9.1 The scope for a compromise

By contrast, in Fig. 9.1(b) there is no logically possible position (or agreement) that could be concluded which would: (a) increase benefits to Party A without making Party B worse off than their maximum concession, or (b) increase the benefits and decrease the costs to B without making A worse off.

The relationship between the actual 'objective' situation and the perceptions of the parties themselves makes yet another difference to whether a negotiation will start, or succeed once started. If the actual situation is (b) and the parties perceive it as (a), then a process of negotiation may begin, but unless one or both parties have considerable success in modifying their rival's maximum concession, then the negotiations are likely to prove abortive. On the other hand, if the parties perceive the situation as being (b), even if it is actually (a),[4] then negotiations are unlikely to begin, unless some form of sham negotiation is conducted for purposes unrelated to a genuine search for a compromise.

C. TYPES OF NEGOTIATING SITUATION

Once parties to a dispute have decided to attempt to arrive at a compromise through negotiation, a wide variety of factors will have an impact on the nature and outcome of the negotiating process, and on whether that process leads to a successful compromise or a complete breakdown of discussions and return to coercive strategies. Factors such as skill of the negotiators, their accountability to constituents, the limits of potential concessions set by the two sides, time pressures, tactics used during the negotiations, incentives for reaching some agreement, the number of disputing parties involved and their disparate goals, all contribute towards the success or failure of face-to-face bargaining.

An obviously important influence is the nature of the relationship that existed between the parties before the dispute occurred, and that likely to exist should a compromise agreement be reached. The nature and success of a negotiation process is likely to be strongly affected by whether it takes place, for example (i) between parties that have to continue some close relationship after a settlement, and also possessed a high level of mutually beneficial inter-action before the dispute or (ii) between parties that have had minimal contact before the dispute commenced and who can return to relative isolation once some compromise settlement has been achieved, as in an international negotiation between two governments between whom there is normally a low level of inter-action, exchange or co-operation. In the former case, it is plausible to assume that the dispute will be one of a series, that the norms for conducting the conflict will be clearly laid down and usually followed, so that negotiations may be simpler. Moreover the fact that some kind of *modus vivendi* has to be worked out, if what both sides regard as a relatively mutually beneficial relationship is to be resumed, presumably exercises some effect upon the probable success of discussions. Conversely, similar pressures towards compromise through a negotiated settlement will not exist in any conflict between previously isolated parties.

1. ISSUES TO BE NEGOTIATED

While prior and anticipated relationships between negotiating parties are likely to be important influences upon the course and outcome of any discussions, the best starting assumption seems unarguably that the style and outcome of negotiations will be most strongly affected by the issues being bargained over – their number, complexity and relative salience to the negotiating parties. Iklé (1964) suggests four basic types of negotiation, although he insists that no real world negotiation ever consists solely of one particular class of issue:

(a) *Extension negotiations*, concerned with the renewal of an existing agreement, or its replacement and enlargement in the light of the first agreement and subsequent experience. (For example, the renewal of a military treaty, an agreement about sovereign base rights, a trade agreement or a commercial contract.) Fundamentally, such agreements are merely continuations of 'the normal', and represent few serious problems for negotiators.

(b) *Innovatory negotiations*, where those involved are concerned to reach an agreement about some entirely new enterprise in which agreement would be of considerable mutual benefit. (For example, agreements about the development of nuclear power, or the establishment of a customs union or common market.)

(c) *Redistribution negotiations*, where some fundamental change in existing arrangements or distributions is desired by one party, and resisted by another. The liberation of a colony, the establishment of a fundamentally different wage structure – or workers' control – or the transfer of political office between leaders of rival factions within a society.

(d) *Normalisation negotiations*, concerned with the termination of undesired, and relatively 'abnormal' conditions, and return to some status quo, or some new but mutually acceptable relationship. Such negotiations are usually appropriate at the end of a conflict process, when a truce, cease-fire, peace treaty, or some other ending of coercive strategies, is desired by both sides.

These last two types of negotiation are mainly relevant to ending disputes, even though elements of all four are normally mixed up in real world conflicts. Negotiations undertaken to end a dispute can be viewed as efforts to bring a mutually costly inter-action to an end and return to something like a 'normal' relationship, even though the normalisation agreement, if achieved, may establish a totally different 'normality' from that which existed before the dispute. However, negotiations at the end of many conflicts also contain strong elements of redistribution as the original issues in the conflict involve some demand for change by at least one party, either in the distribution of valued resources or roles, or in the behaviour of one party and its relationship with the other. Hence, negotiations are likely to be facilitated by the 'normalisation' elements in the situation, and hindered by the surviving 'redistribution' elements. The likely success of the overall process of conflict termination, and of the final process of negotiation, will largely depend upon the relative importance of these two elements in the minds of adversaries, and their leaders.

2. ASYMMETRIC NEGOTIATING POSITIONS

Normally, asymmetric negotiations refer to face-to-face bargaining between a markedly weaker and a markedly stronger party, such as those which took place between Malta and the UK in 1971 over the eventual terms of British withdrawal from the island[5] (Wriggins, 1976). However, another sense in which negotiations may be asymmetric, arises when parties occupy different tactical positions that develop from conflict over a *redistribution* of values in dispute. In such negotiations, any party defending a status quo is limited in the range of bargaining tactics available by the very fact that it seeks no change in some existing relationship with the pro-change party. Why should its leaders agree even to discuss, let alone negotiate, about some problem which is purely the result of the desires of another group, community or government? The status quo is satisfactory. Furthermore, the act of discussion itself may imply that there might be something in the demand for change being advanced! Hence, the initial stance for the *defensive* party in redistribution conflicts is to argue that there is nothing to discuss, that the existing situation is generally satisfactory, and that the only disturbance is the unreasonable set of demands by a greedy and self-seeking minority in the rival party. The *offensive* party, in contrast, will base its claims for a new status quo on the grounds of historic right, changing values, legal justification or shared morality. It will be able to appear 'reasonable' by offering to negotiate about the situation (rather than going immediately over to coercive strategies, which can be held in reserve as a threat should the adversary not agree at once to discussions and concessions) even though it has arisen through its own desire for a change.

Given such an asymmetry, the question arises as to why the defensive party should ever agree to negotiations, especially at the outset of a dispute. The safest tactic would be to argue that there is really nothing to negotiate about. Any sign of willingness to negotiate would place the defensive party in some risk:

(a) That negotiators would feel constrained to offer concessions going some way towards changing the status quo, merely to demonstrate flexibility, or reasonableness, to relevant audiences.

(b) That both leadership and rank-and-file would gradually lower their own expectations and abandon peripheral goals, so that their own image of a satisfactory final status quo would be altered and become more akin to that of their opponents.

(c) Over time, the defensive party's perception of the dispute might change, so that the conflict and any negotiations would become a question of 'normalisation' rather than 'redistribution'. In other words, the leaders of the defensive party and relevant third parties might come to regard the situation about which there is a dispute as 'abnormal', necessitating a change so as to 'normalise' the situation and the relationship with their adversary.

(d) Any concession, even an offer of discussions, might lead to the start of a process whereby the offensive party engaged in 'salami' tactics aimed at gaining a series of individually minor concessions which, when completed, would amount to a major alteration in the status quo (Iklé, 1964). The start of such a process should, therefore, be avoided at all costs.

For these reasons, the defensive party at the start of any conflict over redistribution often adopts the intransigent position that there is nothing to negotiate about in the claim of its opponent. In adopting such a stance the party is running the risk that its frustrated opponent will then resort to coercive strategies so that a decision about whether to negotiate may well occur again at a later stage in the conflict process, when the costs of the coercive inter-action necessitate reconsideration of the choice between compromise or continued coercion. Often in the initial stage of the dispute, the perceived choice lies between intransigence, and the risks that the implied threat of coercion by the opponent can and will be carried out; or accepting some proposal for discussions and a risk of concession and change. The potential costs of intransigence explain the majority of cases in which a defensive party offers to negotiate with its change-seeking rival, in spite of the fact that no real desire for any change or discussion exists. The threat of coercion, if the request for discussions is ignored, becomes too great. In other cases, negotiation in the initial stage of a dispute may be agreed to for several reasons:

(1) To act as a delaying tactic while the bargaining position of the defensive party is improved through building up resources, ally-seeking, or undermining the position and advantages of its rival.

(2) To discover what the opponent 'really' wants. This reason for agreeing to talk is founded upon the common assumption that the opponents cannot want what they appear, publicly, to be demanding, probably because this represents an initial bargaining position from which retreat to a 'realistic' set of goals is possible. Hence, discussions ought to occur, because only through such a process can one side find out the 'true' demands of the opposing party, and work towards some satisfactory solution. (At the same time such discussions will provide an opportunity to convince the leaders of the opposing party of the impossibility of fulfilling their demands, and reducing them to a more reasonable frame of mind: when 'they' understand 'our' position and problems, then they will recognise the unreality of many of their demands!)

Acceptance of a proposal to discuss a grievance or a desire for a change in some status quo may, naturally, still be dangerous for any defensive party bent on not making any concessions to its rival and determined to use discussions (or 'pseudo-negotiations') for its own purpose. However, many of these risks can be minimised by a variety of tactics pursued before negotiations actually begin.

D. PRE-NEGOTIATING TACTICS

Earlier we argued that the process of negotiation could usefully be distinguished from any preceding tacit bargaining designed to coerce or persuade an adversary to abandon the goals in dispute. It is equally helpful to consider the process of negotiation itself having a number of stages, some of which bear a close resemblance to tacit bargaining. In fact, pre-negotiation and attendant manoeuvring for advantage may begin well before the negotiators themselves sit down to work out some compromise settlement. Hence, it is helpful to consider the overall process of negotiation as consisting of three main stages:

(1) *Preliminary bargaining* concerning the terms upon which the involved parties will agree to begin formal negotiation of substantive issues.

(2) *Face-to-face negotiation* in which various strategies and tactics are used by negotiators to obtain an agreement satisfactory to them, and also to their opponent. This stage is accompanied by acts and statements outside the negotiating chamber designed to affect the relative positions of advantage within it.

(3) *Implementation* which involves (i) 'selling' the agreement to the remainder of the party on whose behalf the settlement has been negotiated and (ii) putting the terms of the agreement into operation in such a way as to satisfy the adversary, while ensuring that the adversary implements his part of the agreement.

This three stage progression for negotiations presents an idealised picture, and many negotiation initiatives never get beyond the stage of preliminary bargaining about prior conditions for full negotiations to take place. Others fail again and again when they reach the face-to-face stage, so that the process becomes repetitive rather than progressive. The obstacles and pitfalls even at preliminary stages are immense, particularly when parties are conscious of the importance of the terms on which they enter the negotiating chamber for any subsequent success or failure, and thus spend considerable time and effort manoeuvring themselves into the best possible position from which to agree to negotiate.

Pre-negotiation skirmishing takes a number of forms, and revolves around a number of different issues. The whole process is often known as 'talks about talks'. One of the crucial issues that often plays a part in this pre-negotiating stage concerns the related issues of who is going to be permitted to negotiate, and with what status?

1. PARTIES, STATUS AND NEGOTIATION

Considerable ingenuity is often expended by parties in the pre-negotiation stage of a negotiation process trying to control which individuals, groups or governments they will agree to meet as fellow negotiators, and what the latters' role in such direct exchanges should be. Attendance at, and role within, negotiations are obviously powerful factors in determining the outcome of any talks. Who is excluded and who included can often determine what range of potential outcomes will be considered. Three important elements in this regard are status, the problem of implied recognition, and the effects of these two on the nature and outcome of negotiations.

(a) *Status*. The problem of 'status' at negotiations is a familiar one, especially at the international level. An often quoted example is that it took six months deliberation at the Conference in Westphalia ending the Thirty Years War to decide the order of entry and seating among the numerous delegates, while the 'Big Three' at Yalta solved this particular problem by emerging simultaneously from three separate doors into the conference chamber. Often, however, there are more subtle and influential aspects to the problem of status than the mere question of diplomatic precedence, and refusal to lose face. In many conflicts, the defined status of the parties, once generally accepted, has an important effect upon the relative positions of advantage of the negotiators, on the way the subject matter to be negotiated is defined, and on the outcome of the discussions. Important differences will stem from defining an international conflict as between an 'aggressor' and the 'defender' of a legitimate status quo, or as a 'war of national liberation'. Often, when possible negotiations are being discussed, parties will try to establish their status and relationship in such a way as to give themselves maximum advantage in subsequent deliberations. For example, the Greek-dominated Cyprus Government insisted, after the fighting of 1963–4, that the Turkish leaders should be regarded and negotiated with as rebels against the legitimate government, while the Turkish–Cypriot leaders insisted that both parties were merely representatives of their own communities on the island. The fact that the Greek–Cypriots had remained in an already Greek-dominated political regime when the Turks left conferred no advantageous status on them in subsequent bargaining. In short, the Turkish–Cypriots refused to come to any discussions under the handicapping label of 'rebels', because this would have irreparably damaged their own case, even before substantive talks could begin. Similar problems attended efforts to begin direct negotiations between the British Government and Sinn Fein in 1921. Were the Irish negotiators to come as representatives of an already independent Ireland (if so, half the British case would already have gone by default) or as subjects of the British Crown? (Pakenham, 1972, pp. 77–9).

At the international level this problem of relative status often becomes acute, given the existing legalistic framework. In international or transnational conflicts, either for reasons of precedent or tactical advantage, governments will seldom negotiate with the representatives of non-governmental groups. Thus, given the rigidly hierarchical status ordering of the international system with its emphasis on legally sovereign state entities, disputes that involve other types of entity (communities such as the Kurds, the Nagas or the Palestinians; guerrilla movements such as the Tupermaros, the NLF in Vietnam or the IRA in Northern Ireland; or transnational groupings, such as the nomadic peoples of the Sahel) are seldom amenable to direct negotiation between the parties most directly involved. The difficulty of the Palestinian organisations in making their case known, let alone coercing the Israeli Government into contemplating eventual negotiation with some form of representation of a 'Palestinian entity' is a well-known case in point. The struggles of the Kurds, divided between four separate countries, is another. The difficulty in setting up discussions between the representatives of governmental and non governmental parties is one reason for the intractability of transnational disputes to directly negotiated settlements. A further aspect of the same problem is the refusal of governments to allow other governments or third parties to become involved in conflicts defined as 'domestic', no matter what transnational implications these may have. The Eire Government has frequently been accused of 'interfering' in Northern Ireland in the late 1960s, and the awkward fact that such a transnational conflict does not fit neatly into a 'sovereign state' framework conveniently ignored.

(b) *Implied Recognition.* A part of the problem of establishing some mutually satisfactory status relationship before entering formal discussions is the problem of substantive recognition implied in one party's public willingness to hold talks with another.[6] There are two sides to this particular dilemma: (i) that of an implied recognition of opposing groups or organisations as being genuine parties to a particular dispute (and not merely persons of no status or standing); and (ii) that of an implied recognition that such parties' objectives and claims form part of the overall problem, and have to be included in any bargaining leading towards a final settlement. Thus, agreeing to open even 'talks about talks' with particular governments or groups can have profound implications for subsequent negotiations through a recognition that the discussions must include some representatives and issues previously ignored. The problem of implied recognition is well illustrated by the bargaining that took place before the Paris Peace Talks on the ending of the struggle in Vietnam, and in the endless (and apparently ludicrous) debates about the shape of the table at which delegates would sit in the conference chamber. In effect, both the US and the North Vietnamese Governments were engaged in an attempt to define the nature of the South Vietnamese conflict in their own terms and thus be in a position of distinct advantage once formal negotiation opened. One of the crucial questions was whether there were two, three or four genuinely 'independent' parties to the dispute, and which of these should be represented and in what status at the Paris Peace Talks. The US contention was that the dispute in Vietnam was over an invasion of the South from the North, so that the NLF was merely a military arm of the North Vietnamese Government, operating with the separate state of South Vietnam. Hence, it needed no separate status at Paris. The North Vietnamese and NLF counter to this was to say that the conflict in South Vietnam was a war between the Vietnamese people living there (represented by the NLF) and the alien American aggressors and their stooges (the Government in Saigon), who thus were by no means an independent party and hence had no right to be seated at any negotiations. For these reasons, the question of who was to be present (and in what status) in the negotiating chamber at Paris became an important preliminary bargaining process in its own right, the result helping to determine the nature of the subsequent negotiations and their outcome. Similarly, in many redistributive conflicts, the action of a status quo party in agreeing even to talks about talks with a pro-change party would involve a tacit acknowledgement that there might be some legitimacy in the claims of the latter − an admission to be avoided at all costs in the initial stages of any bargaining.

(c) *Status, Implied Recognition and the Issues in Conflict.* The pre-negotiation manoeuvres that preceded the Paris Peace Talks neatly illustrate our final point in this section. That there is a close connection between the acknowledged status of the parties that eventually negotiate, and the definition of the issues in dispute which are to be negotiated – and ultimately the eventual outcome of the negotiations. The perceived status of the parties to an intra-national dispute, for example, will partly decide whether eventual discussions concern the return of the 'deviant' party to some status quo relationship that existed before the 'deviance', or whether two parties of equal status will negotiate about a wholly new relationship which must be satisfactory to both sides, rather than one that must necessarily conform (even approximately) to some situation existing before the conflict arose. In the Vietnam case, US acknowledgement of the North Vietnamese contention that the regime in Saigon were merely American puppets would have led negotiations into a set of issues relating to the rights of the US to establish such puppets in a basically hostile country; and then to the terms for US withdrawal and transferring power to the NLF in the south of a fundamentally united country. Similarly, had the US definition of the NLF as a mere appendage of the Hanoi regime prevailed, negotiations would have concerned the withdrawal of an alien invading force from the South, and the terms on which two separate Vietnamese entities could learn to coexist. On Cyprus after 1964, any Turkish acknowledgement of their role as 'rebels' against the legal government of the island would inevitably have led to discussions about the terms on which the rebellious community would have returned to a Greek–Cypriot dominated status quo, rather than about the need to hammer out some totally new relationship between the communities on the island.

All these examples illustrate the basic point that the status in which parties in conflict come to any discussions has an important impact upon what is discussed, the way it is discussed, and the outcome of negotiations. Hence, there is often a considerable level of pre-bargaining and manoeuvring (which to an outsider may look either trivial, or meaningless, or merely petty) between parties who realise that this activity is highly relevant for the terms upon which their negotiations will begin, the issues they will have to ignore and the tactics they can use or must avoid. Lack of skill at this stage of the negotiating process may fatally handicap one side at a later stage, so that considerable importance is attached to getting the adversary to come to negotiations on 'the right terms'. Success in such preliminaries can be used to offset disadvantages, or reinforce advantages gained in the previous process of tacit bargaining.

2. 'GETTING THE TERMS RIGHT'

Apart from establishing some advantageous status *vis-à-vis* one's adversary, other tactics for beginning negotiations in an advantageous position are open to parties preparing for negotiations, and pre-bargaining often begins at an early stage of any termination process. We have noted, in another connection, the dilemma of a party to a conflict wishing to open discussions for some kind of compromise settlement, but not wanting to give an impression of weakness or vacillation to its adversary. Often, this leads to a policy of waiting until a substantial advantage has been gained in the conflict (which may never occur), or until a major tactical victory has been achieved, so that peace feelers can be interpreted as a magnanimous gesture both to the adversary and to rank-and-file supporters within one's own party.

A far more usual process, once a genuine desire for some compromise settlement is mutually evidenced by both parties (or, alternatively, once both are under heavy pressure from third parties to come to some compromise agreement) is for both to engage in a series of preliminary manoeuvres which ensure that they will come into a negotiating situation on terms calculated to pre-determine the outcome of the substantive negotiations in their favour. In all such pre-negotiation tactics, the parties use the sanction of their final refusal to take part in any discussions at all, unless the terms for negotiation are satisfactory. For each, the central dilemma in this stage of the process is to estimate the relative desire for negotiations in its adversary as some function of the costs the latter would suffer through a return to coercive conflict behaviour, and of the benefits it perceives it might gain through a relatively 'successful' negotiation. In this situation, a party favouring the status quo will often enjoy an advantage in setting the conditions for negotiations, as its own motivation for any negotiated compromise will be low or entirely dependent upon how unpleasant the pro-change party can make any refusal to compromise.

Common pre-negotiation tactics often aim at preventing undesired but anticipated negotiations taking place, or making sure that they occur in circumstances heavily in one's own favour:

(a) *Calling for negotiations publicly and frequently.* This is in order to demonstrate one's flexibility and willingness to compromise, yet ensuring that no negotiations are ever likely to take place. Such a strategy can be used both for building up a reputation for reasonableness in the light of the universally shared belief that negotiations are in themselves a 'good' thing, and in some sense a substitute for violence and coercion; and also for 'responding' to the expectations and pressures from third parties to the effect that negotiated compromise is both possible and desirable. One common tactic used in such a process is to call for negotiations on terms one knows the opposing party will reject − probably out of hand. This can be done by offering a set of proposals as a basis for discussion, and including one or more conditions that the opponent's leaders are bound to reject, thus putting themselves in the worst possible light. This became such a regular feature of the Soviet−US disarmament negotiations in the late 1940s and 50s that it became the habit to talk of − and look for − the 'joker' provision in any set of disarmament proposals presented by one side to the other (Spanier and Nogee, 1962).

(b) *Denying the existence of particular issues as forming the basis for any conflict.* This is a common tactic on the part of status quo parties in any dispute, and involves a refusal to recognise that any problem exists, except the inexplicably wicked behaviour of the adversary. A corollary, should third party pressure for negotiation become acute, is to agree to negotiate about anything other than the other side's claim − usually 'We will negotiate about the ending of the X's dangerous, costly and unjustifiable actions'. This strategy is often associated with a more general practice discussed in (c).

(c) *Attempting to define what the issues are in the dispute in such a way as to steer negotiation on to issues defined so as to give a marked advantage to the defining side.* The next stage is to try to force this definition of the situation: (i) upon the opposing party − who will normally retaliate by a similar strategy, using a definition of the issues favourable to them; and (ii) upon third parties in the 'audience', as a strategy of indirect influence. The key to this pre-negotiating strategy is that, if one side can 'satisfactorily' establish 'what the dispute is about', then it is a simple matter to decide on this basis what will be discussed at any negotiations. It is possible to see two parties trying this strategy in the dispute over Cyprus which flared up again in August 1974. When discussions were being arranged between the Greek and the Turkish Governments, the Greeks tried to define the immediate negotiating problem as the withdrawal of the Turkish invading force from the island. The Turkish Government spokesman, by contrast, defined the problem as that of achieving a final settlement for the two communities in Cyprus, something the Greeks argued was a second stage problem, that could only be discussed once the Turks had already withdrawn.

This deliberate strategy of defining the issues in a way that gives one's own side maximum advantage in any negotiation should not, however, be confused with the genuine hindrances to beginning negotiations which are the result of markedly different, and genuinely held, definitions of the situation. These can easily lead to a total inability on the part of adversaries to understand their opponents' definition of the problem and of the issues in dispute, and to attendant convictions that the other side is deliberately distorting what the conflict is 'really' about for its own tactical advantage. Earlier in this study, we noted the manner in which conflict situations can be exacerbated by parties approaching a problem with completely different assumptions, perceptions or preference scales and how mutual misunderstanding of *what* the other party sees and wants can lead to increased suspicion and hostility, all too easily confirmed by later behaviour. Differences in definition of the situation arising from cultural backgrounds can, furthermore, affect negotiations both indirectly, by making difficult the development of some minimal level of trust, on which all negotiations must be based if they are to occur; and directly, by preventing even agreement on 'what negotiations should be about'. Additional difficulties stemming from genuinely, as opposed to tactically, different frames of reference, involve differing views of the nature and purpose of the negotiating process itself. Druckman (1973) has mentioned that, in many cultures, the concept of making a 'compromise' agreement has definite connotations of defeat and disgrace, as one's initial bargaining position is assumed to be fundamentally right and based upon unarguable truths, so that retreat becomes impossible. An experimental study of discussions between Greek and American students, for example, indicated that the Greek students regarded settling for a mid-point solution in between two initial bargaining positions as a definite defeat, a feeling not shared by the Americans (Triandis and Davis, 1965).

(d) *'Limiting the bargaining range'*. Akin to attempts to define the issues in conflict favourably is a further strategy aimed at controlling the outcome of a negotiation by limiting what will and will not be discussed, even though it may be admitted − privately − that this will involve excluding issues that the other side regards as essentially part of the dispute. Iklé refers to this as 'limiting the bargaining range'. It is open to either party, but more often used by that possessing a possibly temporary advantage. The basic process involves offering the benefits of negotiation on *some* relevant issues, at the cost of excluding others from consideration. 'We will agree to discuss x, y and s, but not a and b!' (Iklé, 1964). Limiting the bargaining range may be carried out either by controlling the agenda, and hence, largely controlling the nature of any discussion and agreement, or by specifically reserving key issues as items which will not be introduced into the discussion, the sanction being withdrawal from the talks if these items are mentioned. Rigid structuring of an agenda militates against the possibility of any fruitful exploration of the problem, and against any attempts at creatively producing new outcomes. Hence, both parties are always confronted at the pre-negotiation stage with the dilemma of whether to work for: (i) a narrow and inflexible agenda, which limits possible adverse outcomes but also mutually beneficial ones; or (ii) an open and flexible agenda, in the hope that the adversary's representatives will approach the meeting as a problem-solving exercise rather than a hard-bargaining session, and not take advantage of the first party's own flexibility.

(e) *A final pre-negotiation strategy is the practice of using the promise of negotiation itself as an inducement.* Practically, this involves demanding *prior* action by the adversary before allowing negotiations to take place; '. . . We will only agree to negotiate after our opponents have fulfilled the following list of necessary preconditions . . .' Thus, the act of negotiating becomes the reward for prior acts by the adversary, which will probably weaken their bargaining position in any negotiations that follow. Examples of this strategy in operation are numerous from a management refusing to open discussions with unions until a strike is called off, to attempts by the Greek Government to make a cessation of Turkish military activity on Cyprus a precondition for the resumption of talks about a political settlement for the island. Similarly, efforts by the Commonwealth Secretariat and UK Government to encourage discussions between the Nigerian Federal Government and Colonel Ojukwu's regime in Biafra during 1968 were wholly frustrated by the two sides' preconditions for beginning substantive negotiations. The Federal Government insisted upon a prior renunciation of secession by the Biafrans, while the Biafran leaders insisted upon a cease-fire and the withdrawal of all troops to pre-war positions as a pre-requisite for any negotiated settlement. Similar tactics were used by the Icelandic Foreign Minister at a meeting in Geneva of the UN Law of the Sea Conference in September 1975 when he announced that Iceland would only negotiate with the UK on fishing limits after the Royal Navy had been withdrawn from Icelandic waters, and the UK Government had agreed to prevent British trawlers from fishing within the 200 mile zone and to limit their future fish quota to 65,000 tons per annum. In all such cases, the choice placed before the opposing party is whether the opening of negotiations with an inevitably problematical outcome, is worth the prior sacrifice demanded. As such sacrifices often involve the surrender of objectives being sought, as well as some position of tactical advantage in the conflict (by 1968, Federal troops were well into Biafran territory), the normal reaction is a negative one. Hence, the frequent use of this tactic of offering negotiations on unacceptable prior conditions by a party not actually wishing to negotiate but wishing to avoid the general reputation for inflexibility. A frequent counter-strategy often seems to be to reply to such an offer with demands for negotiations 'without prior conditions'. The call for unconditional negotiations is often an indication that one party has worked itself into a position of tactical advantage and wishes to exploit that advantage; or that the party making such a demand is a pro-change party, trying to ensure that half its goals are not deliberately cut off from consideration as the price of merely having others discussed.

E. CONCLUSION

The pitfalls of pre-negotiation manoeuvrings are many, the largest being that a party indulging in them runs the risk of ruining any chance of substantive negotiations that may be genuinely desired. Frequently, several attempts have to be made to reach the stage of face-to-face talks on mutually satisfactory terms before success is achieved. One need only consider the series of abortive manoeuvres preceding the eventual negotiations between the French Government and the GPRA over Algerian independence, which included one occasion when GPRA delegates actually arrived in France only to return without having met French negotiators, to recognise that 'talks about talks' are likely to be long drawn-out, and frustrating for those involved.

However, many conflicts ultimately reach the point of face-to-face contacts between representative negotiators, and some even reach the stage of agreement and implementation of a compromise settlement, even though an on-off process of bargaining (along the lines of the

US–Vietnamese negotiations from 1969–72), may prolong the conflict. Our next chapter discusses in more detail the two stages of face-to-face bargaining, and implementation.

10 The Structure of Negotiations

> . . . the way negotiations are carried out is almost as important as what is negotiated. The choreography of how one enters negotiations, what is settled first and in what manner, is inseparable from the substance of the issues.
>
> Henry Kissinger (1969)

Having analysed the tactics open to both sides in the period preceding direct negotiations, we must now turn our attention to the actual process of negotiating itself, and analyse the elements in the process of settling of conflict by trading concessions and conditional promises on some bilateral basis.

There are a number of important aspects of the process of formal negotiation which will affect the success or failure of any specific case of face-to-face bargaining. However, all negotiations are alike in one fundamental fact; the process takes place within an environment of implicit threat, the ultimate sanction on the other negotiating party for not conceding a vital point being an end to negotiations and a return to some status quo from which negotiation was designed to provide an escape.

A. FACE-TO-FACE NEGOTIATIONS: STRATEGY AND STRUCTURE

Two broad strategies are open to parties approaching a negotiation to arrange a compromise settlement. The first involves an attempt to reach a settlement by 'fractionating' the conflict, the second to settle several issues simultaneously in a 'package' deal.

1. FRACTIONATING ISSUES

Those advocating a strategy of fractionating argue that splitting up the problem to be negotiated into a number of conflict dyads and taking each item issue by issue may facilitate agreement on a limited number of essentially agree-able issues. Further, such a process of extracting agreeable issues from the general context of negotiations and shelving contentious issues liable to wreck them may develop trust and a spirit of compromise among participants, so that a spill-over effect makes contentious issues less intractable at a later stage of the proceedings (Fisher, 1964).

Another advantage is that concentration on specific issues usually involves dealing with practical problems and avoiding symbolic issues or fundamental principles, which are always more difficult to compromise. Hence, the result may be a limited settlement on issues that (initially) present the best promise of agreement, and either a mutual agreement to shelve more contentious items, or a 'spill-over' effect on to contentious items, once mutual trust has been developed.

Against this position, it has been argued that the strategy of 'fractionating' a negotiation into constituent issues and concentrating upon those most amenable to compromise, often involves an avoidance of the 'core' issues of the conflict. Moreover, later settlement of the avoided issues may not occur, simply because they are much less salient to one party than to the other. Other criticisms of the strategy include the argument that, by agreeing *not* to deal with certain issues, one party may be abandoning significant leverage over the opponent. Again, isolating issues may make them more difficult to adjust and compromise over; upon any single issue A and B may have strictly opposed goals so that gain by A represents automatic loss to B. In such a situation, mutual adjustment may, in fact, become more difficult.

2. PACKAGE DEALS

An alternative strategy to that of separating the issues to be discussed is to take a fundamentally opposite course, and suggest a series of major 'package deals', involving the simultaneous settlement of a number of issues forming part of the overall conflict. The principal advantage with such a method, it is argued, is that widening the number of issues may make it possible to effect some form of 'trading', whereby losses in one area offset gains in others, and that this occurs for both parties. This is a familiar strategy in industrial conflict, known as 'log-rolling' and defined as a process whereby one party trades a concession on one issue for a reciprocal concession by its adversary on another separate issue.[1] Experience in such conflicts and also in negotiating experiments indicate that package deals and log-rolling are usually more effective in settling a conflict quickly and to all parties' mutual satisfaction than a strategy of taking a conflict issue by issue, and bargaining on each separately (Froman and Cohen, 1970). The strategy is also frequently used in multi-issue international conflicts. For example, at the Congress of Berlin in 1878 Disraeli, the British Prime Minister would only agree to discuss the independence of Rumania as part of a package deal also involving a settlement of the question of freedom for international navigation along the Danube.

3. THE BASIC SITUATION

Whatever general approaches parties use when engaged in face-to-face meetings, the structure of the negotiating situation remains basically the same:

(a) A set of conditional actions or inactions to be offered as compromises.
(b) A set of outcomes resulting from the mutual acts of both parties.
(c) A set of preferences or a scale of value underlying the range of potential outcomes, at least *ordering* the latter from most to least desirable.

The basic objective of the parties in such circumstances is to arrive at the most preferred of a set of potential circumstances, the range of which will be affected both by their own behaviour and that of the opposing party.

This basic situation can be illustrated in a number of ways. For example, a series of negotiations takes place within an industrial organisation over a new wage structure, in which one possible outcome is no change at all (the management's most preferred outcome, although other elements, such as increased productivity or minimum absenteeism might also enter in the management's overall evaluation), while another is the maximum increase demanded by the union involved (the management's least preferred outcome).[2] In between these extremes are a whole series of outcomes which could result from a negotiation, some more preferred than others by either party. The example is also based on the simplifying assumption that the management would *always* prefer to grant the least increase in wage rates possible, while the union would *always* prefer the largest increase.

The conflict is dyadic, with a single issue in negotiation. It is also unusual because the preferences of the parties negotiating are the exact reverse of each other. In other words, the conflict is one in which the gain of one party is the loss of the other. In real life, of course, one or both parties may prefer to expand the number of issues being discussed, and try to conclude a package deal involving several issues, such as more flexible working hours, longer holidays, or promises to utilise an arbitration procedure in future disputes, so that losses or gains in changing wage levels are offset by losses or gains on other issues. This sort of process will make the evaluation of potential outcomes more difficult for both sides but, nonetheless, the basic structure of the situation remains the same; a number of (more complex) potential outcomes, and at least preference orderings for both parties although probably no longer in reverse order. The negotiations between Israel and Egypt from October 1977 to 1979 may be similarly described. Both governments envisaged a set of more or less satisfactory outcomes to be negotiated, involving a number of inter-related issues; Israeli withdrawal from Sinai, Egyptian oil sales to Israel, some form of self-government for the West Bank and Gaza, some form of security for Israel in the same area, recognition of Israel's existence as a sovereign state, and others. Both could range possible outcomes on the scale of more or less desired compromises, which obviously changed for the two governments as the negotiations proceeded. Both viewed the protracted negotiations as an opportunity for obtaining the best of the possible compromise outcome by using appropriate negotiating tactics. Both arrived mutually at a settlement worse than the best possible for either, but (presumably) better than a return to the status quo ante.

More formally, the structure underlying any negotiation can be modelled as a set of potential outcomes of the negotiations, scaled for both parties in some order of preference or degree of desirability, and with some rough idea of how more or less valuable each outcome is than the others. In a situation where both sides perceive seven possible compromises, depending upon who concedes what over what issues, the initial situation takes the form illustrated in Fig. 10.1.

Note that direct comparisons cannot yet be made *between* the two scales in Fig. 10.1. The fact that outcome 4 appears roughly in the middle of both scales of desirability does not mean that they are of equal value to the two parties, but merely that, out of all the alternatives available at the start of the negotiation, 4 is roughly half as valuable as 7 to A, while 4 roughly twice as valuable as 5 to B. In fact,

4 may be a semi-disaster for B, and only a minimally satisfactory outcome to A.

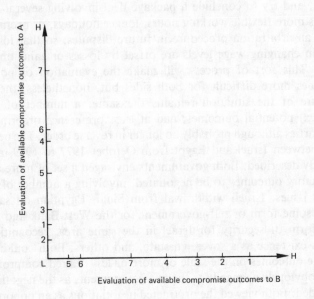

FIGURE 10.1 Initial negotiating situation

Note also, however, that it is apparently a small step in the model to considering the underlying scales of value for each separate party as being inter-changeable, so that the *utility* of particular outcomes can be compared between the parties on a shared utility scale. Whether such a step should be made is always open to question, there being a trade off between the benefits of having the aid of a more powerful analytical model in considering negotiating situations, against the disbenefits of unreality. Inter-party utilities for outcomes are not inter-changeable or directly comparable in the real world, where the only true reflection of how highly things are valued is what sacrifice of other things will be made to obtain them. However, the negotiating situation outlined in Fig. 10.1 will serve as a basis for discussing negotiating tactics open to parties seeking to achieve the best possible compromise.

B. NEGOTIATING TACTICS

Given the structure of a negotiating situation outlined above, what fundamental tactics are open to negotiators seeking their best settlement? It may be that a party enters into particular negotiations with objectives other than achieving the best possible compromise or, indeed, any compromise at all. Iklé has pointed out that parties frequently engage in sham negotiations, and that purposeful negotiations often include large symbolic elements which sometimes assume a greater importance than actually reaching agreement (Iklé, 1964). Three possible reasons are suggested for such *symbolic* negotiating:

(a) *Negotiating for side-effects: bilateral side-effects* as when negotiating can obtain a more accurate appreciation of the adversary's strengths, objectives or determination; *side-effects on third parties* where negotiations are begun to avoid a reputation for inflexibility, or to obtain a platform for making a public case, or for floating proposals and seeing how third parties react to them; or *intra-party side-effects*, when leaders negotiate to bring home the reality of some situation to followers, or to head off criticisms of intransigence from dovish factions, arguing that opportunities for compromise are being lost.

(b) *Negotiating for future effects* in order to establish some kind of 'bargaining reputation' (usually as a tough bargainer who neither bluffs nor reneges) useful for future negotiations undertaken to deal with substantive issues.

(c) *Negotiating for delay* where negotiations, or their prospect, are used to delay the adversary's vigorous prosecution of the conflict, or some feared move. Proposals are put forward not in the hope that the adversary will accept them, but to delay some coercive action, prepare a counter stroke, or provide time to plan alternatives in the breathing space provided. Soviet negotiations with Imre Nagy's Government in 1956 were undoubtedly conducted to enable the Soviets to bring in enough troops to crush the Hungarians and set up a more pro-Soviet regime.

Almost all negotiations contain elements of 'negotiating for effect', but most are mainly concerned with arriving at a settlement of the conflict in question. To achieve this, a number of basic negotiating tactics are available to parties, chief among which are attempting to alter the values assigned to outcomes by the adversary, and attempting to increase the most that the adversary will concede in return for an end to the conflict. The process of seeking the most advantageous compromise can begin even in the earliest stages of the negotiation, however, before any of the basic tactics come into play.

1. STRUCTURING THE AGENDA

We have already commented on how any substantial influence on the *contents* of the agenda (what will and, more important, will *not* be discussed), can virtually determine the course and the outcome of negotiations. Equally obviously, the order in which items are discussed may also have a significant effect upon the course of negotiations. A number of tactics can be used in 'structuring' the agenda. One 'hard-line' tactic is a party's insistence on the discussion of what it defines as salient and vital issues first, so that its own special interests can be ensured before it needs to consider concessions on other points. If the requisite results are not obtained over the issues placed first on the agenda, then the party insisting on prior discussion of these is always in a position to threaten to withdraw from the discussions without having made any concessions, and without revealing its relative indifference to matters in the latter half of the agenda. Both sides attempted to use this tactic at the Vietnam Peace Talks in Paris in 1972, the US delegates insisting upon discussing military agreements first, which would have helped to ensure the viability and survival of the South Vietnamese Government, and the North Vietnamese representatives insisting that political issues should come first on the agenda, for quite the reverse set of reasons. Finally, deadlock was only resolved by an agreement to discuss military and political issues together.[3]

An alternative method aims at developing mutual trust as discussions proceed, and resembles Fisher's strategy of 'fractionating' a multi-issue dispute into issues. Less controversial issues are taken first, in order to allow group processes and negotiating norms to develop before attempts are made to tackle sensitive items. Agreement over initial agenda items will, it is hoped, create an atmosphere which will ease the resolution of more difficult issues taken later on the agenda.

The Irish delegation to the peace talks in 1921 used this tactic to some effect in the initial stages of the conference, dealing first with what Arthur Griffiths referred to as major 'points of agreement' (Pakenham, 1972, p. 140) such as defence arrangements, future trade, sharing of war debts, and fiscal autonomy, leaving until last the difficult issues of possible dominion status for Ireland and the future of Ulster. A derivation of the more general tactic is a tacit agreement not to allow failure to agree on earlier items to preclude discussions of later items.

A somewhat more Machiavellian version of these tactics is for one side to ensure that the first items on the agreed agenda are strongly desired by its opponents, but of peripheral importance to it; and that these are followed by one or two items which are mutually important. The first side then proceeds to argue stongly over the first few issues, but ultimately 'concedes'. When the next items come up for discussion, the first party argues moderately but firmly, and does not give way. The second is then placed in the awkward position of refusing to concede on these issues, in spite of the first party's previous 'conciliatory' behaviour over the first items on the agenda. In such circumstances, various forms of psychological and practical pressures result from having to break already established negotiating norms and operate to make the second party retreat. Other problems in refusing to concede arise from the success of one party in the opening stages of a negotiation, a success which can be ensured by careful structuring of an agenda and suitable negotiating tactics. In cases of preliminary success it is important to note how the costs to an initially successful negotiator of *not* eventually achieving agreement increase the more benefits are gained in the initial stages. One always runs the risk of sacrificing apparent initial success by intransigence later. Hence, it is often possible for the opposing party to negotiate 'hard' during the final stages of negotiations, relatively safe in the knowledge that the other side has already gained high benefits from issues already discussed, and will be more likely to make sacrifices to maintain these initial gains, than might have been the case before those gains became a graspable reality. Archbishop Makarios was able to use this tactic right up to the last minute with the British Government over the detailed implementation of the 1959 London and Zurich Agreements over the future of Cyprus, safe in the knowledge that the British were unlikely to wreck the carefully negotiated tri-partite agreement for the sake of detailed items concerning British bases or economic assistance to the island (Foot, 1964, p. 184).

An extreme version of this tactic is the familiar ploy of the 'last-minute demand', presented only after other outstanding issues have been settled. It is often used in the hope that exhaustion at the end of a long negotiation will increase the temptation to accede and also, on the assumption that few negotiators will consider throwing away the benefits of a final agreement for the sake of intransigence over some last-minute addition. In more formal terms, it is hoped that the adversaries will reckon that the marginal costs of a final concession will be far exceeded by the overall benefits of the final agreement being implemented. However, the tactics may backfire if the adversary is determined to show that it is not the sort of party against whom such tactics work, or if the party using the 'ploy' is perceived as wanting the existing agreement as much as the party subject to the last-minute demand.

2. MODIFYING PREFERENCES OR DESIRABILITY

At a more analytic level, one of the fundamental tactics in negotiation is to change the way in which various outcomes are evaluated by adversaries, so that their preference ordering becomes similar to one's own. This can be achieved either by modifying the preference ordering of possible outcomes, or by altering their position on the underlying scale of desirability, so that particular outcomes are viewed as less undesirable than at the start of the negotiation. The process is illustrated in Fig. 10.2.

Major methods of changing an opponent's evaluation of outcomes involve communication and persuasion, both of which aim at modifying preferences and '. . . concern the way in which the arguments and proposals of each party are understood by the other . . .' (Sawyer and Guetzkow, 1965, p. 474). Communication becomes difficult between parties in intense conflict, so that formal negotiations may be the first opportunity for direct communication and efforts at persuasions between the parties for some time. Even in face-to-face exchanges, communication may still be hampered by conflict attitudes that develop among people engaged in any intense, long-lasting dispute. However, numerous experimental findings in small-group psychology back up diplomatic experience and common sense in proposing that, as communication increases in volume and sophistication, negotiation and compromise become easier. In many 'real-world' and experimental cases, an increase in trust and co-operation accompanies an increase in communication level and facilitates making mutual concessions.

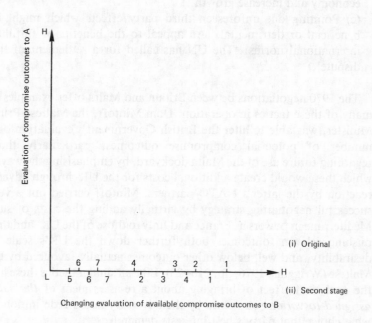

Figure 10.2 Modifying outcome evaluation

The techniques used to alter an adversary's evaluation of an existing range of alternative settlements include providing information, argument, new interpretation or hitherto hidden implications for one's opponent, in order to persuade him that there has been a misleading evaluation on his party, or to re-assess the desirability of the outcomes available. The process consists of persuading the adversary that his own self-interest is not what he thought it was, often by emphasising long-term, in contrast to short-term, benefits, but in other ways by:

(a) Persuading the adversary that the probability of some adverse reaction is much higher than he had previously estimated.
(b) Emphasising some direct benefit which had been ignored, or

perhaps under-played, by the opponent. ('Lowering arms levels will also release men from the forces into the industrial sector of your economy and increase growth'.)

(c) Pointing out unforeseen third party effects which might be beneficial or detrimental. (An appeal to the benefits of fulfilling international norms: 'The UN has called for a settlement of this dispute'.)

The 1970 negotiations between Britain and Malta offer examples of many of these tactics in operation. Dom Mintoff, the Maltese Prime Minister, was able to alter the British Government's evaluation of a number of potential compromise outcomes, particularly those regarding future use of the Malta dockyard, by emphasising the way in which these would create additional costs for the UK through adverse reaction by the latter's NATO partners. Mintoff carried out a very successful negotiating strategy by virtually adding the costs of such Mediterranean powers as France and Italy to those of the UK, and thus pushing relevant outcomes both further down the UK's scale of desirability, and well below other outcomes actually favoured by the Maltese (Wriggins, 1976, pp. 216–25). Like all similar tactics these had the analytical effect of bringing about a re-assessment of *the value assigned to various outcomes* by the adversary and a redefinition of what choice that party's best interests demanded.

However, it is highly unlikely that even the most successful 'persuader' can modify the opponent's preferences enough to make them identical with his own, especially when, as in most cases, negotiators are significantly bound by the expectations of their own constituents. Hence, some residual hard bargaining for concessions must be undertaken if a final compromise agreement is to ensue. In such circumstances, a number of alternative outcomes remain for consideration, most of which are generally acceptable, but where choice of one rather than another will result in gains for A usually at the expense of B. Here, other bargaining tactics come into play.

3. ALTERING THE AVAILABILITY OF OUTCOMES

Hard bargaining tactics frequently involve efforts to decrease or increase the number of alternative outcomes perceived as *realistically* open to an adversary. This depends upon the obvious principle that compromises depend upon the inter-dependent actions of negotiating parties, either in implementing or refraining from particular unilateral courses of action. In other words, reaching a compromise depends upon a process of '. . . We will do this if, and when you do that . . .' or '. . . If you insist upon doing that we will, reluctantly, be forced to do this . . .'. This tactic makes it possible to *reduce* the number of realistic outcomes by making some of them too costly through the addition of other conditional elements making that outcome no longer worth considering; or to *increase* the number available, by bringing in wholly new possibilities or making others more attractive so that they become realistic options for the adversary. The process is illustrated in Fig. 10.3.

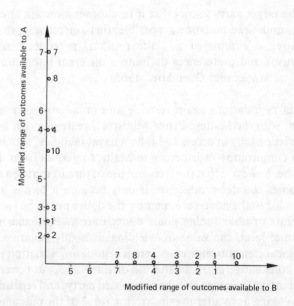

FIGURE 10.3 Altering outcome availability

A number of ways of activating either of these basic tactics are available:

(a) *Reducing Alternatives: Threats and Promises*

Threats as a means of altering the potential costs on courses of action have already been mentioned, and a similar process affects the course of face-to-face negotiation. One way of influencing the range of alternatives seriously considered by the opposing side is to threaten actions which, in the event of the opponent making undesired choices, will lead to outcomes so costly that the choice will actually be discarded. In short, while the potential mix of action and outcome will, with all logically possible outcomes included, be very large, that actually contemplated will be much smaller. One major process in any negotiation is thus to reduce the contemplated set of alternatives by the use of credible threats. (In a similar fashion, one can actually increase the number of alternative outcomes by the use of credible promises.)

> . . . The target party knows that if he chooses a certain alternative, only an undesired outcome is possible; then, effectively, that entire alternative is eliminated . . . the result is a reduced matrix of alternatives and preferences defining a different interaction situation . . . (Sawyer and Guetzkow, 1965)

The Malta negotiations again provide an example of such tactics in operation, with the Maltese Prime Minister threatening that he would allow Soviet or Libyan access to Malta's naval facilities, should he not achieve a compromise satisfactory to Malta's interests from the UK.

It may be, however, that the frequent use of threats during a negotiation becomes counter-productive, if only because it brings into play another value in the adversary, namely the desire not to be seen giving in to threats or abandoning goals under duress. Particularly at the international level, the value of 'yielding' is highly negative. Again, psychological elements may enter into a negotiating situation in which one side constantly resorts to the use of threats to win concessions.[4] Use of threats may antagonise the threatened party, and repetition may be so provoking as to alter the underlying value of the outcomes being negotiated. A particular outcome achieved after being threatened may be regarded as far more costly than the same outcome achieved in the acceptable 'give and take' of negotiation, and hence become much less desirable. Anger, desire not to concede when threatened, and rational calculation of interest may thus alter the value scale underlying a set of outcomes, and have the opposite effect from that intended. Threats may *lessen* the chances of arriving at a relatively successful accommodation, and increase the chances that the status quo will seem preferable to compromise at an otherwise acceptable outcome while being threatened.

The ultimate threat available to negotiating parties is withdrawal from the negotiations and the resumption of coercive conflict behaviour. Such a threat often forms part of an ultimatum involving a deadline. Many negotiators have used this imposition of time limits for agreement either at particular stages of the negotiations, or for the entire 'package'. The risks and advantages of this tactic are obvious. On the one hand, parties run the risk of having their bluff called by the opposing party, and then either having to retreat from a stated position, with an attendant loss of credibility, or find some ingenious excuse for continuing discussions. On the other hand, this particular form of coercion may work, and the adversary consent to a perhaps ill-considered agreement, giving a definite advantage to the party imposing the time limit. One example of such a tactic was the killingly effective ultimatum delivered by Lloyd George to the Irish delegation discussing the Anglo-Irish peace settlement, when he managed to convince them that he had to have an immediate decision on the draft treaty (because he had promised the Ulster Prime Minister the results of negotiations by the following day); that the British had said their last word; and that the alternative was that '. . . both sides would be free to resume whatever warfare they could wage against each other . . .' (Pakenham, 1972, p. 240). After an agonising night of indecision, the Irish delegation signed the agreement, and precipitated a vicious civil war in Ireland over its acceptance.

Sometimes the imposition of time limits can work to the disadvantage of the imposing party. On going to negotiate with the Viet Minh in Geneva in 1954, the French Prime Minister, M Mendes-France, publicly committed himself to the French public to bring back peace or his resignation within 30 days, a commitment the Viet Minh delegates were able to use greatly to their advantage in subsequent bargaining with the French delegation (Randle, 1969). In other circumstances, a mutually agreed time limit may heighten the sense of urgency about reaching a settlement, and be salutary for those concerned in negotiation (Walton and McKersie, 1966, p. 380), even though this does lose opportunities to explore the problem and search for an innovative solution.

(b) Faits Accomplis
In a similar, but more definite fashion, a *fait accompli* can reduce the number of possible outcomes by cutting down available courses of

action open to an adversary. As some form of inter-action between the opponents is likely to be continuing outside the negotiating chamber during the course of negotiation such a modification may occur as the balance of advantage in the dispute changes. On other occasions, a *fait accompli* eliminating certain possibilities as outcomes may be implemented deliberately to reduce the adversary's chances of bargaining over a settlement. In August 1974, for example, the Turkish delegation withdrew from the Cyprus negotiations in Geneva while their army expanded the area it controlled and fought its way south east to relieve a besieged Turkish community in Famagusta. The delegation later returned to the negotiations, having eliminated the Greek opportunity of using the Famagusta Turks as a bargaining counter, and reduced the Greek chance of arguing against a separate, consolidated Turkish enclave on the island on the grounds that it would contain a large number of Greek Cypriots. Israeli doctrines of 'creating facts' provide numerous other examples of *faits accomplis*.

Such examples give an indication of the peremptory nature of the *fait accompli* especially when used in some international negotiations. Essential elements are the ability of one party to present a more limited choice to the other party on some 'take it or leave it' basis, or at least the ability suddenly to eliminate one or more of its adversary's options and thus present a much reduced matrix of choices and possible outcomes. The risk of such a strategy is that the very fact of being presented unilaterally with this reduced choice may so antagonise the adversary that the goal of punishing the other side becomes more attractive and the party's preference ordering changes adversely.

(c) *Increasing Alternatives: Creative Problem-Solving*

In many negotiating situations it is often the case that there is no outcome that *both* parties would prefer to no agreement and a return to the status quo. Given that both have made a careful evaluation of the apparently available range of outcomes, and that their preference ordering and underlying evaluation are not open to any substantial change by persuasion or communication, the only possibility for some final compromise settlement is the emergence of yet further outcomes offering advantages to both sides, or increased values to one party without diminishing those for the other. Development of further alternatives involving innovation rather than selection from existing alternatives, has been called 'creative problem-solving' and contrasted with the 'normal' bargaining process occurring in most negotiations.

'Creative problem-solving' can be illustrated by relaxing our previous proviso about the non-interchangeability of parties' evaluations of outcomes, and imagining the admittedly unreal case of there being a single, shared utility scale. (The nearest real-world conflict to such a model might be a wage-bargaining situation where both parties valued monetary units similarly.) There is always a physical limit to the amount of values available to be shared at any one time, represented by a *utility frontier*. Creative problem-solving can be represented by moving this utility frontier beyond its location which sets limits on what kinds of compromise outcomes can be obtained at the opening of negotiations. Developing new alternative outcomes, the frontier can be moved to include solutions that increase gains all round, as in Fig. 10.4.

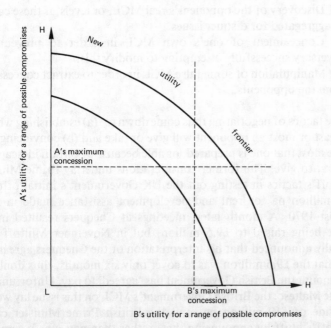

FIGURE 10.4   Increasing the bargaining range via creative problem-solving

4. MANIPULATING MAXIMUM CONCESSION LEVELS

The final major tactic open to those seeking the best compromise is to change the point at which the opponent would prefer no agreement, to a compromise so costly and unpopular as to be not worth having.[5] This Maximum Level of Concession (MCL) a party is prepared to make in order to achieve some form of settlement is obviously flexible and depends upon the fortunes of the party up to the point of negotiation. As a general rule, a party's MCL will be lower, and it will accept more sacrifices for a settlement, the greater its position of disadvantage outside the negotiating chamber. Furthermore, one party's MCL is closely related to its estimate of its opponent's; how much a party will be willing to take will depend upon its estimate of how much its opponent is willing to give.

A major part of a negotiating process is therefore:

(a) Discovery of the opponent's real MCL, or levels, if these can be disaggregated for distinct issues.

(b) Concealment of one's own MCL in order to prevent the adversary successfully attempting to modify this.

(c) Manipulation of some false MCL in order to extract concessions from the opponents.

The tactics of negotiating thus come down to: (a) establishing what is the least or most an opponent will give or take and (b) convincing him of the most that one is prepared, or able because of certain inescapable factors, to give. The former considerations underlay Prime Minister Mintoff's tactics in testing out the UK Government's initial offer of £8.5 million pa for rent and development assistance made in mid-August 1970. A month later, meetings at Chequers resulted in the figure being raised to £9.5 million, but in November Mintoff unilaterally announced that his interpretation of the Chequers agreement was that the £9.5 million was to cover only six months, thus doubling the amount the British Government has 'agreed' to pay. Unfortunately for the Maltese, the British Government's MCL on this issue lay well to one side of £19 million pa, and the British Prime Minister called Mintoff's bluff by announcing that, rather than pay such a sum, the British would, indeed, withdraw from Malta (Wriggins, 1976, pp. 225–7).

A further complexity may therefore be added to the basic structure of a negotiating situation, given that both parties will probably know their own MCL[6] but will often only have some rough conception of the position of their adversary's MCL. Each party's *perceived* MCL for its adversary may be more or less accurate depending upon the optimism or pessimism with which the adversary's bargaining position is viewed. Figure 10.5 illustrates two pessimistic estimates.

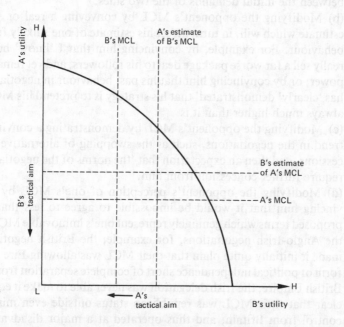

FIGURE 10.5   Actual and perceived bargaining ranges

The precise techniques used to modify the opponent's MCL or the opponent's estimate of one's own MCL, vary widely and include:

(a) Initiating negotiations with a 'prominent demand' as one's initial position. This tactic is especially profitable in negotiations involving status quo and pro-change parties, where the former's

MCL and its initial bargaining position *is* the status quo. (It is rarely the case that a status quo party can use the tactics of reverting to an even more conservative pre-status quo proposal from which to make bargaining 'concessions'.) In such a case, the pro-change party will be able to make an initial 'prominent demand' from which it can go to meet its adversary halfway by making public, if sham, concessions. This puts pressure on the status quo party to 'reciprocate', as it is often assumed that a 'fair' agreement should lie somewhere between the initial demands of the two sides.

(b) Modifying the opponent's MCL by conveying a real or sham estimate which will, in turn, affect his estimate of one's likely future behaviour. For example, by convincing him that I 'know' he can really sell a far worse package deal to his followers, and yet remain in power; or by convincing him that his past behaviour in negotiations has 'clearly' demonstrated' that his strategy is to pretend his MCL is always much higher than it is.

(c) Modifying the opponent's MCL by demonstrating a convincing trend in the negotiations, such as the swopping of alternative concessions, and then an expectation that 'the norms of the negotiation' require further concession from him.

(d) Modifying the opponent's perception of one's MCL by convincing him that it would be impossible to agree to less than the proposed terms which genuinely represent one's immovable MCL. In the Anglo-Irish negotiations, for example, the British negotiators made it initially quite plain that their MCL was allowing Eire some form of political independence short of complete separation from the British Empire; the Irish delegation was never able to make it equally clear that their MCL was republican status outside even minimal control from Britain, and thus operated at a major disadvantage throughout the discussions (Pakenham, 1972, pp. 250–2).

(e) Modifying the opponent's perception of the MCL by exhibiting attitudes, statements or behaviour consistent with one even more intransigent than the opponent's current estimates.

Putting forward a falsely favourable MCL can be part of a more complex tactic involving the construction of a wholly sham bargaining position with which to confront a negotiating adversary. In adopting this tactic, one party attempts not only to project its MCL at a higher level than reality, but also puts forward an initial set of demands well beyond what the opponent's MCL is judged to be. As in Fig. 10.6 the entire projected bargaining range of one party is shifted further into the opponent's set of preferred outcomes, in the hope of convincing the adversary that one's MCL is higher than in reality, and providing a number of harmless and low cost 'concessions' that can be 'grudgingly' abandoned in exchange for similar concessions by the adversary.

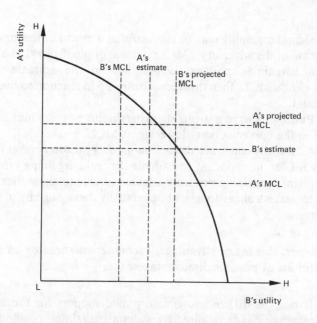

FIGURE 10.6   Actual, perceived and projected bargaining ranges

In plain language, one party 'asks high' and pretends its maximum concessions are small, in order to convince the opposing party that it has little room for flexibility, concession or manoeuvre. In one sense, the adoption of a sham bargaining position is an extension of Schelling's strategy of 'commitment', applied to face-to-face negotiations. Thus, when a concession is actually made, whether it is a sham concession or – at a later stage, if bluffs have been called – a real one, the object is to make this appear a substantial, and probably final retreat. The extent of the 'sacrifice', it is implied, should be appreciated and reciprocated by any reasonable adversary.

A number of advantages and disadvantages attend the use of such negotiating tactics, and their relative success varies. Advantages include:

(a) Sham bargaining may be successful as a means of testing out an estimate of the adversary's MCL; if it was originally too low and the sham bargaining position is well beyond the estimate of the opponent's MCL, then this should show up in reaction to the initial demand.

(b) Putting forward a strong sham bargaining position may actually lead to the opposing party lowering its MCL.

(c) A carefully constructed sham bargaining position makes it more difficult for an opponent to estimate the real bargaining range.

(d) Sham bargaining positions enable one side to show 'flexibility' and to make 'concessions' without actually damaging any of its real interests.

However, this list of advantages is counter-balanced by an equally powerful list of possible disadvantages:

(1) It may be difficult to obtain public support for the kind of 'extreme' demands required by a sham bargaining position, both within one's own party and from third parties whose tacit approval may be essential for final agreement.

(2) Once public support has been roused for an extreme sham bargaining position, it may be difficult to placate later, should 'concessions' have to be made. If rank-and-file followers accept the sham bargaining range and false MCL as 'real', leaders may find themselves in a self-made trap, and be unable to retreat from publicly reiterated positions.

(3) The use of such tactics may cause the opposing party to feel that negotiations are hopeless, with no chance for concessions or agreement, and discussions may be terminated, which may have been the original intention!

(4) Sham bargaining positions may delay agreement, which, again, may have been the intention underlying their use.

(5) The tactic of using sham concessions, may initially demonstrate flexibility, but also set a dangerous precedent for real concessions at a later stage of the discussions. In addition, the party adopting such tactics may gain a bargaining reputation for not holding firmly to its initial position; on later occasions it may wish to do just that.

C. NEGOTIATING STRUCTURE: SOME MODIFICATIONS

The discussion so far contains a number of unreal elements, and needs modification to make the analysis resemble real-world negotiations. For one thing, concentrating upon a model of two negotiating parties consciously choosing optimum or, at least, satisfactory outcomes on the basis of unified preferences puts the analysis straight back into a *Rational Actor* framework. For another, little has been said about the actual negotiators themselves, or about the question of secrecy in negotiations. Finally, the assumption that negotiations invariably occur bilaterally needs to be questioned, given the prevalence of multi-party negotiations, especially at the international level.

1. FACTIONALISM AND INTER-PARTY NEGOTIATION

Abandoning *Rational Actor* assumptions about negotiation emphasises that a major problem for conflicting parties in carrying through negotiations arises from intra-party factionalism, and competing intra-party preference orderings. These are as much a part of negotiation as they are of overall conflict termination.

Factionalism inevitably affects intra-party consensus about any negotiation. It will often have a major impact upon the constraints facing each party's representatives and hence its negotiating position. If intra-party unity can be maintained during delicate negotiations, then the negotiator runs small risk of having his bargaining position undermined by factional disagreements over priorities and preferences for goals, general bargaining behaviour, or MCL. Intra-party disunity is likely to affect negotiations where one party to the dispute has no agreed central leadership, where the degree of intra-party factionalism is high, although formal leaders exist, or where the leadership are in a precarious position in the formal hierarchy of government, community or organisation. (For example, in cases where a national government faces a powerful and critical opposition party, and continued office depends upon maintaining support from a wavering or volatile constituency.) However, the problem of intra-party relations is one that affects every party to a conflict, no matter how hierarchically organised or initially integrated. In negotiation it typically takes the form of a leadership dilemma in convincing rank-and-file followers that the stage has been reached when it is necessary to abandon some goals as a concession to the adversary. In industrial conflicts, this lack of consensus between leaders and followers regarding the need for concessions during negotiations often results from their different structural positions within the party, which lead to differing evaluations of proposals, and the feasibility of achieving goals, or resisting the demands of the adversary (Walton, 1965a). Four possible reasons for this discrepancy are that leaders:

(1) Are more sensitive to issues of an 'institutional' character (precedents, public image, future bargaining reputation, and comparison with other groups).

(2) Can better judge the full implications of some issues (a complex productivity agreement, or an agreement for arms control), while followers can often better estimate the precise impact on their particular aspirations of those parts of an agreement directly affecting them.

(3) Often have more information about their adversary's preferences, MCL and resources, more opportunity to test out their hunches, and more skill in interpreting clues about their adversary's perceptions and aspirations.

(4) Are often more calculating, and can better appreciate the effects of the range of sanctions both sides can invoke, should no settlement result. Such sanctions, if invoked, will often have differential effects upon goals of leaders and followers.

Typically, '. . . a leader has a more realistic view of the situation, considerably in advance of his membership . . .' (Walton, 1965b, p. 4), so that there arises the problem of how to achieve sufficient consenus supporting leaders' view of their party's negotiating position. Intra-party bargaining then becomes crucial for the eventual outcome of the inter-party negotiations.

One skill of a negotiator thus becomes allowing for the configuration of factions and interests that combine within an adversary, and the way in which the negotiating position of the other may change as the balance of forces changes. (Naturally, the same is usually true of the negotiator's own party, and this has led some practitioners to argue that no negotiating position should ever be regarded as fixed, even in the short run, and even for one's own side.)[7] The task of negotiators is thus to '. . . understand the complex motivations and personalities that have gone into the establishment of a position . . .', or else run a greater risk of failure (Barnett, 1971, p. 106).

One basic problem, however, remains how the various factions within their party can be successfully manipulated both prior to, and during the negotiation, so that:

(1) Followers' aspirations, and behaviour reinforce, rather than work against, the negotiating position and tactics adopted by leaders.
(2) Actual negotiators remain isolated from constituencies' efforts to influence their strategies and objectives within the inter-party negotiating process.

Leadership efforts to change intra-party factors assume that they can be used to reinforce, rather than hinder negotiating tactics against the adversary. Raising members' aspirations can support or 'justify' the making of higher demands for concessions. Increasing levels of hostility can create an atmosphere in which leaders' ambitious demands and coercive threats are both more appropriate and justifiable in the eyes of constituents, and more credible in the eyes of the opponents. On the other hand, lowering aspirations and antagonistic feelings may permit the negotiator to behave flexibly, and make concessions deemed necessary.

A wide variety of tactics are available to a leadership group attempting to increase or maintain a high level of intra-party support during negotiations with an adversary. Often, many of the apparently illogical and incomprehensible acts and statements made by leaders engaged in negotiations are symbolic and designed to influence factions and followers within their own party, rather than the adversary with whom negotiations are being conducted:

(a) Creating a low level of expectations among constituents (unless it is desired to create a high level, to emphasise the impossibility of concession to the adversary), so that a poor settlement will be accepted, and a better one appear a triumph.
(b) Excluding individuals and factions from the planning stage

when the initial negotiating position is developed, or from the actual process of negotiation, if it is feared that they would urge higher, or more moderate, demands and more militant, or accommodating, tactics. The danger is that, having been excluded from participation in the negotiation, rival factions might find it easier to condemn eventual agreement between the parties.

(c) Bringing into more direct contact with the adversary those who either doubt the opponent's strength or determination or have an exaggerated idea of the opponent's reasonableness, depending upon whether the leadership's critics are more, or less extreme in their demands.

(d) Invoking personal prestige or political influence to bring dissenting factions into line with leadership views and strategies.

(e) Indulging in 'ceremonial hard-bargaining' to demonstrate that concessions have not been given away without a fight, and that considerable thought and effort have gone into any final agreement.

(f) Indulging in 'going-through-the-motion' bargaining in the initial stages of discussions, but making plain to the adversary that, while appearing to conform completely to constituents' views on basic negotiating positions, nevertheless this is merely a public preliminary to genuine efforts to settle the dispute.

(g) Trying to prevent expectations within the party rigidifying until the negotiating position and strategy of the adversary are clear.

(h) Tacit exchanges with the adversary's negotiator in order to facilitate the communication of *different* information to the opponent and one's own followers. This may be another aspect of informing the adversary that symbolic negotiating behaviour is not to be taken seriously, but it also represents an attempt to signal two ways, and by controlling communication to control also the way in which the adversary and rank-and-file followers learn of each other's views and aspirations, levels of expectation, or attitudes.

Apart from using some of the tactics mentioned above for creating the highest possible level of intra-party consensus, leadership groups usually indulge in efforts to 'manage' available news about the negotiations in order to minimise their own dilemma. This 'news management' occurs whether negotiations are planned to take place in complete secrecy, or whether open or 'leaked' information is being used by negotiators to affect intra-party views and attitudes. Leaders may carry out this strategy in a variety of ways: making public or suppressing information about the discussion; emphasising, or playing down, certain aspects of the negotiation; providing 'background' information, so that news of the discussions can be interpreted within the 'correct' setting; or demonstrating sustained or momentary attention to various aspects of the negotiation process.

2. NEGOTIATORS: DELEGATES OR LEADERS?

Another aspect of maintaining intra-party consensus is the question of who should attend discussions to negotiate an agreement on behalf of the party. Anecdotal hypotheses have been offered concerning whether the attendance of 'top' political leaders (President, Prime Minister, Union General Secretary), as opposed to delegated representatives, makes any substantial difference to the course and outcome of the negotiations. These sometimes contradictory guidelines include hypotheses that:

(a) Top decisionmakers will not commit their personal prestige to discussions unless some settlement has already been substantially agreed by subordinates, so that success and the prestige that goes with success are largely assured.

(b) In certain circumstances, only the presence of top decision-makers will assure the adversary that one side is taking the chance of a negotiated settlement seriously.

(c) The presence of leader–negotiators is an assurance that any agreements reached through negotiation will be accepted as binding by the party making them.

(d) Delegate–negotiators will slow down the process of negotiation, as they are inevitably less flexible than a leader–negotiator (often having to refer back to the leadership for instructions in unforeseen circumstances), especially when provided with a rigid brief from which deviations are not allowed save with express permission. On the other hand, having to refer back to absent leaders can be an advantage for parties who wish to avoid hasty decisions or delay making concessions. Certainly De Valera's absence from the 1921 peace talks was an advantage for the Irish delegation on occasions, although the weapon backfired on them at the crucial moment in the talks.

Such propositions stem from experience in diplomatic and industrial negotiations, and tend to emphasise the relative freedom enjoyed by the negotiator who is also the leader of his party. The argument is often put forward that the success of some negotiations and the failure of others is related to the relative degree of freedom to bargain, manoeuvre and make commitments enjoyed by the leader–negotiator, but lacking in the delegate–negotiator. The constraints of the 'delegate role', and the obligations and stresses inherent in being held responsible for the outcome by superiors and constituents, yet not possessing the necessary authority to compromise, change tactics or make concessions solely in the light of one's own judgement, make it less likely that a negotiation will arrive at a satisfactory settlement. Delegate–negotiators are assumed to be far more cautious in making concessions than leader–negotiators, who are less likely to be called to account by irate superiors, and will have a better chance of handling subsequent discontent. Informal observations from real-world negotiations are supported by evidence from laboratory experiments, several of which show that the obligations of being a 'representative' negotiator for a group militate against making concessions to an adversary, and make deadlock in negotiating games more likely. Even in experimental situations where ending in a deadlock is specifically discouraged, delegate–negotiators as opposed to those who are *not* delegated specific responsibility for outcomes by their constituents, tend to minimise the maximum concessions of each party needed to achieve an outcome, and indulge in 'hard-bargaining' (Druckman, 1973).

On the other hand, there have been numerous occasions when negotiators have agreed to substantial concessions, only to have the settlement repudiated by an absent leader on their return. The classic example of this was De Valera's refusal to accept the Anglo-Irish Peace Treaty negotiated by an Irish delegation led by Arthur Griffiths and Michael Collins, a refusal that led ultimately to the splitting of the Dial Eirann and the Irish Civil War. The balance of pro and con for leaders *not* being present as negotiators is ambiguous.

3. SECRECY

One of the main means by which pressure on leader – or delegate – negotiators can be minimised is for discussions to occur in private, or even for the fact of their taking place being kept secret. Both strategies avoid any chance of intra-group processes having much effect upon negotiations. In formal terms, secret negotiations maximise the separation between the processes of inter-group bargaining and accommodation, and those of intra-group consensus-building and maintenance. Separation of the two processes may be both physical and temporal. In the latter case, leaders can actually conclude a tacit agreement, and then announce to their followers that they are about to enter into negotiations with an adversary. In these circumstances, leaders can concentrate upon influencing the aspirations and behaviour of their constituents, and bringing them into line with what the leaders regard as realistic expectations.

Secret negotiations also offer considerable advantages to leaders by enabling them to concentrate on inter-group bargaining. They permit fuller and free exploration of the dispute, but enable a negotiator to employ the tactics of pointing out what would happen if his constituents actually became aware of, or involved in, the process of reaching a settlement. For example, that membership aspirations would be more ambitious and less flexible than his own, or members would demand broader participation in discussions, thereby making agreement more difficult.

Conventional wisdom about public and private diplomacy at the international level offers some support for these ideas. The Wilsonian doctrine of 'open covenants openly arrived at' has been replaced by an acknowledgement that the more private the discussions, the more flexible and thorough the search for solutions. Little is expected from formal public conferences save 'playing to the international gallery' and the production of propaganda to impress some internal or international audience.

Other advantages of private discussions are that they may permit the making of specific concessions to the adversary without loss of prestige. While visible concessions from a stated, public position are likely to lead to intra-party dissent, 'invisible' concessions do not carry quite the same risk. Secrecy normally permits a wide variety of 'acts of accommodation' in international diplomacy, provided it also:

(a) Allows a negotiator to convey to the other negotiator that the concessions have the support of his own group.
(b) Diminishes the likelihood of the accommodative acts appearing as a 'sell-out'.
(c) Enables a negotiator to explain his actions in terms which accord with his constituents' own values and aspirations.

In short, '. . . the same compromise arrived at secretly may not look nearly as bad as if arrived at openly . . .' (Druckman, 1973, p. 50).

4. 'SELLING' THE FINAL AGREEMENT

Many tactics for maintaining intra-party consensus become relevant when a compromise has been concluded and the negotiators' final problem is having the agreement accepted by members of their party, or ensuring that the provisions are successfully put into effect. The problems of 'selling' a final agreement to the party rank-and-file, rival intra-party factions and even the leadership group itself, are often difficult for negotiators, who have been engaged in long face-to-face discussions, and who may have built up a stable and comprehensive set of negotiating norms with their adversaries. The problem is often compounded by members' aspirations and expectations being inevitably higher than an eventual compromise settlement, even when a party negotiates from the most adverse of circumstances. (Parties negotiating from weakness as well as strength often have inflated ideas about the possibility of successful outcomes from a negotiated settlement.) Hence, the ultimate problem for negotiators is how to persuade the bulk of their party to accept the terms of an almost inevitably disappointing compromise.

Tactics available to negotiators wishing to minimise intra-party influence on the process of negotiation are also relevant to 'selling' a settlement. Tacit agreement by a successful party not to over-emphasise its gains outside the circle of its own membership, and perhaps not even there, help to make the unsuccessful party appear less unsuccessful. Symbolic concessions can help to make a relatively unequal compromise settlement appear more equal in its distribution of benefits. Other tactics include:

(a) Shifting the blame for failure onto other groups, possibly intra-party rivals, or onto structural factors beyond the negotiators' control.

(b) Establishing tacit agreements with the adversary about publicising the progress and the outcome of negotiations.

(c) Using unwritten agreements to cover any concessions that would be repudiated by rank-and-file membership, or by rival factions.

(d) Misrepresenting the level of achievement from the negotiations, by exaggerating minor items conceded by and minimising concessions made to the adversary.

Dealing successfully with rival factions presents more of a problem, as these groups are likely to be better informed than the rank-and-file, and also to have a vested interest in creating trouble for the party leadership, sometimes to the extent of repudiating the negotiated settlement as a 'sell-out'. Two broad strategies for dealing with such rival factions are common. One is to exclude rival factions from accurate knowledge of the course and outcome of the negotiations, thus blunting criticism. This is a dangerous strategy to pursue, particularly as regards the result of any negotiations. Secret results are in themselves suspicious, and suspicion usually leads to harmful rumour, damaging criticism and, ultimately, disastrous discovery. An alternative strategy is to involve rival factions in the responsibility for the final outcome, thus disarming possible criticism by sharing responsibility for any perceived failure among leadership factions. If this can be done without allowing any rival faction to affect the course of the negotiations in any significant manner, then leaders have achieved a master-stroke of intra-party politics against a presumably unwary opposition. By including rival factions in the responsibility for the agreement, while excluding them from its actual formulation, negotiators have the best of both worlds. There have been numerous examples of negotiators 'taking along' representatives of rival intra-party factions to inter-party negotiations, and then not allowing them into negotiating sessions. For example, when negotiating what he knew would be a highly unpopular *detente* with Kenya at Arusha in 1967, the Somali Prime Minister, Mohammed Ibrahim Egal, made sure that his delegation contained representatives of all significant Somali political factions. The latter were subsequently assumed to have endorsed the eventual Memorandum signed between the two governments, and to be committed to implementing its provisions. It is not, however, clear what influence any of the Somali delegation had on the terms of the Memorandum, which was promptly branded a 'sell-out' of national interests by Somali public opinion, once the provisions were published.

5. MULTILATERAL NEGOTIATION

So far, negotiation processes have been treated as though they merely involved two parties that might, it is true, be troubled with internal divisions, but which, nonetheless, could be treated as unified entities in their inter-action with one another. We have also implicitly assumed that no factions within the two negotiating parties could break away and conduct their own separate discussions, nor communicate with one another without the knowledge of their formal leaders or negotiating representatives; and that the roughly hierarchical organisation of the two involved parties would be maintained during negotiations, enabling some form of generally acceptable settlement to be concluded and later implemented.

It hardly needs pointing out that such a model of negotiating is grossly oversimplified. A major oversimplification is that negotiations to settle a dispute, particularly at the international level, seldom involve just two parties, but a number, each with separate interests and objectives, which may coincide or conflict. In many cases, the typical ending of a serious dispute is a formal 'peace conference', or a series of separate, but related, negotiations about different aspects of a complex set of issues in conflict. The ending of British colonial rule in Africa during the 1950s and 1960s was accompanied by a long series of conferences in London, attended by representatives of different parties involved in disputes about de-colonisation. Similarly, negotiations about the future of Cyprus, following the success of the EOKA campaign in the mid-1950s involved a series of conferences which were attended by representatives of the UK, Greek and Turkish Governments, as well as the leaders of the two communities (Greek and Turkish) on the island, and various factions and interests within those two communities.

Increasing the number of participants inevitably complicates the process of negotiation. Each new party brings in new views about desirable outcomes, different preference orderings regarding available solutions, and fresh patterns of contingent behaviour which other participants have to weigh in their evaluations of likely outcomes and advisable negotiating stances. The presence of more than two parties at a negotiation may be beneficial, by increasing the number of potential gains available through a package deal. It may be harmful, in that it reduces the already limited amount of benefits available for distribution. It may be disastrous for parties in a relatively weak bargaining position, who find their potential gains being reduced by the presence of a more powerful partner, willing to sacrifice their benefits in order to achieve its own goals, and then impose the final settlement on reluctant dependents. In general, the presence of a large number of roughly equal negotiating parties makes the finding of a compromise satisfactory to all more difficult, even when some parties possess complementary goals, and reduces the number of issues about which satisfactory agreements can be reached (a type of 'lowest denominator' outcome). By contrast, discussions involving a number of unequal parties often produce a solution satisfactory to the more powerful, but which has to be imposed upon the weaker parties, often more directly involved in some of the issues in conflict, but who make the sacrifices necessary to achieve a 'compromise'. Brest Litovsk was formally a negotiation between Bolshevik Russia and the four equal members of the Quadruple Alliance, but somehow Austrian, Bulgarian and Turkish interests tended to be sacrificed if they clashed with the interests of the German High Command.

While neither of these general principles may apply to specific cases of multilateral negotiations, experience of both international and intra-national negotiations indicates that there is some truth in both. (The conferences to end both World Wars were dominated by the interests of the victorious Great Powers − and even some of the minor 'victors' found their own objectives being sacrificed in the interests of a 'satisfactory' peace treaty.) Even if the parties to the negotiation are arranged in formal alliances there will always be the problem of managing to achieve − and maintain − a common bargaining position against an adversary whose interests obviously lie in breaking up the unity of the opposing coalition.

A major point in analysing the general process of negotiation is, therefore, that settlements are often negotiated through bilateral bargaining between adversaries, but an equally common structure for negotiations consists of a number of parties with differing interests, arranged in rival coalitions, attempting to achieve some settlement most favourable to their own particular interests. This seems a far more realistic model of many negotiations at the international level; of industrial collective bargaining where numerous firms can be involved in negotiations with several rival unions, with occasional interventions from government departments; and of intra-organisational conflicts which involve coalitions of different departments and individuals within the same firm. Multilateral negotiations, apart from being common at many social levels, are inevitably more complex than bilateral negotiations, and any analysis of 'multilateral diplomacy' and similar processes necessarily involves factors such as the process of coalition formation within rival 'parties', the distribution of resources within various negotiating alignments, and the role of 'brokers', mediators, or other third party intermediaries within rival coalitions attempting to reach some comprehensive settlement.

D. CONCLUSION

Introducing the conception of intermediaries in multilateral negotiation emphasises that efforts to terminate conflict and achieve some form of settlement frequently involve some third party, separate from the rival protagonists, and relatively non-committed in the conflict. The nature of real-world conflicts often make it unlikely that parties who have been employing coercion or violence in an attempt to achieve success can reach some compromise settlement unaided, through a process of bilateral negotiation. This principle holds true whether we consider two unified and cohesive adversaries or two loosely structured and internally divided coalitions; or whether we are dealing with international disputes, such as the 'Cod War', communal conflicts, such as that on Cyprus, or industrial disputes such as that between workers and management in Chrysler (UK). In many such cases, the use of mediators, conciliators, arbitrators and other forms of intermediary, underlines that the business of ending conflicts often becomes a triangular process, involving some third party with an interest in bringing the conflict to an end. The remainder of this study concerns the problem of containing conflict and, more specifically, the role played by various third parties in the containment, settlement or resolution of social and international conflicts.

Part IV: Containing Conflict

11 Managing Conflict

... Parliament is, after all, a substitute for violence, a natural safety valve. If MPs abuse each other, we should not be so refined as to wish to eradicate it ...

Julian Critchley MP

Part III dealt with the process of bringing a conflict to an end through bilateral bargaining, tacit or face-to-face. Parties attempt to develop a solution to their conflict by trading threats, promises or concessions, and using conflict behaviour to manoeuvre the conflict into a state where a best solution, from their viewpoint, can be obtained. 'Solutions' can thus cover a wide range of end states for a conflict. Five basic ones may be distinguished:

(a) Victory for one party with all goals achieved, and defeat for the other.

(b) Destruction of one party, or the incorporation of its remnants in another entity, probably the victor.

(c) Isolation, withdrawal or disengagement, whereby conflict behaviour is suspended and inter-action between the parties ceases, although the situation of goal-incompatibility remains.[1]

(d) Settlement, or accommodation, whereby some compromise solution is achieved 'splitting the differences', and allowing both parties to achieve some of their objectives, even if on an unequal basis.

(e) Resolution, whereby the sources of the conflict situation itself are removed, rather than the behavioural or attitudinal components being altered. Both parties achieve mutual gains, or a new range of benefits.

In a paradoxical way, therefore, the entire conflict process can be regarded as an attempt to achieve a solution to the conflict, even though this 'solution' may involve the enforced submission or even annihilation of the opposing party. However, such one-sided solutions arrived at by purely bilateral means on some rule-less, free-for-all basis are not the only way in which parties or societies cope with conflicts, or bring them to a conclusion.

1. TRIADIC MANAGEMENT PROCESSES

Up to this point, we have analysed efforts to end conflicts as two-party processes, essentially without acknowledged rules or limitations on behaviour. However, alternative processes for ending conflicts may involve the existence and activation of accepted rules or norms, or the involvement of some third party, which intervenes in the conflict with the intention of removing the basic situation of conflict, or bringing a particular form of conflict behaviour to an end. Such third party involvements are often attempted when bilateral inter-actions have become disruptive for the remainder of the society. They create a major change in the structure of any conflict where '. . . the basic interaction changes from a dyad to a triad . . .' (Barkun, 1964, p. 8).

Thus, coping with conflicts involves a number of possible structures, depending upon the number of parties involved in the search for a solution, and the relationships of the parties involved:

(a) Bilateral structure, consisting solely of the parties directly involved as adversaries.

(b) Triadic egalitarian structure, where the third party is (formally, at least) of equivalent status of the adversaries, and acts as a facilitator in seeking a solution, rather than a superior imposing a compromise according to some implicit or explicit rules.[2] (This does not preclude the imposition of some 'solution' by a formally equal but actually superior third party.)

(c) Triadic hierarchical structure, where the third party occupies a superior position, role or status within some organisation or society to which the adversaries belong.

Alternatively, arrangements for ending conflicts may be viewed according to whether the processes of searching for a solution involve known and accepted rules, applied by some third party, see Table 11.1. All or any of these procedures may be used by parties who are in a situation of goal incompatibility and subsequent pattern of conflict behaviour, and who wish to end their conflict with some greater or lesser degree of perceived success. However, ending a conflict once begun deals only with the manifest stage of a conflict, and is only one aspect of the process of *managing conflict*. This phenomenon is far more complex than merely waiting until a conflict has developed to a manifest stage, and then trying to bring that stage to an end by compromise.

TABLE 11.1   Ending conflict

No. of parties	Third party role		Conflict behaviour	Likely solutions
Two	Nil	(1)	Unrestricted bargaining: coercion, collaboration or conciliation; may involve use/threat of violence	Isolation/withdrawal. Destruction. Victory/defeat. Settlement, via a negotiated compromise
	Audience	(2)	Restricted by a framework of norms, rules or third party expectations (e.g. strikes, elections, duals)	Victory/defeat. Settlement
Three or more	Intermediary and conciliatory	(3)	Some restrictions provided by presence and actions of third party, but no rule application or legalised sanction by intermediary	Mediated settlement or resolution
	Arbitral or judicial	(4)	Highly restricted by known and formal rules, backed by sanctions for non-conformity	Arbitration award. Legal settlement

2. MANAGING CONFLICT

Most social systems, however simple, possess a range of mechanisms or procedures, either built into the social structure, or consciously employed by members, that help in *containing* conflict situations that inevitably arise between different entities within the society, or in *limiting* the destructive effects of ensuing conflict behaviour. Whether explicit or implicit, the effectiveness of such conflict management procedures can be measured in two ways; their success, in helping parties possessing incompatible goals to find some solution to their conflict, and (if some solution largely satisfactory cannot be found), in limiting the behaviour employed by adversaries during their processes of tacit bargaining, in order to minimise the disruption stemming from the existence of a conflict. In terms familiar to students of International Relations, 'coping with conflict' involves efforts both to achieve pacific settlement of disputes, and to maintain the peace and security of the society itself.

A wide variety of procedures exist to manage conflict, even within similar social systems. Hence, any simple description of 'conflict-containing' procedures is by no means easy. The boundaries of the field are hardly well-defined, and relevant processes and methods not classified in any straightforward manner. A further difficulty is that any number of labels tend to be used indiscriminately. The generic title of *conflict management* is often used interchangeably with other terms, such as 'conflict control', 'conflict regulation', and 'conflict resolution'.

In chapter 1 we referred to the way in which a society attempts to deal with its inter-party conflicts as *conflict management*, and this term will be used to refer to the whole range of techniques employed in any society (a) to prevent the development of conflict situations; or (once these have developed), (b) to prevent them resulting in disruptive and widely destructive conflict behaviour; or (once this has arisen), (c) to halt the undesired conflict behaviour, or remove its source, through some form of settlement agreement, or resolution of the conflict.

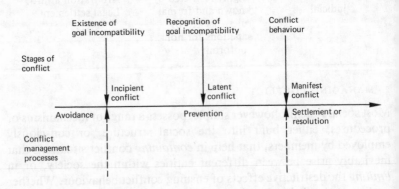

FIGURE 11.1 The sequence of conflict management techniques

This threefold classification of conflict management procedures can easily be related to the developmental continuum of stages in a conflict outlined in chapter 3. (Conflicts will cross the thresholds of that continuum when relevant techniques of conflict management fail to operate successfully at particular stages.) Thus, any processes operating to avoid the development of contentious issues and goal incompatibilities represent *conflict avoidance*; any which contribute to the prevention of undesirable conflict behaviour once some situation of goal incompatibility has arisen, *conflict prevention*; and any activated at the manifest stage, when a conflict involves incompatible goals, hostile attitudes and disruptive behaviour either *conflict settlement*, or, in special circumstances, *conflict resolution*, see Fig. 11.1.

The four processes are the general focus in the remainder of this chapter, and a more detailed analysis of third party approaches to conflict settlement and resolution will be undertaken in the last.

A.   AVOIDING CONFLICT

As the name suggests, mechanisms and processes used for *conflict avoidance* within a society attempt to find some 'solution' by preventing conflicts ever arising. This may seem less paradoxical if our original triadic model of the structure of a conflict is recalled, which makes clear that methods of managing conflict within a society can concentrate upon one or all of its three components. An approach which directs major efforts towards dealing with conflict situations and their development is merely a recognition of the importance of this and every other component, see Fig. 11.2.

Again, if conflicts can arise over a wide variety of issues, then conflict avoidance consists of attempting to ensure that controversies over particular kinds of issue do not arise within the society. In many cases conflicts arise from *resource scarcity* where the current supply of desired objects or states of affairs cannot satisfy all parties, or *position scarcity*, where roles conferring reputation, legitimacy or authority are in short supply, so that parties cannot simultaneously occupy a desired role, or a particular 'behaviour space'. Incompatible goals and a conflict situation arise over who obtains all, or most, of valued scarce resources, whether economic goods, political influence, or some aspect of status and reputation. A version of the Duchess's Law operates: 'The more there is of yours, the less there is of mine . . .' (Boulding, 1962, p. 190).

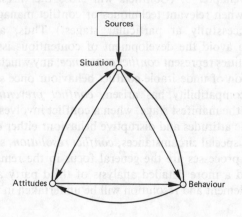

FIGURE 11.2   Basic conflict structure

1. SUPPLYING VALUED GOODS

The first principle of avoiding conflict is straightforward in principle if
not practice. If the primary aim of conflict avoidance mechanisms is to
ensure that situations involving goal incompatibility do not arise, and
if a major source of goal incompatibility is role or resource scarcity,
then conflict avoidance mechanisms must initially concentrate upon
avoiding a scarcity of desired resources or positions. In this way,
relationships between relevant parties will remain co-operative.
However, the structuring of any social system so that situations of
scarce roles and resources seldom arise is easier said than done. Only in
Utopia might there always be enough of anything to satisfy every
individual, group or organisation. Even in Utopia, human beings'
propensity for increasing their wants, no matter how successfully
previous wants might have been satisfied, may eventually place a strain
upon available Utopian resources. In the real world, the chances of
avoiding circumstances that create goal incompatability are even
lower, although role and resource conflict situations may be less salient
in affluent societies, or less frequent in rapidly developing societies,

where more individuals and groups have a chance of fulfilling their, admittedly increasing, aspirations through an increasing availability of goods and services.[3] However, increasing absolute resources will do nothing to avoid conflict situations that originate in a desire to be *relatively* superior to others.

One major means of avoiding the development of conflict situations is, therefore, basically a matter of the management of supply. If 'enough' can be found so that all individuals, groups and organisations satisfy their goals and aspirations, then that social system will be characterised by co-operative relationships rather than conflictful ones. Successful conflict avoidance of this type operates by providing enough of desired resources, so that circumstances in which issues of 'who gets how much' of some good seldom arise. A similar principle operates in connection with negative goals (goals of avoiding some future state), where resources can be devoted to the prevention of unwanted eventualities, such as an outbreak of cholera, the running down of an industry or the continued presence of an alien peace-keeping force in one's country.

2. MINIMISING DEMANDS

A second conflict avoidance strategy may be used separately or to reinforce efforts to supply 'enough' to go around. This is based upon influencing demand, rather than managing supply and attempts to affect the underlying value structure within a social system that determines what individuals or groups come to regard as desirable and deserved objectives. As Mack and Snyder (1957, p. 217) remark, '. . . Different underlying value judgments . . . condition the demand or need for scarce resources and positions . . .', so that in order to avoid the development of conflict situations, it is logical that efforts could be devoted to creating a set of values that militate against the development of too many situations of goal incompatibility.

A major aspect of this strategy could involve a society maintaining a value system such that desired resources and rewards are perceived and evaluated differently by different categories of individual. If a mixed value system can operate, situations of scarcity may be avoided not so much because of plentiful supply, but because of limited demand. If individuals value different resources or roles highly, and define satisfactory rewards in different fashions then, even in non-Utopian situations, there may be 'enough to go around' and situations of goal incompatibility through resource scarcity need not arise.

Again, such a strategy may be easy to envisage in principle, but difficult to put into practice. However, all societies attempt to socialise their members to some degree. Some have tried on a temporary basis to maintain a structure of working values based on concepts of self-denial and self-sacrifice which help to avoid the necessity of groups and individuals competing for desirable social rewards. Still others develop different hierarchies within their overall value system which make different groups and classes seek separate, and in some cases compatible, sets of resources and social roles. In many societies people are socialised into accepting that different generations want, and should have, different kinds of social rewards, and will properly pursue differing values appropriate to particular age groups. The old want and expect different things from the young, partly because of intellectual and biological changes, but also because societies maintain value systems that support concepts of differential rewards and responsibilities according to age. In other societies, the kind of social rewards expected by different social groups depends upon the degree of purity exhibited by particular 'castes'. In still others, expectations about 'proper' social rewards are tied to the possession of different skills and expertise, to different levels of responsibility, or to other accepted indicators of 'merit'.

Value development, or ideological manipulation, as a means of avoiding conflict often take the form of the inculcation of similar values among all members of that society. A resulting paradox is that while totally different values held by separate groups within a society may lead to situations of conflict, yet equally cases where all members of a society share similar values and desire the same goods may also lead to situations of conflict. If all members share the value of self-determination, for example, then a conflict situation may arise if one faction wishes to achieve its own self-determination while others, believing in self-determination for their society, nevertheless also believe in maintaining the integrity of the whole society and not allowing subgroups to fall away. In such a case, a shared value of self-determination, socialised into members of a society, may be just as disruptive as different values socialised into the members. This problem arose acutely for many Third World leaders who, having used the value of self-determination to obtain freedom from colonial rule, found themselves confronting separatist demands within their newly independent countries from groups basing their secessionist claims on that same shared value of self-determination. In one case the Kenyan Government was reduced to arguing that the principle of self-determination only applied to cases of 'foreign' domination, and not to 'multi-racial' societies in Africa – such as Kenya!

Societies may thus both avoid and create conflicts either by inculcating similar or widely different values into their members, depending upon the availability of resources and the degree of incompatibility of the value systems. Theoretically, societies could be built upon complementary values, but this ideal would be difficult to achieve in the most stable of environments, where existing values complemented, explained and justified the social structure and division of rewards among individuals and groups. Rapid social change is often seen as one of the most likely pre-determining factors for widespread conflict, however. This emphasises the difficulty in any society of controlling the diversity and intensity of demands through socialisation and the development of a non-competitive ideological value basis, and hence of minimising the growth of situations of conflict.

3. DEVELOPING SUPER-ORDINATE GOALS

The principles of conflict avoidance discussed so far are efforts to reinforce some threshold at the point in our conflict continuum where situations of goal incompatabilities arise. If any social system can operate so that the barrier between co-operation and incipient conflict is maintained, even for most of the time, then successful conflict avoidance processes are operating within that society. Many societies also rely on the development of shared, over-arching or 'super-ordinate' goals to avoid the growth of conflict situations between parties in that society. One major sociological school of thought argues that the existence of any society is posited on certain widely shared principles which the vast majority of members will be unwilling to sacrifice for particularist interests, however pressing. Personal security and the existence of minimal law and order are usually quoted in this connection, while defence against external interference is also frequently held to be a generally agreed 'public good'. Given the existence of such super-ordinate goals, it can be argued that factional goals are means to achieve these generally agreed ends, and that means can ultimately be changed and accommodated to others' means provided the final ends remain agreed and can be fulfilled. Alternatively, it can be argued that the pursuit of particularist, factional goals will prevent the fulfilment of some super-ordinate goals for society, so that the costs of pursuing such a course of action will eventually outweigh the gains, even to the factions in question, as well as to society as a whole.

Super-ordinate goals can also be created or used to end or prevent disruptive conflict behaviour once a conflict situation has arisen and become manifest. Sherif has argued that this experimental work clearly demonstrates the efficacy of super-ordinate goals in resolving conflict, and specifically that co-operation in achieving some objective highly valued by conflicting parties will initially offset and then relegate to an easily soluble condition previously salient conflicts between parties (Sherif, 1966). It is undoubtedly true that super-ordinate goals can unite erstwhile adversaries. Local opposition to the Belfast motorway scheme in 1973 established an alliance even between Belfast Catholics and Protestants, including para-military organisations. Peter Loizos has commented on how the overarching goal of maintaining 'village solidarity' tended in a Greek Cypriot village both to dampen down intra-village conflicts when they arose, and avoid village to outsider conflicts by establishing the convention of not selling land to outsiders (Loizos, 1975). However, the mechanism appears weak at the level of international society, in spite of the often reported universal interest in the avoidance of nuclear annihilation or preservation of the 'global eco-structure'. Numerous schemes based upon ostensibly obvious supra-national goals, such as the Indus Waters scheme or the Mekong Delta plan have come to grief, and even the Sahara Forest scheme has yet to prove unassailable evidence that it will prevent international conflicts between states involved.

4. THE LIMITATIONS OF CONFLICT AVOIDANCE

The strategies of conflict avoidance outlined above are simple in principle, if difficult to implement. The first two operate either to lessen and simplify complex demands, or increase relevant supply, both operations which are difficult to carry out successfully, especially in any rapidly changing environment which gives rise to new patterns of demand, and increased strain on supply. Furthermore, both seem only likely to work successfully in avoiding conflicts over resources or position scarcity when the goal incompatibility in question arises from the relative distribution of value of resources of roles. However, the provision of enough of the disputed resource whether by increasing supply or lowering demand is unlikely to have any effect upon conflicts over survival, or upon ideological conflict situations, where one party aims at the conversion of the other. The only way of avoiding the latter type of conflict is through the prior development of tolerance for non-conformity and difference. Socialisation rather than sufficiency appears the relevant conflict avoidance technique, unless the ultimate strategy of complete isolation is available, as a last resort.

We do not intend to explore the idea of *conflict avoidance* further. Although social systems possess mechanisms for helping their members avoid conflict situations, few manage to keep them to a minimum, or indeed, to prevent the frequent development of situations of incompatible goals. Moreover, societies of all kinds find it is impossible to keep conflicts incipient, rather than latent or manifest. The thresholds in our conflict continuum present minimal barriers to the progression of conflicts, from the initial stage of goal incompatability to organisation and overt behaviour in pursuit of the desired goals and against the adversary. Hence, one most pressing and realistic problem for conflict management is to cope with latent conflicts, where the conflict situation already exists, even if the conflict has yet to result in disruptive behaviour by one or both parties.

B. PREVENTING DISRUPTIVE CONFLICT

Given that a condition of incipient or latent conflict exists, the means by which a social system contains such a conflict are based on preventing the parties crossing the threshold between a consciousness of incompatible goals, and destructive behaviour in pursuit of those goals, or on influencing the nature of the transition and subsequent behaviour. *Conflict prevention* is a conception that embraces two types of process. Those which:

(a) Prevent behaviour defined within the relevant social system as disruptive or 'undesirable', but which might follow from the development of a situation of conflict.
(b) Attempt to confine conflict behaviour within clearly defined limits of permissible activity.

The first category contains all forms of inhibition or deterrence, such as the threat or use of coercion by some constabulary force, able to impose sanctions for 'disruptive behaviour'. These have previously been referred to as *conflict suppression*. The second includes all measures to limit conflict behaviour within set, recognised and often accepted rules of action, such as formal duels between individuals, legal processes for making awards and decisions, or various types of limited warfare, and will be called *conflict regulation*.

1. SUPPRESSION

Techniques of conflict suppression may conveniently be divided into those which:

(a) *Prevent* non-approved behaviour by the removal or control of the resources necessary for carrying out such an activity. Such methods include all forms of weapons limitation, such as gun control laws, disarmament agreements, or rules about the existence of private military forces or mercenary organisations. (Henry VII's ordinances against liveries in England at the end of the fifteenth century.) The underlying principle is the presumed effectiveness of removing the means of conducting non-approved, violent or destructive behaviour.

(b) *Deter* non-approved types of conflict behaviour through the threat of sanctions imposed by some legalised coercive force. All societies, from tribal to international, utilise threat systems to deter undesired behaviour, usually from some minority defined as deviant. Threat systems differ according to the level of general support for the system and its agents and whether the system is centralised and controlled (police forces and collective security) or decentralised and based upon self-help (lineage linkages in many tribal societies or the 'balance of power' system in eighteenth- and nineteenth-century Europe).[4]

Parties, whether individuals, communities or nations can be stopped from using 'undesirable' conflict behaviour in a number of ways. At the one extreme, they may be deterred by the physical interposition of some respected third party who would suffer physical harm through the continuation or resumption of the conflict behaviour. Examples of this end of the 'conflict prevention continuum' range from the actions of such 'interposers' as the leopard skin chief in Nuer society to the emplacement of a UN peacekeeping force between conflicting parties. In both cases, conflict behaviour may be deterred because of a wish to avoid inflicting damage on the peacekeeping party.

At the other extreme, conflicting parties may be deterred from pursuing their conflict by the existence of some third party able and willing to impose unacceptable costs on the antagonists for any violation of social rules and norms or harm to the third party. This form of 'keeping the peace' is most familiar in the activities of domestic police forces often acting as 'peace officers', but nonetheless possessing the capability, and sometimes the authority, to *enforce* peace. Conflict behaviour is suppressed through the parties' fear of damaging consequences imposed by third parties in response to their pursuit of goals through unacceptable means. The use of armies to enforce peace and suppress conflict behaviour in a domestic setting such as Ulster from 1969–80 is the most obvious example of such conflict prevention. Attempts to create an international army for use by the League of Nations, or a Great Power 'police force' directed by the Security Council after World War II, are examples of attempting to create an international 'law and order force'.

Needless to say, the two extreme forms of maintaining 'the peace' and preventing unacceptable conflict behaviour by interposition or imposition are ideal types. In real world conflicts, the line between peacekeeping and peace enforcement is a fine one, as evidence the problems of the UN force in the Congo, and of the Arab League Peacekeeping Force, sometimes more accurately called the 'Arab League Deterrent Force', in the Lebanon trying to cope with the civil war.

Moreover, while either interposition or imposition may work successfully to prevent the continuation of overt conflict behaviour, this may not be an unambiguous gain. Successful suppression will also result in the continued, sometimes long-term existence of a condition of latent conflict, in which the parties are conscious of a goal incompatability, but are unable to take action to modify the situation in some satisfactory way. Conflict attitudes and perceptions remain unaffected (or, perhaps, change in a more antagonistic direction) and the situation itself unresolved and dormant, ready to burst into life should the threat system break down.

2. REGULATION

Processes whereby attempts are made to regulate conflict behaviour within acceptable limits fall into two basic categories, practically inter-connected and, often, inter-dependent.

(a) Establishing acceptable settlement procedures

This category includes all ritualised conflict behaviours in simple

societies, such as *potlatch* ceremonies among the Tobrian
islanders, and systems of rules regarding compensatory payment
for injuries inflicted, such as *wer-gild* among the Saxon kingdoms o
pre-Norman England, or *dia* among Somali clans. In modern, in
dustrialised societies, a whole range of regulated processes enabl
conflicts over resource allocation, or role occupation to b
prosecuted and decided relatively peacefully within a recognisec
structure of rules.

The general principle of conflict regulation is that conflict behaviou
occurs within a framework of rules whether these are formally enactec
laws, or informal norms of behaviour arising from custom. Th
development of mechanisms for conflict regulation is thus a matter o
creating *behavioural boundaries* for the conduct of conflicts. Often i
simple societies, conflict behaviour becomes ritualised and a substitut
for more damaging action. Eskimo rivals engage in a ceremonia
exchange of insults to drum accompaniment, while competitiv
destruction of one's own property in a *potlatch* ceremony is only one o
the more bizarre forms of ritualised conflict behaviour developed to
avoid the disruptions of violence within a small society.

More usually, mechanisms for conflict regulation do not seek to
replace physical combat with some symbolic contest or activity, but to
establish an elaborate set of rules regarding permissible codes o
behaviour, some of which, as in the European duelling code, ar
merely institutionalisations of actual physical combat (Galtung, 1965)
while others involve a simple agreement to allow some random device
such as tossing a coin, to decide on the outcome of a contest (Phipps
1961). The most frequently encountered prohibitions regulating
various types of intra- and international conflict include rules about:

(a) The nature of the conflict behaviour permitted, which ar
frequently based upon principles of *equalisation* giving parties a
'fair' chance, and *supervision*, to see that no unfair tactics ar
employed.
(b) Where and when that behaviour may be used, often setting
temporal and geographical limits to conflict behaviour as wher
fighting is prohibited on Holy days, or in markets or Mosque
(Lewis, 1961).
(c) Against whom conflict behaviour may legitimately be employed
and who are automatically exempted. Laws of War developed i
western Europe from the time of Aquinas have tended to exemp

'the innocent' from the effects of violence, although recent years have seen the erosion of that category as anyone belonging to a nation or social category has become a 'legitimate' target of violence in war or certain types of domestic conflict (Walzer, 1977, pp. 197–206).

(d) Who may use conflict behaviour. In many forms of regulated conflict a substitute protagonist with requisite skills may be employed to conduct the conflict for a party. This principle has produced such figures as the medieval champion and the modern barrister.

(e) Upon what occasions conflict behaviour may justifiably be employed. Again, a whole structure of rules and norms surround the concept of 'the just war' and rights of self-defence which, at the international level are formally written into the UN Charter.

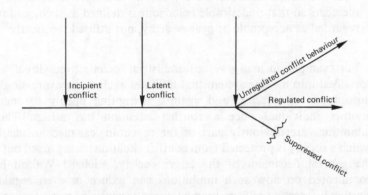

FIGURE 11.3 Effects of conflict prevention strategies

The ultimate result of many efforts to regulate social and international conflict is the development of a system of rules and adjudication: '. . . courts, codes and constables . . .' in Lucy Mair's (1962) phrase. In such a system, conflict behaviour has become thoroughly regulated (some would say ritualised) with rules about procedure, the nature of evidence, what constitutes a right and a wrong, and the scales of compensation for injury. Civil codes represent an institutionalised form of conflict regulation, although in most cases it is still open to the parties (or, at least, one of them) to decide whether to use this particular form of bounded conflict behaviour in an endeavour to achieve the goals in dispute.

Wherever such rules of conflict are successfully developed, the result is to transform *the means* by which incompatible goals are pursued, rather than to prevent any action at all being taken to achieve them, or allow the use of any means whatever that the parties themselves might choose. With this type of regulation, the conflict does move from a latent to a manifest stage, but into limited forms of behaviour that do not produce damage and social disruption, see Fig. 11.3. The same can be said about the second regulatory strategy.

(b) Creating non-disruptive values

Such techniques do not necessarily involve a set of over-riding social values making for total quiescence or withdrawal when confronted with a conflict. However, every society attempts to socialise its members so that undesirable behaviour is defined as such, and not regarded as acceptable or praiseworthy, nor utilised frequently.

For example, in many western industrial societies, individuals are socialised into a value system that militates against the expression of hostility or annoyance, and against attempting openly to coerce another individual once a conflict situation has arisen. These inhibitions are obviously part of the psychological mechanisms by which a society is protected from conflict situations being acted out to the general detriment of the larger society. Richard Walton has commented on how such inhibitions can reduce or even regulate conflict by erecting self-imposed barriers to expressing one's feeling in a conflict, and by establishing social conventions that particular conflicts – say between subordinate and superior in an organisation – are not pursued or even confronted (Walton, 1969, pp. 75–6). If society disapproves of particular forms of expression or behaviour, considering them immature or bad manners, then these may not be used, and the conflict suppressed by one or both of the parties, although it may later be acted out indirectly, and in a sometimes more costly manner.[5]

In general, these social isolation processes may be divided into those concerned with: (i) the acceptability and hence legitimacy of rules and mechanisms for conducting and solving conflicts within society;

(ii) values regarding the nature and desirability of competition and conflict within society; and (iii) attitudes towards the permissible use of non-sanctioned, violent or disruptive forms of conflict behaviour.

3. INSTITUTIONALISATION

The development of a system of law and adjudication from efforts to regulate social conflict is not the only way in which conflict behaviour can move from being bounded by acknowledged rules to having a set of social institutions to contain it and bring about some relatively satisfactory outcome for the parties and for society as a whole. In many ways, the political system of a country in its entirety can be regarded as a means for settling conflicts without recourse to violence or physical coercion. The appearance of the latter phenomena in the political life of a country indicates that the political system no longer fulfils one of its basic functions.

The idea that political institutions are mechanisms for managing conflicts and preventing conflict situations developing disruptively is hardly a new one. Most recently Schattschneider (1960, p. 71) expressed it succinctly by arguing that '. . . All politics, all leadership and all organisation involve the management of conflict . . .' Elections, voting procedures, rules about two-thirds or majority decisions, can all be regarded as behaviours which substitute for other, possibly coercive, means of waging conflicts, or as a means of establishing 'rules of the game' which enjoy widespread support or initially can be imposed upon a society by a dominant group. 'Although elections are not necessarily peaceful . . . the number of violent incidents associated with elections is only a fraction of those that could take place if there were no elections . . .' (Pirages, 1976, p. 72). Where accepted methods of peacefully transferring power from one group to another − for example, the defeat of a major piece of government legislation in the House of Commons − do not exist, then power tends to be transferred violently by a coup or insurrection. Political rules of the game, in fact, transform political conflict into a kind of regulated game.

The conception of political systems as partly devices for conflict management, and for preventing conflict behaviour between competing social groups and classes from becoming wholly disruptive, is perhaps best illustrated in societies where major permanent cleavages exist. In divided societies, conflicts reinforce rather than cut across one another, and give rise to frequent, sometimes permanent antagonisms between the same social groups or communities as parties. The political systems of such countries as Belgium, Lebanon, Cyprus, Sri Lanka, Yugoslavia and Canada face particularly difficult problems of conflict management, although this is not to say that similar strains are not felt, at least from time to time, in other countries with less noticeable divisions.

A variety of institutional structures have been used in such societies to manage conflicts that develop between the constituent groups or communities, and to prevent these conflicts disrupting the entire social system. (Obvious failure of such institutions in the case of Lebanon and Cyprus, and stresses and strains in Canada, Bangladesh and Yugoslavia, emphasise the difficulties of containing conflict in such societies.) On occasions, as Esman (1973, pp. 55–60) points out, these structures are imposed by a dominant community in order to safeguard their interests rather than to prevent conflict, but often these two objectives complement each other, so even in cases where the consti-tutional 'rules of the game' are designed to keep the dominant com-munity dominant, they often also operate to prevent conflicts being pursued to the point of social disruption. Nordlinger (1972) for example, suggests that six institutional patterns have emerged historic-ally in deeply divided and conflict prone societies:

(1) A stable political coalition of elites from the communities in-volved.
(2) A proportionality principle that establishes rules of the game for representation, relative influence and share of social values in dispute.
(3) An alternative set of tacit rules that suppress sensitive issues or keep them out of the political arena through mutual agreement.
(4) A system where communal parties possess a mutual veto on any form of goal-seeking behaviour by others which they regard as harmful to their core interests, or even survival.
(5) A system whereby goals are pursued but the process is marked by constant compromises, negotiation and horse trading.
(6) A system whereby a dominant community buys off seriously disruptive conflict by making concessions to other communities.

Nordlinger also condemns two commonly suggested institutions for managing conflict in divided societies, namely the use of majority decisionmaking and efforts to create an overarching identity which will finally, as Enloe suggests, eliminate conflict situations by eliminating cleavages rather than prevent conflict behaviour between communally separate parties (Enloe, 1977, pp. 152–3). However, one frequent long-term effort to prevent disuptive conflict behaviour in such societies has, in fact, taken the form of efforts to assimilate potentially conflicting communities into a dominant group (what Enloe calls *vanguard* assimilation and Esman *induced* assimilation). This can be done either by co-opting the elite of dominated groups or an entire group or community into a new national identity which will, it is hoped, eliminate ethnic or linguistic differences and lay the foundation for an integrated nation state. (Esman (1973, p. 58) refers to this version of the traditional 'melting pot' theory as *syncretic* integration.) Other examples of different ways of managing conflict in divided societies exist, from the full-scale destruction or domination of a potentially disruptive communal group, through various forms of institutions for conducting a permanent negotiation between the communities making up pluralist systems, to the final expedient of relative isolation of potential parties to potential conflicts by some form of territorial or legal–cultural autonomy. The most familiar form of this last strategy is a federal system which acts '. . . by quarantining explosive issues . . .' and by allowing communities to exercise '. . . significant control over their own territorial jurisdictions . . .' (Enloe, 1977, p. 154).

Although institutional arrangements for preventing disruptive conflict can be very different, they are hardly mutually exclusive, and several processes may be tried simultaneously, in order to contain conflicts arising within these essentially fragile political systems. The point to note is that all of them, as well as the techniques and processes mentioned as appropriate for less seriously divided societies, are established on the basis of an acknowledgement that conflict situations will arise within societies, as well as between them, and that some generally accepted methods must be found of enabling goals to be pursued and conflicts played out without socially disruptive behaviour.

4. SOCIAL STRUCTURE AND CONFLICT PREVENTION

A final aspect of conflict prevention differs markedly from those previously discussed, in that suppression regulation and institutionalisation attempted to prevent disuptive conflict behaviour by the deliberate provision of institutions with the function of dealing with conflict situations. An alternative strategy operates, in contrast, indirectly, and seeks to prevent conflict situations developing into disruptive conflict behaviour through principles of compensation, or self-imposed restraint on action in pursuit of goals. In other words, parties in many social systems frequently find themselves in situations of conflict, but refrain from reacting with behaviour in pursuit of their currently blocked goals because they judge that to do so would result in disruption of other, valued, co-operative relationships. Losses to them would not be offset even by complete success. Many social systems, therefore, succeed in preventing particular conflicts from crossing the threshold into the manifest stage by processes of 'compensation', or by providing sufficient alternative benefits to offset the non-achievement of particular goals, thus causing parties to refrain from action. (Such mechanisms will, of course, cease to operate efficiently when the sacrifices of not achieving the goal in conflict are considered to outweigh the compensatory benefits available through continued quiescence.)

At their simplest, such structures consist of the gradual development of forms of functional inter-dependence, such that the values of maintaining that inter-dependence outweigh the value of using disruptive behaviour, even when parties are involved in an intense conflict situation. The most obvious example of such a structural arrangement is economic inter-dependence within a society, which can motivate individuals and groups towards continued co-operation and non-disruptive conflict behaviour. A somewhat more complex structural arrangement is the establishment of numerous, cross-cutting sub-groupings which develop a criss-cross of group interests throughout a society (Gluckman, 1956). The development of such a cross-cutting, inter-dependent structure (such as kinship ties through inter-marriage, or differing economic, ethnic, religious or linguistic group member-ship)[6] usually has the effect that:

(a) Individuals and groups are mutually linked in many co-operative relationships which offset or negate conflict situations, and reduce the likelihood of disruptive conflict behaviour arising. The growth of such a criss-cross structure in a society also prevents a situation developing where all conflicts in that society occur across one single line of cleavage as in divided societies.

(b) Cross-cutting group loyalties and allegiances develop which serve to bind a social system together via their individual members, and to establish values militating against the use of disruptive behaviour against current adversaries, who may be friends and allies at some future time, or in some other conflict.

(c) Different individuals, groups and organisations come to develop complementary interests over certain issues, and (ultimately) become linked via goals which no group can achieve through its own unaided efforts. The existence of such goals can also lead to the development of positive attitudes between groups, and to expectations of further co-operation and benefits but more important, to a significant, if self-imposed deterrent to allowing any conflicts over other issues to disrupt existing relationships.

The major point above all such structural arrangements is that they put up the costs of employing non-sanctioned conflict behaviour through its effects upon a valued set of relationships. Sanctions are 'built in' to the social structure, and any individual or group in a society must count the cost of rupturing such inter-dependencies, once it is possible to overcome the conditioning of socialisation processes and contemplate the use of disruptive behaviour in order to prosecute a conflict. As emphasised in chapter 1, individuals, groups and organisations are usually involved in both co-operative and conflictful relationships. The costs of disrupting the co-operative relationships will often dampen the desire of parties to cross the threshold from latent to manifest conflict, and ultimately help to resolve that particular conflict. The dampening effect will work best when the co-operative relationship is highly valued, so that the costs of damaging that relationship, by escalating conflict behaviour, will be high and hence highly deterring. It will work least well when the co-operative relationships are few, and not valued highly.

The ideas behind the creation of a social system marked by a high level of cross-cutting groups, and overlapping individual loyalties, have been particularly influential in recent discussions about how the international system might be structured in order to maximise that system's relatively low propensity to contain conflicts at the latent threshold. Ideas about the dampening and compensating features of systems characterised by a high level of inter-dependence, criss-crossing structure, and multiple group loyalties have underpinned much of the functionalist's theoretical approach to international integration (Mitrany, 1966) and practical efforts to minimise the effects of conflict situations that arise between international and transnational parties. The strategy of building up a complex, interlocking network of co-operative relationships where few existed previously, is a major part of the 'functionalist' answer to the problems of international conflict prevention. It is, however, based upon another variant of the Rational

Actor approach to conflict, in that it assumes that increased inter-dependence will alter the values in some cost-benefit calculation about sacrificing co-operation for conflict, and tend to increase costs of disruption even if the benefits remain stable. Various scholars have pointed out that numerous counter-examples exist of cases in which the strongest and most complex set of co-operative relationships have not prevented a serious conflict situation between parties from becoming manifest and developing into most coercive conflict behaviour. Zambian–Rhodesian economic inter-dependence provides but one example.

C. MANAGING OVERT CONFLICT

Discussion of the general process of conflict management has con-centrated upon efforts to cope with conflict in its incipient or latent stages. The final strategies of conflict management are employed once a conflict has crossed the threshold into a manifest condition, but has not taken the path of regulated conflict behaviour, either because one of the parties deems this path unsatisfactory, or because no such path is readily available. *Conflict settlement* and *conflict resolution* are means of arriving at some solution, once a conflict situation has led to the employment of non-institutionalised and disruptive behaviour. In principle, both approaches may be used bilaterally by the parties themselves in efforts to achieve a favourable solution to their conflict. However, in the following comments, attention will be concentrated upon both settlement and resolution as processes involving third parties in some intermediary role.

1. THIRD PARTY INVOLVEMENT

Third parties can become involved in manifest conflicts in different ways. A distinction needs to be drawn between third party activity that is essentially partisan, and that which is intermediary. This is a simple dichotomy, and there are probably more examples of third parties becoming involved in a conflict as participants rather than inter-mediaries. Frequently, third parties enter a conflict and help to bring about a final solution to the conflict as allies of one side or another (Young, 1967–8). The USA, for example, entered World War I on the side of the Allies and against the Central Powers. Many industrial conflicts widen as other unions take action 'in sympathy' with the one originally involved in the conflict situation. In tribal societies, the process of individual 'self-help' involves calling in other, related individuals or lineage segments to help win a quarrel.

The essential point about this type of third (or fourth, or fifth) party activity is that it is intended to help one of the parties win the dispute, or, at least, to achieve an improved outcome. Partisan behaviour can add resources to one or other party in a conflict situation, and assist some favoured party in harming, or bargaining with, its adversary, or in lessening the impact of that adversary's behaviour. Intermediary activity, on the other hand, is undertaken by a third party with the primary intention of achieving some compromise settlement of the issues at stake between the parties, or at least ending disruptive conflict behaviour indulged in by both sides. We therefore make a distinction between the first type of third party activity, undertaken with the aim of assisting one party to 'win' − in that party's own terms − and the second, where the objective is to achieve a compromise. The first represents *intervention* and the second *intermediary* activity.[7]

2. SETTLEMENT AND RESOLUTION

The distinction between the concepts of settlement and resolution of a conflict is one which is becoming increasingly recognised as important in analysing the search for conflict solutions at many social levels. Settlement and resolution will be regarded as activity on the part of one or more third parties wishing to affect some on-going, manifest conflict, and bring it to some conclusion by changing the behaviour, attitudes or goals of the adversaries. Major differences between settlement and resolution, therefore, lie in:

(a) The components of conflict (attitudes and perceptions, behaviour, or situation of incompatible goals) the activities try to modify, and
(b) The acceptability of the eventual solution to the parties directly involved.

While some attention may be paid to indirect efforts to modify extreme conflict attitudes held by adversaries, conflict *settlement* techniques aim primarily at altering conflict behaviour (stopping the use of violence and coercive strategies, or achieving some form of temporary truce); and then reaching a compromise solution in which the parties make 'fair' sacrifices of some of the goals in dispute in order to achieve others. Thus, behaviour is altered, usually in a less violent direction and a process of tri-partite negotiation replaces strategies of outright coercion. (At the same time, efforts may be made to lower the levels of fear, hostility and suspicion within the adversaries, either generally or, at least, at leadership level.) Little effort is usually made to get adversaries to change their goals or objectives, so that settlement techniques tend to leave the underlying goals structure of the parties unchanged, and the conflict attitudes and perceptions of the parties unmodified. Hence, with goals and underlying values remaining basically unsatisfied, and attitudes of fear and hostility often unchanged, the chance of further conflict behaviour breaking out over the same issues at some future date is never wholly removed. For one thing, any compromise settlement, whether arranged bilaterally or through the action of intermediaries is likely to leave at least one party feeling that important goals remain unfilfilled. As with *suppressed* conflict, dissatisfaction is likely to remain until the deprived party perceives some opportunity to re-open the issues and redress the balance. At times, a settlement will have to be guaranteed by the promises, sometimes the threats, of some powerful third party, as with the US role in the March 1979 Israeli–Egyptian settlement. Such guarantees are often an indication of the limitations of a compromise, which has to be shored up externally instead of being self-supporting.

In contrast, techniques of conflict *resolution* aim at providing a solution which is generally acceptable to parties to the conflict, which they themselves have evolved and which for these reasons is self-supporting. Recognising that stopping the disruptive conflict behaviour only affects the most obvious dimension of the conflict, intermediaries using resolution techniques seek to operate on all three components of a conflict, situation, behaviour, attitudes; and help the parties themselves appreciate the nature of the goals which led to the conflict situation, the behaviour and inter-action that ensued from the incompatability of those goals, and the type of percepts and attitudes which frequently accompany involvement in such a process. By directing attention to the three major components of the conflict, such intermediaries can assist the parties themselves to make a clearer analysis of the situation, of one another, and of the range of options available to reach some satisfactory solution, and to remove the conflict between them. In theory, such an approach is always possible, but in practice it is usually supremely difficult. It may be straightforward to end coercive or violent conflict behaviour (although it often isn't); it may be feasible to change perceptions, attitudes and emotions (again, this is not easy, especially in a highly factionalised or decentralised party); but it is inevitably the hardest of all to assist adversaries towards a solution whereby neither opponent abandons any of its basic values, even though some sacrifice of intermediate goals may be called for. Nonetheless, this is what conflict resolution attempts to do.

It is hardly surprising that such techniques are better developed at some social levels than others. At the international level, for example, techniques of conflict settlement are the norm, and efforts to use non-directive techniques of conflict resolution have been few, especially relative to the intra-organisational or inter-personal level, (see Burton (1969) and Doob (1970) for two such efforts).

D. CONCLUSION

Major distinctions between the various forms of *conflict management* that can be employed at different stages of the development of a conflict may be clearer if regarded merely as attempts to deal with the three major components of conflict illustrated by our simple triangular model of basic conflict structure. This model draws attention away from the sequential use of various conflict management techniques as a conflict develops from the incipient, through the latent into the manifest stage, but it does emphasise another point: that the different methods by which any society contains conflict (whether by avoidance, suppression, regulation, settlement or resolution), all differ in the components of conflict they primarily attempt to influence. *Avoidance* techniques aim largely at conflict situations and the value structures likely to lead to the development of incompatible goals. *Prevention* techniques direct major efforts towards attitudes and behaviour, trying in the first instance to build up a structure of values and beliefs that militates against the use of disruptive behaviour, and in the second to ensure that behaviour occurs within a recognised framework of accepted rules. *Settlement* again operates primarily at a behavioural level, although settlement techniques also, at their more sophisticated, operate to change views and beliefs held by adversaries. Finally, *resolution* processes seek to act on all three components, so that values and goals, attitudes and behaviour, can all be brought into consideration during a search for some final, non-imposed and self-supporting solution which deals with all aspects of the conflict and clears the way

Table 11.2   Conflict management technique

Strategy	Method	Tactics	Examples
Conflict avoidance	Ensure that situations involving goal incompatibility do not arise	(i) Provision of enough of desired resources or positions	Increase disputed water supplies in desert region
		(ii) Maintenance of values militating against possession of incompatible goals between individuals or groups	Ideology (or religion) emphasising self-sacrifice or service to others

Stage 1.   Conflict situation develops

Conflict prevention	Ensure that no conflict situation leads to undesired forms of conflict behaviour	(i) Conflict regulation: situation acted out and resolved within accepted rules	Use of legal and political systems. Socialisation of relevant values and attitudes. Develop a social structure making disruptive behaviour too costly.
		(ii) Conflict suppression: inhibition of undesired behaviour through coercion or threat	Security forces; control of arms

Stage 2.   (Unregulated) Conflict behaviour develops

Conflict settlement	Third party aims at stopping conflict behaviour and at reaching some compromise settlement	(i) Intervention (ii) Imposition (iii) Peacekeeping good offices and conciliation mediation	Great-power settlement with 'guarantees' UN force industrial mediator
Conflict resolution	Third party aims to modify all three aspects of conflict (attitudes behaviour and situation-goals and issues) to produce a self-supporting settlement	Non-directive techniques inc: Social case work, Marriage guidance, T-group analysis, Controlled communication	

for the establishment of a co-operative relationship between erstwhile adversaries. The complete range of management processes is outlined in Table 11.2.

Finally, distinguishing various forms of conflict management for analytical clarity does not, once again, mean that they are separate and distinct in the real world of social and international conflict. It is often difficult in practice to tell whether an activity is classifiable as conflict avoidance or prevention. Effects on both situation, attitudes and subsequent behaviour may easily result, and be intended. Moreover, in coping with many conflicts, a wide variety of management techniques may be simultaneously employed. Nevertheless, our suggested classification is a simple one, and will, hopefully, clarify subsequent discussion of attempts to contain international conflicts.

12 Peacemaking

> The *monkalun* has no authority. All he can do is act as a peace-making go-between. His only power is in his art of persuasion, his tact and his skilful playing on human emotions and motives. Were he closely related to the plaintiff, he would have no influence with the defendant, and *mutatis mutandis*, the opposite would be true.
>
> R. F. Barton (1919)

Chapter 9 considered difficulties experienced by parties attempting to reach a settlement of their mutual conflict through bilateral negotiations, and noted that the achievement of some form of compromise agreement presented difficulties whether compromise was worked out from a position of imbalance or stalemate. Third party involvement in this peacemaking process is intended to facilitate a settlement and, under a variety of labels ('mediation', 'good offices', 'conciliation') is part of those conflict management techniques coming into effect once *conflict avoidance* and *prevention* have failed to stop a conflict reaching the stage of destructive behaviour. 'Peacemaking' by third parties is thus a stage beyond 'peacekeeping', the major difference being that, while peace*keeping* activities focus on the behavioural component of any conflict, peace*making* concentrates on goals and attitudes. This is not to argue that 'intermediaries' totally neglect the behavioural component of any conflict in favour of persuading parties to abandon particular goals, or adopt a more positive view of their adversary. Often, intermediaries have to carry out their function of peacemaking while the parties to the dispute continue to use coercive forms of conflict behaviour against one another, so that in the initial stages of any initiative, the task of the third party may be the conclusion of a prior agreement to limit violent conflict as a preliminary to discussions about substantive issues.

At the international level this peacemaking task has been carried out by a wide variety of intermediaries ranging since 1945 from individuals such as the Emperor of Ethiopia and the US Secretary of State, to such organisations as the World Council of Churches and the International

Committee of the Red Cross. Such a heterogeneous collection of inter-mediaries raises questions about factors contributing to the success or failure of an intermediary initiative, and ultimately to the successful settlement of a conflict. What part is played by the prestige and skill of the mediator? What types of dispute, or what stages in the conflict, lend themselves to successful intermediary activity? What techniques does the mediator employ, and which should he avoid? Should the process be private or public?

A. 'MEDIABLE' SITUATIONS

All intermediaries or mediating bodies confront a crucial problem of timing, of when third party initiatives are likely to be acceptable to parties involved in an intense, long-lasting conflict. When is an inter-mediary likely to be relevant, and when irrelevant? In many ways, the question resembles that raised about the overall process of ending a conflict. Factors relevant to leaders considering terminating a conflict bilaterally are also important when they consider accepting, or asking for, the efforts of an intermediary:

(a) The perceived distance from attaining the goals in conflict.

(b) The perceived probability of eventually attaining these desired goals.

(c) The availability of further resources to continue conflict behaviour in pursuit of the desired goal.

(d) The relative value of the goal in conflict compared with other objectives (in economic terms, the 'opportunity costs') and the per-ceived probability of achieving the latter.

(e) The resources already expended in pursuit of the disputed goals, which will add to the desirability of the original goals; and the extent of the existing sacrifices made during the conflict inter-action.

Many students of intermediary activity, both analysts and prac-titioners, have argued that these structural considerations really deter-mine whether any intermediary activity will even begin, let alone succeed, and that intermediaries make little contribution to bringing about a compromise agreement. More often, the parties to the conflict themselves decide, either independently or tacitly, that they wish to arrange a compromise solution, and when this stage is reached, they look around for a convenient third party to act as go-between and legitimiser of their activity.

The basis of this argument is that the key factors determining whether or not a mediation initiative succeeds are the relative positions of advantage of the parties and not the personal qualities of the mediator, or even the prestige of the organisation he represents. Given that nobody really makes significant concessions from a position of strength, and nobody will readily agree to make concessions when they are in a position of relative weakness, no mediatory initiative is likely to have much success unless the two parties have decided to come to some agreement, or one party has decided it must cut its losses and abandon the conflict for a compromise. In either case, almost any mediation effort will succeed irrespective of mediator skills or acceptability.

In the Middle East after 1967, for example, neither Secretary of State Rogers nor Ambassador Jarring was likely to bring about a successful compromise because of the position of overwhelming advantage achieved by Israelis. Why should the Israelis have agreed to compromise when their government perceived itself as holding all the cards in the conflict with the Arab states especially the UAR? (Unless, of course, the UAR would agree to cut its losses to such an extent as to abandon almost all pan-Arab goals.) Similarly, a willingness to make concessions over the Cyprus dispute has been evinced neither by Greek–Cypriots when they were in a dominant position on the island in the period from 1963 to 1974, nor by Turkish–Cypriots thereafter.

If third party initiatives are likely to be unsuccessful in highly asymmetric circumstances, with the balance of advantage tilted significantly in one direction, then a third party's best opportunity might arise in conditions of uncertainty, stalemate or mutual exhaustion. Such circumstances allow us to reconcile the views of those who argue that the parties take a decision to use intermediaries and those who argue that third parties can themselves initiate effective action to help in developing a compromise, and thus genuinely contribute to a peace-making process. In circumstances where the adversaries are uncertain about the likely future course of events, a third party offer of help may be tolerated, or even welcomed. There are always stages in conflicts when both parties are relatively certain about the future and stages when they are much less certain. In the latter case, parties will be unsure about likely future success for their activities in pursuit of the disputed goals, so that they are also uncertain about the relative pay-offs of continuing the conflict, or compromising. Often, the decision to continue or compromise depends, to some extent, upon the changed attitudes and goals of the adversary. In such a situation, a third party can play at least a useful 'communication' role, and this is recognised by parties. Similar positive reactions to a third party's initiatives are likely to arise from circumstances where a long drawn-out conflict has led to mutually recognised exhaustion of resources and options, or to circumstances where neither side is yet exhausted, but where both can recognise a stalemate.

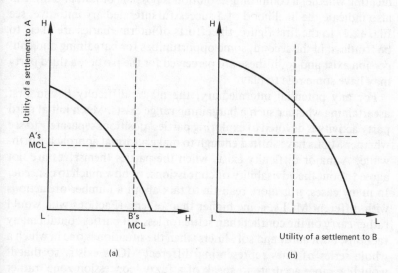

FIGURE 12.1 Intermediary opportunities and bargaining ranges

Apart from the existence of some generally recognised stalemate, or state of mutual exhaustion, parties must also perceive that conditions exist that offer both some advantages, even if they fail to achieve all desired goals. A situation similar to that encouraging bilateral negotiations also assists intermediary initiatives. If the parties' Maximum Concession Levels produce some realistic bargaining range, then the assistance of an intermediary in exploring the dimensions of this range will usually be recognised as helpful. If, on the other hand, the parties' MCLs appear to preclude any chance of a compromise, then any intermediary activity that occurs may merely be symbolic, designed to make a public case, or to demonstrate one's flexibility compared with an adversary's intransigence. Much of the peace-making during the Nigerian Civil War took on this character of a charade, given the Federal Government's consistent unwillingness to consider discussions about anything less than a unified Nigeria, and the Biafran leader's refusal to consider anything less than Biafran sovereignty and possibility a customs union (Stremlau, 1976).

Both circumstances have already been illustrated by a model, indicating whether a compromise solution is possible or not, and this can also indicate the likelihood of a successful intermediary initiative, see Fig. 12.1. In the first figure, the efforts of intermediaries are likely to be fruitless; in the second, some opportunities for bargaining and concession exist and so, if these are perceived for the parties, a third party may have some role to play.

For any potential intermediary, the major difficulty lies in first ascertaining whether such a bargaining range exists. Much initial third party activity is devoted to exploring parties' positions separately to see whether MCLs have shifted enough to make a formal approach worthwhile. A major difficulty exists when the parties themselves are not agreed about the advisability of concessions, or how much to concede. In many cases, it is more realistic to talk about a number of factions with different MCLs, some higher than others. (Factions who would rather carry on the conflict than settle for less.) If parties contain many factions, both hard- and soft-liners, then the situation is one in which a whole series of lines representing different MCLs exists, so that it would be more accurate to speak of a fuzzy 'concession zone' rather than a single, unambiguous MCL, see Fig. 12.2.

An analytical problem is what types of party are especially prone to such 'zoning'. Is the phenomenon common to all parties save the smallest and most tightly disciplined? A problem for all active third parties is, given such a situation, should they undertake activity to strengthen the soft-liners, whose MCL is lower and who are prepared to conciliate in the interests of a settlement. Should third parties intervene – perhaps as mediators, perhaps as supporters – into intra-party conflicts, with a view to strengthening 'doves'? If the answer to this question is in the affirmative, and with mediators with high coercive potential, such an activity is regarded as a legitimate third party function, the next dilemma is how a third party might go about assisting soft-liners within a party engaged in conflict, and whether such action as the publicising of intransigence by the party hard-liners is a help or a hindrance in undermining their position. Powerful and interested intermediaries often use this last tactic in trying to put pressure upon one or other party to make further concessions. There can be little doubt, for example, that the actions of Dr Kissinger and President Ford in publicly underlining Israeli intransigence in the disengagement negotiations were intended to weaken the domestic position of Israeli 'hawks' and to strengthen that of any less intransigent groups within the Israeli Government.

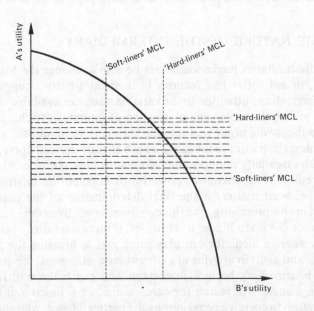

FIGURE 12.2   Intra-party differences over concessions

Alternatively, third parties might be able to alter hard-liners' MCLs by operating on the assumption that hard-line factions within a party are those for whom the current benefits of the conflict outweigh the current costs. Hence, there is a need for alternative benefits for hard-liners to outweigh those sacrificed through their acceptance of any compromise. The difficulties of providing alternatives for hard-liners has already been mentioned but the problem again arises for an intermediary attempting to bring about a settlement. Softening hard-liners is less of a problem for powerful and resourceful intermediaries, as the latter often possess resources necessary to provide additional benefits. Such a course of action is not open to a resourceless intermediary, but an alternative strategy might first be to resolve intra-party disputes between hard- and soft-liners before attempting any action at the inter-party level. The result in the model would be to produce an agreed, relatively coherent MCL, instead of a wide zone of intra-party disagreement.

B. THE NATURE OF THE INTERMEDIARY

That intermediaries might sometimes be able to change the MCLs of parties, or aid softer line factions in their intra-party struggle with hard-liners, draws attention to the variable resources available to third parties and to the more general question of intermediary characteristics. To those who argue that intermediaries are fundamentally irrelevant unless the parties to the dispute have already decided upon peace, these are essentially unimportant. No matter how skilful or blundering, prestigious or unknown, powerful or impotent an intermediary might be, what matters is the final determination of the parties to succeed in compromising, and this decisiveness will overcome anything a mediator can do to hinder it. However, if there is a range of circumstances where a mediator can play some part in bringing the parties together and assist in arriving at a compromise settlement, the qualities of the intermediary become important, and can make a difference between a successful search for compromise, or a fiasco and subsequent return to coercive behaviour by the parties. Hence, while bearing in mind the argument that there are stages in any dispute where the most beautifully handled intermediary initiative has little chance of being taken up, let alone succeeding, there is some benefit in discussing desirable intermediary qualities. These may form one set of variables assisting a compromise settlement. What types of third parties become involved in peacemaking and what are their appropriate qualities?

1. INDIVIDUALS AS INTERMEDIARIES

In everyday language, the concept of an intermediary conjures up a picture of an individual who acts as a 'go-between' for two individuals in an intense conflict between whom communication has broken down. A third party is needed to restore communication and, perhaps, to suggest a compromise or a way out of the dispute that enables both parties to profit. So firmly is this image of 'the' mediator held, that the basic assumption about intermediary activity (especially at the international level), is that it involves a single, usually prestigious figure travelling between capital and capital with a briefcase full of peace plans, compromise solutions and face-saving formulae, ready to produce these as soon as he confronts the leaders of the parties in conflict and hoping that, by use of ingenious arguments and the force of his prestige, one or other of his schemes will provide the long-sought-for solution.

There is some truth in this caricature. At some social levels the mediator often is an individual, and does fulfil the functions of a physical go-between, communicator, or provider of compromise schemes. In many simple societies, for example, single prestigious individuals are often recognised as possessing a formal, accepted role as intermediary in conflicts, helping the parties towards a compromise settlement without using any coercion, save the expectations of the rest of the community that his activity will not be lightly ignored. In certain sedentary and non-sedentary tribes in Africa, a religious or magical leader will act in an intermediary capacity should a conflict develop between individuals, families or lineages. Among the Nuer of the Sudan, leopard-skin 'priests' may become involved in feuds because of their ritual powers, which include performing the rite of the reconciliation ending any feud that has started with the killing of a man. However, there is no threat or coercion behind such an intermediary's offer of assistance, and it is pointless for the leopard-skin chief to proffer his services unless members of the injured party have signified that they are willing to make some kind of settlement without resorting to further violence.[1] Even if this is the case, dignity, reputation and 'face' makes it necessary to refuse publicity to participate in any compromise process right up until the last moment (Mair, 1962, p. 43). (Parallels with international diplomacy need not be stressed.) Similarly, in Ifugao society there exists an office known as the *monkalun*, the occupants of which act for a fee as professional mediators between individuals and exhaust all the arts of coaxing, flattering, scolding, threatening and insinuating, in order to bring about a peaceful settlement to a dispute (Barton, 1919, pp. 94–5).

2. INTERNATIONAL INTERMEDIARIES

In many respects, these activities within simpler societies appear similar to those carried out by single, prestigious figures at the international level. In a large number of disputes since 1945 (and before) a single person has fulfilled the role of a 'facilitator' for constructive discussion which, on occasions, has resulted in a compromise settlement. In such processes, figures such as Hammarskjold, Bunche, Nehru, U Thant, Jarring, Gallo Plaza and Kissinger have, through their roles as representatives of salient international bodies, but also personal stature, mediatory skill and confidence within the conflicting parties, acted as some form of catalyst on the situation, and caused parties to abandon goals, change perceptions and beliefs, cease destructive behaviour, or arrive at some supportable compromise.

It would be misleading to draw too close a parallel between the activities of third parties at individual and at international levels, however. In the latter case, it is obvious that very different types of third parties become involved in inter- or transnational disputes; that the characteristics of these third parties vary tremendously; and that behaviour in the third party role can differ widely from conflict to conflict, and from third party to third party. One has only to compare the position and behaviour of a representative of the All Africa Council of Churches, and the US Secretary of State to recognise such distinctions.

One observer suggests that differences between intermediaries at the international level may best be revealed by dividing them into five basic categories:

(a) The non-involved' and disinterested. (Non-committed and non-aligned states.)

(b) The 'involved', or otherwise 'aligned', the latter category implying that while the third party might not be directly affected by a particular conflict, nonetheless its commitment is generally to one party rather than the other. (Aligned and semi-aligned states.)

(c) Associations and organisations of which both parties are members; for example trade associations or trade union federations, or regional organisations such as the OAU.

(d) Private organisations and individuals, essentially 'outside' the conflict and normally not associated with the parties. (Non-governmental organisations.)

(e) Political organisations taking more or less authoritative decisions for the whole social system, such as the national government, or a trade union's national executive, or the UN (Young, 1967, p. 91).[2]

Certainly, even a superficial historical survey of international intermediaries, or even of the intermediaries in a single, long drawn-out
conflict, reveals the heterogeneity of third party involvement. UN
Conciliation commissions in the Congo in 1960 are counter-pointed by
bilateral Swedish initiatives between Cambodia and Thailand in 1977
or Nigerian attempts to mediate between Angola and Zaire in the same
year. Less formal mediators are as much in evidence in both international and intra-national conflicts, ranging from the efforts of
Quaker intermediaries during the Nigerian Civil War to those of the
Lonrho Corporation in trying to arrange 'peace' talks between Ian
Smith and Kenneth Kaunda over the Rhodesian conflict in 1977. The
number and variety of potential intermediaries is indicated by the list in
Table 12.1 of those who actually became involved in peacemaking
initiatives during the Nigerian Civl War, surely one of the most
mediated of recent intra-national conflicts.

TABLE 12.1   Intermediaries in the Nigerian Civil War 1967–70

Date	Country/ organisation involved	Main mediators	Nature of initiative
(1967)			
(1) January	Ghana	Gen. J. Ankrah	Conference at Aburi, attended by main Nigerian military leaders, inc. Regional Governors
(2) June/July	East African Community	Presidents Kaunda, Obote, Nyrere and Kenyatta	Call for EAC peace mission to be allowed to visit Nigeria
(3) August	Dahomey	Foreign Minister Emile Zinzou	Offer to mediate made to Federal Govt
(4) October/ November	Commonwealth Secretariat	Secretary-General, Arnold Smith	Efforts to arrange talks between Biafra and Federal Govt
(5) December	Vatican	Cardinals Conway and Rochau	Visits to Lagos and Biafra with offers to help open 'indirect' negotiations
(6) November	OAU	Emperor Haile Selassi and five other African Presidents	OAU Consultative Committee set up to place its services at disposal of Federal Govt; visits Lagos

TABLE 12.1—cont.

Date	Country/ organisation involved	Main mediators	Nature of initiative
(1968)			
(7) February/ March	Society of Friends	Prof Adam Curle and John Volkmar	Fostered an indirect exchange of views between Federal Govt and Biafran leaders
(8) March	World Council of Churches	Rev B. T. Molander and G. Murray	Joint Vatican/WCC appeal for cease-fire following visit to both sets of leaders
(9) May	Commonwealth Secretariat	Secretary-General Smith	Meetings in London adjourned to Kampala between Biafran and Federal Govt representatives
(10) June	UK	Minister of State, Lord Shepherd	Visit to Lagos to present UK proposals for informal talks
(11) July/ August	OAU	Consultative Committee led by Haile Selassi	Meetings at Naimey attended by Biafran and Federal Govt delegation; adjourned to Addis Ababa
(12) August	Society of Friends	John Volkmar	Passed views of head of Biafran delegation on to Lagos after failure of Addis Ababa Conference
(13) December	UK	Minister of State, Lord Shepherd	Visit to Lagos, urging invitation to UK Prime Minister for possible mediatory initiative
(1969)			
(14) January	Sierre Leone	Prime Minister Saika Stevens	Circulated proposal at Commonwealth Conference setting up new Committee to mediate on behalf of Commonwealth Prime Ministers
(15) January/ February	OCAM	Presidents Mobutu and Diori	Suggestion of a special OCAM peace mission

TABLE 12.1—cont.

Date	Country/ organisation involved	Main mediators	Nature of initiative
1969—cont.			
(16) March	UK	Prime Minister Wilson	Visit to Lagos for talks with Federal Govt on British initiative and contacts with Ojukwu
(17) July/ August	Vatican	Pope Paul	Pope attempts to bring representatives of two sides together in Kampala
(18) December	UK	Under Secretary of State M. Foley	Visit to Lagos with request for support for British mission to Biafra
(19) October/ December	OAU	Consultative Committee led Haile Selassi	Final effort to bring together Biafran and Federal Govt representatives at Addis Ababa

The variety of potential mediators for inter- or transnational conflicts does not imply, of course, that all types operate with equal frequency. Butterworth's (1978) recent study of 'conflict managers' in the international system shows clearly that the majority of efforts to reduce the intensity of 'serious interstate security disputes' between 1945 and 1974 were undertaken by international organisations 'with a collective security mandate', such as the UN (122 cases), OAS (26), Arab League (16), OAU (13) and NATO (12), or by individual governments led by the US (8 cases) and Ethiopia (4). A different picture might emerge had Butterworth's data contained intra- or transnational conflicts, which are less amenable to intermediary activity from international organisations or other governments, and had the conflict 'managers' been defined less restrictively in the form of 'access' to parties that they obtained (Butterworth, 1976, p. 4). However, this work supports the common-sense impression that intermediary activity since 1945 has become far more a matter for international institutions than used to be the case. It also reinforces LeVine's analysis of mediation since 1815, with its figures suggesting that 'the role of the major powers has been declining (although unevenly) since the mid-nineteenth century . . .', while '. . . international organisations have assumed a pre-eminent position as mediators since World War II, [although] both lesser and major powers remain moderately active . . .' (LeVine, 1972, p. 33).

3. GENERAL INTERMEDIARY QUALITIES

Even though a wide variety of third parties can be active in a peace-making process, most possess common characteristics, which have some effects on their success. Observers are agreed, for example, that a relatively powerless intermediary depends far more upon his own and his sponsoring organisation's perceived impartiality in a dispute, than does an already involved, but powerful third party. Credibility to parties is very closely linked, in the former case to impartiality.

Given that even conflict settlement (let alone conflict resolution) is a process that aims at finding a solution to a conflict through a compromise, rather than an imposed settlement temporarily suppressing conflict behaviour, a variety of characteristics may be associated with some success in finding a solution. Oran Young (1967, pp. 80–90) suggests that necessary qualities for *international* intermediaries include:

(1) Independence, especially from the parties to the dispute.
(2) Prestige and authority, in the eyes of the parties involved in a dispute, and of relevant regional and international observers.
(3) Knowledge, skill and flexibility.
(4) Access to appropriate technological resources and services to enable him to conduct the mediation process rapidly, without having to rely upon either of the two sides for assistance in conducting the process. (Reliance on one side for help, no matter how minor, will begin to destroy the mediator's appearance of impartiality, as well as his independence. Reliance upon either party for facilities will lead to frequent minor procedural conflicts which will exhaust the mediator, his energy and his credit with both sides on trivial differences.)

At other social levels, third parties often possess attributes said to characterise an ideal type of 'disinterested' intermediary. Analysis of mediation in industrial disputes, intra-organisational conflicts and personal quarrels produces a list of qualities said to be helpful in achieving success in any search for solutions:

(a) A high level of professional expertise regarding social structures and processes that are relevant to the conflict.

(b) Low power to enforce a settlement, but a high level of services and competence in a variety of fields that assist in the implementation of any settlement.

(c) A high level of control over the setting of any face-to-face contacts, and the procedures used therein.

(d) A low level of direct interest in the eventual outcome of the conflict.

(e) Moderate, but not extensive knowledge of the issues in dispute, and the background factors associated with the conflict (Walton, 1969).

At the international level it is rare that the latter combination of qualities is evidenced by third parties who are often representatives of governments or organisations having some direct interest in the outcome of the conflict, and often have some power to threaten sanctions for non-acceptance of particular compromises necessary to some settlement. However, a number of shared characteristics or, alternatively, contrasting dichotomies emerge from an analysis of intermediary initiatives at this level. Most salient among these are the shared and familiar quality of impartiality, and the contrasting ones of level of direct interest in the conflict, relative ability to influence and ease of access to the parties.

4. IMPARTIALITY AND CREDIBILITY

Part of the folk-lore of intermediary action is that third parties must possess qualities of impartiality and neutrality if their efforts are to be either acceptable or successful. Without such qualities, it is often argued, only the most powerful third parties will be able to impose their intermediary role and possibly a final settlement (which usually turns out to be anything but final) on the protagonists. With less powerful third parties, both individuals and their sponsoring organisations must appear neutral and act impartially to be acceptable. A mediator, it is often stated 'must have the confidence of both parties' and this confidence will only be forthcoming if he is sufficiently impartial.[3]

The role of intermediary is thus a difficult one to sustain, and this is particularly true of third parties attempting to mediate at the international level. If it is important for the mediator and his supporting body (the UN, the OAU, or his own national government) to be both *credible* and *acceptable* to both conflicting parties, then this is a particularly difficult status to achieve, even though certain 'professionally neutral' countries, such as Sweden or some of the smaller Latin American states, have traditionally been acceptable to conflicting governments. There are a number of reasons for this difficulty:

(a) Any government in alliance with, or even friendly towards, one of the conflicting parties will almost automatically be out of the question. An offer of mediation from such a source may be highly acceptable to one party, who always hopes for a mediator to be in its favour, but to the other, that 'third' party will appear thoroughly biased. This principle explains the utter failure of British mediatory initiatives in Vietnam during 1967, rejected by the North Vietnamese Government and by the NLF mainly because the UK Government were perceived, with some justice, as American 'stooges', and officially because the British had failed to condemn US policy in South East Asia, either publicly or privately.

(b) More subtly, it becomes difficult for any government or international organisation to act as an intermediary if it has either taken up a position upon the conflict in question, or even on any previous conflict which either party could regard as similar or involving analogous principles.[4] The OAU rendered itself powerless as a potential mediator in disputes over African boundaries in the 1960s by passing at its 1964 Cairo Heads of State Conference a resolution to the effect that OAU members agreed to accept and defend African boundaries as they existed at independence. This meant that any government, such as that of Morocco, or the Somali Republic, which had a boundary claim on one of its neighbours would never agree to any mediation initiative by the OAU. That Organisation had made its formal position upon boundary revision plain, so that the result of any intermediary effort would be perceived as a foregone, and adverse, conclusion by the government seeking a change. The OAU similarly tied its hands in the Nigerian Civil War, but over a different principle.

(c) A third point about the difficulty of obtaining a suitable and acceptable mediator at the international level is that, in many cases, the dispute to be mediated is neither purely international nor purely domestic. It may either be international with domestic connotations, as in the 'confrontation' between Malaysia backed by Britain and Indonesia; or domestic with international linkages such as the dispute between Greek Cypriots and Turkish Cypriots, with participation from mainland Greek and Turkish groups and governments. Transnational disputes are among the most difficult for third parties to affect, although similar difficulties attend any attempt by outsiders to act as intermediaries in purely domestic disputes, such as the Nigerian Civil War or the secessionist struggle in the South Sudan. A major stumbling block is the problem of breaking into a sovereign country's domestic jurisdiction, a move statesmen and international organisations are often reluctant to make as it may set a dangerous precedent from which they themselves will later suffer. Another is the refusal of 'legal' governments, often one of the protagonists in the dispute, to allow outsiders to interfere with their own domestic business.

In such intra- or transnational conflicts, the only potential intermediaries may be non-official bodies or private individuals whose activities would not appear to confer any public, formal recognition on non-governmental parties to the conflict. Such third parties have been characterised as 'private' mediators (Curle, 1971) in contrast to representatives of national governments or officials of international organisations. They often are either non-governmental bodies, such as church organisations or the ICRC, or private individuals who are mutual friends of leaders of parties in conflict and can thus be used as unobtrusive go-betweens or even in more positive roles.

However, private mediators themselves suffer from disadvantages in their efforts to 'penetrate' a conflict which in many respects parallel and even add to those handicapping more official third parties. For one thing, the customary channels through which intermediary offers may be initiated are often closed to private mediators. Governments willing to act as intermediaries can operate through normal diplomatic channels, while international or regional organisations, such as the UN or the OAU, have established both formal contacts as well as an accepted reputation for being potential intermediaries. The same opportunities are not immediately open to others who wish to operate at a private, rather than official level.

On the other hand, many private individuals possess more open and frequent access to top decisionmakers than is available through official channels. The part played by informal networks of personal contacts in mediation should never be under-estimated. Again, many potential mediators have access to parties in conflict through some humanitarian activity which already renders services to them, and which may provide an opportunity for intermediary activity. It is often argued that bodies such as the ICRC can use the good-will arising from their humanitarian activity so that this 'spills over' into support for other intermediary activities, although the manner in which the ICRC's activities in the Nigerian Civil War undermined its credibility with the Federal Government should indicate that, in some conflicts, access may be destroyed by an imbalance in the services provided to parties. The ICRC's relief flights into the Biafran enclave undoubtedly assisted the Biafrans to fight on, and were also used as cover for Biafran arms shipment (Stremlau, 1976).

5. INTEREST, INVOLVEMENT AND COERCION

In direct contrast to private intermediaries, government officials or representatives of formal international organisations often possess easy access to conflicting parties at the international level, but can be handicapped in offering themselves as mediating third parties because of obvious interest in the final outcome. This stake in the outcome is also frequently accompanied by some ability to coerce the parties involved into some compromise settlement 'arranged under the auspices' of a mediator with a high ability to extract 'necessary' concessions from one or both sides.

Many observers have argued that in comparing types of inter mediary and forms of intermediary activity, these two dimensions of *coercive potential* and *stake in the outcome* are crucial. The extreme contrast is between third parties who possess a direct interest in any settlement and a high coercive potential and those with no direct interest in the outcome of the conflict, and little ability to coerce either party. However, third parties vary on both these dimensions, and can fall anywhere in the attribute space illustrated in Fig. 12.3.

Such a classification scheme can, obviously, be misleading. For one thing, the coercive potential dimension is inevitably more complex than might be suggested by comparing ideal types of 'powerless' or 'powerful' third parties. One important aspect might be the straight forward material resources available to a third party which could be used to support a settlement, but this is different from a third party's influence over the parties, or ability to coerce them should they prove reluctant to accept an 'offer' of mediation or recalcitrant on a general settlement scheme. Coercive ability can also be possessed asymmetrically by third parties, in that some might be in a position to coerce only one of the protagonists, while others might be able to coerce both simultaneously. It proved a simple matter for the USA to influence the Israeli Government in the Spring of 1974, for example, given the then dependent relationship between Israel and the USA. In contrast, Dr Kissinger had to woo the Egyptian Government with diplomatic gestures and material resources in order to obtain concessions over disengagement in Sinai.

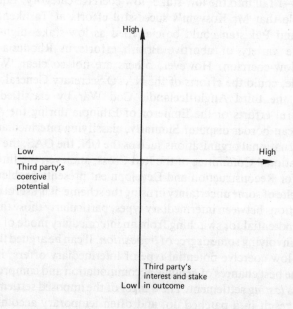

FIGURE 12.3   Classifying intermediaries: Power and interest

Similarly, all intermediaries possess some minimal stake in arranging a successful settlement of the conflict within which they are

active, if only in the sense that success adds to personal satisfaction c
prestige, or organisation reputation. However, many third parties hav
become involved in a dispute through a direct interest in the issues i
conflict, the outcome of which will affect their own future fortune:
Many possess a direct stake in the kind of settlement achieved, nc
merely in the fact of a satisfactory settlement, and thus have difficult
in being accepted as genuinely disinterested. A 'stake' often takes th
form of psychological satisfaction, or increase in status but often ma
add up to actual material rewards, or gains in influence and patronag
with the conflicting parties. All intermediaries cannot be neatly fitte
into such a classification scheme. Dr Kissinger, as a Middle East inte:
mediary, quite clearly falls into the high-stake–high-coercive potentia
category, just as the World Council of Churches activities in the Suda
in 1970–1 fall into the low-stake–low-coercive category. Equally, it i
probable that Mr Kosygin's successful efforts at Tashkent betwee
India and Pakistan could be classified as low-stake–high-coercior
and the variety of abortive British efforts in Rhodesia as high
stake–low-coercion. However, others are not so clear. Where, fc
example, could the efforts of the NATO Secretary General, Dr Lun:
during the third Anglo-Icelandic Cod War by classified? Or th
successful efforts of the Emperor of Ethiopia during the Algerian-
Moroccan border dispute? Similarly, classifying intermediary activit
by international organisations such as the UN, the OAS, the OAU, th
International Committee of the Red Cross, and even the Internationa
Bank for Reconstruction and Development presents problems.

In spite of some uncertainty in using the scheme, it is useful in drawin
distinctions between intermediary types, particularly those third partie
with a potential for switching from an intermediary mode of behaviou
to one involving some degree of *imposition*. It can be argued that the lo
stake, low coercive potential type of intermediary offers, in the lon
run, the best chances of genuine accommodation and compromise, an
hence a *lasting* settlement. The danger of the imposed settlement is tha
it will result in a patched up, and often temporary accommodation
tailored to suit not the interests and objectives of the parties in conflic
but those of the powerful intermediary. The very powerlessness of th
powerless intermediary might be one of the best guarantees of a lastin
settlement, for any resulting compromise will be the result of dis
cussions between the parties themselves, rather than their possibl
reluctant acceptance of a suggested compromise from an intermediar
neither can afford to antagonise. How do relatively powerless thir
parties assist in developing such a solution?

C. INTERMEDIARY FUNCTIONS

Instead of asking the straightforward question about what low stake, low coercion intermediaries actually do, it has become customary to speak about them fulfilling a number of 'functions'. A large number potentially exist, but no single intermediary need carry out all, or even most, of these functions. Just as a 'mediator' need not necessarily be a single individual, but a 'team' (Burton, 1969, pp. 60–5), so intermediary functions need not necessarily be carried out by the same mediating party, or even at the same time. It is possible to talk of 'multiple' intermediaries in cases where a number of different organisations and individuals fulfil different, but complementary functions.

1. INTERMEDIARY FUNCTIONS AND THE STAGES OF MEDIATION

Most observers of mediatory processes agree that the basic function performed by an intermediary is the restoration of contact between the leaders of parties, often when the growth of hostility and coercive behaviour has ended open communication. The rationale underlying this task is that the establishment of 'channels for dialogue' between leaders will make the situation more conducive to negotiation and some de-escalation in the conflict. Beyond this restoration of contact, however, there seems little agreement in the literature on mediation about what intermediaries do, or what they should do in order to achieve success.[5]

Accounts of Quaker international conciliation experiences throw light upon other functions for intermediaries apart from restoring contacts. A general principle underlying Quaker conciliation is the penetration of the 'belief system' of the leaders of parties in conflict, and disrupting those images and attitudes to such a degree that they will be willing to redefine the situation sufficiently to permit some accommodation. Yarrow (1978) reviewing Quaker conciliation processes, suggests a number of basic activities for intermediaries:

(a) Providing a medium of exchange for antagonists who may have no other direct contact.
(b) Personal visitation and contact within and between the conflicting parties.
(c) Listening to each side's perceptions, proposals and rationale.
(d) Identifying conditions which may permit partial solutions.

(e) Assessing realities on both sides of the 'communications gap'.

(f) Proposing small steps away from 'dead-centre' confrontation.

All these seem realistic and modest, in that they do not suggest that an intermediary can have a sudden and electrifying effect upon a conflict, or make an immediate major contribution to its settlement by the involved parties. However, the range of intermediary functions is wider than the list suggested and limiting intermediary functions to the stage when the intermediary makes contact with the leaders of the parties in conflict ignores important functions that occur before actual tri-partite discussions, or even bilateral contact between intermediary and participants begin.

In classifying functions that can be carried out by third parties, it may be helpful to make the somewhat unrealistic assumption that mediation processes 'typically' proceed through four main stages, and that at each stage different third party functions become relevant to the furthering of peacemaking:

(1) Initiatory stage.

(2) Bilateral contacts stage.

(3) Face-to-face discussions stage.

(4) Implementation stage.

These stages do not form any natural progression. They can take place concurrently, and it is not the case that all intermediary initiatives go through all stages. Many mediation processes never get beyond the first stage, as the idea of making any kind of contact with the adversary, even through a third party, is rejected out of hand by one or other of the conflicting parties. Similarly, the move from the bilateral contacts stage through to a direct, face-to-face discussion is often an intensely difficult step to take, and many parties never manage to move into the third stage of mediation. There is a large practical and psychological gulf between maintaining discreet contacts with an enemy through a friendly intermediary, and actually meeting the former's representative directly. Many leaders see great danger in doing the latter, possibly because the chances of being attacked from within one's own party are greater, and the level of commitment of a different order. Most Arab leaders, since 1949 and 1977, constantly refused to enter into direct negotiations with the Israeli Government, and were content to maintain indirect contacts with their opponents.

It has, therefore, frequently been argued that one great service that an intermediary can provide, for parties who do not wish to be seen negotiating, is to keep them publicly apart, and yet maintain a high level of contact on a purely bilateral basis. Negotiations can actually take place 'indirectly', at long distance, by using an intermediary and without coming to actual face-to-face discussions that leaders have too often and too publicly vowed to be out of the question. The drawbacks to this type of indirect negotiation are obvious, and its chances for permanent success slight. An intermediary who continues to act merely as a 'go-between' may be doing a disservice to parties by arranging and prolonging some uneasy truce to the detriment of a long-term settlement. One important intermediary function may be to insist upon eventual face-to-face meetings on the grounds that, without these, no genuine solution will be possible. Needless to say, such 'insisting' will have to be carried out with a maximum of delicacy to avoid wrecking the mediation completely. Moreover, intermediaries are usually in no condition to insist on the acceleration of the peacemaking process, especially if they are genuinely disinterested parties with little ability to coerce. Hence, many intermediary offers remain merely offers, and many others only reach some very basic stage before being aborted. The review of the failure of the many peace initiatives during the Nigerian Civil War set out in Table 12.2 shows that few reached the stage of face-to-face discussions, mainly owing to the refusal of both sides to contemplate any major concessions in the terms on which they would agree to meet one another.

It may be helpful to suggest a modification of our four stage mediatory process, by subdividing the face-to-face discussion stage into two substages. The first of these may be called 'confrontation', for it seems that the initial period of any face-to-face meeting after a long dispute will inevitably consist of fundamentally negative exchanges between participants, particularly of accusations and counter-accusations, of appeals to the third party for support for a particular position in the dispute, of the statement of prepared arguments and counter-arguments, of the rebuttal of the opponents' case, and of the general expression of hostile attitudes and emotions that have developed over the period of the conflict process. Only in a later stage might a meeting become more productive, and cooler consideration of the substantive issues in dispute lead to formulation of settlement suggestions, the development of concessions and the proposal of formal compromise agreements. Discussion might, of course, never reach this point, but if it should, it seems worthwhile to distinguish, at least analytically, between this second stage of the face-to-face

TABLE 12.2 The progress of Nigerian peacemaking

Intermediary	Initiator		Bi-lateral contacts		Face-to-face discussions			Implementation		Outcome
	Proposal made to one side or public appeal for mediation	Third party mediatory initiative	Third party contacts both adversaries with proposal for mediation	Meeting arranged / go-between contact	Parties send delegates to proposed meeting	Delegates seen separately	Face-to-face meetings held	Agreement reached	Terms successfully implemented	
(1) Ghanaian Govt (Gen. J. Ankrah)	X	X	X	X	X	X	X	X	—	Aburi Accords re relationship between Nigerian Central Govt and regions interpreted differently by Biafran and Federal leaders: failure to implement 'correctly' leads to Biafran secession
(2) East African Presidents	X	—	—	—	—	—	—	—	—	Request for a peace mission to visit Nigeria rejected by Federal Govt as 'premature and unnecessary'
(3) Dahomey Govt (Foreign Minister Zinzou)	X	—	—	—	—	—	—	—	—	Offer to mediate rejected by Federal Govt; secession a domestic matter and any initiative should come from OAU

(4) OAU Consultative Committee (Emperor Haile Selassi)	X	—	—	—	—	—	—	Committee visits Lagos to place services at disposal of Federal Govt and assure it of OAU's desire for unity and territorial integrity of Nigeria
(5) Vatican (Cardinals Conway and Rochau)	X	X	—	—	—	—	—	Visit to both Federal Govt and Biafra in endeavour to open indirect negotiations: Biafran Govt to do so only after a cease-fire
(6) Society of Friends	—	X	—	—	—	—	—	An indirect exchange of view's between Gowon and Ojukwu: no proposal of formal mediation
(7) World Council of Churches	X	X	—	—	—	—	—	Call for a cease-fire and negotiation rejected by Federal Govt and Biafrans, latter making condition that negotiations can only follow Federal Govt recognition of Biafran independence
(8) Commonwealth Secretariat (Secretary-General Arnold Smith)	X	X	X	X	X	—	X	Preliminary meetings in London lead to full scale conference in Kampala, but these reveal lack of any bargaining range between Federal and Biafran demands. Conference collapses with no agreement reached and wide gap revealed

TABLE 12.2—cont.

(9) UK Govt (Lord Shepherd)	X	X	X	–	–	–	–	–	Following talks in London with Federal Govt and Biafran representatives, UK proposals taken to Lagos, but initiative founders on Federal insistence of recognition of united Nigeria before cease-fire agreed and Biafran on prior cease-fire
(10) OAU Consultative Committee (Emperor Haile Selassi)	X	X	X	X	X	X	X	–	Initial discussions at Naimey attended by delegates from both sides. Later meetings at Addis Ababa served to reveal that uncompromising positions of two sides not altered and conference collapses
(11) Society of Friends	–	X	–	–	–	–	–	–	Quaker delegation at Addis Ababa pass on views of head of Biafran delegation that sovereignty a symbolic issue, but this not pursued as Federal Govt unsure of whether this was also position of Ojukwu

(12) UK Govt	X	—	—	—	—	—	Lord Shepherd proposes an international team to observe Federal Govt's conduct of war: agreed by General Gowon
(13) Sierra Leone Govt (Prime Minister Saika Stevens)	X	—	—	—	—	—	Previous contact with Biafrans in Freetown leads PM Stevens at Commonwealth PM's Conf. to circulate proposal for tri-partite committee to mediate dispute. Rejected by Nigerian delegation as interfering with OAU
(14) OCAM (Presidents Mobutu and Diori)	X	—	—	—	—	—	OCAM meeting announced setting up of peace mission, but idea dismissed publicly by Biafran leaders and Federal Govt informs OCAM it will only act under OAU auspices
(15) UK Govt (Prime Minister Wilson)	X	—	—	—	—	—	UK PM visits Lagos on 'fact finding' tour and receives Federal Govt approval for meeting with Ojukwu *outside* Biafra: proposal rejected by Biafran leader, who had previously agreed to meeting *in* enclave

TABLE 12.2—cont.

(16) Vatican (Pope Paul)	X	X	–	X	X	Pope, with assistance of President Obote, arranges meeting with representatives in Kampala, but fails to get them into direct discussions
(17) UK Govt (Under Secretary of State M. Foley)	X	–	–	–	–	Proposals to Federal Govt re granting concessions to Biafra and a UK envoy to arrange surrender firmly rejected by Federal Govt
(18) OAU Consultative Committee (Emperor Haile Selassi)	X	X	X	X	–	Discussions arranged by Haile Selassi in Addis Ababa, but Biafran public announcement that these HIM's *own* initiatives led to Ethiopian insistence that meetings remained OAU sponsored and withdrawal of Biafran delegation on eve of conference

dialogue and the former, more expressive stage. We have therefore called this the 'negotiation' stage of the mediation process, and Table 12.3 suggests that an 'ideal' intermediary process will go through five basic stages, in each of which various third party functions may facilitate the process and move towards some compromise settlements.

TABLE 12.3   Stages of mediation

Mediation states	Intermediary functions
(1) Initiatory	Delaying
	Synchronising
(2) Bilateral contact	Defining
	Communicating
	Informing
(3) Face-to-face discussion	Providing a forum
	Suggesting ideas
(a) *Confrontation*	Initiating
	De-committing
	Substitute-proposing
(4) (b) *Negotiation*	Excusing
	Providing resources
	Encouraging
	Managing
(5) Implementation	Supervising and securing
	Guaranteeing
	Legitimising

2. BASIC INTERMEDIARY FUNCTIONS

While our discussion in this section concentrates on those functions fulfilled by an intermediary during the bilateral contacts and face-to-face meeting stages of a mediation, important functions in the preparatory stage should not be ignored. These basically concern the important idea of timing, and can take the form of an *initiating* function, whereby proposals for beginning a peacemaking process come from a third party; a *synchronising* function, whereby the third party ensures that the process begins with both parties, as far as possible, at a similar level of readiness to engage in dialogue, rather than one wanting to talk and the other highly unwilling; and a *delaying* function, in cases where the third party judges that one side's eagerness to engage in dialogue is not yet matched by the adversary's parallel motivation. Assessment of such circumstances is inevitably a subtle matter for third parties, and often explains the long drawn-out process of informally 'taking soundings' that occurs even before a third party proffers its services formally. However, the frequency with which real-world intermediaries ignore basic ground rules of matching parties' motivations for compromise, and attempt to bring together parties manifestly unprepared for any meaningful dialogue or compromise indicates that third parties often use the peacemaking process for their own ends, irrespective of the effects of any failure on the conflict being mediated.

In some conflicts, in the stage between initial explorations or an offer of intermediary services and the development of bilateral contacts, the third party can often fulfil a neglected but nonetheless vital function. This is the function of *defining* relevant parties, and results from third parties often having to make a choice of whom to contact when offering mediatory services, particularly in multi-party conflicts or where parties are split into rival factions. Often, third parties define what become the key parties to a conflict by their own actions. Dealing with one leader or faction within a party split into a number of competing factions, the intermediary may help to identify an adversary with whom the other contending party may usefully deal. Also, by making a choice, the intermediary may help legitimise that leader or faction's claim to speak on behalf of the whole 'party'. A mediator's choice of whom to talk with can act as an implicit sign of recognition. In the act of choosing among competing sub-factions, the final selection may give added status internationally, with the adversary, or throughout that leader's own sub-faction or 'party' as a whole. The AACC's decision in 1971 to mediate between the Sudanese Government in Kartoum and a faction led by Colonel Joseph Lagu within the South Sudanese Liberation Movement undoubtedly strengthened Lagu's position *vis-à-vis* rival groups. Ultimately, it also assisted his emergence as acknowledged leader of the South Sudanese Movement within Sudan, and as the person chiefly responsible for negotiating a settlement with the Khartoum Government.

At this stage of 'long-range contacts', the major functions of a third party are those traditionally associated with a 'go-between', namely *communicating* views, information, ideas and suggestions from one party to another, *informing* each party about the other's perceived willingness to meet and enter into a dialogue, and *interpreting* the stance of one party to another. In fulfilling such functions, the objectives of the intermediary are obviously to affect the perceptions, evaluations and ultimately actions of each party in directions deemed beneficial to the process of peacemaking. Hence the intermediary can select and often manipulate the information that he makes available to one or both sides. Such selection often increases the influence of the third party, at least for a short time and, skilfully used, may facilitate a rapid settlement.[6] The short-term objectives of this process are usually to alter the view of situation and opponent held by each party, and to reduce the tension, fear and hostility developed during the conflict in order to develop some mutual willingness to compromise. However, it is usually impossible to manipulate one or both parties 'impartially' through the selective transfer of information and there also exists a problem of the acceptability of this type of behaviour by an intermediary. An inherent dilemma exists even when a third party has to decide whether to pass on to both parties an accurate picture of one another, including the dilemmas of the leaders, the internal divisions and disagreements, and the pressures working to prevent any attempt at reaching a compromise solution. If the total picture is clearly transmitted through an intermediary to an adversary, it may be that the latter, thus fully informed, will not wait until its rival's internal difficulties are resolved before proceeding to a negotiated compromise. Indeed, its leaders might decide to take advantage of the enemy's divisions and uncertainty, and press on with coercive strategies to win. Completely accurate information may be a two-edged weapon. Even if the information function is satisfactorily performed by the intermediary, it could, under certain circumstances, have a detrimental and 'conflict intensifying' effect.

If an intermediary is sufficiently skilled or fortunate to persuade parties to move out of a bilateral contacts stage, and engage in direct discussions, a new range of functions becomes relevant. Many have to do with arranging and conducting meetings, with the additional complication that those attending are likely to be highly antagonistic, so that the mediator, while conducting discussions, has to retain their perception as reasonably impartial, while trying to influence the parties towards a final compromise outcome.[7]

The main functions of an intermediary, once face-to-face discussions are underway, traditionally include:

(i) Providing ideas or possible solutions, particularly when the parties are deadlocked.

(ii) Initiating proposals which originate from one or other party, but which could not be advanced for fear of revealing weakness or uncertainty.

(iii) De-committing parties by providing some formula by which they can gracefully abandon previous positions to which public act and statements have heavily committed them.

(iv) Acting as a substitute source of ideas or proposals for the two adversaries.

(v) Excusing the parties for making concession, both within the discussions and outside to supporters, by providing an alternative to the superior bargaining position or skill of the adversary as a rationale for concession.

(vi) Providing an 'audience' or 'spur' function through the channelling of expectations from a wider audience that the peacemaking process will continue and some compromise be reached, rather than the whole process collapsing and the conflict be renewed coercively.

In addition to these basic intermediary functions, the third party is often called upon to exercise considerable ability in managing the face-to-face discussions, which can often call for subtle skill in influencing the way in which discussions are directed, paced and timed. These skills are not peculiar to mediatory discussions alone, but apply to almost all meetings which involve a confrontation between two individuals or groups, with some third party attempting to ensure a 'productive' discussion. During both 'confrontation' and 'negotiation' stages, one of the prime tasks of the intermediary will be conducting the meeting in such a way as to maximise the productive openness of exchanges and minimise the level of expressed hostility, disruptive exchanges, accusation, emotional outbursts, and playing to the gallery that occur. Fulfilling this 'easing' function is never simple, but the intermediary can use all his skill to facilitate productive dialogue, provide emotional reassurance to participants, establish helpful rules of procedure for the exchange of views and ideas, and attempt to establish norms within the discussion group which facilitate productive, rather than disruptive, expressions of difference. A major part of this task will be fulfilled by contributing to the reliability of communication between the parties' representatives, often:

(i) By 'translating' or restating statements until sender and receiver agree on the meaning.

(ii) By procedural devices that require one side to make clear that they have truly understood what the other has said and meant.

(iii) By helping to develop a common language within the group which enables those present to deal both with highly emotional feelings or attitudes and the substantive issues which make up the conflict situation.

Often the third party will not be able to fulfil all aspects of the 'easing' function within the meeting, for to do so would imply a probably unprecedented level of control over setting and participants. But, certainly, the skills mentioned above are those which are implicitly put into practice by intermediaries when they reach the face-to-face stage of their activity. Unfortunately, intermediaries are usually caught between the need to facilitate clear and non-divisive exchange between the parties, and the somewhat contradictory need to reach an optimum level of urgency, even of tension in the exchanges, so that momentum towards reaching a solution is not lost. In one sense, this need to maintain momentum is the intra-meeting side of the 'spur' function. Achieving the right level of urgency becomes important because the situation outside the arena of discussion can change rapidly and because opportunities for discussion of the mediation process, especially by 'hawk' factions on both sides, increase the more long drawn-out and unproductive discussions become.

Finally, the third party may find that it has some role to fulful should the peacemaking process produce some final but fragile agreement between the parties. Often, this role may merely take the form of helping to maintain contact and communications between the opposing parties, but frequently other activities are required, as when third parties act to supervise the terms of any agreement, and thus reassure each party that the other is, in fact, carrying out their side of the agreement. Beyond this straightforwad watch-dog role, third parties may become involved in actually guaranteeing an agreement. In the case of a third party with little power, this may be by the involvement of prestige or reputation. In other cases, powerful third parties can themselves guarantee a settlement by implicitly threatening damaging sanctions against infringements. One final service intermediaries may perform of the parties may be to legitimise any final agreement to rank-and-file followers, and thus assist in the 'selling' of any settlement by adding the weight of an impartial reputation for statesmanship to a returning leadership. Sometimes, third parties fulfil a similar function in the event of failure. Returning leaders can avoid blame both by pointing to the intransigence of the adversary and the partiality or lack of skill of the intermediary. The final service of an intermediary may be as a scapegoat.

D. SHORTCOMINGS OF TRADITIONAL MEDIATION

Even after this lengthy discussion, it must be admitted that the record of success for traditionally conceived intermediary activity is by no means a good one, especially at the international level. Powerful intermediaries tend to construct, and often impose settlements that prove to be temporary, merely resting upon the coercive potential of the third party or the short-term willingness of the parties to refrain from further coercion in pursuit of their still retained goals. Powerless and informal intermediaries are seldom able to affect disputes, and frequently fail even to have their offer of intermediary assistance considered seriously by parties in conflict.[8] The world is full of abandoned, unsuccessful mediatory initiatives, and withdrawn or expelled intermediaries who have antagonised the leaders of one or more parties in a dispute.

Critics of conventional third party mediation have argued that the relatively frequent failure of the peacemaking process is inevitable for a number of reasons, not least that intermediaries, however powerless and disinterested, nevertheless represent some interest that clashes with those of the parties, who will inevitably be reluctant to jeopardise their own freedom of action and pursuit of goals by their own chosen means. Furthermore, third parties often represent to the parties yet another uncontrollable and hence disturbing element in their conflict, especially if they impose themselves on the conflict and represent some regional or international body with an interest in the conflict in question. Often, the attitude of the parties in conflict to such potential peacemakers is one of stalling for time by going through the motions of peacemaking without any serious intent of doing anything beyond accepting the surrender of an adversary. Such was undoubtedly the attitude of the Nigerian Federal Government towards numerous well-meaning peacemakers. This attitude is not untypical.

Underlying such comments is a rather more fundamental critique of conventional peacemaking approaches, namely that third parties adopt a particular conceptual framework concerning the nature of intra- and international conflict, and hence a set of assumptions about what possible solutions may be sought. In virtually all cases a traditional intermediary accepts the parties' own bargaining approach to their conflict and their concepts of sacrifice and concession (in 'fair' amounts) being necessary to achieve a settlement. Intermediaries thus aim for some compromise solution, with goals left unsatisfied and attitudes unaltered on both sides. The main change is in the behaviour of the parties, usually involving the abandonment of costly coercion. However, if parties are unwilling to abandon goals or make the sacrifices deemed necessary by the third party, then traditional intermediary activity is likely to be rejected.

Given some validity in this argument, it is not enough for an intermediary to be non-coercive and disinterested in order to ensure that third party involvement will have the highest potential for finding an acceptable solution. There is an obvious need for some new style of third party activity, and for an intermediary that can be both sought and controlled by the parties themselves, so that the intermediary represents no 'danger of sacrifice' to the parties, nor even any 'danger of condemnation'. This possibility only appears viable if third parties can initially adopt an approach to conflict that abandons assumptions about the constant-sum nature of relationships and situations, and also the bargaining approach which characterises most traditional intermediary activity. What is needed is not merely a non-coercive and non-imposing approach by third parties, but one adopting *problem-solving* assumptions where the conflict situation is regarded as one from which mutually beneficial solutions can be developed,[9] and a self-supporting *resolution* of the conflict is possible (Burton, 1969).

In adopting such a problem-solving approach to conflicts, low power, consultant intermediaries may find that the basic intermediary function becomes an educational one of bringing about a redefinition of the nature of the problem among the parties themselves. If they are able to re-conceptualise the conflict and their relationship, then an integrative solution, not involving sacrifices or compromise, can be envisaged as at least a possibility. Using such an approach, an intermediary could help the parties move away from assumptions about the necessity for bargaining, exchanging concessions and making sacifices in a situation of limited resources, or for compromising their way towards a settlement. With such a problem-solving approach, all conflicts may not disappear for good, but certainly the costs of becoming involved in them may be lessened, and the search for solutions eased.

Afterword: Future Directions

At the beginning of this study, we stated that six themes would be pursued and that these would form a framework within which conflicts and disputes, at widely different social levels, would be considered. These themes were:

(i) The basic concepts involved in any analysis of social and international conflict.
(ii) The different types of conflict that could be distinguished.
(iii) The sources of conflicts.
(iv) The major behavioural patterns and processes involved when parties found themselves in situations of goal incompatibility.
(v) Exacerbating and dampening factors and influences upon conflict processes.
(vi) The various forms of conflict termination from victory or extermination, to a solution reached with the assistance of some third party.

We have now dealt with these themes, some in greater detail than others, but all within the framework of continuing research into the nature of human conflict. We have tried to trace out parallel tactics for the winning of international and industrial disputes; have noted analogous problems confronting parties wishing to terminate a conflict inter-action both within organisations and within an urban ghetto; have discussed common psychological influences that affect people in intense conflicts, whether this is between people as individuals, or people as representatives of an embattled minority in a multi-cultural country. In all of these discussions, we have attempted to underline the unity of the subject matter under study, and the fact that insights from one, conventionally separate, social level can help inform and add precision to the analysis of conflicts in other social levels, or in other environments.

However, when all this is admitted, the results of our survey will inevitably be disappointing for, at a very fundamental level, this study is profoundly non-theoretical; and if conflict research is to have any practical, as opposed to esoteric, value then the end result must be tried and tested theories about social and international conflict, which enable us to make predictions about causes, course and outcomes with some degree of accuracy. This will involve making, with some confidence, statements of the nature; the greater the degree of X present (elite factionalism, for example) then the higher the levels of Y and Z and the greater the probability that A will occur. The absence of such assertions, and their more accurate, quantified brethren currently beloved by econometricians and politi-metricians, is a notable feature of this present volume, particularly as progress towards more precise, empirically based, and genuinely theoretical formulations is a noticeable current feature of many of the disciplines relevant to our survey of the components of conflict, and of conflict processes. *The Structures of International Conflict* lacks even the list of rather vague hypotheses, with their non-operationalised concepts and non-specified relationships between the dependent and independent variables in each hypothesis to be found in many books and survey articles. Neither can this study be termed historical, or even descriptive, for we have made strenuous efforts to discuss conflict processes at a high level of abstraction, to point out common structures and processes in a wide variety of conflicts on a comparative basis, and to 'get beneath' simple descriptions of 'what happens' in particular cases of phenomena that everyday language labels 'conflicts'.

In one sense, however, it might be rather unfair to class this study as non-theoretical. A better description might be that it is a *pre-theoretical* work, which concentrates upon clearing away preliminary difficulties to establishing a genuine, theory-building approach to the analysis of social and international conflicts. Hence, our concentration upon linguistic efforts to clarify concepts, and make them more precise and upon the development of classification schemes with clear distinctions between categories that help to dissect the subject matter of conflict research into component parts for further exploration and analysis. From such an initial basis, it may be possible to advance this new field of study towards the development of genuine, empirically based conflict theory, via the systematic discovery of solvable problems, answerable questions, and (ultimately) falsifiable propositions, developed either from empirical study or logically deduced from theoretical propositions that have themselves been validated by other empirical work. We hope that it is in this direction that conflict research will proceed over the next few years, rapidly rendering this present study obsolete with a flood of new findings and empirical generalisations about conflict structures and processes drawn from the referent world of the 1980s and 90s – no matter how much the world appears to change, at least as regards the surface details of conflicts and disputes.

Again, the contribution of this present survey to any advancement of conflict research may not be negligible if it helps people to think about the problems of wars, urban riots, confrontations, damaging strikes, interpersonal friction, and inter-ethnic struggles in new ways, and to adopt fresh perspectives on the nature of their circumstances, and their options for future relationships and inter-actions. This change does not necessarily involve the adoption of the fashionable device of 'lateral thinking' – but new insights can be gained by posing old problems in a different way and by considering different types of entity, inter-action and relationship from those which form the bases of accepted disciplines. In one sense, the adoption of a 'conflict research perspective' on society, both inter- and intra-national, does involve the adoption of a new 'paradigm' (to employ Thomas Kuhn's most misused word. If this present study has contributed towards shifting the boundaries and categories of 'conventional wisdom', and the fashions of thinking about the world and its conflicts, even in a minor manner, it will have been worth the time and effort.

Notes

INTRODUCTION

1. A further argument is that international and intra-national conflicts are so inter-connected that, in real life, it is impossible to separate them. Cases such as the dispute between Somalia and Ethiopia in the Ogaden, and between Indonesia and Malaysia give weight to such arguments.
2. This raises the problem of conditions under which such a transfer of insights may validly be made; this 'rules of transfer' problem has yet to be satisfactorily solved.
3. The point is made in similar terms by Quincy Wright (1951, p. 199).

   . . . A society in which there was no internal conflict would be one in which no individual or sub-group could formulate its own purposes and act to achieve them. A society of that character would be an entity guided by a single purpose and a single method . . .

4. Two recomended are by Mack and Snyder (1957) and Fink (1968).
5. For example, in the chapters on negotiation we have avoided discussing formal mathematical or game theoretical approaches to bargaining, on the grounds that actual decisionmakers approach problems of how best to negotiate in a manner far removed from that posited by formal analysis. Our approach in this sense is intended to be 'behavioural'.

CHAPTER 1

1. Richard Walton makes a similar point when he distinguishes between two aspects of inter-personal conflict within organisations: (i) *disageements* over substantive issues, such as organisational structures, policies and practices; competition for the same resources; and differing conceptions of roles and role relationships; and (ii) inter-personal *antagonisms* or emotional differences involving negative feelings between parties (Walton, 1969, p. 73).
2. Limited goods societies exist at the very margin of subsistence, where material goods are, in fact, in very limited supply. This obviously influences individuals' perceptions of the availability of other valued 'goods'. A basic assumption is that the society is a closed system, and an overall increase in the supply of material and non-material goods is out of the question. Hence, any one person's increase must be taken from

another; limited goods societies are perfect examples of zero-sum situations (Foster, 1965).

3. Report in the *Guardian*, 27 March 1973.

4. As we note later one of the tendencies during intense conflicts is for the parties to align themselves on opposite sides of more and more issues, and perceive that they are in opposition on many issues apart from those underlying the original dispute. Thus, gradually, circumstances of total 'confrontation' arise, where the mere fact that one party is pursuing a particular goal in one area is enough for its adversary to pursue an opposed goal.

5. The nature of co-operation has been neglected by conflict research, save for the implied assumption that it is the reverse of conflict, or an aspect of 'peace'. A similar state of affairs characterises sociology, and one noted sociologist has stated that 'co-operation' is a wholly worthless concept as far as sociology is concerned (Bernard, 1957).

6. When enquiring about 'the sources' of a dispute, a good rule of thumb is to ask what factors, once removed would lead to a cessation of the conflict behaviour.

7. Insights into many aspects of the approach can be gained from the growing literature on the nature of human aggression, especially Ashley Montague, 1973; Gunn, 1973; Megargee and Hokanson, 1970.

8. Violence, in this connection, refers to *the killing or injuring of people*, and *the destruction of property*. Some scholars, notably Galtung (1968), have developed the concept of 'structural violence', which is (roughly) applied to conditions in which a person is prevented by social deprivation or political repression from fulfilling his own aspirations (e.g., a situation in which a minority population is kept in deprivation with respect to the majority, but where there is no overt, violent behaviour because of the weakness of the minority and efficient policing by the majority).

9. Report in the *Guardian*, 31 May 1972.

CHAPTER 2

1. They refer to such an example as a 'conflict of understanding', but the situation is fundamentally similar to Aubert's (1963) concept of value dissensus, and the normal understanding of an 'ideological' conflict (Glenn *et al.*, 1970).

2. Horai (1977, p. 89) refers to such strategies as 'attributional influence', defining it as '. . . one or more parties' attempt to restructure the causal explanations of others . . .'.

3. It may also be that achievement of agreed goals leads to a differential distribution of *benefits* among the party or parties pursuing them. Achievement of independence for Namibia, although a goal shared by the leadership of SWAPO, by many of the rank and file Ovambos, and by members of other tribal groups in South West Africa, would nevertheless bring different kinds and levels of benefits to each party.

4. To repeat the argument outlined, while conflict situations arising from distinct ideologies may be different in their consequences from those

arising in circumstances of shared values, nonetheless, ideological conflicts can be treated as situations of goal incompatibility. Fundamentally, conflicts of 'value' arise from circumstances in which the goals of one party are to make members of the other party conform to particular beliefs, attitudes or (at least) patterns of behaviour; while the goals of the other party are to maintain their current beliefs, behaviour and attitudes (and, perhaps, even convert the first party in a reciprocal fashion). The goals of 'Convert to our ways' are thus mutually incompatible with the goals of 'Remain as we are!'

5. The way in which the issues were defined during the mid-1960s in the conflict between Somalia and Kenya over the latter's Northern Province.

6. Psychological evidence exists to the effect that, if certain goals of two groups are in conflict, there is a tendency for members to experience that even more interests are in conflict than was originally the case. Both cognitive balance (Heider, 1958) and cognitive dissonance theories (Festinger, 1957) support such contentions.

CHAPTER 3

1. McClelland's work on the structure of international crises shows clearly that the amount of information exchanged by governments on the brink of violence increases rapidly and changes in character as does the information exchanged between the parties and their environment. Similarly, his work on 'normal' inter-action flows between governments demonstrates that friends and foes are characterised by widely different patterns of information exchange (McClelland and Hoggard, 1969; McClelland, 1961; 1964).

2. Part of the difficulty of studying conflict processes is that, quite simply, relevant over-time data is difficult to obtain, so that much investigation takes place using static models or frameworks. There are significant exceptions to this observation, of course, such as Richardson's pioneering work on the dynamics of arms races and the works of his followers; McClelland's studies of international inter-action and particularly crisis points; and the Stanford studies of changing perceptions and attitudes among decisionmakers during an international crisis (Richardson, 1960; McClelland, 1961, 1964; Holsti, 1972; Holsti and North, 1965).

3. In the context of international relations, Burton has characterised such situations as *non-war* as opposed to the more positive implications of the term *peace* (Burton, 1962).

4. Another version is in terms of differences between *covert* conflict and *overt* conflict.

5. After an intense costly conflict, one of the resultant benefits may be that the winner can extract reparations for the latter's conduct of the conflict even to punishing ex-leaders for war crimes.

6. There is an element of self-fulfilling prophecy in such preparations.

7. Report in *The Times*, 8 May 1972.

8. An alternative conception of *polarisation* can be applied to the overall social system within which conflict takes place, and is defined as a process whereby all individuals, groups, collectivities and organisations gradually

coalesce around the two adversaries and their opposed goals, leaving no 'middle ground' occupied by parties who take different, or less extreme positions than the antagonists. The polarisation of American society over the question of slavery during the 1850s and of British society during the General Strike of 1926 are examples of this conception, which is fundamentally a matter of drawing every 'moderate' group into two 'militant' camps.

9. Osgood's (1962) work represents a rare attempt to consider the nature and problems of de-escalation.

10. In a formal sense, Sisson and Ackoff (1966) suggest that escalation can be an increasing *degree* of conflict where the gap between the value of an outcome to Alpha without Beta's intervention and the value with Beta's intervention increases markedly; or of increasing *intensity*, where the costs of Alpha and Beta's combined losses increases; or of increasing *propensity*, where more and more of Alpha and Beta's outcomes are adversely affected by each others' actions.

11. This form of escalation is a decision taken by default. Other forms, such as the intensification of fighting by the introduction of a new weapon, or the opening of a new front in a war or the IRA's decision in 1973 to extend the bombing campaign to mainland Britain, need a deliberate positive decision, whereas the policy of 'more as before' needs no decision at all. Indeed, a negative decision has to be taken to end such a strategy.

12. Edelman points out that similar processes make dovish factions in opposing parties inter-dependent, but Singer's arguments help to explain why the amplifying effects are less effective in this case.

CHAPTER 4

1. Sperlich has challenged the dominating assumptions of psychological balance through tension reduction or avoidance of stress (which he refers to as 'consistency' or 'harmony' theories). Instead, he proposes that individuals possess variable tension requirements, so that different circumstances may be regarded as psychologically comfortable or uncomfortable by different individuals, or the same individual at different times. On occasions, individuals may actively seek sources of stress in order to optimise tension with respect to their current requirements, and seek conflict rather than trying to avoid or resolve it (Sperlich, 1971, pp. 166–7).

2. Organisations develop structures and practices to reduce the potential for stress and anxiety on their members (for example, by 'insulating' leaders from direct danger and also from direct experience of the results of their decisions).

3. Holsti selected John Foster Dulles as an example of an extremely inflexible, 'closed mind', capable of rejecting any information that (i) did not conform to his beliefs about the Soviet Union, its leaders and their intentions; or (ii) might do damage to his existing 'image' of the international environment. Holsti (1967) and Finlay *et al.* (1967).

4. The picture in Allport's experiment showed a razor in the hands of the

white man, but – at a very early age – the razor 'jumped' into the hands of the Negro in the perception of many children, because they had been led to believe that a razor was a particularly 'Negro' weapon.

5. In this context recall General Westmoreland's claim that 'Asiatics don't feel grief in the same way that we do'.

6. Druckman has even noted the development of strong group loyalties to imaginary nations during simulations. Players developed feelings of group loyalty and bias against other 'countries' and players in large-scale Inter-Nation Simulations, even though the simulated world was entirely artificial. Druckman concludes that this is a persuasive demonstration of the search for group identity being a basic universal psychological process (Druckman, 1968).

7. IRA tarring-and-feathering exploits have demonstrated to girls in the Belfast Catholic community the dangers of having any friendly contacts with British soldiers in Northern Ireland.

8. Janis coined the term 'mindguard' for a member of a group of decision-makers faced with a difficult decision during a crisis, who takes upon himself the role of suppressing dissenting views of the problem. He ensures that such deviant voices do not reach those members chiefly concerned with the decision and subject to the most stress and greatest need for a high level of support brought about by consensus (Janis, 1972, pp. 41–2)

9. The normal process of identification, so that 'our' group is virtuous, moral, free from sin, peaceloving and wise – thus meriting loyalty, obedience and sacrifice – assists in dehumanising an enemy who must (by merely extending the argument) be the opposite; bad, immoral, aggressive, treacherous, greedy and not quite human.

CHAPTER 5

1. A similar phenomenon occurs at levels besides the international. Teenage urban gangs often appear to identify with a defined area in a city, and be prepared to defend their 'turf' with almost the same determination as Russians resisted German invasion of their homeland in 1941.

2. White's list included Northern Ireland, Bosnia, Alsace-Lorraine, the Sudetenland, Algeria, Israel, Kashmir, South Korea, Formosa, South Vietnam and the Sino-Indian border areas (White, 1969, p. 31).

3. The situation in Ireland provides an example of two interlocking, 'alien–intruder' images, with the Protestant community in the north regarding their local Catholic minority as intruders within Ulster, and the Irish Catholics regarding the northern Protestants, in turn, as alien intruders into Ireland itself. In 1975, IRA and Sinn Fein propaganda in the north began to refer to the Protestant majority there as 'colonists'.

4. In another context, Coser has pointed out how the maximum level of group hostility is always reserved for traitors and heretics, whose views and activity form a basic threat to the ideology and unity of the group, by revealing that alternative views can be developed and that 'orthodoxy' is merely orthodox, and not truth (Coser, 1956).

5. Exiles or refugees are usually bad sources of information about the

general mood inside the country from which they have just fled and about the views and attitudes of the bulk of 'the people'. For one thing, refugees are likely to try to supply their hosts with information that they think hosts want to hear. For another, refugees are unlikely to have emigrated unless they disliked their old regime, or felt that they had been badly treated (which may, indeed have been the case). Refugees tend to be hostile rather than neutral witnesses.

6. The numerous instances in which 'puppets' have turned round and disobeyed their so-called 'masters', or have continued to act in the same manner once the strings and supports have been withdrawn, should make us wary of applying the term 'puppet' too easily to groups or individual leaders. One has only to think of Stalin's relations with Tito, or the almost total failure of the USA to make Ngo den Diem implement a successful land reform programme in South Vietnam, to realise that one should be cautious in assuming total control by one government over another. White quotes McGeorge Bundy as saying, on one occasion:

. . . Anyone who thinks that the lines of influence from Washington are like so many strings to so many puppets has never sat at the pulling end . . . (White, 1970, p. 313)

7. The inter-active perspective offers interesting possibilities for ending the conflict, for if the enemy's behaviour depends to a large extent upon ours, then the former's can be altered by an alteration in our behaviour. If the enemy's behaviour, by contrast, is relatively immutable, springing from essential greed, aggression, love of domination, or search for power, then nothing we do will make any difference to it. The key factor in an inter-actionist view of conflict behaviour is the degree to which the two parties' behaviour is, in fact, inter-dependent, offset by the frequent inability of parties in conflict to perceive this inter-dependence.

CHAPTER 6

1. 'Legitimised' actions are those which the target party accepts as being the right of the acting party to undertake, and where compliance should be forthcoming on a voluntary basis. This is not the same as 'legitimate' behaviour which is merely legally permitted.

2. The distinctions drawn above are purely for analytical clarity, and do not imply that parties in the real world are faced with an either/or choice of conflict strategies. All four may be employed, consecutively or simultaneously.

3. '. . . Almost any conflict can be seen as an attempt by one government to influence another government to do or say something, or not to do or say something . . . a conflict is a situation in which one government wants another government to change their mind with regard to something they have done or are threatening to do. There is some decision they could make that would avoid a clash . . . some decision or action by the other country is required in a relatively short time span . . .' (Fisher,

1969, p. 9). Fisher's use of the term 'change their mind' applied to a government may be rather misleading.

4. Iklé makes a useful distinction between *threats* and *warnings*, when both are used to affect the behaviour and goals of another party. Threats imply that the occurrence of the future harmful event depends very much upon the final decision of the threatener himself; whereas warnings involve a future harmful event that will probably occur irrespective of the actions and decisions of the warner, but is heavily dependent upon the future acts and decisions of the warned (Iklé, 1964, p. 62).

5. The ultimate stage in such a strategy would result in complete disruption of an existing (and presumably desired) inter-action, and the complete *isolation* of the opposing party. Cutting off all contact can be a highly potent form of conflict behaviour at all levels, from the inter-personal to the international.

6. 'Disruption' is often taken to involve violence and physical damage, aimed (i) at preventing an opponent from continuing to operate; or (ii) neutralising, injuring or eliminating the other party. However, we intend to use the term in a similar manner to that of Specht, meaning tactics used with the main objective of preventing

> . . . the target system from continuing to operate as usual, i.e. to disupt, but not to harm or injure or destroy. These latter are the goals of the tactics of violence . . . (Specht, 1969, p. 10)

7. See reports in the *Sunday Times*, 2 January and the *Observer*, 9 January 1977.

8. Prime Minister Wilson records of a meeting with Ian Smith in October 1965 that the Rhodesian leader

> . . . could not get away from his obsession, which he repeated in these talks and, indeed, on almost every occasion whenever we met. This was the assertion that the people of Rhodesia – the Europeans – knew that their country and their lives were at stake, and that the situation facing them was exactly that facing Britain in 1939 . . . (Wilson, 1971, p. 148)

9. For a full listing of non-violent conflict behaviour, see Sharp (1973).

10. For example, in 1956 over 10,000 Japanese people occupied a site intended for a US base, successfully preventing its use by the third party involved (Specht, 1969).

11. The high level of inter-dependence in modern societies often means that third parties become involved in conflicts as inadvertent cost-bearers, given that cost-imposing behaviour by one party frequently affects beneficial inter-action between target party and third parties. In many strikes, major costs are borne by third parties through a spill-over process, whereby actions by workers or management withdraw services from customers, or the general public – in a rail or power strike, for example. In some cases, these costs are deliberately used as a weapon by one party to bring indirect pressure on its adversary, while in others they are an ostensibly regretted but acknowledged side-effect.

12. For example, in 1974, the Istrian Refugees Association placed a full page

advertisement in *The Times* regarding Yugoslav policies over Trieste obviously with a view to influencing non-involved parties. Interestingly, in view of the argument in this study that conflict behaviour comes in many forms, not all involving violence, the advertisement began in the following manner:

> . . . Instead of throwing a bomb, kidnapping a diplomat or pirating an aeroplane, we are publishing this advertisement. This is the means that we have chosen to inform the public opinion about a problem and about a risk which is not only ours but which concerns all the Western European countries . . .

CHAPTER 7

1. It could be argued that, in reality, the use of positive sanctions also implies a threat; namely that the benefit will be withheld or withdrawn in the event of non-compliance. However, there is a fundamental psychological difference between being threatened and being offered benefits which may not materialise and this affects the way in which people react, and hence the nature of the strategy. See Baldwin (1972) for a more detailed argument.

2. . . . a lower rate of success makes threats more salient in international than domestic politics . . . observers will tend to over-estimate the role of threats relative to promises in international politics and underestimate the role of threats relative to promises in domestic politics . . . (Baldwin, 1971, pp. 30–1)

3. The implicit message in the use of (possibly minimum) force and violence is 'We are hurting you a little *now* to show what we can – and will – do in *future*, in the event of your non-compliance/aggression/failure to . . .'

4. More formally the actual pay-off from any given course of action is the *utility* of the outcome to B (roughly, the benefits minus the costs); and the likelihood of that outcome occurring is the *subjective probability* – the latter depending upon B's decision to pursue a specific set of options, and A's decision (uncertain in B's eyes) to implement his threat or promise.

5. A fourth possibility is that the behaviour is designed to alter the fundamental structure of the situation itself – e.g. by producing more of the value in dispute – so enabling one to achieve goals through structural change.

6. Cottam (1967) makes the interesting point that, on occasions, countries 'signal' to one another by the medium of mob-protest, in which sponsored attacks on embassies or other symbols of the disapproved country take place, the mobs often having been recruited, paid and transported to the spot by government agents. In 1965, counter mobs were used on each other's embassies by the Tunisian and UAR Governments, following President Bourghiba's suggestion that Israel be recognised on the basis of the 1947 boundaries. After the mob has burned the embassy or the information service, governments often pay for the damage to the property and apologise – privately.

7. A change in the composition of a leadership group often creates an

expectation, among that group's followers and rival sets of decision-makers, that some major change is likely and that very expectation creates an environment in which bringing about change becomes easier. The 'honeymoon period' of a newly installed American President is partly explained by the fact that both bureaucracy and American public (as well as other governments), expect that the new broom will sweep clean, and are prepared to tolerate – and even encourage – some changes.

CHAPTER 8

1. This was especially so in the case of members of one particular union involved in the strike, where union rules limited the duration of strike pay, and the workers had to rely upon voluntary contributions to a special 'strike fund'.

2. After three years the original 175 strikers were reduced to only 31. For an account of the decision of the strikers at Fine Tubes that 'three years is enough', see *The Times*, Thursday 14 June 1973.

3. Some authors, notably Coser, have discussed conflicts in which institutional termination points are 'built in' to the structure of the conflict process itself, thus providing unambiguous signals that the conflict has come to an end, and one or other party is 'the winner' (Coser, 1961, pp. 347–8). Efforts to extend this concept to conflicts that do not share this game-like quality of recognised rules for ending have not been wholly convincing. The only finding that emerges is that symbolic 'termination points' can be found, provided they are recognised as such by both parties. Such symbolic points can be geographical (the capture of a key town or region), temporal or numerical (round figures). More often, they represent a qualitative change in some aspect of the conflict, rather than an increase or decrease of some already established pattern of behaviour (Schelling, 1963, pp. 54–7).

4. Perhaps the position achieved by the management of Fine Tubes Ltd is an example of this rare situation in which one side can gain all its goals in spite of all the efforts of its adversary. At the international level, the extreme example of such a situation might be total victory in war (Rome after the Punic Wars, the Allies after 1945, or the NLF in South Vietnam in 1974), but even at this level conflicts are rarely pursued to the extent of rendering the adversary wholly helpless, so that most wars are 'limited', in this sense.

5. The fact that such calculations are difficult does not mean that they are never made in practice. All political leaders have to make decisions of this nature, based on more or less subjective assessments of uncertain situations. Decisions to terminate a conflict – or to continue it – *are* made, and hence must be made upon ambiguous information and subjective criteria.

6. Aristotle, *The Politics*.

7. More formal analysis involves combining costs and benefits into a calculation of the *Utility* of settlement to a party. However, parties in real life appear to keep considerations of costs and benefits rather separate. (Given the difficulty of combining them into a single expression, this is

hardly surprising.) Hence, it seems more realistic to continue to treat them as separate elements in discussing any decision about ending a conflict.

8. Concentration upon incremental, additional costs (or benefits) does no mean that total sacrifices or gains have no impact on leaders' decisions Nor should we forget the point that total costs already incurred will affec leaders' evaluations of additional costs yet to be incurred (Edmead, 1971)

9. In some circumstances, perceptions of the parties may be complementary – that is, A sees itself on the verge of victory, while B recognises it is abou to suffer a major defeat. However, it would be quite feasible for partie to possess widely differing evaluations of their positions of relativ advantage. Both may genuinely believe they possess a decisive advantage or one may see a condition of stalemate while the other believes it is nearing victory. One see itself as about to lose while the other perceives only a stalemate. The complications of such non-complementary perceptions o the position for the process of ending a conflict hardly need emphasising

10. To which remark the Austrian Foreign Minister, Czernin, is said to have sadly observed: 'Just like ourselves'.

11. An interesting example of such a relatively restrained offer of terms from a complete victor are those offered by Hitler – not usually considered the most moderate of men – to the Pétain Govenment in 1940. Hitler's offe was calculated as one that Pétain could accept without being disowned by his own supporters, and which could be sold to the people of France. To de this, Hitler had to restrain Mussolini who wished to add terms favourable to Italy which would probably have made the whole Vichy settlemen unacceptable, even to Pétain.

12. This will have to be done with the greatest delicacy to avoid what might b termed the 'kiss of death effect' – approving so much of a particula faction that it becomes regarded merely as a stooge.

CHAPTER 9

1. Recall the behaviour of the Turkish delegation to the August 1974 cease fire talks over Cyprus, at one stage negotiating in the knowledge tha Turkish forces on the island were about to begin a massive offensive t enlarge their bridgehead and capture more of the island. When the offensive occurred, the Turks withdrew from the talks, and, following military success, returned to new talks in an even stronger negotiating position.

2. In this connection, note Milburn's important point that any 'concession must involve a major and obvious sacrifice of values, goals or resources if i is to be *perceived* as a concession by the opposing party (Milburn, 1961) What seems a major concession to the party offering to sustain a sacrific often appears in a quite different light to their adversary. To the Israel Government in the period 1967–73, for example, withdrawal from Sina might have appeared to be a major concession; to the Government of th UAR, on the other hand, such a move would have involved no significan sacrifice, so it could not be perceived as any kind of concession on the par of the Israelis. Similarly, the PLO's promise to allow all Israelis currentl

living in Israel to remain in any new, multi-ethnic Palestinian state, rather than only those living there before 1967 or 1948, was obviously regarded as a major concession by the Palestinians. However, Israelis potentially affected already actually possessed both the fact and (in their eyes) the right of residence, so their view of such a Palestinian concession was that it amounted to nothing of the sort.

3. An often neglected factor in this situation was that Egyptian and Israeli envoys were about to meet informally in Washington under US auspices and with the approval of the USSR — a plan that was subsequently wrecked by Nasser's moves and the Israeli responses.

4. This latter possibility is not unusual, given that the leaders of parties in dispute often overstate their claims, to avoid both making any real concessions should the time come to 'concede', and charges of insufficient devotion to the pursuit of party goals from the ranks of their own followers.

5. Events in this negotiation demonstrate that an ostensibly weaker party may be able to employ tactics giving it unexpected advantages in dealing with its adversary — in the Maltese case by involving third parties' interests and threatening future actions that adversely affect these. (Allowing the Libyans or Soviets future use of base facilities on the island as a means of alarming NATO powers.) The third parties may then put pressure on the 'stronger' negotiator to make concessions.

6. The actual conclusion of an agreement itself almost inevitably confers status. Having signed a peace treaty with Israel, the Egyptian Government can hardly deny Israel's right to exist, no more than the British Government, having concluded the Anglo-Irish Treaty in 1921, could deny the representative status of Sinn Fein and the Dial Eirann.

CHAPTER 10

1. A particular type of log-rolling tactic is the 'tie-in', where one negotiating party introduces an issue, usually remote from those being discussed, and offers to agree a compromise on the issues already negotiated (and usually near settlement) if the new issue is settled to its satisfaction. The implied argument of this, last-minute tactic is 'If you accept the minimal cost of *also* agreeing this final item we have introduced, then you will finally receive the benefits of the compromise we are both nearing; if not, you run the risk of there being no settlement.' Success in using the tactic often depends on the desirability of the compromise to the party facing the 'tie-in', but also on that party's estimate of the value of the settlement and 'tie-in' to its adversary. For example, at one stage during the 1963 Soviet–US negotiations about a nuclear test-ban treaty, Mr Krushchev proposed a 'tie-in' between a test-ban treaty and a non-aggression pact, but this was rejected by the US. (Cohen and Cohen, 1974, p. 15).

2. Initial demands in both industrial and international negotiations often take the form of 'blue skies' proposals, representing much more than the asking party actually hopes to gain from the bargaining, but serving as an initial basis for negotiation and an opportunity for 'making concessions' that do

not really diminish actual gains by the asking side.

3. On occasions, especially in Soviet–US negotiations, the only way out of similar *impasse* has been either (i) to agree to have no agenda at all – which leads to aimless discussion – or (ii) to have a rotating agenda, whereb each party discusses its own agenda on alternate days, a device that wa adopted during the negotiations for the nuclear test-ban in 1958–61.

4. This point was well made by de Callieres at the beginning of the eighteent century:

... Menaces always do harm to negotiation, and they frequently pus one party to extremities to which they would not have resorted withou provocation. It is well-known that injured vanity frequently drives me into courses which a sober estimate of their own interests would lea them to avoid . . . (de Callieres, 1919, p. 25)

5. In negotiations between firms it has been called the 'threat point'; in labou management relations, the 'resistance point'; and in political negotiations the 'minimum disposition'.

6. Iklé and Leites make the point that, in many real-world situations politica negotiators seldom go into an intra- or international negotiation with an very clear idea of their own or their adversary's MCL.

... They may feel that such estimates might reduce flexibility and th capacity to put pressure on the opponent. The tendency not to estimate bargaining range is also fostered by the fact that real negotiations ar immensely more complex . . . since most arguments involve a grea many bargaining ranges which must be combined into an overa bargain . . . (Iklé and Leites, 1962, p. 22)

7. An alternative view is that the intra-party bargaining that precedes th presentation of one party's negotiating position is often so complex tha the eventual 'platform' may become virtually immoveable, as modificatio would mean a long-drawn-out renewal of intra-party negotiation an factional in-fighting, which will be avoided at almost any cost.

CHAPTER 11

1. Isolation or disengagement involves a positive bilateral decision to sto actively pursuing their goals without actually abandoning them, eithe publicly or in pivate; and, in many cases, avoiding further inter-action c any sort on the issues in conflict, and sometimes any varieties of inte action at all. The concepts resemble that of 'avoidance' (Boulding, 1962 Holsti, 1966).

2. Michael Barkun comments that the remainder of a society can perform th function of 'implicit mediation' in a conflict, solely through their expecta tions that the conflict process will be conducted and settled within define limits (Barkun, 1964).

3. For an argument to the effect that rapid increases in social wealth crea more conflicts than they avoid, see Olson (1963).

4. Many anthropologists have pointed out that threat systems can be base

upon formal or informal human agencies and processes (the wise, the wealthy, or even the entire community); or upon supernatural agencies (such as ancestor spirits, ghosts or gods). In many simple societies, the latter often seem to be the most effective intra-societal deterrent force (LeVine, 1961, pp. 10–11).

5. An indirect mode of pursuing a conflict is, for example, when '. . . Manager A opposes an expansion plan proposed by B ostensibly because of inadequate documentation but, in reality because B has ignored A on some important occasions in the past . . .' (Walton, 1969, p. 3).

6. Gluckman (1966, pp. 12–14) lists the creation of overlapping kinship ties as one of the major means by which the Nuer of the Southern Sudan prevent disruptive conflict among various villages while LeVine (1961, p. 10) includes economic inter-dependence among his five mechanisms for 'resolving' conflict within local tribal communities.

7. Both should be distinguished from a third type of activity by third parties, namely *imposition* where some powerful third party imposes a cessation of conflict behaviour upon the parties involved, and may further impose some unpopular compromise by threatening direct sanctions for non-compliance. The USA and the Soviet Union, for example, might try to impose a Middle East settlement on Israel and the Arab states by threatening the use of armed force.

CHAPTER 12

1. In this case, the leopard-skin priest may invoke supernatural powers by threatening a curse, and thus coerce parties into accepting the necessity for mediation and an attempt at compromise. However, the level of coercion in the overall process appears minimal.

2. Each of these types of intermediary will possess varying levels of ability to impose some solution on the parties involved.

3. This statement raises crucial problems of what happens when the intermediary loses the confidence of one or both parties to the conflict, how this occurs, and what steps (if any) the intermediary can take to restore his position with all those involved. Note the misadventures of Ambassador Jarring *vis-à-vis* the Israeli Government, especially following the public unveiling of Jarring's own proposals for a Middle East settlement in 1970.

4. When the All African Council of Churches offered its services as a mediator in Sudan in 1971, this was viewed with considerable disfavour by the South Sudanese Movement, owing to a previous WCC-AACC fact-finding mission to the Sudan 1966 having published a report favourable to the northern Sudanese Government in Khartoum. Church organisations were also handicapped by the fact that they had a long history of missionary work in the southern areas of the Sudan, and were thus involved in the dispute at least as perceived contributory causes.

5. Young (1967) has suggested that the methods open to intermediaries at the international level may be summarised as: (1) persuasion; (2) enunciation; (3) elaboration; (4) initiation; and (5) interpretation. Many of these parallel

our ideas about mediatory functions, but some of the categories seem to broad to give much indication of the exact nature of the third party actions or intentions.

6. Young underlines the importance of this function at the international leve and the power it gives the mediator to facilitate the achievement of settlement by such tactics as

> . . . the suppression of information where such information might b disruptive, timing the delivery of various messages, selecting material fc emphasis and de-emphasis, and even distorting messages in appropriat directions . . . (Young, 1967, p. 34)

Others have made the same point about industrial mediation, arguin that '. . . Control of the communications structure generally facilitate attempts at persuasion and also coercion . . .' (Stevens, 1963, p. 129); an that '. . . at times the mediator's ability to alter or block the flow c information may be crucial . . .' (Lovell, 1952, p. 28).

7. The intermediary may help to bring about direct discussions by decreasin the perceived risks of failure of such discussions, because he is assumed t possess skills that will (a) facilitate a dialogue, and (b) assist towards th discovery of a new compromise that might satisfy both parties just su ficiently to make an agreement workable. To a large extent, the operatio of this factor will depend upon the reputation of the intermediary, an upon past successes. As very few intermediaries at the international leve get a chance to operate more than once – Dag Hammarskjold, Ralp Bunche and Henry Kissinger are three exceptions to this rule – the chanc of building up a useful reputation for success seems limited.

8. There are obvious and recent exceptions to both these statements (fc example the success of the AACC in the Southern Sudan dispute) but ou generalisation about lack of success is broadly supported by the historica record.

9. For a review of this *consultant* approach, see my forthcoming *Peac making and the Consultant Role* (Gower Press, 1981).

Bibliography

. Abrahamsson, 'A Model for the Analysis of Inter-Group Conflict', in B. Hoglund and J. W. Ulrich (eds.), *Conflict Control and Conflict Resolution* (Copenhagen: Munksgaard, 1972).

. M. Alexander and T. L. Saaty, 'The Forward and Backward Processes of Conflict Analysis', *Behavioural Science*, 22 (2) (1977) 87–98.

. T. Allison, *Essence of Decision; Explaining the Cuban Missile Crisis* (Boston: Little, Brown, 1971).

. W. Allport, *The Nature of Prejudice* (Reading, Mass.: Addison Wesley, 1954).

. Ardrey, *The Territorial Imperative* (New York: Athenaeum Press, 1966).

. Asch, 'Opinions and Social Pressure', *Scientific American*, 193 (5) (1955) 31–5.

. F. Ashley M. (ed.), *Man and Aggression*, 2nd ed. (New York: Oxford University Press, 1973).

. Aubert, 'Competition and Dissensus; Two Types of Conflict and Conflict Resolution', *Journal of Conflict Resolution*, VII (1) (1963) 26–42.

. A. Baldwin, 'The Power of Positive Sanctions', *World Politics*, XXIV (1) (1971) 19–38.

. H. Banks, A. J. R. Groom and A. N. Oppenheim, 'Gaming and Simulation In International Relations', *Political Studies*, XVI (1) (1968) 1–17.

. Barkun, 'Conflict Resolution Through Implicit Mediation', *Journal of Conflict Resolution*, VIII (2) (1964) 121–30.

. Barnett, *Observations of International Negotiations*. Transcript of a Conference at Greenwich, Conn., June 1971 (New York: Academy for Educational Development, 1971).

. F. Barton, *Ifugao Law* (Los Angeles: University of California Press, 1919).

. J. Bartos, 'How Predictable Are Negotiations?', *Journal of Conflict Resolution*, XI (4) (1967) 481–96.

. A. Bauer, 'Problems of Perception Between the United States and the Soviet Union', *Journal of Conflict Resolution*, V (3) (1961) 223–9.

. A. Benton, 'Accountability and Negotiations Between Group Representatives', *Proceedings of the 80th Convention of the American Psychological Association*, 1971.

. A. Benton and D. Druckman, 'Constituents' Bargaining Orientation in Intergroup Negotiations', *Journal of Applied Social Psychology*, 4 (2) (1974) 141–50.

. Bernard, 'The Sociological Study of Conflict' in *The Nature of Conflict* (Paris: Unesco, 1957) pp. 33–117.

R. R. Blake and J. S. Mouton, 'Comprehension of Own and Outgroup Positions Under Intergroup Competition', *Journal of Conflict Resolution*, V (3) (1961) 304–10.

A. A. Blum, 'Collective Bargaining: Ritual or Reality?', *Harvard Business Review*, XXIX (6) (1961) 63–9.

T. V. Bonoma, *Conflict; Escalation and De Escalation* (Beverley Hills: Sage, 1976).

K. E. Boulding, *The Image; Knowledge in Life and Society* (Ann Arbor: University of Michigan Press, 1956).

K. E. Boulding, *Conflict and Defense: A General Theory* (New York: Harper & Row, 1962).

U. I. Bronfenbrenner, 'The Mirror-Image in Soviet–American Relations' *Journal of Social Issues*, XVII (3) (1961) 45–56.

J. W. Burton, *Peace Theory; Preconditions for Disarmament* (New York: Alfred Knopf, 1962).

J. W. Burton, *International Relations; A General Theory* (Cambridge: Cambridge University Press, 1965).

J. W. Burton, 'Conflict as a Function of Change' in A. V. S. De Reuck and J. Knight (eds.), *Conflict in Society* (London: Churchill, 1966) pp. 370–401.

J. W. Burton, *Conflict and Communication* (London: Macmillan, 1969).

J. W. Burton, 'The Resolution of Conflict', *International Studies Quarterly*, XVI (1) (1972a) 5–29.

J. W. Burton, 'Some Further Comments – In Reply to Criticism', *International Studies Quarterly*, XVI (1) (1972b) 41–52.

R. L. Butterworth, *Managing Inter-State Conflict; 1945–74* (Pittsburgh: University Center for International Studies, 1976).

R. L. Butterworth, 'Do Conflict Managers Matter?', *International Studies Quarterly*, XXII (2) (1978) 195–214.

D. T. Campbell, 'Common Fate, Similarity and Other Indices of the Status of Aggregates of Persons as Social Entities', *Behavioural Science*, 3 (1) (1958) 14–25.

A. H. Cantril Jr., 'The Indian Perception of the Sino-Indian Border Clash', *Public Opinion Quarterly*, XXVIII (2) (1964) 233–42.

R. Cassady Jr., 'Taxicab Rate War; Counterpart of International Conflict', *Journal of Conflict Resolution*, I (4) (1957) 364–8.

S. Chase, *Roads to Agreement* (New York: Harper & Row, 1949).

R. Cohen and S. Cohen, *Peace Conferences: The Formal Aspects*, Jerusalem Papers on Peace Problems No. 1 (Jerusalem: Hebrew University, 1974).

L. A. Coser, *The Functions of Social Conflict* (London: Routledge & Kegan Paul, 1956).

L. A. Coser, 'The Termination of Conflict', *Journal of Conflict Resolution*, V (4) (1961) 347–53.

R. C. Cottam, *Competitive Interference in Twentieth Century Diplomacy* (Pittsburgh: University of Pittsburgh Press, 1967).

A. Curle, *Making Peace* (London: Tavistock Publications, 1971).

J. C. Davies, 'Towards a Theory of Revolution', *American Sociological Review*, VI (1) (1962) 5–19.

F. C. de Callieres, *On the Manner of Negotiating With Princes*, trans. by

A. F. Whyte (New York: Houghton Mifflin, 1919).

A. V. S. De Reuck, 'Controlled Communication; Rationale and Dynamics', *The Human Context*, VI (1) (1974) 64–79.

M. Deutsch, 'Trust and Suspicion', *Journal of Conflict Resolution*, II (4) (1958) 265–79.

M. Deutsch, 'Conflicts; Productive and Destructive', *Journal of Social Issues*, XXV (1) (1969) 7–42.

M. Deutsch, *The Resolution of Conflict* (New Haven: Yale University Press, 1973).

M. Deutsch and R. M. Krause, 'The Effects of Threat on Interpersonal Bargaining', *Journal of Abnormal and Social Psychology*, 61 (2) (1960) 181–9.

M. Deutsch and R. M. Krause, 'Studies of Interpersonal Bargaining', *Journal of Conflict Resolution*, VI (1) (1962) 52–76.

L. W. Doob (ed.), *Resolving Conflict in Africa; The Fermeda Workshop* (New Haven: Yale University Press, 1970).

M. P. Doxey, *Economic Sanctions and International Enforcement* (London: Oxford University Press, 1971).

D. Druckman, 'Ethnocentrism in the Inter Nation Simulation', *Journal of Conflict Resolution*, XII (1) (1968) 45–68.

D. Druckman, *Human Factors in International Negotiations* (Beverley Hills: Sage, 1973)

D. Druckman and K. Zechmeister, 'Conflict of Interest and Value Dissensus; Propositions in the Sociology of Conflict', *Human Relations*, 26 (4) (1973) 449–66.

H. Eckstein, 'Introduction; Towards the Theoretical Study of Internal War' in H. Eckstein (ed.), *Internal War; Problems and Approaches* (New York: Free Press, 1964).

M. Edelman, 'Escalation and Ritualisation of Political Conflict', *American Behavioural Scientist*, 13 (2) (1969) 231–46.

A. Eden, *Facing the Dictators* (London: Cassell, 1963).

F. Edmead, *Analysis and Prediction in International Mediation* (New York: UNITAR, 1971).

C. H. Enloe, 'Internal Colonialism, Federalism and Alternative State Development Strategies', *Publius*, 7 (4) (1977) 145–60.

M. J. Esman, 'The Management of Communal Conflict', *Public Policy*, 21 (1) (1973) 49–78.

L. Festinger, *A Theory of Cognitive Dissonance* (Stanford: Stanford University Press, 1957).

L. Festinger, H. W. Riecken and S. Schachter, *When Prophecy Fails* (Minneapolis: University of Minnesota Press, 1956).

C. F. Fink, 'Some Conceptual Difficulties in the Theory of Social Conflict', *Journal of Conflict Resolution*, XII (4) (1968) 412–60.

J. Finlay, O. R. Holsti and R. R. Fagen, *Enemies in Politics* (Chicago: Rand McNally, 1967).

R. Fisher, 'Fractionating Conflict' in R. Fisher (ed.), *International Conflict and The Behavioural Sciences* (New York: Basic Books, 1964).

R. Fisher, *International Conflict for Beginners* (New York: Harper & Row, 1969).

H. Foot, *A Start in Freedom* (London: Hodder & Stoughton, 1964).

G. M. Foster, 'Peasant Society and the Image of Limited Good', *American Anthropologist*, 67 (3) (1965) 293–315.

G. M. Foster, *Tzintzuntzan; Mexican Peasants in a Changing World* (Boston: Little, Brown, 1967).

E. Frenkel-Brunswick, 'Intolerance of Ambiguity as an Emotional and Perceptual Variable', *Journal of Personality*, XVIII (1) (1949) 108–43.

L. A. Froman and M. D. Cohen, 'Compromise and Logroll; Comparing the Efficiency of Two Bargaining Processes', *Behavioural Science*, 15 (2) (1970) 180–3.

J. Galtung, 'Institutionalised Conflict Resolution', *Journal of Peace Research*, 2 (4) (1965) 348–96.

J. Galtung, 'On the Effects of International Economic Sanctions', *World Politics* XIX (3) (1967) 378–416.

J. Galtung, 'A Structural Theory of Integration', *Journal of Peace Research* 5 (4) (1968) 375–95.

J. Galtung, 'Conflict as a Way of Life', in H. Freeman (ed.), *Progress in Mental Health* (London: Churchill, 1969).

C. Geertz, 'Primordial Sentiments and Civil Politics in the New States' in C. Geertz (ed.), *Old Societies and New States* (New York: Free Press, 1963).

S. A. Gitelson, 'Why Do Small States Break Diplomatic Relations with Outside Powers? Lessons from the African Experience', *International Studies Quarterly*, 18 (4) (1974) 451–84.

A. I. Gladstone, 'The Conception of the Enemy', *Journal of Conflict Resolution*, III (2) (1959) 132–7.

E. S. Glenn, R. H. Johnson, P. R. Krimmel and B. Wedge, 'A Cognitive Inter-Action Model to Analyze Culture Conflict in International Relations', *Journal of Conflict Resolution*, XIV (1) (1970) 35–48.

M. Gluckman, *Custom and Conflict in Africa* (Oxford: Basil Blackwell, 1956).

C. L. Gruder, 'Relations with Opponents and Partner in Mixed-motive Bargaining', *Journal of Conflict Resolution*, XV (3) (1971) 403–16.

C. L. Gruder and N. Rosen, 'Effects of Intra-Group Relations as Inter-Group Bargaining', *International Journal of Group Tensions*, I (4) (1971) 301.

J. Gunn, *Violence in Society* (Newton Abbot: David & Charles, 1973).

T. R. Gurr, 'A Causal Model of Civil Strife', *American Political Science Review*, LXII (1968) 1104–24.

K. R. Hammond, 'New Directions in Research on Social Conflict', *Journal of Social Issues*, 21 (3) (1965) 44–66.

A. Haque, 'Mirror-Image Hypothesis in the Context of the Indo-Pakistan Conflict', *Pakistan Journal of Psychology*, 8 (1973) 13–22.

J. C. Harsany, 'Bargaining in Ignorance of the Opponent's Utility Function', *Journal of Conflict Resolution*, VI (1) (1962) 29–38.

F. Heider, *The Psychology of Interpersonal Relations* (New York: John Wiley, 1958).

M. G. Hermann and N. Kogan, 'Negotiations in Leader and Delegate Groups', *Journal of Conflict Resolution*, XII (3) (1968) 332–44.

F. Hirsch, *Social Limits to Growth* (London: Routledge & Kegan Paul, 1977).

E. J. Hobsbawn, *Primitive Rebels* (Manchester: Manchester University Press, 1959).

. Hoffman, 'The Functions of Economic Sanctions', *Journal of Peace Research*, 4 (1) (1967) 140–60.

. Hoglund and J. W. Ulrich (eds.), *Conflict Control and Conflict Resolution* (Copenhagen: Munksgaard, 1972).

. J. Holsti, 'Resolving Conflict Internationally; A Taxonomy and Some Figures', *Journal of Conflict Resolution*, X (3) (1966) 272–96.

. R. Holsti, 'The Belief System and National Images; A Case Study', *Journal of Conflict Resolution*, VI (3) (1962) 244–52.

. R. Holsti, 'Cognitive Dynamics and Images of the Enemy', in J. C. Farrell and A. P. Smith (eds.), *Image and Reality in World Politics*, Chap. 2 (New York: Columbia University Press, 1967).

. R. Holsti, *Crisis, Escalation, War* (Montreal: Queens-McGill University Press, 1972).

. R. Holsti and R. C. North, 'The History of Human Conflict', in E. B. McNeil (ed.), *The Nature of Human Conflict* (Englewood Cliffs, N.J.: Prentice Hall, 1965).

. C. Homans, *Social Behaviour: Its Elementary Forms* (London: Longman Green, 1961).

. Horai, 'Attributional Conflict', *Journal of Social Issues*, 33 (1) (1977) 88–100.

. Huizer, 'Land Invasion as a Non-Violent Strategy of Peasant Rebellion', *Journal of Peace Research*, 9 (2) (1972) 121–32.

. C. Iklé, *How Nations Negotiate* (New York: Praeger, 1964).

. C. Iklé, *Every War Must End* (New York: Columbia University Press, 1971).

. C. Iklé and N. Leites, 'Political Negotiation as a Process of Modifying Utilities', *Journal of Conflict Resolution*, VI (1) (1962) 19–28.

. L. Janis, 'Groupthink', *Psychology Today*, V (6) (1971) 43–76.

. L. Janis, *Victims of Groupthink* (New York: Houghton Mifflin, 1972).

. Jervis, 'Hypotheses on Misperception', *World Politics*, XX (3) (1968) 454–79.

. Jervis, *The Logic of Images in International Relations* (Princeton, N.J.: Princeton University Press, 1970).

. Johnson, *Revolutionary Change* (Boston: Little, Brown, 1968).

. Katz, 'Consistent Reactive Participation of Group Members and Reduction of Inter-Group Conflict', *Journal of Conflict Resolution*, III (1) (1959) 28–40.

. Kecskemeti, *Strategic Surrender* (Stanford: Stanford University Press, 1958).

. C. Kelman, 'Patterns of Personal Involvement in the National System', in J. N. Rosenan (ed.), *International Politics and Foreign Policy*, Chap. 26 (New York: Free Press, 1969).

. C. Kelman, 'Violence Without Moral Restraint', *Journal of Social Issues*, 29 (4) (1973) 25–62.

. F. Kennedy, *Thirteen Days* (London: Macmillan, 1969).

. A. Kissinger, *The Necessity for Choice* (New York: Harper & Row, 1960).

. A. Kissinger, 'The Vietnam Negotiations', *Foreign Affairs*, 47 (2) (1969) 211–34.

. L. Klingberg, 'Predicting the Termination of War; Battle Casualties and Population Losses', *Journal of Conflict Resolution*, X (2) (1966) 147–61.

R. E. Klitgaard, 'Gandhi's Non-Violence as a Tactic', *Journal of Peace Research*, 8 (2) (1971) 143–53.

S. S. Komorita and M. Barnes, 'Effects of Pressure to Reach Agreement on Bargaining', *Journal of Personality and Social Psychology*, 13 (3) (1969) 245–52.

A. Lall, *Modern International Negotiation* (New York: Columbia University Press, 1966).

H. Lamm and N. Kogan, 'Risk-Taking in the Context of Inter-Group Negotiation', *Journal of Experimental and Social Psychology*, VI (3) (1970) 351–63.

R. Lee, 'Religion and Social Conflict: An Introduction' in R. Lee and M. E. Marty (eds.), *Religion and Social Conflict* (New York: Oxford University Press, 1964) 3–10.

E. P. LeVine, 'Mediation in International Politics; A Universe and Some Observations', *Peace Research Society (International) Papers*, XVIII (1972) 23–43.

R. A. LeVine, 'Anthropology and the Study of Conflict', *Journal of Conflict Resolution*, V (1) (1961) 3–15

K. Lewin, *Dynamic Theory of Personality* (New York: McGraw Hill, 1935).

W. H. Lewis, 'Feuding and Social Change in Morocco', *Journal of Conflict Resolution*, V (1) (1961) 45–54.

P. Loizos, *The Greek Gift: Politics in a Cypriot Village* (Oxford: Blackwell, 1975).

C. P. Loomis, 'In Praise of Conflict and its Resolution', *American Sociological Review*, 32 (6) (1967) 875–90.

J. L. Loomis, 'Communication and the Development of Trust and Cooperative Behaviour', *Human Relations*, XII (4) (1959) 305–16.

H. G. Lovell, 'The Pressure Lever in Mediation', *Industrial and Labor Relations Review*, VI (1) (1952) 20–30.

G. Lüschen, 'Cooperation, Association and Contest', *Journal of Conflict Resolution*, XIV (1) (1970) 21–34.

R. W. Mack, 'The Components of Social Conflict', *Social Problems*, XII (4) (1965) 388–97.

R. W. Mack and R. C. Snyder, 'The Analysis of Social Conflict; Towards an Overview and Synthesis', *Journal of Conflict Resolution*, I (2) (1957) 212–48.

L. Mair, *Primitive Government* (Harmondsworth: Penguin Books, 1962).

M. E. Marty, 'The Nature and Consequence of Social Conflict for Religious Groups' in R. Lee and M. E. Marty (eds.), *Religion and Social Conflict* (New York: Oxford University Press, 1964).

G. Marwell, 'Conflict Over Proposed Group Actions: A Typology of Cleavage', *Journal of Conflict Resolution*, X (4) (1966) 427–35.

G. Marwell and D. R. Schmitt, *Cooperation; An Experimental Analysis* (New York: Academic Press, 1975).

A. Mazur, 'Increased Tendency Towards Balance During Stressful Conflict', *Sociometry*, 36 (2) (1973) 279–83.

E. I. Megargee and J. E. Hokanson (eds.), *The Dynamics of Aggression* (New York: Harper & Row, 1970).

T. W. Milburn, 'What Constitutes Effective Deterrence?', *Journal of Conflict Resolution*, III (2) (1959) 138–45.

T. W. Milburn, 'The Concept of Deterrence: Some Logical and Psychological Considerations', *Journal of Social Issues*, XVII (3) (1961) 3–11.

S. Milgram, 'Behavioural Study of Obedience', *Journal of Abnormal and Social Psychology*, 67 (4) (1963) 371–8.

S. Milgram, *Obedience to Authority* (London: Tavistock, 1974).

C. R. Mitchell, 'The Involvement of External Parties in Civil Strife', *International Studies Quarterly*, XIV (2) (1970) 166–94.

D. Mitrany, *A Working Peace System* (Chicago: Quadrangle Books, 1966).

P. A. Munch, *Crisis in Utopia: The Story of Tristan da Cunha* (London: Longmans, 1971).

C. A. McClelland, 'The Acute International Crisis', *World Politics*, XIV (1) (1961) 182–204.

C. A. McClelland, 'Action Structures and Communication in Two International Crises; Quemoy and Berlin', *Background*, 7 (1) (1964) 201–15.

C. A. McClelland, 'Access to Berlin; The Quantity and Variety of Events 1948–1963', in J. D. Singer (ed.), *Quantitative International Politics* (New York: Free Press, 1968).

C. A. McClelland and G. Hoggard, 'Conflict Patterns in the Inter Actions among Nations', in J. N. Rosenan (ed.), *International Politics and Foreign Policy*, 2nd ed., Chap. 57 (New York: Free Press, 1969).

M. B. Nicholson, 'Tariff Wars and a Model of Conflict', *Journal of Peace Research*, 4 (1) (1967a) 26–38.

M. B. Nicholson, 'The Resolution of Conflict', *Journal of the Royal Statistical Society*, 130 (4) (1967b) 529–40.

E. A. Nordlinger, *Conflict Regulation in Divided Societies* (Harvard University: Center for International Studies, 1972).

R. D. Nye, *Conflict Among Humans* (New York: Springer, 1973).

C. Oglesby and R. Shaull, *Containment and Change* (New York: Macmillan, 1967).

M. Olson Jr., 'Rapid Growth as a Destabilising Force', *Journal of Economic History*, XXIII (4) (1963) 529–52.

G. Orwell, 'Politics and the English Language', in *Shooting An Elephant and Other Essays* (London: Secker & Warburg, 1953).

C. Osgood, *An Alternative to War or Surrender* (Urbana, Ill.: University of Illinois Press, 1962).

F. Pakenham, *Peace by Ordeal* (London: Sidgwick & Jackson, 1972) first pub. 1935.

W. R. Phillips, 'The Dynamics of Behavioural Action and Reaction in International Conflict', *Peace Research Society (International) Papers*, XVII (1970).

T. E. Phipps Jr., 'Resolving "Hopeless" Conflicts', *Journal of Conflict Resolution*, V (3) (1961) 274–8.

D. Pirages, *Managing Political Conflict* (New York: Praeger, 1976).

R. F. Randle, *Geneva 1954: The Settlement of the Indo-Chinese War* (Princeton, N.J.: Princeton University Press, 1969).

A. Rapoport, *Fights, Games and Debates* (Ann Arbor: University of Michigan Press, 1960).

L. F. Richardson, *Arms and Insecurity* (London: Stevens, 1960a).

L. F. Richardson, *Statistics of Deadly Quarrels* (London: Stevens, 1960b).

M. Rokeach, *The Open and Closed Mind* (New York: Basic Books, 1960).

S. Rosen, 'Cost-Limits for Preferences in Foreign Policy Issue Areas', *Peace Research Society (International) Papers*, XVII (1971) 61–73.

S. Rosen, 'War Power and the Willingness to Suffer', in Bruce M. Russet (ed.), *Peace, War and Numbers* (Beverley Hills: Sage, 1972).

B. M. Russett, 'The Calculus of Deterrence', *Journal of Conflict Resolution* VII (2) (1963) 97–109.

J. M. Salazar and G. Marin, 'National Stereotypes as a Function of Conflict and Territorial Proximity; A Test of the Mirror-Image Hypothesis', *Journal of Social Psychology*, 101 (1977) 13–19.

N. Sanford, 'Dehumanisation and Collective Destruction', *International Journal of Group Tensions*, I (1) (1971) 26–41.

J. Sawyer and H. Guetzkow, 'Bargaining and Negotiation in International Relations', in H. C. Kelman (ed.), *International Behaviour*, Chap. 13 (New York: Holt, Rhinehart & Winston, 1965).

E. E. Schattschneider, *The Semi-Sovereign People* (New York: Holt, Rhinehart & Winston, 1960).

T. C. Schelling, 'An Essay in Bargaining' in *The Strategy of Conflict*, Chap. 2 (New York: Oxford University Press, 1963).

T. C. Schelling, *Arms and Influence* (New Haven: Yale University Press, 1966).

T. C. Schelling, *The Use of Force in the Nuclear Age* (London: IISS, 1968).

G. Sharp, *The Politics of Non-Violent Action* (Boston: Porter Sargent, 1973).

M. Sherif, *The Psychology of Social Norms* (New York: Harper & Row, 1936).

M. Sherif, *Group Conflict and Cooperation; Their Social Psychology* (London: Routledge & Kegan Paul, 1966).

S. Siegel and L. E. Fouraker, *Bargaining and Group Decision-Making* (New York: McGraw Hill, 1960).

G. Simmel, *Conflict* and *The Web of Group Affiliations* trans. by K. H. Wolff and R. Bendix (New York: Free Press, 1955).

H. A. Simon, *Administrative Behaviour*, 2nd ed. (New York: Macmillan, 1957).

J. D. Singer, 'Escalation and Control in International Conflict: A Simple Feedback Model', *General Systems Yearbook*, XV (1970) 163–73.

J. D. Singer and M. Small, *The Wages of War* 1815–1965 (New York: John Wiley, 1972).

J. D. Singer and P. Ray, 'Decision-making in Conflict: From Interpersonal to International Relations', *Menninger Clinic Bulletin*, XXX (5) (1966) 300–12

R. L. Sisson and R. L. Ackoff, 'Towards a Theory of the Dynamics of Conflict', *Peace Research Society (International) Papers*, V (1966) Philadelphia Conference.

P. A. Sorokin, *Social and Cultural Dynamics*, 4 vols. (New York: American Books, 1937).

J. W. Spanier and J. L. Nogee, *The Politics of Disarmament* (New York: Praeger, 1962).

H. Specht, 'Disruptive Tactics', *Social Work*, XIV (2) (1969) 5–15.

P. W. Sperlich, *Conflict and Harmony in Human Affairs* (Chicago: Rand McNally, 1971).

R. Stagner, *Psychological Aspects of International Conflict* (Belmont, Calif.: Brooks/Cole, 1967a).

R. Stagner, 'The Analysis of Conflict', in R. Stagner (ed.), *The Dimensions of Human Conflict* (Detroit: Wayne State University Press, 1967b).

A. A. Stein, 'Conflict and Cohesion; A Review of the Literature', *Journal of Conflict Resolution*, XX (1) (1976) 143–69.

C. Stevens, *Strategy and Collective Bargaining Negotiation* (New York: McGraw Hill, 1963).

A. Storr, *Human Aggression* (London: Pelican Books, 1968).

H. R. Strack, *Sanctions: The Case of Rhodesia* (Syracuse, N.Y.: Syracuse University Press, 1978).

J. J. Stremlau, *The International Politics of the Nigerian Civil War* (Princeton, N.J.: Princeton University Press, 1976).

Sun Tsu, *The Art of War* trans. by Samuel B. Griffith (London: Oxford University Press, 1963).

H. Tajfel, 'Experiments in Intergroup Discrimination', *Scientific American*, 223 (5) (1970) 96–102.

K. Trevaskis, *Shades of Amber; A South Arabian Episode* (London: Hutchinson, 1968).

H. C. Triandis and E. E. Davis, *Some Methodological Problems Concerning Research on Negotiations Between Monolinguals*, Group Effectiveness Research Lab. Report No. 28 (Urbana, Ill.: University of Illinois Press, 1965).

J. Urry, *Reference Groups and the Theory of Revolution* (London: Routledge & Kegan Paul, 1973).

P. Wallensteen, 'Characteristics of Economic Sanctions', *Journal of Peace Research*, 5 (3) (1968) 248–67.

R. E. Walton, 'Two Strategies of Social Change and Their Dilemmas', *Journal of Applied Behavioural Science*, I (2) (1965a) 167–79.

R. E. Walton, 'Leadership Strategies for Achieving Membership Consensus During Negotiations', *Proceedings of the 18th Annual Meeting of the Industrial Relations Research Association* (December 1965b).

R. E. Walton, *Interpersonal Peacemaking* (Reading, Mass.: Addison Wesley, 1969).

R. E. Walton and R. B. McKersie, *A Behavioural Theory of Labor Negotiations* (New York: McGraw Hill, 1965).

R. E. Walton and R. B. McKersie, 'Behavioural Dilemmas in Mixed-Motive Decision-Making', *Behavioural Science*, 3 (1966) 370–84.

M. Walzer, *Just and Unjust Wars* (London: Allen Lane, 1977).

J. J. Wanderer, 'An Index of Riot Severity and Some Correlates', *American Journal of Sociology*, 74 (3) (1969) 500–5.

J. W. Wheeler-Bennett, *Brest-Litovsk; The Forgotten Peace* (London: Macmillan, 1938).

R. K. White, 'Images in the Context of International Conflict; Soviet Perceptions of the U.S. and U.S.S.R.', in H. C. Kelman (ed.), *International Behaviour*, Chap. 7 (New York: Holt, Rhinehart & Winston, 1965).

R. K. White, 'Three Not-So-Obvious Contributions of Psychology to Peace', *Journal of Social Issues*, XXV (4) (1969) 23–40.

R. K. White, *Nobody Wanted War* (New York: Doubleday/Anchor, 1970).

R. K. White, 'Misperceptions in the Arab–Israeli Conflict', *Journal of Social Issues*, 33 (1) (1977) 190–221.

R. I. Williams, 'Some Further Comments on Chronic Controversies', *American Journal of Sociology*, 71 (6) (1966) 717–21.

R. I. Williams, 'Conflict and Social Order; A Research Strategy for Complex Propositions', *Journal of Social Issues*, 28 (1) (1972) 11–26.

H. Wilson, *The Labour Government 1964–70* (London: Michael Joseph, 1971).

W. H. Wriggins, 'Up for Auction: Malta Bargains with Great Britain 1971', in I. W. Zartman (ed.) *The 50% Solution* (New York: Doubleday/Anchor, 1976).

Q. Wright, *A Study of War* (Chicago: Chicago University Press, 1942).

Q. Wright, 'The Nature of Conflict', *Western Political Quarterly*, IV (2) (1951) 193–209.

C. H. Yarrow, *Quaker Experiences in International Conciliation* (New Haven: Yale University Press, 1978).

O. R. Young, *The Intermediaries: Third Parties in International Crisis* (Princeton, N.J.: Princeton University Press, 1967).

O. R. Young, 'Intermediaries and Interveners: Third Parties in the Middle East Crisis', *International Journal*, XXII (1) (1967–8) 52–73.

P. G. Zimbardo, 'Pathology of Imprisonment', *Society*, IX (6) (1972) 4–8.

Index

341